ARNDT'S STORY

Asia Pacific Press is based in the Crawford School of Economics and Government at The Australian National University. Asia Pacific Press is a specialist publisher on economics, development, governance and management in the Asia Pacific region.

As well as book publishing, Asia Pacific Press also houses the influential journals *Asian–Pacific Economic Literature* and the *Pacific Economic Bulletin*.

The **Institute of Southeast Asian Studies** (ISEAS) was established as an autonomous organisation in 1968. It is a regional centre dedicated to the study of socio-political, security and economic trends and developments in Southeast Asia and its wider geostrategic and economic environment.

The Institute's research programs are the Regional Economic Studies (RES, including ASEAN and APEC), Regional Strategic and Political Studies (RSPS), and Regional Social and Cultural Studies (RSCS).

ISEAS Publishing, an established academic press, has issued almost 2,000 books and journals. It is the largest scholarly publisher of research about Southeast Asia from within the region. ISEAS Publishing works with many other academic and trade publishers and distributors to disseminate important research and analyses from and about Southeast Asia to the rest of the world.

ARNDT'S STORY

The life of an Australian economist

Peter Coleman, Selwyn Cornish, Peter Drake

Asia Pacific Press
The Australian National University

Institute of Southeast Asian Studies
Singapore

Co-Published by ANU E Press and Asia Pacific Press
The Australian National University
Canberra ACT 0200
Email: anuepress@anu.edu.au
This title available online at: http://epress.anu.edu.au/arndt_citation.html

© 2007 ANU E Press and Asia Pacific Press

This work is copyright. Apart from those uses which may be permitted under the Copyright Act 1968 as amended, no part may be reproduced by any process without written permission from the publisher.

First published in Australia by
Asia Pacific Press
Crawford School of Economics
and Government
The Australian National University
Canberra ACT 0200
Ph: 61-2-6125 4700 Fax: 61-2-6125 0767
Website: http://www.asiapacificpress.com

First published in Singapore by
ISEAS Publishing
Institute of Southeast Asian Studies
30 Heng Mui Keng Terrace
Pasir Panjang
Singapore 119614
E-mail: publish@iseas.edu.sg
Website: http://bookshop.iseas.edu.sg

Asia Pacific Press ISBN 978-0-7315-3810-2   ISEAS ISBN 978-981-230-449-0

National Library of Australia Cataloguing in Publication entry

> Coleman, Peter, 1928- .
> Arndt's story : the life of an Australian economist.
>
> Bibliography.
> Includes index.
> ISBN 9780731538102 (pbk.)
> ISBN 9781921313172 (online)
>
> 1. Arndt, H. W. (Heinz Wolfgang), 1915-2002. 2. Australian National University - Biography. 3. Economists - Australia - Biography. 4. Economists - Southeast Asia. I. Drake, P. J. (Peter Joseph), 1932- . II. Cornish, Selwyn. III. Title.
>
> 330.092

Editors: Jan Borrie and Clare Shamier
Photo editor: Jessica Miller
Design: Annie Di Nallo Design

CONTENTS

List of illustrations	vi
Abbreviations	viii
Note on sources	x
Note on authors	xi
Preface	xiii
Prelude— Bettina Arndt	
H.W.A.—The man and his marriage	xiv
Part 1—Peter Coleman	
1. From Kaiser to Hitler	1
2. Oxford made him	13
3. Arndt in the internment camp	32
4. Chatham House	42
Part 2—Selwyn Cornish	
5. Passage to Australia	56
6. The University of Sydney	68
7. Public intellectual	75
8. Ruth's trip to Europe	87
9. New horizons	96
10. Canberra University College	104
11. Canberra	119
12. South Carolina	130
13. Politics	146
14. Economics and policy	171
15. Geneva	195
16. A new lease of intellectual life	206
Part 3—Peter Drake	
17. Economic development in practice: it all began in Jakarta	224
18. The Department of Economics, RSPS, 1963–80	236
19. Sukarno's Indonesia	257
20. Suharto's Indonesia	265
21. Other parts of Asia	274
22. Retirement	293
Postlude—Bettina Arndt	
Chez Arndt	312
Notes	317
References	321
Index	325

LIST OF ILLUSTRATIONS

1. Professor Fritz Arndt teaching his beloved chemistry
2. Fritz Arndt, bedecked with honorary medals, sitting for a bronze bust made for the German Chemical Society
3. Heinz and his sister Bettina
4. Heinz holidaying with friends in Viareggio, Italy 1934 and his brother and sister Bettina
5. A young German in Oxford
6. Dapper young man
7. Heinz and his sister Bettina in England, circa 1937
8. Heinz and Ruth in Cambridge, 1940
9. Relaxing in Switzerland
10. Interned and sent to Canada, 1939
11. The future Mrs Arndt, Ruth Strohsahl, 1939
12. Heinz and Ruth in their student days at London School of Economics, 1939
13. Heinz with his mother Julia at Ruth and Heinz's wedding
14. Ruth with her mentor, Marjorie Rackstraw
15. Wedding, Hampstead, 12 July, 1941
16. Their first Australian beach, 1946 with son Chris
17. Arndt family in Ainslie
18. Heinz with his young family—Chris, Bettina and Nick
19. Ruth playing the piano at one of her migrant parties, with Heinz looking on
20. Neighbours in Hurstville, Noel and Joan Butlin, 1945.
21. Arndts in the Deakin front garden, then set in a bush landscape
22. Family holiday on the South Coast
23. Ruth on her favourite back terrace
24. Heinz and Ruth share a moment at Tuross Lakes
25. Heinz painting landscapes in Geneva, 1960
26. Heinz and Ruth in Canberra
27. The well-dressed BBQ chef
28. With Sir Robert Menzies, circa 1958
29. On the ACT Advisory Council, 1961
30. Heinz's office at Coombs
31. Such a happy man

32. In Dehli
33. Heinz with Premier Sun of Taiwan
34. Heinz with Yip Yat Hoong and Kiyoshi Kojima
35. Heinz with Jan Tinbergen
36. With SA Premier Don Dunstan and US economist Paul Samuelson, 1973
37. In Banda Aceh
38. With Raj Krishna, Bangkok
39. In Indonesia, with Dennis DeTrey (World Bank), Ir Tungky Ariwibowo (Industry Minister) and Marzuki Usman (later Tourism Minister)
40. With Ross Muir, Peter Drysdale, Toshi Kinoshita, Hal Hill and Kazuo Imai
41. Juwono Sudarsono (current Indonesian Defence Minister), Clara Juwono (CSIS, Jakarta) and Moh Arif (the latter a close friend from Malaysia)
42. Heinz and Professor R.M. Sundrum, staff member of Economics, RSPAS, 1971–90
43. In Indonesia, one of many happy dinners
44. Heinz with students
45. A good mix of (mainly) former students, Helen Reid, Hal Hill, Ross McLeod, Chris Manning, HWA, Howard Dick, Andrew Elek, Anne Booth, Tony Reid and Peter McCawley
46. Heinz at the home of Bessie and Vic Camino, Heinz's closest friends from the Philippines
47. In 1995 Gadjah Mada University, Yogyakarta, one of Indonesia's leading universities, launched the Arndt Scholarship Scheme
48. With Professor Nopirin, Dean, Faculty of Economics, Gadjah Mada University and Colleagues
49. HWA, Stuart Harris and Ross Garnaut
50. The academic family, including Ruth as ANU council member at Bettina's ANU graduation, 1971
51. At Bettina's wedding to Dennis Minogue, 1977
52. Ruth with Nick's son Gregory, 1986
53. Heinz with Chris's girls Sara and Emma
54. Heinz at Cottesloe Beach with Sara and Virginia, circa 1980
55. Heinz with Bettina's older son Jesse playing tiddlywinks, circa 1986
56. Arndt family gathered for 50th wedding anniversary celebrations, 2000
57. Last portrait with Ruth
58. Heinz meets his great-granddaughter Charlotte, 2002
59. Recent Arndt gathering Bettina's daughter, Taylor, Nick's sons, Benjamin and Gregory, Nick's wife, Catherine, Bettina and sons Jesse and Cameron and brother Nick
60. Chris' daughters Sara and Virginia, Bettina with her sons, Jesse and Cameron at the launch of the H.W. Arndt Building at The Australian National University
61. The H.W. Arndt Building opened in 2005

ABBREVIATIONS

AAJRP	Joint Research Project on ASEAN–Australia Economic Relations
ABC	Australian Broadcasting Corporation
ACT	Australian Capital Territory
ADB	Asian Development Bank
ADIEP	Asian Institute for Economic Development and Planning
AIPS	Australian Institute of Political Science
AJHP	Australian Journal of History and Politics
ALP	Australian Labor Party
ANU	Australian National University
ANZAAS	Australian and New Zealand Association for the Advancement of Science
APEL	*Asian–Pacific Economic Literature*
ASEAN	Association of Southeast Asian Nations
BIAS	Board of the Institute of Advanced Studies (ANU)
BIES	Bulletin of Indonesian Economic Studies
CHOGM	Commonwealth Heads of Government Meeting
CSO	Central Statistical Organisation (India)
CUC	Canberra University College
DMZ	Demilitarised Zone
ECAFE	United Nations Commission for Asia and the Far East
ECE	United Nations Economic Commission for Europe
IEA	International Economic Association
IMF	International Monetary Fund
IPA	Institute of Public Affairs
IPB	Institut Pertanian Bogor (Indonesia)
ISI	Indian Statistical Institute
LSE	London School of Economics
MIT	Massachusetts Institute of Technology
NEDO	National Economic Development Office (United Kingdom)
NGO	non-government organisation
NSW	New South Wales

OECD	Organisation for Economic Cooperation and Development
OPEC	Organisation of Petroleum Exporting Countries
PAFTAD	Pacific Trade and Development Conference
PAP	People's Action Party (Singapore)
PNG	Papua New Guinea
PWU	Plantation Workers' Union (Malaysia)
RAAF	Royal Australian Air Force
RSPS	Research School of Pacific Studies (ANU)
RSSS	Research School of Social Sciences (ANU)
SEANZA	Southeast Asia, New Zealand and Australia
SGS	School of General Studies (ANU)
SSRC	Social Science Research Council
UNCTAD	United Nations Conference for Trade and Development
UNDP	United Nations Development Program
UNIDO	United Nations Industrial Development Organisation
UNTAD	United Nations Trade and Development Commission
USSR	Union of Soviet Socialist Republics
WEA	Workers' Educational Association (United Kingdom)

NOTE ON SOURCES

The bulk of the personal papers of Professor H.W. Arndt are located in the National Library of Australia. Heinz made four deposits of papers in his lifetime: in 1981, 1988, 1993 and 2000, the first under the Taxation Incentives for the Arts scheme. The papers deposited in 1981, 1988 and 1993 bear the catalogue number MS 6641; those deposited in 2000 have not yet been catalogued (their accession number is Ms ACC00/158).

Further papers were deposited at the National Library after Heinz's death; these papers have not been catalogued (their accession numbers are Ms ACC02/132, ACC02/147 and ACC02/174).

Further papers, of a more personal nature, including letters between Heinz and Ruth, are in the possession of Bettina Arndt.

Peter Drake drew heavily on his correspondence with Heinz, which began in the mid 1960s and continued up to the time of Heinz's death in 2002.

Included in The Australian National University Archives are three staff files that contain material relating to Heinz's appointments, leave and various administrative activities at Canberra University College and the ANU. These files bear the catalogue numbers 1922/1–3. Information elicited from these files was used in Parts 2 and 3.

Material from the Archives of the London School of Economics and Lincoln College, Oxford, was drawn on in the writing of Part 1.

Heinz's published memoir, *A Course Through Life* (The Australian National University, Canberra, 1985) was an invaluable source throughout the writing of this book. Information from Heinz's *Asian Diaries* (Chopmen Publishers, Singapore, 1987) was drawn on for the writing of Part 3.

Walter Arndt's memoir, *A Picaro in Hitler's Europe* (Xlibris Corporation, Philadelphia, 2001) was consulted in the writing of Part 1.

The authors acknowledge invaluable information obtained from conversations with the following: Max Corden, Ross Garnaut, Bob Scott, Joan Butlin, Peter and Lena Karmel, Hal Hill, Walter Arndt, Karen McVicker and Malcolm Treadgold. They are also grateful to Robert Stove for editorial assistance.

NOTE ON AUTHORS

PETER COLEMAN is a writer and editor. His books include *The Heart of James McAuley: life and work of the Australian poet* (1980); *The Liberal Conspiracy. The Congress for Cultural Freedom and the Struggle for the Mind of Postwar Europe* (1989), on the role of intellectuals in the Cold War; *Obscenity Blasphemy Sedition: censorship in Australia* (1963), an inquiry into 100 years of Australian censorship; and the autobiographical *Memoirs of a Slow Learner* (1994). He was editor of *Quadrant* for 20 years, including several years as co-editor with H.W.Arndt, and of *The Bulletin*. He has also edited a number of books including the mould-breaking *Australian Civilization* (1962) and more recently *Double Take. Six Incorrect Essays (on political correctness)* (1996). He served in the Federal Parliament (as the Member for Wentworth) and NSW Parliament (when he was Leader of the Opposition and Minister for Revenue and Chief Secretary, responsible for prisons, police, boxing and pornography).

SELWYN CORNISH graduated in economics with first class honours from the University of Western Australia. He is a Visiting Fellow in the School of Economics and the Head of Toad Hall at the ANU. His major research fields embrace the development and application of macroeconomics in the 20th century, and biographical studies of economists. He has written on Keynes and Australia, and wrote the entry on Keynes for the *Biographical Dictionary of British Economists* (2004). His publications include *Full Employment in Australia. The Genesis of a White Paper* (1981); *Roland Wilson. A Biographical Essay* (2002); *Giblin's Platoon. The Trials and Triumph of the Economist in Australian Public Life* with William Coleman and Alf Hagger (2006); and the entry on 'Australasian Economics' in the *Revised New Palgrave Dictionary of Economics* (2008). He is an Associate Editor of the forthcoming *Biographical Dictionary of Australian and New Zealand Economists*, and is writing the *History of the Reserve Bank of Australia 1975–2000*. In 2004 he was appointed a Member of The Order of Australia for services to secondary education in the ACT.

PETER DRAKE graduated B.Comm. Honours (First Class) from the University of Melbourne in 1962. Heinz Arndt supervised his PhD studies at the Australian National University which were completed in 1966. In his career as an academic economist Peter became expert on monetary systems and financial development, working on Malaysia, Singapore, Indonesia and the Pacific island economies. His books include *Financial Development in Malaya and Singapore* (1969); *Money, Finance and Development* (1980); *Currency, Credit and Commerce: Early Growth in Southeast Asia* (2004). Peter was Professor of Economics, Deputy Vice-Chancellor and Principal of the University of New England, Armidale, before becoming the founding Vice-Chancellor of Australian Catholic University in 1991. In 2003 he was appointed a Member of The Order of Australia in recognition of his contributions to university leadership, the study of economics and the delivery of overseas aid.

BETTINA ARNDT is a social commentator, writing a newspaper column published across Australia and features for *The Australian Women's Weekly*. Originally trained as a clinical psychologist, she became well known in the 1970s as one of Australia's first sex therapists. As editor of the sex education magazine, *Forum*, she spent ten years talking about sex on television and radio and teaching sex counselling to doctors and other professionals. Turning her attention to broader social issues, she commenced writing for other magazines and newspapers. She returned to Australia in 1991 after spending five years in New York where she wrote a syndicated newspaper column and added two children to her family of three. She was for 17 years a member of the ANU council and has served on government committees reviewing child support and family law, IVF, ageing and childcare. Her most recent book is *Taking Sides* (1995).

PREFACE

Heinz Wolfgang Arndt was proud to be called an Australian economist. He was Australian by choice, economist by profession, and excellent in both respects. He was born and educated in Germany, but in the 1930s his family fled from the Nazis and Heinz received his higher education in Oxford. After a short internment in Canada during World War II, Heinz returned to England, married and began his career as an economist. In 1946, that career took him to Australia, where he happily spent the rest of his life.

Just as Heinz's young manhood exemplified a common European reaction to Hitler's regime, so his life and career in Australia personified four central elements of the nation's social and economic development in the second half of the twentieth century. These features were postwar immigration, engagement with Asia, the expansion and maturation of universities and the philosophical and practical shift from state to market authority in the allocation of resources. In this book, we tell, from three different perspectives, Heinz's story as a young European and then as a leading participant in important aspects of the postwar development of Australia.

Peter Coleman
Selwyn Cornish
Peter Drake

PRELUDE
H.W.A.—The man and his marriage

Why doesn't Heinz have a gong? The question had come up many times. It did seem odd that my father hadn't received an honour at any time in his distinguished career. So about 2001, a group of people decided to put his name up. Eminent people lined up to be referees. Former heads of Foreign Affairs, government ministers and prominent academics—the list was impressive.

Nothing happened. Finally, Heinz confessed to me that he had had an offer but had turned it down. What's more, he mentioned that he had had an even more salubrious gong proposed by the Fraser government many years earlier but had said no to that as well. The reason? Ruth didn't approve of such baubles.

Ruth Arndt was a formidable woman. That was always part of the attraction for my father. Her feisty nature was apparent well before they met, when she stood up to the Nazis as a schoolgirl, which ultimately led to her escape from Germany. By the time they were introduced at a party in London, she had endured some tough years working as an *au pair* before landing on her feet through a scholarship to the London School of Economics. There the tall, attractive brunette studied hard but also greatly enjoyed a lively student social life, with female students outnumbered 10 to one by their male colleagues. Perhaps unsurprisingly, Ruth had little interest in getting involved with anyone from Germany, but Heinz persisted, and she eventually succumbed to his charms.

They became quite a team: the elegant, rather stiff young academic with his warm, forthright, immensely capable wife. Within six years, they were in Australia, Heinz having accepted a lectureship at Sydney University when it became clear that despite making a splash with his first book, it would be difficult for a German academic to further his academic career in Britain.

But it still wasn't easy. Economist Noel Butlin had to pretend the couple was Danish to persuade their landlady to allow the Arndts into their shared accommodation. The young couple never spoke German to each other. They were keen to distance themselves from their origins and in years to come would often express irritation at aspects of the German character. 'I don't know why German politicians always have to shout!' Heinz once grumbled to my brother Nick.

While Heinz settled easily into his university community, it was Ruth who had the harder task of creating a new home for her family. 'I don't know how your mother kept her courage and determination having come so far to a place that wasn't the least bit welcoming,' comments Noel Butlin's widow, Joan, describing Ruth's extraordinary capacity to befriend people and make the most of her situation.

From the beginning, it was a very modern marriage. Heinz, who often appeared formal and reserved, was a very involved husband and father 'He did all the washing up! That was unheard of,' comments Joan. 'And he was a wonderful father. Unashamedly demonstrative which was quite rare in those days.' Joan remembers vividly Ruth's decision to return to Europe to see her parents in 1949. She had barely seen them since her escape 16 years earlier and had been saving every penny to pay for the trip. When she discovered she was pregnant, the couple decided she should go ahead. It was Heinz's attitude that astonished the Butlins: 'He supported her going off by herself. He didn't say, "Over my dead body", as many men of that time would have done.'

The result was that I was born in England, with my pregnant mother travelling on her own with her two young sons and returning eight months later with the three children, including a six-week-old baby. Despite caring for two young boys on a ship crowded with Australians, many of whom were far from friendly to a young mum with a foreign accent, Ruth wrote to Heinz almost every day of that difficult journey—twice on the day I was born.

It was in Canberra that Ruth really came into her own. Heinz had a chair at Canberra University College, which later merged with the ANU, but she was the one who connected them into the community through the lively migrant education classes she held in our home. There would be 20 to 30 people crammed into our tiny living rooms—Dutch, Germans, Poles, Latvians, Italians. Few of them were able to talk to each other but they had Ruth as a conduit, with her remarkable capacity to connect with people, even if she couldn't speak their language. A friend recently remembered watching Ruth at a long lunch with two Japanese women who could speak only a few words of English. Ruth knew no Japanese but sat there cheerful and unfazed, chatting away, making do with a mixture of sign language and a few friendly words.

Ruth became the unofficial social worker and confidante to the entire community and Heinz would drive our tiny Ford Anglia—one of the first cars in the area—ferrying pregnant women to hospital and accompanying bewildered migrants to deal with government bureaucracies. Ruth was always right in the thick of it, helping out families and gathering a collection of what Heinz always called 'Ruth's lame ducks', who needed extra care. So when one of her Polish students had all her clothes burnt by a jealous husband who wanted to 'try to keep her at home', Ruth was the one who found her something to wear and forced the man to come to his senses. At the time, Ruth and Heinz and their three young children were living in a fibro prefab with no electric appliances, only woodchip water heaters and a fuel stove. Running such a household was hard work but their home was always filled to the brim with people and alive with sing-songs around the piano, led by Ruth belting out everything from hymns to nursery rhymes to encourage her students to practice their stumbling English.

And so it was that Heinz was dragged far from his cultured, academic background into the real world. Yet he remained very much the cultured European, making strenuous efforts to keep up his knowledge of languages. After he died, we found in his wallet a hand-drawn graph giving a rigorous self-assessment of his competency in reading, comprehension, speaking and writing in English, German, French, Italian, Indonesian, Latin, Dutch and Spanish. He added a postscript noting some knowledge of Chinese, Polish, Turkish and Japanese, but sadly too little for formal rating.

He always retained his distinctive English accent, that he somehow passed onto his second son. Anne Booth met Heinz when she arrived in Canberra in 1971, back from a spell in London to become a research student in Heinz's department. 'I thought at the time (and the thought was to strike me on many occasions in Australia and South East Asia over the next three decades) that there was very little in Heinz's manners, speech or style of dress to suggest that he had ever spent a week in Australia, let alone most of his working life,' she says, mentioning the line in *My Fair Lady*: 'His English is too good which clearly shows that he is foreign.'

The man was rarely seen without his coat and tie, even on the beach or at picnics, which he always greatly enjoyed. He loved Canberra, delighting in the surrounding countryside and particularly the birdlife. He was a skilled landscape painter and had a great love of music, with very distinctive tastes. A friend vividly remembers him complaining: 'One forgets how vulgar Beethoven can be!' He had a huge collection of records but when the ABC started its FM classical music program, he stopped buying records and was very happy to listen to music with his tinny little transistor radio held to his ear—to the irritation of his wife and children. His son Chris made strenuous efforts to improve the quality of his listening experience by buying him expensive CD players, but he always reverted to the little radio.

The Arndt Sunday lunches were famous, as visiting academics were entertained over the renowned Arndt roast and *apfelstrudel*. Ruth had perfected the art of the grey roast in her British *au pair* era—a culinary skill that was later to bring her into conflict with her son Nick, who married into a French family. Nick mentions one occasion when Heinz was carving the roast and he noticed it was still a little pink in the centre. He asked Ruth to put it back in the oven for another 20 minutes, but luckily one of the guests offered to take the offending portion, bravely admitting he preferred it that way.

It didn't matter. Lively conversation was a far more critical component in the Arndt home entertainment, with Heinz always delighting in holding forth to a captive audience but Ruth adding cheerfully to the mix. She remained, all her life, a staunch social democrat committed to bettering the lives of underdogs. This meant she was singularly unimpressed by pomp and circumstance, by honours and titles. This professor's wife was undaunted by even the most intimidating of circumstances. Heinz would often come home from dinner parties shaking his head in amazement at the confidences she had managed to extract from eminent dinner partners during the course of the evening.

This was a woman never afraid of voicing her opinion and indeed of telling others what was good for them. After the Arndts moved away from the migrant community in Ainslie, Ruth turned to teaching evening German classes. In the 1950s, her students included Max Bennett, an ex-sailor whose wife, Shirley, was secretary to another ANU professor. Ruth asked Max about his job. He explained that he was working as a radio announcer. 'You can do better than that!' came the blunt response. 'In later years I realised she was right,' says Max ruefully.

When Peter Karmel was appointed to the ANU as Vice-Chancellor, Ruth contacted his wife, Lena. 'She had a little talk to me because she thought I was going to say the wrong thing as a Vice-Chancellor's wife,' said Lena, adding, 'I did say the wrong thing quite often, sometimes deliberately.' The two became very close friends.

Despite her prodigious energy, Ruth, like many women of her generation, constructed her working life around her family and ended up with a messy, unsatisfying career, shifting from migrant education to teaching in a private school to some rather difficult years in the public service. She was never able to practise her profession because her social work qualifications were not recognised in Australia, which was a bitter disappointment. Heinz left 350 boxes of papers to the National Library. Ruth destroyed all her papers except for half a dozen items, including a letter from the government informing her that her British qualifications were insufficient.

Given Ruth's unwavering commitment to her left-wing political beliefs, she was far from happy when Heinz did an about-turn and shifted his political allegiance. She never forgave him for resigning from the Labor Party over Gough Whitlam's uncritical support of China. Politics became an increasing source of tension between them.

For a man who adored leaping into the fray and participating in public debate, this wasn't easy for Heinz. Whenever some major public issue was in the news that Heinz felt strongly about, he would yearn to toss off a letter to the editor or write a newspaper opinion piece. Sometimes he wouldn't be able to resist and would whip something off, put it in the mail and then spend days in agony, knowing he was going to be in the doghouse when it was published.

Margaret Easton, his secretary of 35 years, remembers one such occasion, when he was longing to express an opinion on some issue that was bound to annoy Ruth. After days of agonising, the letter appeared—published under Easton's name. He had persuaded her to sign it.

In their last few years together, Ruth was increasingly immobilised due to various ailments. Her steady stream of visitors was often subjected to lectures on a variety of topics from Heinz, who so hankered after an audience. As the visitors left, Heinz would show them out and a carefully chosen few would receive a brown paper bag containing a copy of *Quadrant* magazine containing one of his articles, discreetly delivered just outside the front door.

I vividly remember one occasion when I took him to task for allowing Ruth to constrain him from indulging in his favoured role as a public intellectual. He was indignant. 'That's what I love about her. Her strength, the passion of her convictions,' he said. In the weeks after she died, he told me he had often turned around, sensing her presence in their Deakin home. 'I even dream she's still nagging me,' he said, a little wistfully.

PART ONE

1

FROM KAISER TO HITLER

The year of Heinz Wolfgang Arndt's birth, 1915, was not a good year for a German boy to be born in. Such a boy would soon know that his country had been defeated in a great war, that the Emperor had abdicated and a republic had been proclaimed amid putsches, revolutions, assassinations, unemployment and malnutrition. By the time Arndt was seven, Germany would endure hyperinflation. When he was 10, the first volume of Hitler's *Mein Kampf* would be published.

In the 1920s there would be an economic recovery and the explosion of a dazzling 'Weimar' culture, which seemed to make Berlin the cultural capital of the world. But by the time Heinz was 14, the Great Depression would devastate the economy, and the year he turned 18, Hitler's National Socialists would begin a radical transformation of Germany. If he were a Jew or partly Jewish, he would be driven from his trade, business or profession. It would become prudent and even necessary to emigrate. Most of those who did not would be murdered.

Heinz was born in Breslau, then the most important city in eastern Germany. It had been a Polish town (Wratislawa) until Frederick the Great incorporated it into Prussia during the 1740s after the Silesian War. Two hundred years later, after Germany's defeat in World War II, it became Polish again. It was 'ethnically cleansed' and renamed Wroclaw. German Breslau disappeared as totally as had Pompeii.

Wilhelmine Breslau had been cultured, prosperous and progressive. Its universities, scientists, philosophers and musicians helped set international standards. It was also a tolerant city: its German–Jewish symbiosis was more advanced than anything in the United States or Australia. For many Germans it exemplified the civilising mission of the Second Reich: nothing like the Dreyfus Case, they believed, would have been possible in Breslau, and perhaps they were right.

The Arndts were good examples of this symbiosis. They were thoroughly assimilated, had long since Teutonicised their Jewish name (Aaron) and had adopted Lutheranism. Arndt's paternal grandfather, a Hanseatic merchant who had prospered in African trade, had married a tall, blonde and beautiful 'Aryan' daughter of a Bavarian thespian family. The Arndts immersed themselves in German culture, especially science and music.

Heinz's father, Fritz Georg Arndt, moved to Breslau in 1911. He was a brilliant organic chemist, who took a position as an assistant in the University of Breslau when his Kiel Professor was appointed to a chair. This was still the Breslau of parades on the Kaiser's birthday, of Mahler concerts and breakfasts at Kempinski. It was also a place for work, not *savoir-vivre*. As Walter Laqueur, himself a child of Breslau, put it: 'There was no aristocracy or high society as in Berlin, no royal merchants as in Hamburg, no artists' quarter as in Munich.' But it produced a disproportionate number of leading scientists.

The anglophile Fritz Arndt joined the English Club and there he met Julia Heimann, whom he married in March 1914. (The name Julia was, in Heinz Arndt's amused opinion, ostentatiously classicist.) She was twenty-two. Both her parents were Jewish, although Julia was baptised before her Lutheran wedding. Arndt coolly described his mother as 'pretty (on the plump side), ostensibly studying archaeology at the University, but much more interested in riding, novels, dancing, tennis and social life'. Heinz's younger brother, Walter, was less detached: 'Mother was fragrant, soft, and round, all in pastel shades like the more lyrical chocolate-box tops; quite accessible but too full of energetic leisure time projects, and later, alarming educational or gymnastic schemes.'

When World War I began in August 1914, almost every able-bodied man in Breslau readily enlisted to fight for the Kaiser. Although the army rejected Fritz because of his varicose veins, the authorities used his amazing linguistic skills in propaganda and censorship. Then, in October 1915 at the age of 30, he was appointed to a newly created Chair in Chemistry at the Darülfünun (House of Science), known otherwise as the Islamic University of Constantinople. He had become a part of the technical aid that Germany gave to its ally Turkey. His mission was to establish the first chemistry department in Turkey, devise a Turkish technical terminology and write textbooks for Turkish students. He liked to say that he was selected as much for his gifts as a linguist as for his reputation as a chemist.

The infant Heinz was in Constantinople for two years. The family lived well in Ayas Pasa, near Taksim Square in Pera, beside the Bosphorus. They had Turkish servants and a German nanny. Heinz's brother, Walter, was born in Constantinople, but when his mother became pregnant with Bettina, it was thought best that she and the two boys return to Breslau and to German medical services. (Heinz had contracted para-typhoid in Constantinople. It took him months to recover and it continued to affect his walking.)

The Germany to which they returned was dramatically different from the confident country they had left. It had become a land of strikes, mutinies, military defeats and political crises. In November 1918, Germany surrendered. In the same month the Anglo-French forces occupied Constantinople and expelled all Germans, including Heinz's father.

When the family was at last reunited in Breslau, it was a Germany of foreign occupation, revolution, inflation, an unpopular republic and shortages of all kinds, especially food. Heinz's father did not mourn the passing of the Hohenzollerns or the weakening of *Junker* traditions. He was *Republiktreu*, a Wilsonian liberal idealist who supported free trade, opposed nationalism and rejected the Social Democrats as the party of the uneducated. But he had only a minimal interest in politics (his wife had none). His devotion to research and his appointment as an associate professor relieved the stagnation of life in the once confident Breslau.

There was also a housing shortage. At first the family lived on the top floor of Heinz's maternal grandparents' mansion in Kaiser Wilhelm Square (later Adolf Hitler Square). Heinz's first memory was of this house—and of the Kapp Putsch, a monarchist uprising in March 1920 against the new Weimar Republic. One night during the abortive uprising, his mother moved his cot away from a nursery window that had been shattered by the fire of machine-guns.

The hyperinflation of the early 1920s drastically reduced the income from investments on which his grandparents lived, but they kept their art treasures and one or two maids. There was also an old liveried retainer, like Chekhov's Firs, fit for errands, stove-feeding and boot-polishing. Heinz's grandfather, Paul, began his day reading a liberal newspaper, the *Breslauer Neuste Nachrichten*. (His wife, Marie, read the arch-conservative *Schlesische Zeitung*.) He then devoted himself to browsing through histories, in various languages, of art and of the Papacy. He would occasionally take Heinz to a *Konditorei* café to stuff himself on cream cakes and ice-cream. He once took him to watch the 'six-day' bike race in the vast *Jahrhunderthalle*, built in 1912 to commemorate the liberation of Prussia from the Napoleonic yoke. Heavy, bald, with watery blue eyes, a huge nose and dangling lip ('one of the ugliest men I have ever known'), Paul was, Heinz said, 'my closest companion'. His grandmother was more distant. She reminded the children of Britain's Queen Mary. They never heard her laugh loudly, speak quickly or raise her voice. She played golf.

Each afternoon Heinz would go to their apartment on Kaiser Wilhelm Square where, after kissing his grandmother's hand and shaking his grandfather's, he would do his piano practice. Then he would do the homework for his first school, the Weinhold Academy, a *Privat-Reform-Schule*, which he remembered best for his discussions with his schoolmates of the mark–dollar exchange rate in the era of the Great Inflation. He never forgot that at one point the US dollar was officially worth 4,200,000,000,000 marks.

The inflation ended abruptly after Chancellor Gustav Stresemann established the new mark. For young Heinz, however, an era of personal instability now began. The year 1925 marked what he called 'a great divide': the divorce of his mother and father. In an affectionate, unpublished tribute, Heinz presented his father as a loving parent, a kind friend, a distinguished scientist, a gifted linguist and an exuberant personality with a love of music, sport and jokes, which he recorded in a notebook. He was also a difficult man to live with: 'nervous, ready to give vent to minor anxieties, such as the punctual posting or safe arrival of letters'.

> My father would go to the lab around 8.30 a.m. on a two-stroke motorbike. (At no stage of his life could he afford to buy, or even consider buying, a car.) He would come home about 1 p.m. for lunch, lie down for a thirty-minute nap, and after another three hours at the lab, come home for dinner about 6.30 p.m. All his life he suffered from asthma, much aggravated by one of the chemicals on which he worked. For years he tried to combat it by breathing and shouting exercises, which reverberated through the apartment: later for years he would give himself anti-histamine injections. The asthma added to extreme sensitivity to noise which made him a very bad sleeper, one reason why, as long as I can remember, he slept in his own bedroom adjoining his large study. Constant admonitions that he must not be disturbed during his afternoon or early morning sleep punctuated our lives as children. He was an inveterate smoker, but only pipe and (black Brazil) cigars which he chewed nervously at one end as fast as he burned them at the other, leaving small plugs in ash trays all over the apartment.

Fritz Arndt came to believe that his wife was having an affair with 'Feo-Weo'—Wilhelm Furtwängler, the great conductor—and perhaps with other men. In any case, one day in 1925 he called the children together in the sitting room and informed them that their mother had decided she could not live without Freddy von Cramon, a Breslau businessman, and she wanted a divorce. (This was also the period of Fritz's greatest contribution to science, the Arndt–Eistert Reaction, a very useful procedure for synthesising certain classes of molecules and increasing the length of the carbon chain.)

Heinz, who took his father's side in this painful disruption of their lives, wrote of it with a brevity and coolness that conceals pain: 'We were shocked as much by the social stigma that attached to divorce in German middle class circles as by the prospect of separation from her.' Walter tells a more emotional and surely more accurate story: their mother left them, he wrote, 'maimed and numbed, his childhood blighted and his sense of worth destroyed. He had taken her part in the guilt reckoning. He still did. Yet he had felt abandoned. He belonged to her, but she was gone.' She wrote 'urgent, searching letters' but Walter's replies were merely 'polite, empty'. How could the children touch on 'the monstrous central topic'?

Fritz was deeply hurt by his wife's departure and never forgave her. (He later married his housekeeper.) The divorce, however, brought Fritz and Heinz closer to each other. They sat together around the HMV gramophone playing Brahms over and over again. The father took the children on holidays—to Budapest and Venice. They bathed together in the Lido. He played chess with the children. At Sunday lunch, he gave marvellously comprehensible little lectures on Albert Einstein's relativity theory or Niels Bohr's model of the atom (he translated Bohr into German from Danish). He also took pains to develop Heinz's mastery of English. At some meals conversation was permitted only in English. There were also English reading evenings. The children saw their mother once a year in the summer.

This great divide in Heinz's childhood coincided with his enrolment at the Kaiser Wilhelm Gymnasium. The school found him a difficult young man: 'I got the worst marks that had ever been known in my Gymnasium for behaviour,' he said. A student who behaved even moderately received a first, and very bad students received a second. Some boys guilty of atrocious behaviour received a third. Heinz received a fourth.

ARNDT'S STORY

Sibling rivalries exacerbated the tension produced by the divorce. The younger brother and sister ganged up against the first-born. 'My brother was extraordinarily clever,' Heinz said. 'He was much so better at everything than I was. That worried me all my school life. I was intensely lacking in self-confidence because of this. In my last years at school I got better.'

Walter recalls a typical quarrel. Heinz was devouring the works of Leonhard Frank, whose popular and revolutionary novels depicted the struggles (usually doomed) of a free-spirited young man against the repressive ethos of school, society, capitalism and militarism. Walter picked up Frank's *Das Tor zur Welt* and flicked through its pages derisively. An enraged Heinz seized the book from his hands and tore it up.

These schoolboy rivalries soon gave way to the wider political tensions created by the rise of Adolf Hitler. The family's Jewishness meant nothing to them. They were all part of the German–Jewish symbiosis. They had no wish to be considered Jewish, but it would have been vulgar to have been ostentatiously non-Jewish. Both of Heinz's parents professed Lutheranism and he had been baptised in the Lutheran Church. None of his grandparents was a practising Jew, although his Breslau grandfather occasionally made a donation to the synagogue. 'Religion played no part in our home. After a short religious "crisis" induced by a fashionable and persuasive young parson during my "confirmation lessons" when I was about 15, I turned my back very firmly on religion and have never since quite rid myself of a now old-fashioned atheist zeal.'

Even at school, the Jewish question had never been important. One or two Jewish boys would leave class during the religious instruction period. So did a couple of Catholic boys. It was all a bit mysterious. ('What were they up to?') But these boys looked like everyone else and no one thought much about it. Just as Catholics had missed out, it was assumed, when Luther reformed the Church in the sixteenth century, so, it was also assumed, Jews had missed out at the time of Jesus. No doubt in God's good time they would all catch up and become sound Lutherans. The students heard or read nothing of Russian pogroms, Viennese anti-Semitism, even the Dreyfus case. The murder of Walter Rathenau in 1922 or Rosa Luxemburg in 1919 could have happened in Outer Mongolia for all they heard about them from their teachers.

Yet there was space in the textbooks for combating 'foreign lies' about Germany's war guilt and for recording the sufferings of ethnic Germans in the 'lost' territories, for whom each month the school collected compulsory dues. The teachers were nationalist and *revanchist*, and some of the schoolboys, who had little feeling for the old soldiers' *Fronterlebnis* (experience of the wartime front), even mocked their wooden limbs, iron crosses and pot-bellied appearance that would afterwards be made world-famous by Erich von Stroheim.

The Great Depression, however, weakened the appeal of this sort of Weimar irreverence—or turned it against itself. Walter Laqueur tells of a typical incident one Sunday on his way home from a family outing on the Oder. As his steamer's little orchestra played *Nun ade, du mein lieb Heimatland* ('Now adieu, you, my beloved homeland'), a swimmer climbed on to the ship and wiped his bottom with the Black-Red-Gold flag of the Weimar Republic. There was a great roar of laughter.

Yet there was no laughter among the Sunday crowds of unemployed workers in the Breslau streets when their quarrels culminated, as they often did, in murder. When Hitler spoke in Breslau, from the ramp of the castle in Kaiser Wilhelm Square, he began to draw vast crowds. His speeches were anti-capitalist, anti-bourgeois, anti-monarchist, anti-Semitic, anti-Slav, populist, nationalist, socialist and, above all, *revanchist*. Anti-Semitic riots followed his visits. The local papers published lists of Jews and sponsored anti-Semitic petitions. One by one, Heinz's fellow students joined the Hitler Youth. The teachers began to speak of a new dawn coming: bliss was it in that dawn to be alive.

Many liberal or conservative Germans still clung to a determined, almost neurotic, optimism. Even in January 1933 when Hitler was appointed Chancellor, he swore allegiance to the Weimar Constitution. There was a Nazi torchlight procession through Berlin's Wilhelmstrasse (and another in Breslau), but there was at first little indication of a radical Nazi revolution. Some conservatives thought they had captured the National Socialists. Hitler would not last very long, they said. 'We have hired him!' declared the Prussian aristocrat Franz von Papen. (The populist Nazis despised 'the vons'.)

But the optimism was short-lived. Hitler announced an election for March 1933 and Nazi terror dominated the campaign. The National Socialists broke up meetings and shot opponents. Nazi postal workers opened letters and Nazi technicians bugged telephones. Nazi journalists, civil servants, academics and trade unionists demanded the abolition of the 'Jewish republic' and the purge of the media, civil service, universities and trade unions.

The National Socialists won only 44 per cent of the vote (they did better in Breslau with 50.2 per cent), but the Reichstag granted Hitler dictatorial powers for four years. All parties except the National Socialist German Workers Party were dissolved. Workers deserted their trade unions and joined the Nazi *Betriebszellen* (factory cells). The Nazi Labour Front became the voice of the working class. The national flag and national anthem were abolished, so were the federal Constitution and states' rights. The persecution of the Jews began. Social democrats, communists, Catholics and nationalists joined the National Socialists in singing the Horst Wessel Song on public occasions.

Sebastian Haffner, then a Berlin lawyer and later the author of *Defying Hitler* (2000), recalled the tale that every Prussian schoolchild knew—of the miller of Potsdam. Frederick the Great wanted the demolition of a windmill that spoiled his view. He offered to buy the mill. The miller did not want to sell. Frederick threatened to seize and destroy it.'Just so, Your Majesty,' said the miller,'but I still have the High Court in Berlin.'The mill, writes Haffner, can still be seen to this day.

But judges who kept the law against Frederick the Great did not stand up to Hitler. When Nazi thugs entered the law courts shouting '*Jude verrecke!*' ('Death to the Jews!'), court officers announced:'Jewish gentlemen would do well to leave the building.' Nazi lawyers sniggered as the Jews left. The student revolution extended to Christians. In Munich, Friedrich Reck-Malleczewen observed a Hitler Youth, his soft face contorted in fury, rip a crucifix from a classroom wall and fling it out of the window, shouting, 'Dirty Jew!'

Still, for many Germans, life went on normally. They strolled the streets or danced in the open air. Cafés, cinemas and dance halls were full. Aryan journalists, film-makers, actors, singers and musicians saw career opportunities and took them.

Heinz's Breslau grandmother died as Hitler took power. Years afterwards, Heinz wrote of her husband

> A few days later, in his seventy-seventh year, clearly believing that whatever purpose his life might have had was now gone, he took a huge overdose of sleeping pills. To the horror of my mother who had come to take charge of the situation, the dose was barely sufficient. For seven days she and the family doctor dreaded that he would wake up. Fortunately he died and thus saved himself the fate that befell most of his Jewish relatives in the following years.

In a matter of weeks, Heinz's father was dismissed from the University of Breslau. However widely honoured he had been for the Arndt–Eistert Reaction, he still, as far as the Nazis were concerned, had a Jewish grandfather.

At the end of March 1933, the English economist Lord Beveridge, of the London School of Economics (LSE), was chatting in a café in Vienna with fellow economists Ludwig von Mises and Lionel Robbins. Someone opened an evening paper listing the names of leading German professors being purged under racial laws. The list included Fritz Arndt. Beveridge and Robbins decided immediately to set up an organisation, based in the LSE, to help all German scholars dismissed by the Nazis to find academic work in Britain.

Soon afterwards, the LSE teachers and administrators agreed to contribute deductions from salaries to an Academic Assistance Fund. Beveridge then persuaded the nuclear physicist Lord Rutherford to be its president. The Council of the Royal Society, the oldest and most respected of British societies of scientists, then provided offices in Burlington House, London.

On 22 May 1933, a sombre letter was sent to *The Times* announcing the formation of the Academic Assistance Council. It was drafted in a low key in clear awareness that, in this pre-Holocaust period, public concern about the careers of German Jewish academics was serious but limited. The Royal Society had strongly urged that any appeal be based on academic freedom and liberal civilisation, and not be specifically Jewish. It also suggested that no signatory of any appeal be Jewish.

The letter of appeal was signed by 41 famous scholars, but only the Australian philosopher Samuel Alexander was Jewish. The signatories included Lord Rutherford, the economist John Maynard Keynes, the poet A.E. Housman, the historian H.A.L. Fisher and the Australian classicist Gilbert Murray. It is a historic letter and can be quoted at length

> Many eminent scholars and men of science and University teachers of all grades and in all faculties are being obliged to relinquish their posts in Universities of Germany.
>
> The Universities of our own and other countries will, we hope, take whatever action they can to offer employment to these men and women, as teachers and investigators.
>
> But the financial resources of Universities are limited and are subject to claims for their normal development which cannot be

ignored. If the information before us is correct, effective help from outside for more than a small fraction of the teachers now likely to be condemned to want and idleness will depend on the existence of large funds specifically devoted to this purpose. It seems clear also that some organisation will be needed to act as a centre of information and put the teachers concerned into touch with the institutions that can best help them.

We have formed ourselves accordingly into a provisional Council for these two reasons. We shall seek to raise a fund, to be used primarily, though not exclusively, in providing maintenance for displaced teachers and investigators, and finding them work in universities and scientific institutions.

We shall place ourselves in communication both with Universities in this country and with organisations which are being formed for similar purposes in other countries, and we shall seek to provide a clearing house and centre of information.

The issue raised at the moment is not a Jewish one alone; many who have suffered or are threatened have no Jewish connection. Our action implies no unfriendly feelings to any people of any country; it implies no judgment on forms of government or on any political issue between countries. Our only aims are the relief of suffering and the defence of learning and science.

The Academic Assistance Council's rooms in Burlington House became an academic labour exchange and dispensary of honoraria to dismissed scholars. One of the first to be helped was Fritz Arndt, who was appointed to the Department of Organic Chemistry at Oxford.

At the very time, in 1933, when German professors were being dismissed under the Aryan Laws, a new University Law in Turkey was converting the old Islamic Ottoman University of Constantinople into the secular University of Istanbul, with new faculties of Medicine, Law, Science and Letters. President Kemal Atatürk seized his opportunity. A tragedy for Germany became an extraordinary stroke of luck for Turkey, as Kemal recruited some 50 German (and Austrian) scholars to his new university.

They included such famous figures as the economist Wilhelm Roepke, who inspired Ludwig Erhard's 'economic miracle' in postwar West Germany; Fritz Neumark, who reformed Turkey's income tax system and later became Rector of Frankfurt University; the philosopher Hans

Reichenbach, who founded the Berlin school of logical positivism; the mathematician Richard von Mises; the sociologist Gerhard Kessler; the surgeon Rudolf Nissen; and Fritz Arndt, who returned to his old chair.

Arndt lectured in Turkish, became a Turkish citizen and was known as modern *kimya'yi Turkiye'ye getiren adam*—the man who brought modern chemistry to Turkey. He held the chair until he retired in 1955.

As the Arndt family began fanning out across Europe, Heinz's brother, Walter, joined his father in Oxford and enrolled in Oriel College. He later moved to Poland, where he planned to learn his uncle's business in the sugar mill, but found himself in the Polish Resistance before escaping to Istanbul. Their sister, Bettina, finished school in Oxford before moving to Vienna to study art, escaping back to England the day before German troops arrived. Heinz's mother remained in Berlin with her second husband until they too moved to Istanbul, where her husband died. She was later married again to a Czech diplomat and lived in Prague before fleeing with her husband to London.

Heinz remained in Germany for most of 1933. He finished his written examinations under Weimar and did his oral examinations under Hitler. He then joined a labour service set up by the Social Democratic Party to arrange work for the young unemployed. This gave him time to see if the Nazi madness would be as short-lived as many still thought it would be. For six months, he lived in an idle textile mill near Gorlitz, chopping rocks six hours a day for use in road repairs. For the rest of the day, he and his companions played chess, hiked, painted or did fatigue duty. In August, they were billeted in villages to help farmers with the harvest.

It was soon clear that Hitler was no flash in the pan. While Heinz was chopping rocks, his fellow students in Berlin built a ceremonial bonfire, onto which they hurled books by Jewish writers, in the enthusiastic presence of the Minister for Culture, celebrated editor and orator Dr Goebbels. In the same month, the famous philosopher Martin Heidegger delivered a rectorial address in the University of Marburg, calling on all German intellectuals to repudiate the old discredited liberalism and rally around Hitler. 'German students are already on the march!' were Heidegger's own words. In August the first list of *émigrés* to lose German citizenship included the satirist Kurt Tucholsky, the dramatist Ernst Toller and the novelists Heinrich Mann and Lion Feuchtwanger. The surge of Nazi popularity was becoming irresistible.

The old Germany was almost dead. German civilisation had submitted to the German Reich, as Friedrich Nietzsche had predicted. The Prussia of Kant, of truthfulness, humanity, honour and selfless service, had been taken over by the *canaille*. The Bavaria of Catholic faith and tradition had given way to a fanatic racism. Conservatives of the old Germany fled or became internal *émigrés*.

By October, Heinz decided to follow his father to Oxford. His earlier ambition to become a German diplomat was now ridiculous. Any idea of attending a Nazified German university was unthinkable. The prospect of an Oxford education offered some hope. The young German said goodbye to his Hamburg grandparents, turned his back on the New Order and took the ferry to England with a sense of liberation.

2
OXFORD MADE HIM

Heinz's arrival in England in October 1933 had elements of farce. Eager to practise his English, he struck up a conversation on the cross-channel ferry with an affable Englishman who turned out to be a homosexual attracted to the good-looking if confused young German. At Oxford, he disconcerted the Lincoln College porter by addressing him as 'sir'. On his first morning, he attended the matriculation ceremony in the Divinity School, but was unable to understand a word of the Vice-Chancellor's address, which was, as it happened, delivered in the Latin spoken by English dons. To show how cooperative he could be, he joined the Lincoln boat club, in which he rowed badly and without pleasure.

But such gaucheries in no way weakened his determination. 'I intend to get a first!' Heinz told his bemused friend John Douglas Pringle, later editor of the *Sydney Morning Herald*. He had decided that the best option open to him, as a foreigner and a refugee, was an academic career in political science. For this, a first-class degree was a necessary prerequisite. He would read modern greats (philosophy, politics and economics), the recently created variation on traditional greats (ancient history and philosophy) and he would do as brilliantly as he could.

Oxford enchanted Heinz. Unlike the German universities, it was left of centre and pacifist. Its union had recently passed the resolution: 'This House will not fight for King and Country.' Students and dons took easily to Heinz: this tall, dark, grey-eyed, somewhat mid-Victorian foreigner, who played the piano, tennis and chess and was a bit of a swot. But he remained an outsider.

Two men broke through his reserve. One was Tom Baily, a son of the vicarage, who read theology and planned to be a vicar himself. They became close friends. Tom invited Heinz to meet his family in the Lake District. Heinz invited Tom to meet his father in Istanbul, swim in the Bosphorus, sail on the Sea of Marmara and see the sights in old Stamboul.

Fifty years later, Heinz recalled this friend of his youth in a heartfelt memoir called *Canon Baily*. Tom was, he wrote, 'the complete English country gentleman'. Tall, slim, blond, always in flannels and tweed, with a long woollen scarf on cool days, he was 'a conservative with few illusions, an amused spectator of the follies of mankind'. His favourite reading was

The Times, Jane Austen, Anthony Trollope and railway timetables.'He read the Barsetshire novels over and over again.' (He later became a regular reader of the Sydney sex education magazine *Forum* edited by Heinz's daughter, Bettina, whom he had christened.)

'For well over thirty years Tom tended his parish, conducting his Sunday services, marrying and burying parishioners all of whom he knew by name, baptising their children, visiting the sick, often on quite remote farms up the fells, taking Sunday School, helping run community organisations and carrying out all the tasks nowadays assigned to social welfare workers and counsellors. I never once heard him refer to religion.' Heinz was sure his friend no longer believed in the Anglican creed or even in God. But he did his duty year in and year out.

Heinz also accepted the family legend that his sister, Bettina, had turned down a proposal of marriage from Tom, who remained in love with her to his dying day, never marrying, but dividing his life between his duties as the Vicar of Shap and his attachment to the Arndt family.

Heinz's other friend at Oxford was his mentor and moral tutor, the philosopher Harold Cox. Even more than Tom Baily, Cox shaped Heinz's understanding of Englishness—or Britishness, since this dry, reserved don who dressed always in the compulsory flannels and tweed had been born in Glasgow and attended Glasgow High School. 'I now realise,' Heinz subsequently recollected,'that his friendships with undergraduates reflected his repressed homosexuality, but I was too innocent at the time for the thought to have occurred to me, and in all the years of close companionship there was never an overt or covert hint or word or gesture from him. He took mildly amused note of my successive girlfriends, but never expressed the slightest desire to meet them.'

Cox listened patiently each week to Heinz's essays on the assigned topics. He would never intimate that he had heard these brilliant and devastating arguments countless times already. He would, however, ask probing questions, 'raising doubts, compelling me to clarify, distinguish, qualify, think'. He also taught Heinz about food and wine, painting and architecture. He introduced him to Ravel, Debussy and Stravinsky—a new musical world for a refugee from Breslau brought up in the self-sufficient heritage of the German–Austrian classics.

They took holidays together in Spain, Spanish Morocco and Istanbul. They also toured England in Cox's MG sports car. Once while they were sitting on a Norfolk beach at Overy Staithe, near Burnham Market, the

German hydrogen-powered airship, the *Hindenburg*, flew in from over the North Sea, its engine noise drowned by the roar of the waves. It was, in the propaganda of Dr Goebbels, an exemplar of National Socialist achievement. Heinz and his companion were struck by its daring beauty. As Heinz put it in a letter to a girlfriend, it was 'extraordinarily nice'.

The conservative Cox was distressed, however, by Heinz's gradual shift into the orbit of the Communist Party. Their association cooled and they lost contact. They met only once in the 36 years after Heinz left Oxford. He always recalled with pleasure the understated way Cox had initiated him into English civility. 'I hope you are getting better,' a friend said to Cox, who was suffering from cancer. 'I won't be getting better,' he replied. He took his own life soon afterwards.

However much Heinz admired British phlegm, liberalism, even humour, he would not pretend to be other than German. It was his nationality. He signed his letters, teutonically, 'Heinz Wolfgang'. He went to meetings of the German Club. He kept in touch with his German relatives. He was confident that the hysterical crowds worshipping Hitler in Dr Goebbels' propaganda films did not reflect the millions of Germans who opposed the Nazis. His own austere moral code, which his English friends mocked, was more Prussian than Bloomsbury.

Something of his tensions, uncertainties and dual loyalties surfaced suddenly in March 1936—two and half years after he left Germany—in his response to John Ford's film *The Informer* (1935). Based on the novel by Liam O'Flaherty (1925), it is the story of an Irishman (played by Victor McLagen) who betrays his country, is tortured by conscience and is condemned to death by a secret IRA court. In a long letter to a girlfriend, Pauline, Heinz wrote

> I don't think I have ever seen a film which produces a particular atmosphere—the atmosphere of this tense nationalism, the underground work, the lowness and struggle of those rebels, and all that mixed with that devout Catholicism—so powerfully and vividly. It has swept me off my feet and I am amazed at myself. None of the sentiments which the film represents and glorifies appeals to me. I detest that nationalism, the spirit of lawlessness and revolt, I approve of the surrender of the rebel to the law, I have no understanding for [*sic*] the religious sentiments by which these men and women are swayed.

> And yet the film carried me away to an extent which even now, after half an hour, seems almost incredible. It appealed to all that is irrational in me and that was enough to overpower everything else; maybe I am less rational, more sentimental than other people, which I would not like to believe. It is simply that we do not always think and reason but instead let ourselves drift and float on a current of instinct and emotion. That same instinct, the same emotions which drive nations mad, which make them swerve, as in a dream, in joy, anger, hate, pride and above all profound fear down to another crash and another short awakening before the current sweeps them away again. Any are mad [*sic*] is no reason for going mad ourselves, and an experience like mine tonight is a good warning to train one's mind against these forces by showing their latent power in our strangely built minds, or as the Germans would say, souls.

It was no easy matter to abandon 1,000 years of German culture and proclaim, with the leftist playwright Ernst Toller, *Ich War Ein Deutscher* ('I used to be a German'). But undergraduates' travel tales about the friendly Nazis increasingly repelled Heinz. At the last meeting he attended of the German Club, the speaker began his talk with a 'Heil Hitler' salute and then spoke for an hour about Hitler's Autobahnen. For a moment, Heinz thought of joining the Jewish Society.

He found some relief in left-wing politics. 'These were the thirties. We lived politics.' Students were overwhelmingly on the left. This meant they detested Mussolini and Hitler, admired Franklin Roosevelt and Jawaharlal Nehru, and despised Ramsay MacDonald, Stanley Baldwin and Neville Chamberlain. They were against nationalism and militarism, fascism and Nazism. They were also anti-capitalist because 'an economic system characterized by periodic disastrous depressions, chronic unemployment and stagnation, extreme inequality of wealth and income, and an ethic of each for himself and devil take the hindmost, was hopelessly inefficient as well as immoral'.

In the course of his five years in Oxford, Heinz began as a Wilsonian liberal, became a fellow-traveller of the Soviet Union and ended as a non-party communist. When he arrived in October 1933, he was still, like his father, committed to moral absolutes and opposed to violence. He noted Joan Robinson's *The Economics of Imperfect Competition* (in 1933, the *dernier cri*), but did not need her rigorous proofs that there were unemployed workers in England. (He had watched the Hunger Marchers parade through the bleak Oxford streets.) He still shared his father's scepticism about the political wisdom of the uneducated proletariat, but he dropped in on the communist October Club, read the Webbs' *Soviet Communism: A New Civilisation?* (1935) and devoured the works of the Left Book Club. The one book that bowled him over was Beverley Nichols' passionate pacifist polemic, *Cry Havoc!* (1933), with its theme that 'Patriotism is an Evil—in every country'. Hitler must be stopped, they all believed, but without war or rearmament.

However much Heinz 'lived politics', his plans for an academic career depended on his getting a first-class degree. At first, he enjoyed his course immensely, 'plunging into one subject after the other with naïve and argumentative excitement: philosophy, economics, history, politics—and English. I worked on my English every day. The tutorial system with its requirement of writing two essays a week for three years taught me to write as nothing else could have done.' G.M. Trevelyan's social history especially thrilled him: it was a revelation that history was not, as he had been taught in Breslau, about kings and wars, but about ordinary people. 'He worked like a dog,' his brother said.

But Heinz was soon disenchanted. Oxford was in a stale period. He had arrived two or three years too early. He found philosophy 'anaemic'—until late in his course when he read A.J. Ayer's *Language, Truth and Logic* (1936). Economics was likewise limited—again, until late in his course, when he read Keynes' *General Theory* (1936). Politics was also dull—until he discovered Karl Mannheim's *Ideology and Utopia*, yet another revelation from 1936. (The German version had been published years before, but it was the controversy engendered by the English version that excited Heinz—and that deepened his commitment to communism.) One of his tutors, the conservative John Maude, advised Harold Cox that Arndt was 'unteachable'—that is, too argumentative and dogmatically left-wing.

At the end of June 1936, Heinz unburdened himself to his friend Pauline: 'I have no hopes whatever for a first.' In July, he tried to explain himself

> As so often before I felt so utterly futile and silly, so superfluous all the time. I bore everybody else with continuously talking about it. And yet the stake is so immense. Everything, whether I shall be able to lead the life I want to lead, to do those things for others

which I feel myself able to do, all my fortunes of [*sic*] the rest of my life, depend on what my examiners will think of my performance during those 30 hours two weeks ago and those few minutes on the 17th which I still have before me.

As it happened, he got his first. In March 1937, the Assistant Registrar certified that

…it appears by the Registers of the University of Oxford that Heinz Wolfgang Arndt Lincoln College satisfied the Examiners in the Final Honour School of Philosophy, Politics, and Economics in Trinity Term, 1936, and was placed by them in the First Class; and having, in accordance with the Statutes of the University, kept the prescribed residence and passed all necessary Examinations, was on the fifteenth day of October 1936 formally presented and admitted to the degree of Bachelor of Arts.

The next career move would be a doctorate of philosophy, an Oxford DPhil, for which he needed a scholarship to supplement his monthly remittance of £20 from his Uncle Leo in Poland and the modest fees he earned as a college tutor. After New College turned him down ('My German nationality decided the matter'), Lincoln awarded him a scholarship of £120 a year. It was enough. He was now that new phenomenon: a research student—part of 'an unorganised and socially unimportant fringe of the student community', neither don nor undergraduate, with no standing compared with the honours schools.

In October the Board of the Social Studies Faculty cautiously accepted the theme he selected for a thesis: 'The place of Romanticism in English political theory during the nineteenth century.' It would draw on his German and English experience. In Germany, his teachers had discussed the old *völkisch* theories of race, blood, folk-soul and nation. He knew that these ideas had taken a National Socialist direction (although Nazis had tended to shun them as high-faluting). Yet in England a broadly related set of ideas—Romanticism—had led to Burkean Conservatism, far less sinister than National Socialism, but also, in Heinz's judgement, suspect. How did they differ?

He wrote again to Pauline

> I want to find out how much there is in English political theory
> of that 'political Romanticism' which was enormously in vogue in
> Germany and which is in fact the precursor of Nazi and Fascist
> political theory. Romanticism is a bad word and I have to use it
> in default of a better one. It is really the anti-rationalist theory of
> the State and of Society, the emphasis on a *Stande-Staat* i.e. a class
> structure resembling feudalism, the stress on history and tradition,
> the revival of religion, the emphasis on feelings and passions
> as opposed to reason and the intellect, the birth of nationalism,
> the view that the State is everything, that men are unequal (the
> *Führerprinzip*), anti-liberalism, anti-French Revolution, the reaction
> against the 18th century, and so on. These doctrines have had
> comparatively few exponents in England (Coleridge, Burke, Carlyle,
> Disraeli and some others), but it may be worthwhile to find out
> what there is of them, and particularly why rationalism has been
> so strong in England and has withstood them so well. Most of the
> people with whom I have discussed the subject did not think much
> of it. I think it's worthwhile.

He slogged away for two years, trying to convince the dons. Three factors made his task harder. The first was the limited resources available to research students in Oxford; even so great a university suffered from English provincialism. 'The facilities of research at Oxford are inferior to London,' Heinz wrote. 'The Bodleian, with its subsidiary libraries, the fine law library of All Souls, and several smaller libraries, provide most of the material the ordinary Research Student needs. There is however a shocking dearth of even the most essential foreign literature and, even apart from that, almost every student will find occasional journeys to the British Museum or the Public Record Office or other libraries in London necessary.'

The second problem was that he had become a disciple of Karl Mannheim. The sociology of knowledge that reduced political philosophies to class-based, self-serving programs was, for him, a 'tremendously exciting discovery', a revelation. You no longer asked if an idea was true or false; you looked for its social function. The application to society and politics of absolute moral standards now became 'naïve' and 'shallow', and books written in that spirit were now 'unreadable'.

But the Oxford dons found Mannheim's relativism uncivilised, intolerable and Germanic. What mattered to them was the truth or falsity of a proposition, not its sociology. Heinz was aware that (as he put it, mimicking donnish style) 'a certain orthodoxy in the general approach and in the choice of subjects is not considered a disadvantage'. He also knew that his best chance of getting Oxford University Press to publish his thesis was to study under an influential supervisor and to produce a work that 'does not offend the traditional code or political and academic orthodoxy (the second qualification is generally a corollary of the first!)'.

Yet he could not complete his thesis and, at the same time, abandon his convictions on which it was based. How was he to find a supervisor who had even a minimal sympathy with Heinz's mixture of Mannheim and Marx? He was allocated to Denis Brogan, who declined. He was transferred to Harold Beeley, who was more sympathetic but left Oxford soon afterwards. The Board of Faculty then suggested that Heinz find a supervisor himself.

He sounded out Ernest Barker at Cambridge, who was 'quite useless'. (It would have involved travelling to Cambridge once a month in the hope of catching Barker at home during his lunch hour 'amidst distractions caused by numerous small children'.) Finally, he was assigned to G.D.H. Cole, who generously put his enormous private library at Heinz's disposal but was otherwise 'not helpful'. Heinz never found the right supervisor.

A third factor making academic life difficult for him was the Spanish Civil War. It dominated everything (including his thesis) in the way that the Vietnam War did academic life 30 to 40 years later. The left saw the war as a contest between a Popular Front of socialists, idealists, liberals, democrats and all men of good will on one side of the barricades, and fascists, clerical-fascists, monarchists, national socialists, militarists and reactionaries of all kinds on the other. The right saw the war as a battle for God and civilisation against Stalinists, anarchists, dissident communists and leftist dupes of all kinds.

British intellectuals from George Orwell to Stephen Spender supported the Popular Front, almost to a man. 'Did you read in the papers this morning of the horrible mess in Spain?' Heinz wrote to Pauline in May 1937

> Not without provocation Government aeroplanes bombed the German battleship *Deutschland* on Saturday as she was lying

off Ibiza—where she had no business to be; result: 20 dead, 70 wounded. Further result: immediate Cabinet meeting in Berlin; five German warships bombed a town at the south coast, in Government hands, for one hour and a half. Also an Italian submarine sank a Spanish merchant vessel: 50 drowned. God knows how this business is going to end. There is nobody to stop the Germans going on with their atrocities. In Germany the people have been told of an 'unprovoked murder of scores of brave German sailors' and obviously they are furious and could support the Government in anything they wish to do. It is only by letting Germany and Italy play havoc in Europe that the Western countries can buy peace for a little while longer.

Heinz now moved forward from liberalism, as Spender had put it in 1937. There was no longer time to waste on popular or conservative diversions. ('Where are you going to be during the Coronation?' he asked Pauline in April 1937. 'I shall probably spend the day in the Bodleian. The only question is how to spend the evening as quietly as possible.') He had become a committed fellow-traveller of the Soviet Union and the Communist Party. 'There could no longer be any doubt,' Heinz wrote, 'about the need to work with Communists who were foremost in the struggle. We listened enthralled to [Clement] Attlee, Nye [Aneurin] Bevan, Jimmy Maxton and Harry Pollitt at Popular Front rallies. We applauded Esmond Romilly going off to fight in the Communist-led International Brigade.' He saw no need to modify his enthusiasm as Stalin took over the Spanish government. In 1937, he applauded Koestler's *Spanish Testament* (1937), with its 'moving account of Franco's persecution of Spanish Communists', but not Orwell's *Homage to Catalonia* (1938), with its moving account of the communists' persecution of Spanish anarchists.

Heinz wrote to Pauline about Attlee's passionate speeches to the Oxford Labour Club in February 1938, when Franco was winning the civil war and Hitler was being rapturously welcomed into Austria, now as part of the Reich. 'He was given an extraordinary reception. At the conclusion of his last speech (he had to address crowds who had assembled in three different places) hundreds of undergraduates and townspeople carried him on their shoulders all through the High to Carfax, through the Corn, the Broad, the Turl and through Brasenose Lane to the Radcliffe Camera where he had a car waiting. 'The speeches were 'sound and interesting', but the Labour Party was still too 'flabby' compared with the Communist Party, especially in its opposition to Hitler, Franco and Mussolini.

Heinz's postgraduate years, which began with the Spanish Civil War, ended with the Munich crisis of September–October 1938 and the British government's appeasement of Hitler. If Spain made him a fellow-traveller, Munich made him a committed, if non-party, communist. Mannheim's relativist sociology had already undermined Heinz's belief in absolute moral standards and his opposition to revolutionary violence. Heinz now saw these former principles of his as the ideological weapons of the ruling class.

There was also a personal influence: his American friend Leslie Epstein (later Falk). Epstein was Jewish, a Rhodes Scholar studying microbiology and 'one of the gentlest and most charming persons I have ever met'. Thirty years after Munich, Heinz recalled his furious arguments with Epstein.

> He gradually convinced me that communism was the only rational approach to the world's problems. In his gentle but scientific way, he argued convincingly that the end justifies the means. To condemn revolution was the obvious tactic of the ruling class. How, without violent revolution, could the 'New Civilisation' of the Soviet Union have been achieved which the Webbs had just described so eloquently on the basis of first-hand knowledge? I remember, about this time, reading the famous discussion between H.G. Wells and Stalin which turned largely on the issue of ends and means and being impressed by Stalin's impeccable logic.

It was this logic that enabled 'many of us to shrug off with an uncomfortable shudder' whatever parts of the reports of Stalin's purges they could not dismiss as capitalist propaganda. They must prepare, Heinz maintained, for war against Hitler in support of the Soviet Union and not for more appeasement.

Later he was to say that 'I insufficiently understood the importance of political liberty', but there was no denying at the time 'the joys of being a Communist'. They alone, he said, had the true faith and understood the laws of history and progress. They alone looked at society scientifically and rationally. They despised those around them who were still in the fetters of superstition and reactionary ideology.

'We also enjoyed "the camaraderie of a secret society" (even when Party duties were legal) working selflessly for the world-wide revolution.' Finally, there was the less selfless appeal of a working-class doctrine that left no doubt that 'leadership in the struggle and power after victory belonged to the intellectual elite'—that is, to Heinz and his comrades.

Heinz spent his last days in Oxford assembling gas masks in the Oxford Town Hall and digging air-raid shelters near the Natural Science Museum. His friends' letters reflect the conflicting moods of that desperate autumn of 1938. In mid-September, as Chamberlain flew to Berchtesgaden to meet Hitler, Heinz's German–Jewish friend Ira, who was holidaying in Zürich, tried to see a brighter side: she was 'not at all proud of Hitler's achievements', she told 'Heinzle', but it can't be denied that 'he has done a lot for Germany. A few years ago, nobody would have thought of listening to the speeches of a German chancellor as they do now. And for an English Premier to go and see him, why, it would have been unthinkable. I wonder whether he was sick in the plane.'

Later in the month, Pauline wrote to Heinz: 'I have just heard Hitler's speech and the first English translated précis of it in my room by myself. I managed to feel slightly happier by the end of the original, as I had feared that it would be something far worse and that it would immediately precipitate us into war. But somehow the English translation followed by accounts of military precautions which are being taken in this and other countries completely depressed me again.'

Tom Baily's mother, Mary, was often in touch with Heinz during the crisis. Shortly before the Munich conference in late September, she wrote

> I feel perhaps it is better to say nothing until after this conference but I fear and hope that I may not have to be completely ashamed of my country. I am almost certain that you must be greatly disturbed in your mind and heart, and I just wanted to show that my husband and I are not unmindful of you and trust you will always rely on our friendship and affection.

A few days later, and immediately before the Munich conference, she wrote again.

> You would be looking at the situation with the mind of a true German, just as I hope a true Englishman will look at it. I hope the true and real German mentality will arise and triumph over the dark sinister rule of Dictatorship and Nazism. I feared you might think England was afraid to stand up with her friends and that we

might be refusing our help to Czechoslovakia. I am by no means a convinced admirer of Chamberlain. I wish very much that Eden were back in the Cabinet. I have not been very pleased with the *Times* lately. In their rather blunt way nearly everybody here just says 'Hitler must be put a stop to'.

Britain and France did not, however, 'put a stop' to Hitler. They agreed to his absorbing the hitherto Czech-controlled Sudetenland. A desperate Tom Baily wrote to Heinz

There is a faint chance now of coming to some reasonable settlement in Europe. Very faint, perhaps, but still there. I'm sure that the most justifiable war is likely to end in the victory of little but wickedness and folly. But the price has been dreadful. It is reassuring to find people here [in Sheffield] inclined to be very ashamed. Very few of them would like to look a Czech in the face. So you'll see that I'm not quite in accordance with your views. I shall continue to vote unrepentantly for the National Government.

Heinz's mood was angrier. 'I recall almost physically,' he wrote many years later, 'the nauseating mixture of disgust and relief we felt when Chamberlain returned from Munich bringing "peace in our time".'

Heinz had by now fully committed himself to the pro-Soviet, anti-Nazi cause. Only five years after he had left Germany, anti-Jewish pogroms (*Kristallnacht*) had exploded in Germany. Late in 1938, an exhibition opened in Berlin in the Reichstag building designed to expose 'Jewish infamy', from the horrors of ritual animal slaughter to communism, surrealism and pornography and on to the Weimar *Judenrepublik*. The exhibition culminated with photographs of hollow-cheeked Jewish prisoners in Dachau's concentration camp. All Berlin students were compelled to visit the exhibition. Heinz applied for British naturalisation.

This turmoil made it harder for Heinz to find a detached voice for his thesis. By now it was clear that he had a great gift for research. The problem for the dons was to turn him from an argumentative communist into a scholar and academic.

Years later, Heinz agreed that his thesis was a poor one. It was not just his Mannheimian sociology, with its rejection of the idea of objective truth, which offended the dons. His understanding of British politics, especially

English conservatism, was superficial. Put bluntly, Heinz did not seem to know what he was talking about. His examiners would not give him a DPhil. They offered him a BPhil instead. But a BPhil was regarded as a public declaration of failure to obtain a DPhil. Heinz preferred to rewrite and resubmit his thesis in a year or two.

Meanwhile, he was unemployed. Manning Clark, who had just arrived in Oxford from Melbourne, told him of plans to establish a Department of Political Science at Melbourne University. Heinz wrote to MacMahon Ball, asking if it would be worthwhile applying to him for whatever vacancies might occur. He gave the names of G.D.H. Cole and Harold Laski as referees, but nothing came of it.

His hope now rested on the application he had made in September for a Leverhulme Research Studentship (£150 a year) at the LSE, where Mannheim conducted seminars, and which seemed a far more sympathetic centre than Oxford. He discussed his problems with Ivor Jennings of the LSE, who encouraged his idea of writing a sociology of *Verwaltungsrechtslehre*—the jurisprudence of administrative law. (This would certainly mean going to London because there were no books on it in Oxford.) They finally settled on the theme of the *Rechtsstaat* or the Theory of the Rule of Law. (Jennings said Heinz was 'the only student I have met who understood what the subject was about'.)

Heinz submitted his proposal to the Leverhulme Selection Board

> During the last ten years the problem arising out of the conflict between the traditional doctrine of the 'Rule of Law' and the actual development of modern administrative law has been one of the most hotly debated questions among political scientists and jurists in this country.
>
> I therefore propose (i) to investigate the history of the doctrine and its development (a) by English lawyers and English constitutional and legal theory; and (b) by German, French, Italian, and perhaps American, jurists. I shall attempt to place each writer in his philosophical, political, and social background, showing particularly how the doctrine changed with changing political and economic conditions.
>
> Secondly (ii), I intend to consider how far any such theory can be sustained in modern conditions. I can, of course, not yet indicate

what my conclusions will be. But I expect that I shall largely follow Mr Jennings with whose standpoint I agree in most respects. I shall devote special attention to those aspects of the doctrine which are immediately relevant to the practical problems of modern administrative law: such as the doctrine of the separation of powers and governmental functions; and the questions of the desirability of a separate system of administrative courts; of delegated legislation and jurisdiction; and of the English notion of the special immunities of the Crown as far as it concerns the responsibility of the State for the actions of its servants.

Harold Beeley, his old supervisor, supported the application: 'He has read widely in both the philosophy and the political theory of the period [the nineteenth century], German as well as English. From this unusual knowledge of its background, his work derives a richness of content and a sense of proportion.' Beeley added, in a reference to Mannheim: 'At the same time he is never unaware of the relationship between movements of thought and the social conditions in which they arise.'

G.D.H. Cole also wrote in support: 'I think very highly of his work. He has an excellent understanding of the background of English political thought in the eighteenth and early nineteenth centuries; and he writes good English. He has shown very good capacity as a research student, and in my view his thesis is of admirable quality. He is well worth helping to continue his researches.'

Ernest Barker had this to say

Mr Arndt has a lively and eager mind; he has a grip of modern philosophy; and he has already covered a wide field. He has the advantage of having combined a previous German training with the Oxford course of 'Modern Greats'; and he has been able to look at his subject, if I may use that phrase, through both German and through English spectacles—or, in other words, to consider it both from outside and from inside. Mr Arndt has still to simplify his style and to make his thinking more concrete; but he shows promise of bringing an original mind, and an original point of view to the interpretation of English political ideas.

Herman Finer, of the LSE, who was a member of the selection board, added his voice: 'He is a person of abnormally mature intellect, has a rapid intelligence, and is [a] brilliant thinker. He has a most engaging manner and is extremely well informed.'

Finally, Ivor Jennings wrote: 'Since Dr. [sic] H.W. Arndt is likely in due course to obtain some academic post, it would be useful both for him and the School to have him associated with us.'

Heinz's application was successful and he promptly enrolled at the LSE. It was 'a wonderfully exhilarating place' at its height as a centre of intellectual activity. There were Mannheim, Jennings, Lionel Robbins, R.H. Tawney, Eileen Power, Nicholas Kaldor, Frederic Benham, W.A. Robson and Friedrich Hayek. 'I saw much,' Heinz wrote, 'of Laski, [Herman] Finer and Robson, the triumvirate of Fabian political scientists who—far more than the predominantly conservative group of economists—were largely responsible for the "red" label attached to the LSE.'

Above all, he found himself working with and among 150 postgraduate students, many of whom were to be among the leading social scientists of the English-speaking world. These students welcomed Heinz in their journal with an ironic *Who's Who* entry

> At present waiting for various people to make up their minds
> (a) for his Oxford examination, whether they will give him the D.Phil.;
> (b) for the Home Secretary, whether he will grant him the certificate of naturalisation;
> (c) for himself, whether he prefers London to Oxford or vice versa.
> Subject: politics and sociology; Hobbies: politics and music; Passions: politics and—never mind.

His politics remained Marxist and communist. He attended a Marxist study group of students and junior staff and made his friends among 'party members' and supporters. 'I did not join the Party—if only because my naturalisation was held up through some muddle in the Home Office and I did not want to endanger it by political activity.'

In 1939, he published his first major academic paper, 'Bentham on administrative jurisdiction', in the *Journal of Comparative Legislation*. He was 24. He was almost certainly the last person to examine the original draft of Bentham's *The Constitutional Code* (1830), then in the University College Library, but later destroyed by German bombers. His conclusion conveys his position and mood.

> Bentham realised—and he was perhaps the first to realise—that capitalism needed not only freedom from restraint but also efficiency of control where control was still possible. He realised that even a free economic system needs as its precondition an efficiently organised administrative system to look after the essentials of a stable social order. This insight saved him from the stupidities, and therefore, also from the cruelties, of the fanatics of *laissez-faire*.

The large number of governmental functions that Bentham laid down included the supervision of water, sewage and drainage; health inspection of schools, lunatic asylums, prisons and workhouses; and the maintenance of medical services in the armed services, certain hospitals and lazarettos. Heinz concluded that Bentham's discussion of 'the problem of administrative jurisdiction is not yet irrelevant to our own conditions'.

This period at the LSE was not only intellectually exhilarating, it was personally exciting. One momentous development was Heinz's birthday party in Bloomsbury in February 1939. When he was asked how he felt about inviting a German refugee girl, Heinz was unenthusiastic. He was more interested in meeting English girls. But the German girl came anyway—and 'that is how I met my wife'.

The girl was Ruth Strohsahl from Cuxhaven, a fishing town on the Elbe, down-river from Hamburg. Her mother was a leader of the Social Democratic faction in the city council and her father was the editor of the Social Democratic paper. There were no prominent National Socialists in Cuxhaven, but young men, including Ruth's boyfriend, gradually joined Hitler's party (they were often attracted by the Nazi uniform).

When Hitler became Chancellor, Ruth's father was briefly imprisoned and the swastika raised over the newspaper building in which the family lived. National Socialist officials searched their apartment. Louts, enraged by the peace badges that Ruth and her mother wore on their coat lapels, insulted them in the street. In her final examination in Germany, her *Arbitur*, she characteristically wrote an essay criticising National Socialist economic policy. It was called 'Problems of our time'. The education authorities failed her and advised the school that she would have no place in the New Order unless she was removed from the influence of her parents.

Her Social Democrat teachers, determined to help, quickly found her a job as an *au pair* girl in England, where she arrived in 1935. She was 17, knew no one and owned a total sum of 10 shillings. At first, she worked *au pair* in London and Berkshire, and then enrolled in the LSE to study sociology, with the idea of becoming a social worker. She lived on two small grants, one from the International Student Service and one from George Strauss, a backbench MP. From time to time, her mother sent her parcels of clothes from Germany.

Meanwhile, Germany occupied all of Czechoslovakia. Franco took Madrid. Italy invaded Albania. But more sensationally, in August 1939, Hitler and Stalin agreed on a Pact of Friendship. At the airport in Moscow, the Red Army band played the Horst Wessel Song to welcome the Nazi Foreign Minister, Joachim von Ribbentrop, for the signing of the agreement.

The pact at first shook—yet later deepened—Heinz's communist loyalty. At first, it was 'unbelievable'. In this, the most critical moment, 'a deal with the enemy by those whom we had come to see, indeed whom we knew to be, the leaders in the struggle against fascism!' His misery soon turned to agony. Three weeks later, Hitler and Stalin partitioned Poland. In Wroclaw, or Hohensalza, as the Germans called it, two German soldiers began arresting prominent Jews, including Heinz's Uncle Leo. Leopold, a former major in the Imperial German Army, demanded to see the commanding officer. Within minutes, he was shot dead. In Warsaw, Heinz's Aunt Lala (Countess Ilnicka) was made to watch as her Jewish husband was executed.

To Heinz's astonishment, the Communist Party denounced the war against Hitler as shadow-boxing while the imperialists of Britain and France prepared to attack the Soviet Union. 'It was grotesque.' For two full days and one night, Heinz argued against the new pro-Hitler line with an American communist who was the leading party member among the remaining research students. In the end, the American 'supplied me with all the arguments I so badly needed to enable me to remain loyal to my communist faith in the face of this enormous about-turn'.

Heinz managed to persuade himself that Chamberlain and the French Premier, Édouard Daladier, were scheming to turn the German war machine against the Soviet Union, that the future of socialism and progress depended on the defence of the 'socialist sixth of the world' and that the national interest of the Soviet Union was the touchstone of right and wrong in world affairs.

In London, however, Heinz had more mundane problems. When early in September 1939 Britain declared war on Germany, most of the LSE staff joined the government or armed services. The Ministry of Economic Warfare took over the school buildings and the remaining staff and students, including Heinz and Ruth Strohsahl, moved to Cambridge.

Heinz resubmitted his Oxford thesis for the DPhil and again the examiners rejected it. 'I had my viva [viva voce examination] with [A.D.] Lindsay and [E.F.] Carritt, and they failed me again for the DPhil although they gave the BLitt. Cole sent me their confidential report to the Board of the Faculty; it was very nasty. They seem to have misunderstood entirely what I wanted to show in the thesis and then declared that "this thesis is of course not original".'

They also complained again that Heinz showed 'a very inadequate understanding of how English politicians actually thought and acted' and was too concerned with fitting the facts into a preconceived system, which he accepted too uncritically. 'In the viva which lasted for two solid hours I had spent more than half an hour in what was practically a political argument with Lindsay. Well, it can't be helped now. I shall take the useless BPhil because it will enable me to explain how I spent my last two years at Oxford.'

Heinz now completed an *apologia pro vita sua*, which he called *The Social Outlook of British Philosophers*. It was his response to *An Autobiography* (1939) by R.G. Collingwood, a leading British philosopher and historian at the time, but it was also a statement of what Heinz had learned in Oxford about the English intelligentsia.

The theme of Collingwood's memoirs is his polemic against Realism, especially Oxford Realism, the philosophy that had supplanted Idealism, just as Idealism had supplanted Utilitarianism. The Realist doctrine is that nothing is affected by being known, that the authentic philosophical attitude is sceptical, critical and detached, and that philosophy can give no moral guidance. Oxford Realism, according to Collingwood, made its followers dupes of every adventurer in morals and politics.

Collingwood went further. He completed his book in the shadows of Munich and he condemned Realism as the principal cause of British appeasement of Hitler, of British moral capitulation. The Realists and the British intelligentsia who followed them were propagandists for fascist nihilism. What was needed was a return to Idealist philosophy as a guide to life and morality.

Heinz gave Collingwood's critique of Oxford a more Marxist or Mannheimian interpretation. The problem was not so much that the Realists had abandoned their function as public mentors but that the progressive forces in society had abandoned the Realists. Utilitarianism had been the philosophy of the rising bourgeoisie. Idealism had been the philosophy of the established bourgeoisie. Realism was the philosophy of the bourgeoisie in decline. The rejuvenation of philosophy would come about, according to Heinz, only by association with the working class and socialism.

> I see little reason to suppose that an intelligentsia largely recruited from the ruling class and for a large part dependent for their livelihood and comfort on the existing social system would throw themselves into the fray on behalf of the truth as I see it.

But Heinz also struck a note of caution against triumphalism. His conclusion demanded that the intellectual commit himself actively and with every instrument at his command to furthering what he believed to be true and right.'It [also] asks him to preserve his intellectual and moral integrity, his preparedness to criticise the forces whom he supports (and on whose support he rests), knowing that events may prove him wrong and that he may be left to rot by the wayside.'

He submitted his apologia—part manifesto, part *cri de coeur*—to the New York journal *Science and Society: A Marxian Quarterly*. It was accepted for publication; by the time it appeared, however, Heinz was interned in a camp for enemy aliens on the other side of the Atlantic—'rotting by the wayside'. In May 1940, his nationality was still German and therefore he was an enemy alien. With Hitler's troops 20 miles away, the order from Whitehall was blunt:'Collar the lot!'

3
ARNDT IN THE INTERNMENT CAMP

'Please attend Hampstead Police Station on 3rd October 1939 at noon, and bring with you all papers regarding your nationality and those connected with your profession or business'.

So began Heinz Wolfgang Arndt's ordeal as an enemy alien. The Chamberlain government had not intended it to be an ordeal. Determined to avoid the undiscriminating mistreatment of aliens that had occurred during World War I, it established 120 tribunals throughout Britain whose mandate was to assess the loyalty of some 73,500 foreigners. It was to classify them in three categories: A (dangerous; to be interned); B (of uncertain loyalty; to be restricted); or C (friendly; to remain at liberty). The majority would be C.

Heinz—24, single, MA (Oxon.), research student at the LSE, of German nationality—duly reported to the Hampstead police for a preliminary check of his papers. In the next week, in Hampstead Town Hall, a tribunal formally classified him C. He was practically as free as an Englishman. When the government commandeered the LSE buildings for the war effort and Arndt moved with the remaining students and staff to Cambridge, he immediately applied to do national service.

The government's liberal policy, however, lasted barely six months. In April 1940, the Wehrmacht occupied Denmark in a few hours and Norway in a few days. In May, it conquered Holland and Belgium, and in June, France. An invasion of Britain was now expected daily. Aliens became targets of official and popular suspicion. The British Ambassador to Holland warned his countrymen to keep an eye on 'refugees' who were often disguised spies. The popular journalist Beverley Nichols, whose ridiculing of mindless patriotism had so delighted Arndt when he was an Oxford undergraduate, now demanded the internment of all Germans without exception, whatever their anti-Nazi pretences. Their dirty tricks, he wrote, would 'make your hair stand on end. Particularly the German women.' On 7 May, Churchill replaced Chamberlain as Prime Minister and issued the order already cited: 'Collar the lot!'

Accordingly, after lunch on a brilliant spring Sunday on 12 May 1940, the Cambridge police 'collared' Arndt. He outlined his trials in the next months in his regular letters to Ruth Strohsahl, whom he planned to marry.

The letters were written daily, then weekly, and all of the regulation-length 24 lines. They did not tell the full story. Arndt chose his words with care to make sure they passed the British censors. He also tried hard, sometimes too hard, to be cheerful. But he gave a characteristically clear record of the main events and of his gradual change of mood from confidence in his early release to despair that he might remain imprisoned for years.

Heinz spent his first night in a convent in Bury St Edmunds, which served as a temporary detention centre. His letter of 14 May was almost desperately reassuring

> Don't worry, little one. It is not very comfortable here, but there is nothing to complain about. The soldiers and especially the officers are extremely nice and polite. There is no indication whatever as to when we shall come out. But I am quite enjoying my holiday, and I could hardly have more pleasant company (with one exception). Be good and work hard. Think of me, little one, and don't worry about us.

On 15 May, he described the plans for a *Volkshochschule* or camp university: 'I shall take a class on British government and possibly one on political theory, economic historians etc etc.'

In his letter of 16 May, he described 'the crowd in the camp'

> There are about 250 altogether. Most of them Jewish refugees but also some non-refugees, among others the second son of the [Hohenzollern] Crown prince…Most of the people are dons or students who treat their condition philosophically, cheerfully or stoically. The grumblers are only two or three. This is largely due to the extraordinarily considerate, polite, and gentlemanly treatment which we receive from the officers in command.

A week later, the internees were moved to an Aliens' Internment Camp at Huyton, near Liverpool. Heinz described it on 27 May

> It is a housing estate, fairly large, like a village. Some 2300 internees live in houses and tents. All people under 26 including myself in tents. Most of the administration is run by us. I have been elected 'father' to a village of tents with 200 people.

> Could you please send me a parcel containing food, sewing material, a mirror, soap, toothpaste, my thin combinations, my light brown shoes, cigarettes? We are not allowed any newspapers or BBC news. We therefore know nothing about the war situation. But don't write about it.

He also asked Ruth to send to *Science and Society: A Marxian Quarterly* in New York a biographical note about him to be appended to his forthcoming article, 'The social outlook of British philosophers', his Marxising lament for English intellectuals.

By 17 June the internees had been moved again, to Douglas on the Isle of Man. The move was, however, temporary. The camp adjutant informed them that they would soon be moved to Canada, which, like Australia, had agreed to take in dangerous internees whose presence in England might weaken the war effort. (New Zealand, South Africa and the United States refused to take any enemy aliens.)

Arndt was not able to send any letters during the two weeks of the voyage to Canada on the motor-ship *Ettrick*. In any case his experiences were too squalid for him to tell Ruth about them in detail. He almost lost not only his British optimism but his Germanic stoicism. To ease the humiliation, he kept a diary in letter form

> 3 July: She is a troop-carrier with large rooms (mess-decks) with low ceilings. One thousand internees were crammed together in three such rooms. At first conditions were indescribable. There were ventilators but the portholes had to remain closed.
> 4 July: By 4 p.m. practically everyone was sick who had not managed to get on deck.
> 5 July: After breakfast we organised a large cleaning campaign. Working from 10 a.m. till 2 p.m. we got the place fairly clean and more or less tidy…One grand Viennese spent an hour playing the accordion and singing with himself…One lies about reading or playing cards and enjoying the fresh air. The food is, on the whole, good and very plentiful.
> 6 July: Things have been much better today. The obstructionists are relatively few; but they give enough trouble. On the whole, people are good and willing to co-operate, considering the fact that they have been interned for eight weeks and are now being shoved

across the Atlantic like cattle. These young people take their fate stoically and with as much humour as they can muster. There are some older people who are leaving their wives and children, their property and position in England. They are pretty miserable and a few have broken down and can hardly be comforted.

7 July: In the morning when one shift of 300 people was taken on deck, a sergeant, while trying to push people back, suddenly pulled out a long large rubber truncheon and started beating ten, fifteen people right on the head as hard as he could. He had simply lost his head and temper.

It was a disgusting performance in front of the eyes of the [German] prisoners of war who no doubt enjoyed this re-enactment of concentration camp scenes. The sergeant even tried to grab a rifle with bayonet from one of the sentries. An announcement from the Command was made that the sergeant would be punished.

9 July: I played a lot of bridge and game of chess. Bridge now for very high stakes—half a bar of chocolate or two cigarettes. There is, of course, some thrill and sense of adventure in this sudden departure to a wholly new country and continent. And if it weren't for the enforced separation from you, the worry about your safety, and my dislike of leaving England I might be able to abandon myself pretty fully to this sense of excitement.

10 July: This morning I heard in a fairly authentic form the rumour that a ship with internees and prisoners of war [*Arandora Star*] was torpedoed off the coast of Ireland and sunk with the loss of 3000 men [the correct figure was 600].

13 July: Before breakfast we had reached the St Lawrence River and went upstream. The weather was wonderful and we enjoyed one of the most beautiful sceneries [*sic*] I have ever seen.

Soon it became necessary for some to go to the lavatory. I spent the next three hours trying to get permission for them. This has been one of our worst troubles during the whole voyage. We were locked up in our decks and unable to go to the lavatory. For two nights we had an epidemic of diarrhoea. It took us hours of argument with the sergeants—no officers were visible—until they allowed at first buckets to be put up inside the barbed wire and when they proved wholly inadequate permitted people to go one after the other to the lavatories. The scenes do not suffer description. It was simply ghastly.

We docked at 1.30 p.m.…. The Colonel in command being unable to cope with disembarkation proceedings raged about shouting at everyone. A little Jewish boy was kicked by him and beaten with his stick…At 7.30 p.m. at last we were taken off the ship…By about 8 p.m. we once again reached barbed wire…Most of our things were put into green bags with our names on them.

15 July: When the green bags were opened it was soon found that the sergeants and privates had used the unrivalled opportunity of the night search to steal on a colossal scale. Money, watches, pens, cigarettes, lighters, everything of value had been appropriated.

At the same time our luggage was put up in a long row in the street. Here the robbery started again. The soldiers stole several typewriters in front of the eyes of their owners. [Later a military court of inquiry was set up.]

16 July: We are really being well and adequately fed.

17 July: An internee, who had the day before tried to attack another one in a hut and had been put into the camp hospital as mentally disturbed, apparently tried to break out of the hospital and was shot by a passing sergeant of the guard through the thin wood of the hospital wall.

In the first letter Arndt posted to Ruth from Canada (dated 17 July), he summed up the horrors of the trip to Québec in these spare words: 'Our crossing was not frightfully comfortable.' He added: 'I was very miserable when I arrived here and it dawned on me that I may never get out of this until the war is over. I am now more composed.'

19 July: Send me a pipe.

Meanwhile in England, protests at the treatment of internees were being organised by a range of refugee, professional and academic organisations. There were also two major debates in the House of Commons in July and August. Why, MPs asked, was it necessary to intern so many aliens with consequent hardship to their families? Why was it necessary to detain category-C aliens at all? Why arrest Sebastian Haffner, author of the anti-Nazi book *Hitler: Jekyll or Hyde?* (1941) Or Franz Borkenau, the anti-Nazi, anti-communist author of *The Totalitarian Enemy?* (1940) Or the famed Dada artist Kurt Schwitters? Or the journalist Heinrich Frankel, author of *The German People Versus Hitler?* (1940) Why were thousands of less well-known anti-Nazis detained? Why was it necessary to deport the internees to Canada and Australia, with the obvious risk of U-boat attacks? Was the government aware that Nazi broadcasters were able to tell the world that Britain was now like Germany and had interned all its Jews?

One polemic, a Penguin Special, *The Internment of Aliens* by François Lafitte, was especially influential. Published in November 1940, it attacked the government's panic of the previous May, exposed the hysterical xenophobia of some journalists and documented the mistreatment of the refugees. The government, Lafitte concluded, 'has declared war on the wrong people'. When he republished his book 48 years later, he conceded that the fear of German invasion and conquest in 1940 was perfectly rational. He also recalled the internees' understandable fear of being turned over *en masse* to the Nazis (as had happened in France), but he found 'astonishingly little' that he wanted to rewrite.

Meanwhile in Canada, the internees formed a refugee committee to negotiate with the camp authorities over grievances. There were two factions: one cooperative, one confrontationist. The spokesman for the first was Count Lingen, the Kaiser's grandson and a cousin of King George VI. Internee and chemist Anthony Michaelis described him as 'tall, blond, blue-eyed, and sportive-looking, always immaculately dressed and clean shaved'. He had won the internees' respect on the *Ettrick* by the efficient way in which, ankle-deep in faeces and vomit, he had organised squads of cleaners with gumboots, mops and buckets to restore hygiene and order. Michaelis was one of the cleaners. The incident led another internee, Max Perutz, the biochemist (later a Nobel Prize winner), to declare this Hohenzollern scion 'King of the Jews'.

One of Count Lingen's memoranda began: '*Hoeflichkeitswegen ist es wuenschenswert, dass die Internierten nicht sitzen bleiben, wenn der Kommandant durch die Huetten oder durch das Lager geht.*' (As a matter of courtesy, it is desirable that internees do not remain seated when the Commandant passes through the huts or the camp.)

Many internees were impatient with the Count's old-style diplomacy. Rejected by their native country as Jews, arrested in their country of adoption as enemies, they were now treated as Nazis. The circumstances favoured confrontation. Their first and continuing demand was that their correct status be acknowledged: they were not prisoners of war who had fought for Hitler, but refugees from Hitler. Some, like Arndt, had already had close relatives murdered by the Nazis. They should not now be fingerprinted, locked in their huts at night, have machine-guns trained on their camps and be forced to wear striped clothes with red patches. Orthodox Jews should be able to observe the Saturday Sabbath and not be forced to have their hair cut.

One of the most active of the confrontationist groups was the communist cell led by Hans Kahle of the OGPU, the former Soviet secret service (and later a Stasi agent in East Germany). It included the brilliant German physicist Klaus Fuchs, who later spied for the Soviet Union when working on the Manhattan (atom-bomb) Project at Los Alamos, New Mexico. Members of this cell purported to find in the refugees' grievances evidence of the basically fascist policies of the British and Canadian 'imperialists'. They also saw an opportunity to win back the support they had lost over the continuing Hitler–Stalin alliance of August 1939. Arndt, torn between both groups but committed to neither, drafted letters for both.

The subject of grievances ranged from the restrictions on internees' letters (number, length, content) to the harassment of internees who preferred courses in the camp university to camp duties in the latrines, gardens or kitchens.

A more serious grievance arose out of the decision of the Canadian authorities in October to segregate Jews and Christians. The Jewish internees considered the policy anti-Semitic: their quarters were two abandoned, sooty and leaking railway sheds with five cold-water taps and six latrines for 720 men. They went on a hunger strike. A disciplinary officer told them that Canadian workmen would soon make the camp habitable, but if they persisted in striking they would be locked in the sheds with the heating cut off and would then be transferred to the Nazis' camp, Camp R. The Jews gave up their strike but not their bitterness.

In drafting complaints about medical and dental services, Arndt was sometimes able to draw on his own experience. On their arrival in Québec, the internees were promptly inoculated against typhoid. They were also vaccinated. But other services were inadequate. The Camp Committee instructed Arndt to describe the unsatisfactory ophthalmic treatment in the camp: 'The oculist who comes to the camp is often unable to treat the patients for lack of the requisite instruments here in the camp. It would be very desirable if urgent cases could also be sent to the oculist in town where they could receive proper treatment.'

In the case of dentistry, however, Arndt reported his own case

> I was taken to the dentist on August 13 with three other internees. There were two cases who had bad holes in their teeth. One had a broken gold filling. I suffered from an abscess. As we came in we were informed by the dentist that he was only allowed to perform extractions. The two internees with bad holes, in spite of the fact that they suffered acute pain and had been wanting to see the dentist for days, thereupon refused to have their teeth extracted and returned without having received any treatment.
> The internee with the broken gold filling found that he merely had the gold filling put back into place, although the dentist stated that the tooth underneath was beginning to decay.
> The dentist dealt with two, if not three, patients at the same time and was working under extreme pressure. He looked at my abscess for two or three seconds and stated that the tooth would have to come out. Then he attended to another patient and when he returned I assented to the extraction whereupon he gave me a local anaesthetic. While the anaesthetic was taking effect an orderly made me sign a form on which I could merely recognise some such words as 'Work done satisfactory'. Then minutes later the dentist reappeared, extracted the tooth, held it up before my eyes, and, without looking at the wound again or dealing with it in any way, went away. The dental orderly gave me some water to rinse my mouth with after which I left.

After Arndt had been drafting complaints for some months, the Camp Commandant informed him that his name was now included on a list of internees suspected of 'communist leanings' and therefore of being pro-Hitler and 'hostile' to Great Britain and the Empire. Fearing that these suspicions might jeopardise his hope of returning to England, or of being naturalised as a British subject, Arndt demanded to see the evidence against him and he put in writing his loyalty to the British cause.

He did not and, because of censorship, could not write to Ruth any of these worries. His letters to her remained cheerful, sometimes nostalgic, and only very occasionally gloomy

> 12 September: Dearest little one, don't get killed. I live and wait for you. One does feel like praying, because one is so helpless. It is silly. It is much better to hope and to be optimistic, confident.

> 15 September: On the whole camp life is quite comfortable, the food is excellent, and we can earn some pocket money by doing cleaning work, and there is a very well stocked canteen. We have a lot of concerts, recitals etc, sport competitions as long as the fine weather lasts…all that can't make one forget the barbed wire, the waste and the worries for those in England. And one feels 'lonely' among the crowds of people and even friends.

One program featured the concert pianist Helmut Blume (later Dean of the Faculty of Music at Montreal's McGill University) as well as a harmonica player and a Grosses Wiener Potpourri culminating in community singing. In the 'university', Arndt lectured on English liberalism, Romanticism and the rule of law. He also prepared camp students for the McGill University 'matric'.

> 22 September: The memories of Cambridge, hundreds of them, of London—Keats Grove, Hampstead Heath and LSE are with me every day and every night. They are the best thing I have here; but even they are not enough…
> 27 October: The food is shamefully good, compared with what you probably get. I am getting awfully fat…My dearest little one, your picture hangs by my bed and you smile at me when I go to sleep.

The war news was bad, including the bombing of English cities in the Battle of Britain and British shipping losses to German U-boats in the Atlantic. Britain and the Empire were still almost alone. The United States remained neutral and the Soviet Union was still allied with Hitler. The internees followed as best they could the battles in Greece: 'We cheer the Greeks to the echo every day.'

At last in November there were good omens. The Home Office sent Alexander Paterson to Canada to sort out who was and was not an enemy alien. A classically educated prison commissioner, active Christian, chain-smoker and whisky-drinker, Paterson arrived in Canada on 18 November and interviewed the internees daily. He ordered most of them freed as soon as possible. His report was humane, generous and sceptical

> Many so far lost their emotional control that I had to keep them after the interview was at an end, rather than that their comrades in the queue outside should witness their condition. While smoking a

cigarette with me they recovered their composure, but it was then necessary to wait till their cigarette was at an end, for it was not any more desirable that they should face the company with a cigarette in their mouth, than with tears on their cheeks. So the time passed.

On 1 December, Heinz wrote his last Canadian letter to Ruth

> Good news today for the first time in 6 months. I shall probably be back in England shortly and may be free again in 2 or 3 months. Last week a high civil servant of the H.O. [Home Office] was here to sort out those, among C cases only, who will be sent back to England and those who want to join the A.M.P.C. [Auxiliary Military Pioneer Corps]. He was very nice to me, advised me strongly not to join up but to go on with my academic work. He said he would try to send me on the second ship, possibly soon after Xmas. We shall go to an English internment camp and have to apply for release from there…

Heinz was allocated to the first ship, the *Thysville*, a requisitioned Belgian steamer. They crossed the Atlantic via Iceland to avoid U-boats. There were no guards, the food was good, the cabins warm, the sheets clean. He arrived in Liverpool on 11 January 1941, after a crossing of 25 days, escorted by the Royal Canadian Navy and the Royal Air Force.

4
CHATHAM HOUSE

Heinz left the internment camp a changed man. He had endured the humiliation of unjust arrest and deportation as an enemy alien. He had been toughened as one of the leaders of the internees in constant, often bitter, unreasonable and sometimes merely tactical disputes with the camp authorities. He had run the camp 'university'. He had been stigmatised as a communist troublemaker. The eight months behind barbed wire had not destroyed his pro-British idealism, but they had indubitably tempered it. On his return to England, he was no longer the uncertain scholar. He was his own man. He was 25.

One thing at least was certain: he was going to marry Ruth Strohsahl. She was, throughout his internment, his principal contact with the world and the centre of his private life. His letters to her, despite restrictions and censorship, have a warmth and passion entirely missing from his earlier correspondence with previous girlfriends.

He also began sorting out his association with the Communist Party. In Québec he had been, as noted earlier, in 'intimate daily contact' with the communist cell led by Colonel Kahle, who held him to the party line, as his communist mentors had done at Oxford and the LSE. Now released from the isolation of the camps, he found it harder to conform.

He would not at the time discuss the communist activities in the camps. In February 1940, he published excerpts from his diary of the voyage to Québec in the leftist magazine *Tribune*, which numbered among its wartime editors no less a figure than George Orwell. His story was headed 'This must never happen again'. It did not mention Colonel Kahle or his faction.

The tensions finally dissolved on 22 June 1941, when Hitler invaded Russia and the communist policy switched to total support of the war in defence of the USSR. Heinz was, however, still sceptical

> I found the patriotic fervour of the Communists almost as distasteful as their previous anti-war line. Over the next year or so, as I still maintained contact with some party members and even did occasional donkey work for them—translating, editing, looking

up facts for party literature—I could not get out of my head the 36 hours of my conversion to the anti-war line.

I felt ashamed. I gradually realised that in becoming a loyal Communist (that I was only a fellow traveller, not a party member, did not matter since the party had my allegiance) I had surrendered my intellectual integrity, not by kowtowing to views I did not believe in but, more corrodingly, by convincing myself that the party was right.

Illumination, in Heinz's case, derived not from a formal political treatise but from a novel: Arthur Koestler's *Darkness at Noon* (1940). Its depiction of the self-destruction of the intellectual, 'by the very process which I had experienced in a small way, cured me thoroughly'. He now found the Communist Party and Marxism–Leninism to be 'destructive of all intellectual integrity'. He remained a social democrat, a Keynesian, a supporter of the British Labour Party and a foundation member of the non-communist left.

Resuming his Leverhulme Studentship at the LSE, Heinz completed his research on the rule of law, but he had become disenchanted by the 'intellectual flabbiness' of academic political science and sociology. They seemed to be little more than journalism mixed with pedantry. Did economics, he wondered to himself, offer 'more solid mental nourishment' as well as a more realistic prospect of social reform?

The man who turned Heinz Wolfgang Arndt, political scientist and sociologist, into H.W. Arndt, economist, was Paul N. Rosenstein-Rodan, the founder of structuralism and of development economics. (He coined the expression 'underdeveloped' in place of 'backward'.) A Central European, like Heinz (born in Cracow, he had taught at the University of Vienna), 'Rosi'—to give him his often-used nickname—was in 1941 the full-time Secretary of the Committee on Post-War Reconstruction of Chatham House—that is, the Royal Institute of International Affairs.

The liberal and socialist members of this committee disagreed totally about how best to reconstruct Britain, and its secretary badly needed a reliable research assistant. Still unemployed—his only paid work since his release had been a month's teaching at Loughborough Grammar School and some casual research jobs for the think-tank Political and Economic Planning Institute—Heinz applied for the position.

Rosenstein-Rodan appointed him on a trial basis for two months. Reappointment would depend on his usefulness to Rosenstein-Rodan (which Rosi had no doubts about) and on a security clearance from the Home Office (which finally reported in September, some weeks after Heinz had started work, that 'Arndt is a convinced anti-Nazi and there appears to be no reason why he should not be employed at Chatham House'). The duties of Heinz's new job included weekly service as a Westminster City Council Fire Guard in St James Square from 6pm to 8pm.

Heinz's new salary of six pounds a week, combined with Ruth's earnings as a social worker (she had taken her diploma in 1940), was enough for the couple to plan a future together. On 12 July, they married at Hampstead Registry Office. On 28 July, Heinz reported to work at Chatham House.

The economists on the reconstruction committee included James Baster, A.G.B. Fisher (author of *The Clash Between Progress and Security*, 1935), J.M. Fleming, R.F. (Roy) Harrod (the biographer of Keynes), Hubert Henderson, Peggy Joseph, James Meade (then chief economist for the economic section of the British Cabinet Office), Joan Robinson (whose books included *An Essay on Marxian Economics*, 1942) and Barbara Wootton (who wrote *Freedom Under Planning*, 1945). Other members represented opposing political parties: the Conservative Party parliamentarian Henry Brooke, later Home Secretary, was chairman of the committee; and the Chairman of the Liberal Party, Sir Andrew McFadyean (who had been active in the campaign for the release of the interned, category-C enemy aliens, such as Heinz). Non-economists included F. Ashton-Gwatkin of the Foreign Office, who had been a member of the doomed Runciman Mission to Prague shortly before the Munich crisis, and J.V. Wilson of the Chatham House Research Department, who later became head of the New Zealand Department of Foreign Affairs.

The stage was set, if not for a Dutch concert, at least for a confrontation. From the first meeting, the basic disagreements between the committee's planners, market economists, Keynesians, protectionists and free traders were plain. Their best way ahead, they decided, was to consider as impartially as possible the successes and failures of the economic policies of the major powers—the United States, the United Kingdom, France and Germany—in the years between the wars.

Heinz was told to draft a report. He accepted the assignment with enthusiasm. It would even be a sort of oblique autobiography, as he examined the Germany and Europe of his disrupted childhood and youth. He wrote nine chapters in five months, roughly a chapter every two to three weeks (two weeks to read the secondary sources and about a week to write each chapter). When he had added a tenth chapter, he had completed the report that was to become his first book, *The Economic Lessons of the Nineteen-Thirties*.

This remarkable speed was, as Heinz said in later years, explained by his ignorance. He had not been trained as an economist and lacked professional caution. At Oxford he had never understood the microeconomics he had 'read' and macroeconomics was still 'in a state of great confusion'. He had picked up many of his ideas of economic policy from John Strachey's *A Programme for Progress*, published by the Left Book Club in 1940, which had concluded that the basic lesson of the 1930s was the central importance of economic planning. The Nazis had, in Strachey's view, demonstrated this plainly: 'Nowhere but in Germany,' wrote Strachey, 'did the revival of the nineteen-thirties reach within even a close approximation to full employment.' The Nazis put the unemployed back to work by massively increasing government spending on public works, especially armaments, supplemented by wage, price and exchange controls. Progressive governments must, according to Strachey, use the same techniques for their different purposes. Indeed, Strachey went on, they were already using them to wage the war, and the same controls must be maintained in peacetime.

The immediate abolition of capitalism, Strachey argued, might still be politically impossible, but 'there can be no general decontrol after this war. The only real issue before us is, who is to do the controlling? The horse is bitted and bridled. Who is to hold the reins? Who is to be the rider?'

Suitably balanced by opposing (if weaker) arguments, this was to be a theme of Heinz's report. The guiding hand throughout, however, was Rosenstein-Rodan. Whatever was fresh in the report, Heinz said, was due to Rosi. One example was Arndt's treatment of the British abandonment of the gold standard on 21 September 1931. Within the rules of the gold standard, the only way of correcting the dramatic deterioration of the British balance of payments on current accounts in 1931 was by deflation and the reduction of prices and incomes—especially the wages of industrial workers—to a level that would slash imports and stimulate exports. This would almost certainly have resulted in bitter social suffering and class conflict on a scale that the country would no longer tolerate. The national government of Ramsay MacDonald chose instead to abandon the gold standard and depreciate the pound. Generally considered at the time to be a disaster of the first magnitude, it was in fact 'the first important step towards helping Britain out of the depression, the stimulus which the depreciation of the pound had imparted to the British economy, was probably the decisive factor in the early British recovery'.

A mere research assistant would not have dared present such an argument to the committee without the encouragement and backing of Rosenstein-Rodan. There were, however, many other such cases. In particular, Arndt's Report also followed Rosi in attributing the severity of the Great Depression to 'structural disequilibria' in the world economy — an early hint of what was later called 'structuralism'. Arndt further wrote

> …the catastrophe of the world depression of 1929–33 cannot be attributed to the internal instability of the advanced industrial countries alone. It was not merely a phase of the 'trade cycle'. The world depression would not have [been] nearly as severe and disastrous in its consequences if it had not been for the fact that ever since [World War I] the economic structure of the world and of individual countries had been in a state of acute disequilibrium which the existing world economic system proved quite incapable of correcting and the consequences of which it aggravated. These disequilibria, most of which appeared as maladjustments in the balances of payments of different countries but which in reality represented fundamental maladjustments in the economic structure of the countries concerned and of the world as a whole, were too large to be corrected by market forces within the framework of an international monetary system, such as the gold standard. At the same time they prevented the gold standard from functioning smoothly and with the American slump of 1929 led to its complete breakdown.

Arndt concluded

> The correction of maladjustments in the world economy of the magnitude of those which confronted the world after the last war [that is, World War I] and [which] will again confront it at the end of this war cannot be left to market forces. The necessary adjustments will have to be carefully planned if we are to avoid a repetition of the international economic chaos of the inter-war period. It is important to see what this implies.
>
> Firstly, there must be a conscious policy designed to ensure the requisite changes in the productive structure of the various

national economies: 'advanced planning of the types of changes required—changes in the amounts of labour and capital employed in particular industries, in the types and volumes of commodities produced and the methods of production, and the planned execution of these changes.' This may necessitate 'direct orders and compulsory powers'.

Secondly, control of the volume and directions of international trade and investment will be essential in the post-war years when most countries will be faced with acute disequilibria in their balances of payments.

Thirdly, there is an 'inescapable' need for international co-operation, 'if not supranational economic authorities'.

Arndt's concluding words in the report are this almost ringing rejection of free trade and capitalism

> The significance of this for our problem is obvious. It means that there is much to be said for superseding the free rule of market forces, by commodity controls, by long-term contracts in trade, so as to effect a compromise between the need for change and adjustment and the desirability of reducing to a minimum that instability which is inherent in the operation of the market mechanism and which exacted a terrible price in terms of social insecurity and economic loss during the inter-war period.

Some critics might argue, Arndt conceded, that this advice appeared to re-enact the international economic chaos of the past. 'The argument cannot be lightly dismissed,' he said—but he went on to dismiss it very lightly indeed.

Again, Arndt would not have offered this analysis to the committee without the backing of Rosenstein-Rodan. For his part, Heinz was so impressed by the analysis that he persuaded ('badgered') Rosi into writing his 1943 article on 'Problems of industrialisation of Eastern and South-Eastern Europe', which is usually considered the starting point of development economics as a distinct branch of the discipline.

In his treatment of the Nazi economy, Heinz echoed Strachey as much as Rosi. He stressed the lessons to be learnt from the successes of Nazi economic policy. 'The Nazis alone achieved complete economic recovery, in the sense of the full use of all available productive resources, by means of an expansionist monetary policy.' Their outstanding achievement was the abolition of unemployment linked to the creation of a war machine that in 1939 and 1940 was able to overrun Europe. Their method was the gradual extension of state control into every corner of the economic system and the total abolition of the rights and liberties of the citizens. Yet these same techniques—planned state intervention, exchange control and the manipulation of foreign trade—'may well be applicable in a worthier cause'.

Heinz remained modest and sceptical about his Report. He wrote to his father in Istanbul: 'I can never inform anyone that I am doing "reconstruction" work without blushing to the roots of my hair.'

He went on, however

> I am under no illusion that our plans for Europe will ever be realised or will even affect the course of events appreciably. The chances of this country having a decisive say in the future settlement of Europe are smaller I feel than many people here assume. Still, I feel, that it is a good thing, if some people spend some of their time while the war is still going on in thinking about the problems that will face us all when the war is over, and sooner or later it will end, at least in Europe. Chatham House is not exactly the ideal place for reconstruction thinking. There are few people here who have ever entertained the [idea] that at the end of this war Europe may not return to the *status quo ante*. And there are few with whom I have any common ground in my approach to all these questions. My justification is that on [the] ten most important economic problems of a more technical character agreement is possible and enlightenment is urgently necessary. And if I did not have the job someone else would in all probability be less progressive.

Whatever Heinz thought of Chatham House, he inevitably benefited from the committee's expert criticism of his draft chapters. There was some measure of agreement with the amended final text of the chapters on the economic history of interwar Europe and the United States, but no agreement was possible over the decisive and tenth chapter on the lessons to be learned from that history. The concluding paragraphs make plain why

> Economists in the past have tended to concentrate attention on the problem of the optimum allocation of the world's productive resources for the maximization of world output: they have paid far too little attention to the advantages of stability and certainty. They have been fascinated by the uncanny way in which market forces—the 'invisible hand'—tend, with certain qualifications which have been more or less freely admitted, to readjust the allocation of resources to any changes in the framework of demand and supply so as to reproduce optimum conditions; they have tended to ignore the costs in terms of instability which this process involved. These costs were not only social costs—the disruption of established communities, the uprooting of people, personal insecurity—but measurable economic costs—losses due to uncertainty, high risks, and transitional unemployment, or underemployment of resources.
>
> To give but one example, the gain which the peasants of Rumania derived from the long-term contracts which the Nazis concluded with Rumania cannot be measured in terms of the prices they received for their produce alone. These prices may have been higher or lower than the prices ruling at any moment in the world market. But they were stable. This enabled the peasants to grow their crops with the assurance that what they sowed in the spring, they would be able to sell in the autumn. The Nazis, in turn, benefited from being able to rely on an assured supply of the commodities they needed.
>
> We are far from underestimating the importance of ensuring the most efficient use of the world's resources. Changes in methods and forms of production will constantly have to take place. What we do plead for is [that] the economic advantages of the optimum allocation of resources at any one moment should be weighed against the social and economic advantages of instability.
>
> The significance of this for our problem is obvious. It means that, quite apart from any other considerations, there is much to be said for superseding the free rule of market forces, by commodity controls, by long-term contracts in international trade, and in other ways, so as to effect a compromise between the need for change

> and adjustment and the desirability of reducing to a minimum that instability which is inherent in the operation of the market mechanism and which exacted a terrible price in terms of social insecurity and economic loss during the inter-war period.

Since the economists, not to mention the lay members of the committee, could never reach agreement on this supposed lesson of the 1930s, Rosi persuaded them to agree on two things. One was to publish the report under Heinz's name alone. The other was to include Dissenting Notes by committee members so disposed (only Sir Andrew McFadyean wrote one).

The first decision was an extraordinary stroke of luck for Heinz. A book on economic history and policy sponsored by the Royal Institute of International Affairs and published by Oxford University Press, drawing on the deliberations of some of the most famous British economists (James Meade later won a Nobel Prize and Joan Robinson was expected to), would have been beyond the wildest dreams of the recently unemployed young man who had not long before been released from internment in Québec and who had just turned to economics. It was a decisive event in Heinz's life.

The second decision, which was reasonable, even inevitable in the circumstances, placed Heinz in the centre of often angry controversy. Although the book was finished in 1943, it was published early in 1945, shortly before the momentous British general elections that were to settle the structure and spirit of postwar Britain. Its espousal of the social and economic planning associated with the British Labour Party ensured that it became the target of Conservative Party and Liberal Party rage. It was also a welcome addition to Labour propaganda, an academic companion volume to the more popular Keynesian polemic *Full Employment* (1944) by Lord Beveridge, and the National Government's White Paper on employment policy.

The Workers' Educational Association (WEA) recommended that its classes study Heinz's book together with Beveridge's and the White Paper—and Heinz certainly did his bit 'to spread the gospel'. (Churchill on the other hand, quoted Friedrich [August] von Hayek in one of his election speeches.)

McFadyean's Dissenting Note opened the argument. Rejecting out of hand the idea that the failures of the past—which had been caused by restrictions on freedom of enterprise—could be remedied by further restricting that freedom, McFadyean declared it absurd to condemn as *laissez-faire* an economy in which the exchange of goods and services had been hampered at every turn by tariffs, quotas, rings and monopolies and bedevilled by the gigantic burden of unproductive and Great War-related indebtedness. As for postwar reconstruction in an underfed and undeveloped world, it would be, McFadyean said, perverse to seek restriction rather than expansion. In a final stroke, he noted Heinz's defence of the *Front Populaire* in France—which had governed from 1936 to 1938—and its destruction by conservatives who left the industrial working class resentful and embittered, and left the direction of French industry and finance in the hands of men who 'were prepared to deliver themselves up to Hitler rather than risk another attempt from below to oust them from their position of privilege'. McFadyean saw this analysis not only as superficial but as 'calculated to offend even Frenchmen who find much to deplore in the events of the last four years preceding the war'.

Supplying a footnote to McFadyean's dissent, A.G.B. Fisher, at this stage Price Professor of International Economics at Chatham House, added: 'Professor A.G.B. Fisher has read the above Dissenting Note and is in substantial agreement with it.' In his memoir, *Recollected in Tranquillity*, written some 20 years later, McFadyean wrote that he saw no reason to revise his dissent from *The Economic Lessons*.

F.W. Paish took up the McFadyean theme in his review in the specialist periodical *Economica* in May 1945. He mocked Heinz's assertion that, while there must be 'direct planning of international economic intercourse' after the war, the form this planning might take was only a 'secondary' consideration

> I do not think that Mr Arndt can be very familiar with the working of the machinery of economic planning, even under the unifying pressure of a common enemy, or he would hardly regard these questions as secondary. In some circumstances a human pilot in an aircraft may be preferable to an automatic pilot. But if the choice is between an automatic pilot and a dozen human pilots, all with different views as to the correct course and all wrestling for the controls, there can be little doubt which the passengers would prefer.

Changing his metaphor, Paish concluded: 'It may well be true that after its previous accident our world was both inadequately treated and discharged from hospital prematurely; but that is hardly an argument for keeping it this time in splints for the rest of its life.'

But the most telling critique of all was an apparently mildly worded but devastating review in *The Spectator* by F.A. Hayek, the widely respected LSE economist whose *The Road to Serfdom* (1944) drew totally opposed lessons from the 1930s. Hayek found that although the 'young research assistant' who wrote the report exhibited 'industry and ability', he relied entirely on secondary sources ('and not always the best'), lacked perspective and was strongly partisan. Arndt repeatedly quoted the Marxian Strachey, an economist of no standing, but neglected the authoritative F.A. Haight. Arndt also assumed that any opposition to the New Deal was reactionary and that the machinations of big business were to blame for any bad developments in the economy. Propaganda of this sort, Hayek considered, might be treated as a minor blemish in the work of a private person, but was not acceptable in a report of the Royal Institute of International Affairs. Hayek also called Heinz's bluff over his attempts at balance: 'As regards the conclusions, the author himself finds it necessary to mention, as an "argument that cannot be lightly dismissed", the contention that his "advice for the future appears to re-enact the international chaos of the past". The four pages in which he attempts to refute this charge are among the least convincing in the book.'

In other words, Hayek charged Arndt with naïvely dismissing his Report's likely critics and with having recommended still more of that disruption of the markets that had devastated the international economy between the wars.

A shaken Heinz wrote to the Royal Institute: 'I hope that Chatham House were [sic] not too shocked by Hayek's vicious treatment of the book.' Inevitably, however, it was. One Chatham House official declared: 'The Group does not wish to be held responsible in any way for the Report.'

Heinz also felt compelled to write almost apologetically to Hayek (who was, as it happened, one of Rosenstein-Rodan's teachers in Vienna). He conceded that he too would have given the book an 'extremely unfavourable' review because 'when I began to write the report I knew even less economics than I do now'.

The only moderate responses in mainstream publications were N.B. Dearle's anonymous but sympathetic notice in the *Times Literary Supplement* and a balanced review in *The Listener*—also anonymous—which cautiously noted: 'It is safe to say that nowhere else is to be found such an authoritative account of the tangled events of the 1930s. This report deserves to be read and carefully studied.' (Until 1974, *Times Literary Supplement* house style mandated anonymity for all its contributors. Unsigned pieces in *The Listener* were, by contrast, comparatively rare.)

None of the committee members publicly defended the report or Heinz. They relied on the words of the Foreword: 'The subject is obviously controversial and the Group decided not to attempt an agreed text, but to publish the document [*sic*] together with such dissenting notes as were submitted. Mr Arndt assumes responsibility for the text.' Although the 2,000 copies of the book (price 12.6d.) soon sold out, neither Chatham House nor Oxford University Press considered publishing a new edition.

At least the election in July was, to Heinz's delight, a landslide for the Labour Party—and indirectly for the underlying ideas of *The Economic Lessons*. He had been active in door-to-door canvassing and in taking Labour voters to the polling booths. As the results came in that evening, 'we cheered ourselves hoarse in the city office of the *Manchester Guardian*' (he was then living in Rochdale).

Well after the elections, academic reviewers of his book were more generous to it. The Harvard economist Alvin H. Hansen reviewed it favourably in the *American Economic Review*. In Australia, an even more sympathetic Herbert Burton took up *The Listener*'s theme that most readers 'will be thoroughly grateful for an extremely valuable survey of the economic history of the leading industrial countries in the period from 1919 to 1939'.

This economic history was indeed the aspect of the Report in which Heinz had the greatest confidence. It alone, in his view, would have justified a reprint of the book, which the Economist Bookshop came to call 'a modern classic'. After almost 20 years, in 1963, Frank Cass and Company Ltd decided to reprint it. In 1994, Gregg Revivals reprinted it again. Then in 1996, more than 50 years after its first publication, Heinz included the first chapter of the report on the 1920s in his *Essays in International Economics 1944–1994* (1996). It would, he wrote, help readers compare the world situation of the 1920s with that of the 1990s. He added a prefatory note cautioning his readers about his own changes of position

> Rosenstein-Rodan was the founder of the structuralist school of development economics and his structuralist ideas strongly influenced my analysis. There are also echoes of the Keynes–Hansen stagnation thesis, of pessimism about trade as the engine of growth and other themes now distinctly unfashionable. There

is not a word about the collapse of money supply which Milton Friedman later identified as the main reason for the severity of the Great Depression.

In 1944, at the time of publication, *The Economic Lessons* had an immediate and dramatic consequence for Heinz's career: it placed him among England's younger economists; it created him as a public intellectual; and it won him a new job.

Heinz's contract with Chatham House expired in September 1943. ('I leave with regret,' he wrote.'I have enjoyed the two years of work here and I know that I have greatly profited from them.') With the war still raging (the Allies had just invaded Italy and the Russians had taken Smolensk), his plan was to volunteer for the Intelligence Corps, but out of the blue J.R. Hicks of Manchester University, encouraged in this by Rosenstein-Rodan, offered Heinz a position as Assistant Lecturer in Economics. The Labour Exchange gave him permission to change his employment; and now, a decade after his arrival in England, he was on the first rung of the English academic ladder in a department headed by one of the most acclaimed economists in England (and later a winner of the Nobel Prize in Economics).

Hicks was not sure what manner of economist Rosi had persuaded him to take in. His first words to the new assistant lecturer were: 'Well Arndt, you are a bit of a dark horse.' He set him to giving the first-year lectures, more or less as published in his new book, *The Social Framework: an introduction to economics* (1942), which started with population and went on to the social accounts.

Heinz finally learned some economics by trying to teach it. He later began lecturing on macroeconomics. Other non-British economists in the shrunken wartime department, such as Hans Singer, Hla Myint and Conrad Leser, encouraged and helped him. Myint would explain any difficult points raised by students. ('One student, in particular, gave me nightmares. He would sit with an indulgent smile playing around his lips while I squirmed. His name was E.J. Mishan.')

Heinz also gave lectures to enthusiastic WEA classes throughout the length and breadth of Lancashire, Cheshire and Derbyshire. This gave him endless opportunities to promote *The Economic Lessons of the Nineteen-Thirties* and also 'eked out my somewhat meagre salary'—the more necessary after the birth of his first son, Christopher, in November 1944.

An assistant lecturer was contracted on an 'up or out' basis. After the return to the department of the liberal Professor John Jewkes, who was completing his anti-socialist polemic, *Ordeal by Planning* (1948), there was no prospect of an 'up' for the socialist Arndt. He applied for such jobs as were advertised, including one for a senior lectureship at Sydney University. Expecting no result from that quarter, he did not, in any case, feel adequately qualified for Sydney.

When an offer came, he consulted his 'Australasian mentor', A.G.B. Fisher (who, it will be recalled, had concurred publicly with McFadyean's spirited rejection of Heinz's recommendations in *The Economic Lessons*). Fisher advised him to take the offer. He also introduced him to E.R. Walker of the Sydney University Economics Department, who was visiting London. A meeting at the Savoy was arranged, and Walker easily persuaded Heinz. Hicks congratulated his temporary assistant lecturer and predicted that Heinz would have a chair in five years. The unemployed Heinz thought this was a joke in poor taste.

At the same time, the Secretary of State finally granted Heinz the Certificate of Naturalisation, for which he had first applied before the war. On 13 July 1946, Heinrich (or Heinz) Wolfgang Arndt formally assumed the privileges and obligations 'to which a natural-born British subject is entitled or subject'. On 18 July at New South Wales House on The Strand, he took the Oath of Allegiance before the NSW Commissioner for Affidavits and swore by Almighty God to be faithful to His Majesty King George VI. On the same day, Ruth Emma Auguste Arndt signed a Duplicate Declaration of Acquisition of British Nationality.

Heinz booked himself, his wife and son on the Blue Funnel liner *Sarpedon* for the nine-week voyage to Sydney via the Cape. They arrived in Australia's largest city on 10 October. He spent the time on board writing notes for the lectures he would give in Sydney.

PART TWO
5
PASSAGE TO AUSTRALIA

Heinz's appointment as assistant lecturer at Manchester was for three years, beginning on 29 September 1943. The custom, in those days, was that when an assistant lecturer had not obtained a lectureship by the end of his or her appointment, he or she should seek employment elsewhere. With the return to the university of a number of economists—John Jewkes and Eli Devons among them—who had spent the war in government service, Heinz thought that his chances of promotion would be limited. This was not only because the number of positions in economics was small. Heinz also believed that when Jewkes, Manchester's second Professor of Economics, returned to the university, the differences between his political opinions and Heinz's would create difficulties. Jewkes, in fact, did not favour Heinz's reappointment. Whether J.R. Hicks would have endorsed Heinz's reappointment is not entirely clear. The chances are, however, that Hicks would not have supported an application from Heinz had he submitted one, which he did not.

It was for these reasons that Heinz began in 1945 to look for other employment. He saw advertised a position in the Ministry of Labour and National Service that he thought might be suitable. Accordingly, he wrote to his Treasury friend, Teddy Kahn: 'Much as I enjoy teaching, I always turn green with envy when I hear of this sort of civil service job!...Not that I dislike the academic life; on the contrary. But I am beginning to get rather doubtful whether I shall get very far in it.'

Heinz and Jewkes were teaching in the same Economics I course and Heinz was getting on badly with Jewkes. In fact, Jewkes had publicly admonished him for altering the content of the Public Economics and Finance course without obtaining authority from the Board of the Faculty. For Heinz, this rebuke was a humiliating experience and it sent him a warning that Jewkes would not look kindly on his reappointment.

Several university posts for economists were becoming available in British universities as student numbers rose. In large part, this rise was occurring because ex-servicemen were beginning tertiary studies, or restarting courses that the war had disrupted.

Advertisements appeared for positions at Corpus Christi and Pembroke Colleges, Oxford; at the Universities of Exeter, Newcastle and Durham; and at the LSE, these last involving tutorships in trade union studies. Heinz applied for the positions at Durham and the LSE, but was unsuccessful, though Durham granted him an interview. He then placed an advertisement in the *American Economic Review* for a position at an American university, informing the Secretary of the American Economic Association that it 'had long been my hope to spend a year or two in the United States. Now that the war is over, this ambition may be realisable, and it has occurred to me that the "appointments" page in the American Economic Review might help me to find a suitable temporary job.' The advertisement appeared in the December 1945 issue and was seen by the Chairman of the Economics Department at McGill in Montreal. He wrote to Heinz, saying that McGill had a suitable vacancy and asking Heinz whether he was interested in applying for it.

At much the same time, Heinz was confiding to Peggy Joseph (an economist friend at the National Institute of Economic and Social Research, with whom he had worked at Chatham House) about the problems he was having with Jewkes and Hicks. Also, he told her of his pessimism about continuing at Manchester after his three-year appointment expired in mid 1946. He mentioned to her a conversation he had recently had with Hicks, who had told him that he should not expect to be reappointed. Peggy reminded Heinz that Rosenstein-Rodan would shortly be leaving University College, London, and as a consequence there might be opportunities there. In addition, she drew Heinz's attention to a number of research fellowships that were becoming available at the National Institute. She suggested that he should tackle Jewkes, which he did, but with little effect. The result with Jewkes was much as it had been with Hicks.

When Heinz informed Peggy of this unproductive meeting, she replied that she was

> ...sorry to hear there is nothing to be hoped from Jewkes. It is very depressing, but there seems to be a general sort of wave of xenophobia—that is perhaps too strong a word, but there is a definite preference for second-rate second-generation Britishers over much better more recent arrivals. I think the same sort of thing is preventing Nicky [Kaldor] from being given [P.B.] Whale's

> Readership [at the LSE], quite apart from [Dennis] Robertson's chair [at the LSE]—for which I should have thought he'd be much the best candidate.[1]

Joseph was not the only person in whom Heinz confided at this stage. He also explained his career difficulties to Tom Wilson, a friend from his student days at LSE who was now at Oxford. Wilson wrote to Heinz, gratifyingly saying: 'The Manchester University people are swine. Why on earth are they treating you so badly…Are Hicks and Jewkes mad? They have a very small staff and I doubt if many of their people in the civil service will return to Manchester. Where on earth do they think they will get anyone half as good as you?'

At any rate, Heinz decided not to apply for the position at McGill because in late January 1946 he received, quite out of the blue, a cable from the University of Sydney. It informed him that the university proposed to offer him a senior lectureship in economics. Heinz had applied for the job after noticing an advertisement for it in *The Times*, even though he had considered the application at the time to be a long shot. He had then promptly forgotten about it. So it came as a great surprise, even a shock, when he received a letter from the Dean of the Faculty of Economics at Sydney, Professor Sid Butlin. This letter advised him that his application had been successful and requested that he notify the university as soon as possible of whether he intended to accept the offer.

When Heinz told Ruth she was at first opposed to the idea of going to Australia. She expected that, with the end of the war, it would soon be possible for her to visit her parents, whom she had seen only briefly on one occasion since she left Germany in 1935. Her mother's health had recently deteriorated and she was naturally reluctant to be separated from her by such a distance.

Heinz, on the other hand, was enthusiastic about the Sydney offer. He quickly contacted his former colleague at Chatham House A.G.B. Fisher, for advice. A New Zealander, Fisher had worked in Australia during the 1930s as Economic Adviser to the Bank of New South Wales in Sydney, and later was briefly Professor of Economics at the University of Western Australia. He informed Heinz that Ronald Walker (a senior Australian economist, who had taught at the University of Sydney in the 1930s before becoming a professor at the University of Tasmania, and who was then beginning what was to become a distinguished career in the Australian diplomatic service) was visiting London. When

Heinz arranged a meeting with Walker on a Sunday morning at the Savoy, where Walker was staying, Walker was able to convince him that he should accept Sydney's offer. Heinz promised Ruth that they would stay in Australia for two, or perhaps three, years at the most; they would then return to England. With this firm undertaking, Ruth reluctantly agreed.

Winning Ruth's approval proved to be simple in comparison with a number of other difficulties that had to be resolved before the Arndt family set sail for Australia. There were concerns about the salary scale and superannuation benefits; about when exactly the university expected Heinz to begin his classes; about arrangements for housing in Sydney; about the availability of suitable shipping to Australia; and about the status of Heinz's application for British citizenship.

Butlin wanted Heinz to be in Sydney by mid 1946. For Heinz, however, so quick a start was impossible, because examinations at Manchester would not be completed until the end of June. That hurdle was soon surmounted when Butlin wrote to reassure Heinz that he

> ...should not worry unduly about the lecture problem. The first post-war year is so chaotic in any case that the exact content of the third-term work for this particular generation of students need not be taken too seriously. They have had as prescribed reading Haberler[2] and they should by this time have had several rather general lectures on the trade cycle so that if you feel disposed to talk Keynes out of your head it will meet the case...In other words, don't feel any need to do a large job of preparation for the few lectures that remain.

Decidedly more difficult than the question of lecture content was the chronic shortage of suitable accommodation in Sydney. Butlin warned Heinz: 'Housing in Australia is difficult, but not to be compared with England's problems...I may be able to fix something which would do while you looked around. But no promises!' What Heinz wanted was a house with two or three bedrooms, at least one living room and a bathroom. Because he and Ruth had no furniture of their own, their home would have to be fully furnished. Having paid only two guineas a week for furnished accommodation in London and Manchester, he told Butlin that he would be 'horrified' if he had to pay more than three Australian pounds. As a concession, he assured Butlin that he would be happy to pay a month's rent in advance to secure a 'roof over our heads'.

Shipping to Australia was especially scarce at the time. For a while it seemed that Heinz might have to travel ahead of Ruth, but he quickly dismissed the idea. He then thought that it might be possible to fly to Australia via Istanbul, where he could break the journey and visit his father. After making inquiries, however, he discovered that the travel allowance provided by the University of Sydney made air travel financially impossible. In the end, he was able to secure a berth on the Blue Funnel liner *Sarpedon*, an old and small (11,000 tonnes) coal-burning steamer. She was the third passenger ship to make the journey from Britain to Australia since the end of the war, the first two having brought to Australia mainly war brides whom Australian servicemen had married in Britain or in Continental Europe.

Of all the matters that had to be finalised before the Arndt family set sail for Australia, that of Heinz's British citizenship proved to be the most vexing. Having satisfied the five-year residency requirement for citizenship in 1938, Heinz had applied for naturalisation just before the outbreak of war. The war, however, delayed the process, which had still not been concluded by the time he accepted the Sydney offer. Heinz wrote to the Home Office explaining that he wanted the matter completed by the time he left Britain for Australia. The Home Office replied that, since he was going to Australia, there was now no need for him to take out British citizenship at all. Heinz was furious with this response, writing to Butlin that

> …this is an utterly unexpected blow the importance of which I need not emphasise. In the first place, it is clear that Sydney University may have the most enormous difficulties in getting me and my wife past the Australian immigration authorities if we are still technically 'enemy aliens'. Moreover, to be quite frank, I should have the most serious qualms…of going to Sydney at all without having received British nationality. Naturalisation in this country is something for which I have now waited impatiently for nearly thirteen years and I could not help feeling that it might be foolish to risk it even for the sake of the advancement and interesting experience which the Sydney post means to me. That there might be that risk is apparent in that I do not know what qualifications I should have to fulfil and what new delays would ensue before I could get naturalised in Australia (the more so as the failure of my application here might have an adverse effect on my application in Australia). Nor do I know whether naturalisation in Australia might

not prejudice my eventual return to this country if, as (to be frank again) I now think, I shall want to return after some years. For all these reasons it is, as you will agree, essential that I should try at all costs to get this disastrous decision reversed as soon as possible.

Butlin agreed that Heinz should indeed try to finalise his British citizenship before he left Britain, to avoid possible antagonism from the Australian immigration authorities towards enemy aliens. He offered to assist Heinz by getting his colleague F.A. Bland, Professor of Public Administration at the University of Sydney (and soon to become a member of the House of Representatives in Canberra), to make inquiries through the Australian High Commission in London. Attempts were also made to enlist the help of members of the British government. Heinz sought assistance from the Vice-Chancellor of Manchester University, from senior colleagues (including Jewkes) and from the local MP, George Benson. To Benson, he wrote

> My position now is that I have to withdraw my acceptance of the Sydney job unless I can get this Home Office decision reversed, for I cannot afford to risk the prospect of my naturalisation, for which I have waited for thirteen years, for the sake of however good an academic job. I have no means of knowing how long it would take to get naturalised in Australia. Moreover, I cannot be sure that naturalisation in Australia would not prejudice my chances of returning to this country after a few years. Lastly, I have been told by Sydney University that without making their offer of the post conditional upon my prior naturalisation, they would greatly prefer it if I could obtain my British nationality before leaving this country, partly no doubt because my entry into Australia would be greatly complicated if I were still an 'enemy alien'.

These representations to the British authorities proved, in the end, successful. Heinz was notified of his British citizenship in July 1946, shortly before he left Britain.

The *Sarpedon* carried 159 passengers, of whom 41 were children. Among these passengers were servicemen returning to Australia and war brides; others were taking up jobs in Australia. There was also the newly appointed Irish Minister to Australia and the Australian singer Dorothy Helmrich, who was returning home after many years in Britain. There was a medical doctor who later became the President of the Australian Medical Association, and three Irish Dominican priests, of whom one was later to become the Bishop of the Solomon Islands. There was a businessman who was going to Sydney to establish a plastics factory, several engineers and the newly appointed Professor of Chemistry at the University of Sydney, with whom Heinz was to have many conversations before the *Sarpedon* finally docked in Sydney.

In 1946, the Suez Canal had not yet reopened for passenger shipping, so the route to Sydney lay around the Cape of Good Hope. The trip was to take nearly nine weeks.

Several decades later, Ruth gave a talk entitled 'A passage to Australia' to the Australian National University Women's Group, which covered her family's voyage to Australia. Life on board ship, she explained, might appear to some to have been a luxurious experience. To be sure, there were stewards who looked after their cabins, there was duty-free alcohol and cigarettes, all the meals were prepared for passengers and there were new places to visit along the way. But Ruth recounted that travelling at sea with an infant was especially difficult. While there was a nursery, it did not accept toddlers, because there was only one childcare assistant on board and that assistant could not keep watch of quick-moving children. 'So all the looking after of Christopher,' Ruth explained

> …had to be done by ourselves. My husband loves playing competitive games, bridge, chess, anything, and could have had a wonderful time on that journey. He kept a diary on the voyage out, and I was quite appalled when I looked at it recently to read how much time we both spent looking after such a small boy. No wonder there are so many entries in his diary which read 'on duty again' from 6 to 11 am.

Even so, Heinz did find enough time to write up a series of the lectures that he had promised Butlin he would give soon after he reached Sydney.

For Ruth, much of the voyage to Australia was tedious. Once the English coast was left behind, little land could be seen, except for the outline of the Canary Islands, until they arrived at Cape Town more than three weeks later. After the *Sarpedon* left Durban, there were 16 days of nothing but water until they reached Fremantle. It rained for most of the trip, and the rain cleared only as they approached the west coast of Australia.

The tedium was, admittedly, broken somewhat at Cape Town, where they were met by the brother of a Cambridge friend, who was very hospitable and who took them sightseeing. Three days later they enjoyed the beaches at Durban. 'But,' Ruth added, 'both Cape Town and Durban were our introductions to apartheid…In both places we saw whites pushing blacks off the footpaths and make [sic] them walk in the gutters, and park benches were marked "for whites only".'

In Durban, the crew of the *Sarpedon* learned that seamen on a sister ship were being paid higher wages than they were. As a consequence, they decided to go slow across the Indian Ocean. This inconvenience was followed by strikes in the Australian ports: 'It didn't worry us,' Ruth said, 'for the voyage across the Indian Ocean was probably the most enjoyable part and we were glad to have extra time in each Australian city on the way.'

On the ship, there was a social committee that planned entertainments, such as brains' trusts and fancy dress dances. Heinz resumed his hobby of sketching, mainly fellow passengers. A major drama occurred when one of the radio officers had a burst appendix halfway across the Indian Ocean. The ship had to slow down as the ship's doctor performed the operation; an ambulance was waiting when the ship docked at Fremantle, but Ruth later heard that the man had died.

The passengers, including Ruth and Heinz, eagerly looked forward to the ship's arrival at Fremantle. As Ruth was later to write, 'Everyone who approaches Australia from Europe by sea falls for Fremantle and Perth and wishes they could get off there. It always looks lovely, and the weather is almost always delightful.' That was certainly the case the day the Arndts stepped on Australian soil for the first time.

Soon after the ship docked, they went for a walk in Fremantle and lunched at a café. According to Ruth's account

> We had what must have been the best meal in my life because I remember it so clearly. It consisted of a very large steak, something we had not seen for many years and probably larger than any I had ever seen before. On top sat two fried eggs, and with it fried tomatoes and sprinkled all round the plate chopped-up lettuce. We enjoyed it so much that we went back to the *Sarpedon*, collected some of our friends and took them to that café where we had the same meal all over again.

At each of the Australian ports—Fremantle, Adelaide and Melbourne—they had introductions to economists from the universities. In Melbourne, Wilfred and Marjorie Prest[3] met them at the boat and took them for a walk through the Botanical Gardens with an old LSE friend, Dick Hayward (who later held a high position in the United Nations Secretariat in New York). Also in Melbourne, Heinz was introduced to Joe Burton, the economic historian who had reviewed *The Economic Lessons of the Nineteen-Thirties* for the *Economic Record*, and who was later to appoint Heinz to the Chair of Economics at Canberra University College. They were invited to the homes of the relatives of friends from the boat; Ruth was later to recall that '[w]e admired the stately homes in Toorak and South Yarra'.

When finally they arrived in Sydney on 10 October, they were greeted at the wharf in Woolloomooloo by Joyce Fisher, Butlin's secretary, and driven to a boarding house in Manly, where they rented a room for the first month. For the first few months in Sydney, they moved into and out of a number of houses and flats. Butlin had placed several advertisements for accommodation in local newspapers before their arrival, but he had not had great success. He managed to secure the Manly flat because it was not the peak holiday season. At four guineas a week, it struck him as exorbitantly expensive, but, as he told Heinz, 'in the circumstances it seems the best thing to do'.

The flat included a verandah, small kitchenette, a laundry and a bathroom that had to be shared with the occupants of two other flats. But it was on the ground floor and the building was located in a quiet and pleasant neighbourhood. Butlin tried to reassure Heinz that 'Mrs Arndt will like the location even if the flat leaves much to be desired. The main thing is that it will give you a chance to look elsewhere and will be at least a headquarters while you are getting to know Sydney.' He hoped that some of his inquiries would eventually bear better fruit, adding, 'I don't think you will find living in Manly a very great hardship.'

Particularly amusing to Ruth's family in Europe, when she wrote to tell them of her safe arrival in Sydney, was the sink. This sink, as she explained in a talk she gave much later about her early Australian experiences, was 'hung out of the window. It may have had something to do with the plumbing, or merely to save space. When we told our friends and relatives, they wrote and asked: "What happens when it rains?" The bathroom with its gas heater was another mystery and we used it as little as we could. I spent the first month mainly sitting with Christopher on the little harbour beach at Manly.'

After a few weeks at Manly, they found another holiday cottage, this time at Narrabeen, a beachside suburb on Sydney's upper North Shore. Living at Narrabeen meant three hours of travelling for Heinz each day, between home and the university. At Narrabeen, Ruth later recalled, they were introduced 'to the dunny in the backyard and to red-back spiders'. When the summer arrived, they had to vacate the house. They were in fact about to rent or buy a tent when they found a room in a boarding house on Kambala Road in affluent Bellevue Hill, which was closer to the university. While the Bellevue Hill residence saved the long travel times from Narrabeen to work and back each day, the rent absorbed almost 40 per cent of Heinz's salary. Clearly there were limits to how long the Arndts could endure this sort of thing.

When it came to housing in Sydney—and in other Australian cities—just after the war, people took whatever they could obtain. Restrictions imposed on dwelling construction, to divert resources from private uses to the war effort, had created a backlog of housing demand. Ruth's later claim that '[o]ur first Christmas was not a happy one' was an understatement. This unsatisfactory situation was overcome when Butlin's younger brother, Noel (a lecturer in economic history at the University of Sydney), and his wife, Joan, offered to share with them a subdivided house that they were occupying in Hurstville in the southern suburbs of Sydney.

The arrangement with the Butlins was not ideal, but it was clearly better than what Sydney had thus far provided for the newcomers. But there was another reason why it had become necessary to secure more adequate and stable housing: Ruth discovered that she was pregnant with Nicholas, who was born at King George V Memorial Hospital on 14 July 1947.

As to Heinz's first impressions of Sydney, he was at first reminded of cities in England, particularly because of the two or three-storey terrace houses that were to be found in many of Sydney's inner suburbs. He later conceded that this was a very superficial impression, for the light, vegetation and climate were all strikingly different from what he had experienced in

Europe. There also seemed to him to be important differences between the British and Australians in their attitudes, traditions and customs. As he was later to write in *A Course Through Life*

> The first impression of Sydney in 1946, after a voyage of 14,000 miles and nine weeks half way round the world from Liverpool, was—that one was back in Liverpool: English looking, English speaking people with part-Cockney part-North-Country accents, the same Victorian Gothic public buildings, the same inner suburbs of working-class terrace houses badly in need of coats of paint, the same petrol and butter rationing (the latter to conserve supplies for Britain). But not quite the same, and the differences quickly grew on one: abundant meat—steaks bigger than we had seen for six years—abundant sunshine, the beautiful harbour and beaches, the olive-grey gum trees, and subtly different attitudes. Most agreeably, there was an almost complete absence of the outward symbols, so conspicuous in Britain, of social class (Arndt 1985:10).

He was soon telling friends and former colleagues that he harboured no regrets about his decision to accept the Sydney appointment. A Manchester colleague, the political scientist Max (later Lord Max) Beloff, wrote to him on Boxing Day 1946: 'I am pleased that you are finding so many opportunities in Australia and don't regret Manchester. If they don't treat their "office boys" as you rightly call us a bit better, they will colonise them very widely, to their own loss, I venture to think.'

To Beloff, Heinz wrote in January 1952 affirming that he had

> …at no time regretted coming out here. The chief advantage to me…is the obvious one that, by leaving England for Australia, you exchange the position of Third Mate on a large liner for that of captain (or, at least something like it) of a tug…Australians are not, by and large, an intensely cultural people, but there is a sufficiently large and keen minority with intellectual interests to satisfy most of one's needs in this respect and the social prestige of university people is, generally speaking, at least as high as in England.

In 1953, Heinz wrote to Dick Spann, another of his former Manchester colleagues, and one who was about to join the University of Sydney: 'Sydney is, I still think, a lovely city—for its superb site and surroundings rather than what men have made of it.' Of academic existence in Australia, he told Spann: 'Frankly, to me, the chief merit of professional life here has been that you enjoy a status far superior to that which your abilities would secure for you in a much larger country like Britain.' Nevertheless, even as he wrote this, he readily acknowledged that 'this may be much less important to a less vain person than myself'.

6
THE UNIVERSITY OF SYDNEY

The University of Sydney, Australia's first university, was founded in 1851. When Heinz started teaching there, its students were overwhelmingly undergraduates. Some were taking master's degrees, but most Australians studying for doctorates were enrolled at either British or American universities. In 1946, student numbers were swollen by ex-servicemen, who were encouraged to enter universities on generous scholarships as part of the Commonwealth government's program of postwar reconstruction.

Between 400 and 500 first-year students were enrolled in courses offered by the Economics Department. Of those, about one-third were studying full-time and two-thirds were part-time students, who attended classes in the evening after they had finished work. For the benefit of part-time students, lectures were often repeated in the evening. There were two lectures each week, but no tutorial classes for pass students; honours students in individual courses attended an additional tutorial class.

Heinz was responsible for establishing a system of tutorials for pass students, which were conducted by the students themselves. He called for volunteer monitors, whom he briefed on the key aspects of the topic to be discussed and who reported back to him in the event of difficulties encountered during the tutorial. While these classes were optional, they were popular because many students appreciated the additional opportunities such events provided to discuss and clarify aspects of the course in smaller tutorial groups.

When Heinz arrived at the university, the Department of Economics was located in the old Gothic sandstone buildings that stood on an elevated site overlooking the city. Heinz's office, on the third floor, looked out across the central quadrangle to the carillon. His close colleagues were Sid and Noel Butlin, who had been so helpful to him earlier on; Hermann (later Sir Hermann) Black, who had studied under Joseph Schumpeter at Harvard and was to become a long-serving chancellor of the university; John La Nauze, whose special fields were the history of economic thought and British economic history (and who was later to become Heinz's colleague at the Australian National University); and Kingsley Laffer, a microeconomist, who pioneered the study of industrial relations in

Australia. Other members of the department included Stuart Rutherford, Cyril Renwick, G.A.J. Simpson-Lee, Max Hartwell and Kurt Singer.

There was a second chair in economics, which had been offered to Ronald Walker (who had declined it) and which remained unoccupied. Heinz fixed his eye on the vacant chair, almost from the moment of his arrival at the university, hoping that he would in due course be appointed to fill it.

He got on well with all of his colleagues, especially the Butlin brothers. Of Sid, Heinz later wrote to Dick Spann that he 'is an odd bird, very intelligent and personally pleasant and helpful, but rather reserved and secretive in some ways, keenly interested in the Machiavellian game of university politics, and very good at it. I always got on very well with him and still do.'

Heinz quickly secured the respect of his colleagues for the dedicated and conscientious approach he took to his academic responsibilities. Unstinting in the time he devoted to his work, he impressed everyone with his energy, enthusiasm and dedication. Within a year of the Arndts' arrival in Sydney, La Nauze wrote to Heinz's economics tutor at Oxford, Robert Hall (later Lord Roberthall), to tell him about Heinz's work ethic. Hall replied by saying that he 'was glad to hear that Arndt was fitting in and [I] agree that he takes life too seriously. It used not to be a German academic fault but has become one.'

Heinz also acquired a reputation for being an excellent teacher. He could be demanding and unforgiving to those students who were not prepared to take academic work seriously, but conscientious listeners usually praised his lectures for their clarity and thoroughness. He took great pains to prepare himself for lectures, falling into the habit of writing the lectures out in full during the preceding summer university vacation, thereby freeing the academic year for taking classes and conducting research.

Every now and then he was accused of tending to mark down female students, although he always strenuously denied ever doing so. Some of his students, particularly those who were members of the Liberal Party, such as William McMahon (the future prime minister) and Gordon Barton (the co-founder of IPEC, the international transport group), criticised political views that he would express from time to time. These were, however, exceptions. Most students appeared to appreciate the policy context within which Heinz discussed the fundamental concepts of macroeconomics.

Of his lectures at Sydney, Heinz wrote in 1985 that he

> ...intensely enjoyed teaching. My lectures, I am afraid, were not very rigorous, no mathematics except for a few diagrams and the simplest algebra—and even these struck terror into the hearts of nine-tenths of the students, a majority of whom suffered from obsessional maths-phobia. I had virtually no mathematics myself and precious little systematic knowledge of economic theory. I learned this gradually by teaching. My chief concern was to pass on to students some of my own excitement about Economics as an exercise of the mind and as a guide to better policies in the post-war world. That economic theory could effectively guide policy, I and most of my generation of economists did not seriously doubt (Arndt 1985:13).

The economics program at Sydney included a general introductory course in first year, microeconomics in second year and macroeconomics in third year. There were also optional courses in mathematical economics, econometrics, industrial relations, economic history, history of economic thought, government (political science) and public administration. More than 300 students, on average, attended Heinz's third-year classes. The course in his first two years covered money and banking in the first term, trade-cycle theory in the second term and the state and economic life in the third term. In his final two years at Sydney, he covered income theory in the first term, money and banking in the second term and public economics in the third term.

Heinz based his course in income theory on Keynes, as interpreted by Alvin H. Hansen's *A Guide to Keynes* (1953), Dudley Dillard's *The Economics of John Maynard Keynes* (1948) and L.R. Klein's *The Keynesian Revolution* (1947). These texts he supplemented with two of Joan Robinson's books, *Introduction to the Theory of Employment* (1937) and *Essays in the Theory of Employment* (1937), Hicks's 'Mr Keynes and the Classics: a suggested simplification' (1937) and Tom Wilson's *Fluctuations in Income and Employment* (1940). Honours students were set Keynes's own *General Theory* (1936), Seymour Harris's *The New Economics* (1947) and works by Michal Kalecki, James S. Duesenberry and Franco Modigliani. For the course on money and banking, students were encouraged to read R.S. Sayers' *Modern Banking* (1938), A.F.W. Plumptre's *Central Banking in the British Dominions* (1940) and Thomas Balogh's *Studies in Financial Organisation* (1947).

Since there were no comparably recent and authoritative studies of Australian banking and the monetary system, Heinz was forced to fall back, when considering those topics, on the *Report of the Royal Commission on the Australian Monetary and Banking Systems*. Because this was outdated—it had been completed as long ago as 1937—and, in any case, was not entirely appropriate for his purpose, Heinz soon resolved to write a book himself on the Australian banking and financial systems. This came to fruition some 10 years later with his book *The Australian Trading Banks* (1957). For the course on international monetary economics, he used Roy Harrod's *International Economics* 1949), Fritz Machlup's and Joan Robinson's writings on the theory of foreign exchanges and articles on contemporary issues such as the dollar shortage.

Heinz was justly proud of his initial batch of Sydney students. Among those who became academics were Harry Edwards (a Professor of Economics at Sydney and Macquarie and later a member of the House of Representatives in Canberra and a shadow minister), Alan Hall, Don Lamberton, Noel Drane and Alan Barnard; among those who became central bankers and public servants were Don Sanders, Jack Wright, Gordon Menzies, Jack Donovan, Ken Foreman and Roy Fernandez.

Because he participated in debates on current economic policy and scarcely concealed his political views, Heinz was often sensitive to allegations of political bias in his lectures. In April 1949, he wrote to Warwick Fairfax, publisher of the *Sydney Morning Herald*, responding to a critical article Fairfax had written in that newspaper about personal political opinions expressed in classes by university teachers. Though Fairfax had not named Heinz, he did name others.

Heinz responded by admitting to Fairfax that there 'is no doubt that the politically controversial character of many of the problems on which economics sheds light presents a special problem to the teacher of economics'. Yet it was Heinz's view that 'all teachers of economics in my acquaintance are painfully aware of this problem; you would find that most of them tend to lean over backwards in their anxiety to cope with it'. 'The fact is,' Heinz went on, 'that, while economists, like scientists in all other fields, disagree on a host of questions, there are also a great many important matters on which the overwhelming weight of professional authority is on one side of an argument.'

As well as teaching, Heinz was expected to conduct research, and to publish the results. He did this at Sydney with an eagerness and enthusiasm that was to mark his entire academic career. Before he had left Manchester,

Oxford Economic Papers had accepted for publication a paper of his entitled 'Productivity in manufacturing and real income per head in Great Britain' (1944), and the *Review of Economic Studies* had agreed to publish an article on 'The monetary theory of deficit spending: a comment' (1946).

His first publications in Australia covered the International Monetary Fund (IMF) and the projected International Trade Organisation. His paper on the IMF, 'The International Monetary Fund and the treatment of cyclical balance of payments difficulties' (1947), appeared in the *Economic Record* and was the first of many articles to appear in that journal in the next 40 years. Heinz had written it originally for the Australian and New Zealand Association for the Advancement of Science (ANZAAS) conference in Perth in August 1947. In the event, Heinz was unable to travel to Perth, so it was read for him by Professor Gordon Wood of Melbourne, the President of Section G of ANZAAS (Economics). Wood wrote to Heinz after the conference saying that the paper 'was generally accepted as a first class piece of work and as a splendid curtain-raiser for the declaration two days later by [Hugh] Dalton [the British Chancellor of the Exchequer] of the inconvertibility of sterling. That gave it both point and added interest in the discussion.'

The major research Heinz conducted in Sydney was not in the field of applied macroeconomics—the core subject of his teaching—but rather in Australian economic history. Here his chief collaborator was Noel Butlin, later to become Australia's leading economic historian. With Butlin, Heinz examined the work of T.A. Coghlan, the eminent Sydney statistician of the late nineteenth and early twentieth centuries. Heinz and Butlin reworked Coghlan's estimate of the gross domestic product for New South Wales in 1891, and the *Economic Record* published their findings. Also, Heinz published an article (this time in the *Economic Journal*) on Coghlan as a pioneer of national income estimation; never again did that august journal publish Heinz's work. Heinz and Butlin recovered much of the information they needed for these two papers from the storerooms of the office of the NSW Statistician, Stanley (later Sir Stanley) Carver.

Another major research project that Heinz embarked on when he was in Sydney—again, with Butlin's assistance—was a study of foreign investment in Australia between 1864 and 1914. This was sparked by Heinz's interest in the balance-of-payments adjustments required to accommodate external flows of capital. The research involved collecting quantitative data from the *Australasian Insurance and Banking Record* and other contemporary publications. Some of this work was funded by two grants awarded by the Commonwealth Research Grant Scheme (a precursor of the present Australian Research Council scheme). In his application for the first grant, Heinz stated that the purpose of the research was to fill an important gap in Australian economic history and to illuminate a number of unresolved problems of economic theory.

The research was expected to examine several fields: first, a number of historical and theoretical problems, including the effects of foreign investment on the industrial structure and distribution of company ownership in Australia. Second, the relations between capital imports and the balance of payments (as a check on Roland Wilson's indirect estimates of capital inflow for the same period). Third, the nature of the monetary transfer mechanism (along the lines of Jacob Viner's studies for Canada and Wilson's for Australia).[4] Fourth, the relationship between capital imports and the trade cycle, focusing on the effect of changes in the flow of capital imports on the level of economic activity in Australia, and the effect of domestic economic conditions on foreign investment. Given the nature of the material, Heinz found himself unable to work with a research assistant. He had engaged one, from the proceeds of the research grants, but he never tried to do so again.[5] As to the work itself, it did not get very far. In fact, no results of it were ever published, though some of the theoretical issues were to resurface in several of his later publications.

As well as this historical work, Heinz's research in Sydney included several projects undertaken for the Commonwealth Bank and the Commonwealth Treasury. L.G. (later Sir Leslie) Melville, Economic Adviser to the Commonwealth Bank, and chairman of the United Nations' Sub-Commission on Employment and Economic Stability, commissioned Heinz to prepare a paper on 'The causes and consequences of inflation in the postwar world' for his work for the United Nations.

Melville later wrote to Heinz congratulating him on the quality of this paper. 'I heard,' Melville wrote, 'many comments of praise for your original draft from the staff of the United Nations, members of the Sub-Commission, and the staff of the International Monetary Fund who had copies.' In fact, Melville informed Heinz that he was 'quite sure that without your draft the Sub-Commission would never have produced a report and, although the final report [of the sub-commission] is perhaps not very good, it did help to set the machinery of the United Nations in action and will, I hope, prove of some value.' For this work, Heinz received £50.

A paper on the 'Impact of immigration on the Australian economy', commissioned again by Melville, this time for the Commonwealth Bank, was published in the bank's *Statistical Bulletin* for October 1950. It was one of five reports on the subject contributed by various authors.

In this paper, Heinz argued that immigration had demand and supply consequences. Moreover, there would not necessarily be a balance between the two. In the current circumstances of full employment, it was clear to him that the demand effects, at least in the short term, would exceed the supply effects. Heinz took the opportunity to hammer home the point that the Australian economy was hopelessly overstretched at the time, and that some reduction in investment, defence expenditure or consumption was necessary. As he put it: 'If defence, investment and consumption claims are pushed regardless of the adequacy of available resources, the allocation will, in effect, be left to the haphazard force of inflation. The consequences will be not merely social injustice, but a disorganisation of the economy which will not permit even small proportions of each of these claims to be satisfied.' What Heinz was saying, in other words, was that conflicting policy goals had to be reconciled by policymakers. In particular, they would need to choose between greater immigration on the one hand and less expenditure on the other, if inflation was to be avoided.

Heinz's work for the Commonwealth Treasury was commissioned early in 1949 by Fred Wheeler, later Secretary to the Treasury. At this stage, Wheeler was in charge of the Treasury's division handling macroeconomic policy. Heinz was asked to undertake an 'urgent job' of drafting a memorandum stating an economic case for the retention of economic controls under the Commonwealth's defence powers. It had to be completed within three weeks and for this labour Heinz was to be paid 100 guineas.

Of the payment, Heinz admitted to Ruth that 'it's outrageous, but of course very nice for us! I expect it will be quite a sweat but still easier than any alternative way of earning that much extra.' To his father, he wrote that he had gone to Canberra for the day: 'a dreary day there,' he said, 'drafting and redrafting, but a very pleasant trip there and back in the private plane of the Governor of the Commonwealth Bank—most luxurious and comfortable.' Altogether, though Heinz had been in the country for little more than three years, he was clearly making his mark in the rather small community of Australian economists.

1. Professor Fritz Arndt teaching his beloved chemistry

2. Fritz Arndt, bedecked with honorary medals, sitting for a bronze bust made for the German Chemical Society

3. Heinz and his sister Bettina

4. Heinz (left) holidaying with friends in Viareggio, Italy, 1934 and his brother Walter (right) and sister Bettina (top left)

5. A young German in Oxford

6. Dapper young man

7. Heinz and his sister Bettina

8. Heinz and Ruth in Cambridge, 1940

9. Relaxing in Switzerland

10. Interned and sent to Canada, 1939

11. The future Mrs Arndt, Ruth Strohsahl, 1939
12. Heinz and Ruth in their student days at London School of Economics, 1939
13. Heinz with his mother Julia at Ruth and Heinz's wedding

14. Ruth with her mentor, Marjorie Rackstraw (right)

15. Wedding, Hampstead, 12 July, 1941

16. Their first Australian beach, 1946 with son Chris

17. Arndt family in Ainslie

18. Heinz with his young family—Chris, Bettina and Nick

19. Ruth playing the piano at one of her migrant parties, with Heinz looking on

20. Neighbours in Hurstville, Noel and Joan Butlin, 1945

21. Arndts in the Deakin front garden, then set in a bush landscape

22. Family holiday on the South Coast

23. Ruth on her favourite back terrace

24. Heinz and Ruth share a moment at Tuross Lakes

25. Heinz painting landscapes in Geneva, 1960

26. Heinz and Ruth in Canberra

27. The well-dressed BBQ chef

7
PUBLIC INTELLECTUAL

Heinz was determined, almost from the moment he stepped foot on Australian soil, to avoid being the typical academic economist who confined himself to teaching undergraduates and conducted esoteric research that lacked practical application. Rather, he expressly intended to become a public intellectual, using the media and speaking engagements to raise issues of social importance. Soon after he arrived in Sydney, he wrote to a friend in England

> In the few months since my arrival in Australia I have been impressed by the apparent lack of interest in, and ignorance about, public affairs in general and international affairs in particular among the people one meets outside the University. This is a complaint that one hears often enough in Britain, too. But ignorance and apathy seem still more widespread here…The result of this apathy, in turn, is a certain provincialism in politics. Politicians are careful to concentrate on bread-and-butter issues; debates of principle are shunned; theory is suspect. A 'big job' for adult education.

Heinz quickly embarked on a one-man crusade to repair this deficiency. His energy and commitment to various political, social and economic causes were truly remarkable. Soon his name became a household word in Sydney and Canberra, and to a lesser degree in the other state capitals. He submitted articles and letters to the *Sydney Morning Herald* and other newspapers; he wrote a regular column for the *Australian Observer* (a fortnightly review edited by Allan Fraser, the federal Labor member for Eden-Monaro in southern New South Wales), signing himself 'An Economist'. He gave talks to the NSW branch of the Australian Institute for International Affairs, presented papers to conferences sponsored by the NSW branch of the Economic Society of Australia and New Zealand (and its Victorian and Canberra branches) and by the Australian and New Zealand Association for the Advancement of Science. He was a frequent contributor to the *Current Affairs Bulletin*, published by Sydney University's Department of Tutorial Classes, and he presented news commentaries on ABC radio.

This wasn't all, for he continued the practice that he began in Manchester of giving lectures under the auspices of the Workers' Educational Association (WEA). Throughout his Sydney years, he regularly lectured in Manly and other northern suburbs for the WEA and was often a featured speaker at its annual summer school at Newport. In 1947, he travelled to Newcastle to deliver a lecture at the Henry Lawson College of the Newcastle branch of the Australian Labor Party (ALP), speaking on the subject 'Does immigration affect our standard of living?'. At various times he addressed the Institute of Accountants (on inflation control), the Christian Social Credit Movement (on bank nationalisation) and the Singleton Rotary Club (on aspects of European affairs). For the Sydney University Department of Tutorial Classes, he gave 10 lectures in 1948 on Fabian socialism.

On the odd occasion he declined an invitation to present a talk or give a lecture, but he did so reluctantly. In 1950, he turned down an invitation to speak at a conference sponsored in Sydney by the Democratic Rights Council, an organisation associated with the Communist Party of Australia. He explained this by saying: 'I am unable to convince myself that the motives of the Council's activities are what they pretend to be. While I gladly recognise the integrity and genuine democratic convictions of some of the persons associated with the Council I am not prepared to co-operate with those who exploit liberal principles for their own illiberal ends.' To reject an invitation to speak on subjects of national importance was, for Heinz, the exception rather than the rule.

In the four years that he spent in Sydney, Heinz got to know many of the leading academic, bank and government economists in Australia. He had several conversations with L.F. Giblin, the grand old man of Australian economics, who was writing his history of the Commonwealth Bank as a central bank. On several occasions, Heinz travelled to Canberra, where he met senior economists working in the Commonwealth Public Service, at the Australian National University (ANU) and at Canberra University College (CUC). During his first visit to the national capital, he read a paper to the Canberra branch of the Economic Society of Australia and New Zealand. Held in the lecture room of CUC, the meeting was chaired by Roland Wilson. Heinz's paper dealt with Keynes's writings on wages and the relationship between wages and employment; this subject had been inspired by a review he had written of Seymour Harris's book *The New Economics*.

In 1949, Heinz went to Canberra again to discuss the work he was doing for the Treasury on the constitutional and legislative basis of economic controls. In 1950, he and other prominent Australian economists were summoned to a meeting in Canberra arranged by Fred Wheeler to discuss whether Australia should revalue the pound. On this occasion he held long conversations with Trevor Swan, J.G. (later Sir John) Crawford and Gerald Firth.[6] Another person whom he met in Canberra was David Bensusan-Butt, who was on secondment to the Treasury from the Economic Section of the British Cabinet Office. Bensusan-Butt later became a close friend and colleague of Heinz's in the Department of Economics in the Research School of Pacific Studies at the ANU.

Other economists whom Heinz came to know well when he was in Sydney were H.C. Coombs, the Governor of the Commonwealth Bank; R.I. (Dick) Downing, future ABC chairman, who was to become Heinz's closest friend; and the Canadian–American economist Benjamin Higgins, who had taken up a short-term appointment at Melbourne University as Ritchie Research Professor of Economics. Heinz also met Sir Douglas Copland, then the Vice-Chancellor of the ANU, when Copland came to Sydney to discuss possible candidates for appointment to the foundation chair of economics at the national university. Afterwards, Professor W.K. Hancock, the director-designate of the Research School of Social Sciences at the ANU, visited the University of Sydney to discuss the establishment of the school and the leadership role he foresaw for the ANU in the social sciences in Australia. At these meetings, Heinz adopted a somewhat jaundiced view of the ANU, arguing that the national university was likely to denude the state universities of much of their talent base, staff and research students.

In his twice-yearly trips to the University College at Armidale (then affiliated with Sydney University, but later the autonomous University of New England), Heinz met Eric Russell, who was to become Professor of Economics at the University of Adelaide and one of Australia's most distinguished economists. Russell taught in Armidale the same course that Heinz was teaching in Sydney; for this reason, Heinz was expected to collaborate with Russell and to attend examiners' meetings at the University College.

On many occasions, Heinz used his expertise as an economist to speak at public forums on the leading economic issues of the day. Immigration and inflation were two such topics that drew his early attention, but there were others. One was whether Australia should join the new international monetary institutions that had been established at the Bretton Woods Conference in 1944. The ALP was hopelessly divided on the issue, with the Left vehemently opposed to Australia becoming a member of the

International Monetary Fund (IMF) and World Bank, while the Right supported Australian membership. This division was responsible for Australia failing to become a foundation member of the two institutions, though when Australia finally decided to join in 1947 it was allowed all the privileges of a foundation member.

Heinz strongly supported Australia's membership. In a letter published in the *Sydney Morning Herald* in December 1946, he wrote

> To those who, like Mr [E.J. ('Eddie')] Ward [the Minister for Transport and External Territories], fear the iron hand of aggressive American capitalism in the velvet glove of the International Monetary Fund, I would say this: the USA undoubtedly stands today for a dogmatic and extreme form of capitalism, repugnant to many people in many countries, and means to impose her views on the new international economic order wherever possible. But the correct defence, if defence is needed, is not to stand aside, but to join the new international organisations and thus strengthen the hands of those countries which, like Great Britain, can be expected to represent and promote a more progressive outlook. Refusal to join merely strengthens the voting power of the block [*sic*] inside the Fund…I might add that, in the short time since my arrival in this country, I have been astonished at the lack of knowledge, even among some of those with opinions on the matter, of the detailed provisions of the Bretton Woods Agreement, and in particular of the many safeguards of the interests of the purely capitalist economies of the American variety which have been emphasised in the scheme (*Sydney Morning Herald*, 20/12/46).

He was to take a similar view a few months later in a well-publicised debate at the Darlinghurst branch of the ALP. In the debate, he opposed Ward (the sitting member for East Sydney, an inner Sydney electorate that included Darlinghurst), who was the government's strongest critic of Australia's membership of the Bretton Woods institutions.

Heinz also spoke publicly on the dollar problem: the inability of many countries, including Britain and Australia, to earn sufficient American dollars to pay for the goods and services they wanted from the United States. Speaking at a lunch-hour meeting in the Sydney University Union in September 1947, Heinz argued that the immediate solution to the dollar problem was for the United States to maintain full employment in its domestic economy. It could thereby increase its demand for imports, reduce its capacity to export and encourage greater exports from other countries. This was the same approach that had been taken by Australian spokesmen during and immediately after the war—the so-called 'positive approach', or 'full-employment approach', which had been formulated by leading Australian economists, including Giblin, Melville and Coombs.

To this policy, Heinz added that devaluation should be contemplated by countries experiencing chronic dollar shortages, among them the United Kingdom. He recommended, too, that the United States should lend more freely to other countries and that deficit countries—including Australia—should be prepared to borrow from the United States. To the argument that America's substantial productivity gap was the major reason for the dollar problem, Heinz thought that bridging the gap in the short term would be a tall order, considering that it was so wide. Much better, he thought, to reduce deficit countries' export prices in American markets, by devaluation. While it was true that devaluation would raise the import costs of deficit countries and thereby feed inflation, and while he admitted that demand in the United States for some imported goods was relatively price inelastic, nevertheless it was correct, Heinz argued, for the United States to call on countries to devalue, especially sterling-bloc countries.

Implied in much of Heinz's approach to the dollar problem was criticism of the Australian government's policy of refusing to borrow in the United States. Such borrowing, to be sure, would augment debt repayment obligations in the future. On balance, though, Heinz thought the risk was worth it. Provided 'we make sure that borrowed dollars are providentially spent on projects which will develop the Australian economy, and not squandered on semi-luxuries like petrol for pleasure motoring, films or tobacco, there is a strong case for exploring the chances of obtaining a substantial dollar loan now'. Of course, should it prove impossible to borrow sufficient dollars, or if devaluation failed to correct external imbalances, cuts in dollar imports would have to be resorted to by imposing various controls. But such cuts, he argued, should 'not be allowed to reduce the total volume of trade more than is absolutely necessary'.

As to Australia's domestic economic policy, Heinz was highly critical of the Chifley government's strategy of maintaining excessive levels of aggregate demand. Here, he was at one with the majority of Australian economists, among them the architects of Australia's full-employment policy. Contrary to recent belief, there was nothing Keynesian about the way economic policy was conducted in Australia in the late 1940s and early 1950s. An economic policy based on the economics of Keynes would not have permitted the number of unfilled vacancies to rise above the numbers registered as unemployed, which was the case at the time. The consequence of excess demand was clear: a rate of inflation by 1949 that exceeded 10 per cent and was accelerating well before the outbreak of the Korean War in 1950. Heinz supported the view associated with Copland, who pointed out that excess demand was reducing labour productivity as large numbers of poorly trained and unskilled workers were attracted into Australian manufacturing industries. In effect, Australia was suffering not from a deficiency of aggregate demand and mass unemployment, as had been feared would be the case once the war was over, but from excess demand and chronic over-full employment.

Just a few days before the announcement of sterling devaluation in September 1949, Heinz predicted in one of his news commentaries on ABC radio that devaluation was imminent. After giving the talk, he told Ruth that if the 'sterling should, after all, be devalued, I shall have a field day; already I have been pestered by all the papers'. What he failed to predict, however, was that Australia would itself devalue with sterling by the full amount against the US dollar. Instead, he had speculated that Australia would go only part of the way with sterling. Considering the country's strong balance of payments and tight labour markets, it beggared belief that the government would act so irresponsibly. But he failed to take account of the government's desperate need to shore up its rural political support only months before the 1949 federal election.

Heinz did not join the ALP until after he moved to Canberra in 1950. This was because he was reluctant to join a political party before his naturalisation was approved, a principle that he had steadfastly adhered to when he lived in Britain. But that principle did not stop him from expressing political views, which he did publicly, frequently and in a robust and forthright manner. He opposed, for instance, the Menzies government's Anti-Communist Bill, informing Allan Fraser that 'I am opposed to the whole principle of the Bill'; he was a signatory to a letter signed by staff at Sydney University who were opposed to the Bill.

Among the first things he did in Sydney was to join with some of his Sydney University colleagues, including Noel Butlin and Kingsley Laffer, in the establishment of the Fabian Society of New South Wales. He was elected its research officer and was responsible for arranging the production of seven publications, the most significant of which was one setting out a case for bank nationalisation. In 1947, Chifley had announced the government's intention to nationalise the private banks. As a member of the *Royal Commission into the Australian Monetary and Banking Systems* in the 1930s, Chifley had written a minority report supporting the nationalisation of the banks. In 1945, however, he had been persuaded by Coombs and others that nationalisation would not be needed and that legislation giving the central bank—then the Commonwealth Bank—additional powers to control the banks would itself ensure that the banking system would function in harmony with the government's economic policies.

Yet the fear that the private banks would challenge successfully in the High Court the constitutional legality of important provisions of the 1945 bank legislation rekindled Chifley's fears about the banks and the likelihood that they might oppose government policy. In 1947, the High Court invalidated Section 48 of the 1945 banking legislation. It did so in terms that seemed to open other, and more significant parts, of the legislation to the danger of successful challenge in the courts.

An Act passed in Federal Parliament in 1947 gave the Commonwealth the power to acquire the shares of all private trading banks (in return for compensation to be assessed by a special Federal Court of Claims) and the power to prohibit private banks from undertaking banking business in Australia after a specified date. In the event, the Act was challenged in the High Court. By a majority judgment, the legislation was declared *ultra vires*, on the grounds that the prohibition on private banking infringed Section 92 of the Australian Constitution. The Commonwealth appealed to the Privy Council in London, but that body upheld the High Court's verdict.

The Fabian Society's pamphlet supporting bank nationalisation was written largely by Heinz, with the assistance of Noel Butlin. It sold more copies than any of the society's other publications, thanks in large measure to the 40,000 copies purchased by Chifley for distribution to party members, government officials and the public. In the pamphlet, Heinz took the view that the inherent weakness of the 1945 legislation made it necessary to secure public ownership of the banking system, for the purpose of maintaining full employment. He argued, further, that a publicly owned banking system would provide improved banking services.

As well as writing the Fabian pamphlet, Heinz explained at several public forums why he supported the nationalisation of the private banks. After an address he gave at Sydney University, he was challenged by an arts student, Mary Walsh, to answer some of the concerns she had about the government's bank-nationalising intentions. In particular, she wanted to know how the nationalisation of the banks might prevent or mitigate a slump originating from overseas. Heinz responded by saying that, while 'there is nothing we can do to prevent the impact on Australia of a foreign slump', what 'we can do and must do is at least prevent the repercussions of the initial impact on industrial incomes and employment. The government must, mainly by means of deficit budget policy, maintain home incomes; at the same time, efforts must be made to maintain or stimulate home investment.' It was here, he said

> …where credit policy comes in. By themselves the private banks are hopeless in such a situation. Adequate action by the banking system presupposes effective central bank control (such as envisaged in the 1945 legislation) or by nationalisation. Since the courts have held that the Commonwealth Government does not possess adequate powers of control under the Constitution, while there is no reasonable doubt that it has the power to nationalise the banks, there is the course which it has decided to take.

Walsh then asked Heinz whether nationalisation of the banks would arrogate excessive power to the government, to which Heinz agreed that economic power should not be highly concentrated, whether in private or in state hands. Yet he was adamant that

> …there are some purposes so important and urgent that, whether we like it or not, we must endow the Government with adequate power to enable it to pursue them effectively…Anyone, therefore, who concedes…that nationalisation is economically essential for the prevention of poverty and mass unemployment in depressions, but refuses to allow the Government the necessary powers, in effect merely expresses a value judgement on the relative importance and urgency of preventing poverty and unemployment, on the one hand, and say national defence, on the other. He says, in effect, that national defence is important and therefore

we must give the Government adequate powers, poverty and unemployment are not important and therefore we are entitled to refuse the Government adequate powers. In some degree, that does seem to be precisely the situation.

To her question about the inefficiency of government enterprises compared with privately owned businesses, Heinz responded by saying that, while 'I do not…deny that the maintenance of efficiency in a public enterprise presents problems', it was 'the primary characteristic and virtue of public enterprise that it makes possible to put the public interest above profit considerations in these cases where there is conflict'. Here he referred to A.C. Pigou's classic work, *The Economics of Welfare* (1920), in support of his case. He rejected the idea of a national referendum that would seek public endorsement of bank nationalisation on the grounds that the Chifley government had been re-elected to office scarcely a year before and thereby possessed a mandate to govern. Besides, referenda were held to alter the Constitution and this was not at issue in the current case. Very soon, of course, the question of whether the Act to nationalise the banks was constitutional became the issue.

Walsh, however, was not convinced by Heinz's arguments. She wrote to him again with further questions. He became rather cross, thinking now—perhaps correctly—that his interlocutor was not the naïve university student he had thought she was, but rather a political activist with an axe to grind. To her questions of an economic nature, he responded abruptly by saying: 'Your reply shows that you do not understand the most elementary principles of a practical full employment policy.' To the claim that the majority of Australians seemed to prefer a private banking system to a state-owned one, Heinz replied

> It must be remembered that the press in this country is a tight monopoly of the opposition parties and points of view, that the banks and big business are prepared to spend, and are spending, unlimited funds in support of their privileged position and to influence the public by propaganda, however unscrupulous, against the government's proposal. I know from personal experience that it is hardly possible for the other side to make itself heard in the press or at meetings.

To her claim that, while poverty and unemployment were tragic for those who found themselves in these conditions, there was nothing the government could do about them, Heinz responded by saying that 'this statement would be laughable if it were not tragic. Do you really believe in *laissez-faire*? In the teeth of all the evidence of the history of the last 100 years and all informed opinion today as far to the right as Professor Bland and beyond? Think again!'.

In addition to this exchange, Heinz wrote several letters to the *Sydney Morning Herald* on the issue of bank nationalisation. The paper opposed the government's nationalisation policy; Heinz defended that policy. Several of the letters were published. One of them took the form of a reply to a correspondent who had claimed that bank nationalisation would not allow impartiality in the administration of the nationalised banks. In a private banking system where decisions were based on commercial criteria, an aggrieved customer could go to another bank. This, the correspondent said, would not be possible if the government operated all the banks. Heinz dismissed this contention, asserting that the safeguards implied in a privately owned system were only partial: commercial considerations, for example, often discriminated against small customers who lacked influential connections. As he put it: 'There has always been the risk of discrimination based on personal motives. And co-operation in such matters between banks, as well as the normal difficulties in obtaining accommodation from any bank but that with which a firm or individual is already connected, have always rendered the possibility of resort to a competing bank somewhat illusory' (*Sydney Morning Herald*, 26/8/47).

Moreover, he saw no reason why a system of appeals could not be devised to meet the problem, were it to arise in a nationalised banking system.

In another letter to the same newspaper, in which Heinz took issue with an editorial criticising nationalisation, a vital sentence was deleted from the published version. This had the effect of changing completely the intention of the letter. Instead of giving clear support to the government's policy, it appeared that Heinz was endorsing a court challenge to the government's legislation (*Sydney Morning Herald*, 23/9/47). In his letter of protest to H.A. McClure-Smith, the *Sydney Morning Herald's* Editor-in-Chief, Heinz complained: 'What I find most disturbing about this incident is that most of the people to whom I have mentioned it have retorted: "What do you expect?" Rightly or wrongly, there seems to be a general conviction that anyone who writes a letter to the *Herald* which does not conform to the policy of the paper runs the risk, if the letter is published at all, of having it mutilated for political purposes.'

McClure-Smith replied that his paper was publishing a balanced collection of letters and that no lesser person than the Prime Minister himself had commended the *Herald* for its impartial coverage of the government's bank policy. For Heinz, this simply reinforced his view that the paper was politically biased and deserved the contempt in which it was held by the general public.

In 1997, Heinz was asked by the editor of the *Canberra Bulletin of Public Administration* to contribute an article on the fiftieth anniversary of the Chifley government's policy to nationalise the banks. Looking back, Heinz found it hard to believe that this blatant act of socialism had occurred in Australia only 50 years before. He now thought the decision was 'incredible' and, while he made no attempt to justify his earlier support for bank nationalisation, he did acknowledge that 'the devastating unemployment and rural and urban poverty [experienced during the 1930s had] instilled widespread doubt about the validity of the capitalist and financial system'.

The bank nationalisation episode was Heinz's major venture into the political arena when he was at the University of Sydney. But there were other political issues that also drew his attention. On the Cold War that had recently broken out between the United States and the Soviet Union (this was the time of the Truman Doctrine and the Marshall Plan), he took what he believed to be a critical attitude towards both superpowers. In a letter sent to the *Australian Observer* in July 1947, the purpose of which was to criticise the support that periodical gave to 'the American point of view on the major international issues', Heinz said that his 'own preference is for a critical attitude equally towards the USA and Russia'.

When another paper at the time asked him why he was a socialist, he replied candidly that there were two sets of reasons, one economic and one non-economic. Socialism, he claimed, was capable of greater efficiency than capitalism: less competition meant less waste of scarce resources; there was the possibility that public ownership would provide greater economies of scale; socialism was likely to overcome the problem of externalities; there would be more incentives for workers; and it was more likely that full employment would be maintained in a socialist system than in a capitalist one. As well as these economic arguments for justifying socialism, Heinz asserted that there were moral reasons why he chose to be a socialist. For him, the 'basic objection to capitalism' was the uneven distribution of income for which it was responsible, inequalities of social status and the irresponsible use of power based on wealth. Further, he objected to what he called the 'spirit of capitalism', by which he meant its underlying selfishness, the emphasis it placed on competition and rivalry and the ethos of the 'devil take the hindmost'. He believed, in short, that the 'capitalist individualist system has placed a premium on objectionable traits'. As for himself, Heinz said that he wanted to live in a country that placed a premium on cooperation and service, rather than one that glorified aggressive competition and acquisitiveness.

This was certainly a bold and uncompromising statement of support for socialism. Nevertheless, to some of his old friends, Heinz appeared to have undergone a fundamental shift of political allegiance since he had left Britain. He was now a proclaimed Fabian socialist and about to become a paid-up member of the ALP, a party mainly of social democrats. In effect, he had turned his back on his youthful dalliance with communism.

Tom Wilson wrote to him in October 1949, saying that Heinz's former Sydney colleague Max Hartwell had told him in Oxford 'about the opening of your eyes to the menace of Stalin the Beast. Perhaps in another ten years you will also see that socialism is a menace. You are slow-witted but you seem to make progress in the end…Are you a professor yet? If not, I presume you will be one soon.'

8
RUTH'S TRIP TO EUROPE

In 1948, after two years in Australia, Ruth decided that she wanted to visit her parents in Germany and take the children with her. Heinz's university commitments made it impossible for him to accompany her. Though three years had passed since the end of the war in Europe, it was still difficult for foreign civilians to travel to Germany. Private citizens generally were not permitted to visit the country, so it was uncertain whether Ruth would be allowed to do so. The annual quota of visitors was usually filled by businessmen, and even then, there was a sizeable waiting list. Heinz called on the assistance of the Labor parliamentarian Allan Fraser, who contacted John Burton, the Secretary of the Department of External Affairs, to see whether he could secure the necessary entry permits for Ruth.

In the application for a permit, Heinz explained that Ruth had left Germany as a political refugee in 1935—when only 20 years old—and had not seen her parents since then, except for one day in 1939, when they met her in London during a cruise. Her parents were now both over 60, neither was in good health and both were eager to see their daughter after so many years.

'It is for this reason,' Heinz wrote, 'that my wife was somewhat reluctant to come to Australia when I was offered my present appointment by Sydney University in 1946, and that, but for my acceptance of the appointment, she would now have the opportunity of inviting her parents to visit her in England.'

Burton worked through the Military Permit Office attached to the British Foreign Office and finally was able to obtain a permit for Ruth for a 30-day visit, valid for June–July 1949. It was fortunate that Cuxhaven, where her parents lived, was in the British Zone of West Germany.

Ruth had originally intended to leave Sydney in May 1949, but when she discovered she was pregnant again, the trip was brought forward. With three weeks' notice, she and the boys set sail for England on the *Esperance Bay* on 1 March. The plan was to spend some time in England completing formalities and visiting friends, and then to travel to Cuxhaven. Heinz had contacted his former Oxford friend, Tom Baily, who by this stage had taken up his post as Anglican cleric at Shap in England's northwest. He asked Baily whether Ruth might stay with him during the latter stages of her of her confinement. Baily readily said yes. So from Germany, Ruth would travel back to England, have the baby and then return to Australia later in the year.

For more than six months, a stream of letters passed backward and forward between Australia and Europe. In his letters to Ruth, whom he invariably addressed 'Dear Darky', Heinz informed her with copious detail of his activities, whom he had met, conditions and events in Australia and, above all, how he was missing her and the children. Ruth, for her part, recorded the difficulties that she and the children experienced on the long sea voyages, the state of Europe, the joys and tribulations of meeting her family and various members of Heinz's family, meetings with friends and, eventually, the birth of Bettina.

Scarcely a fortnight had elapsed since Ruth's departure when Heinz wrote a letter to her, addressed to the ship at Fremantle, saying

> All the time I think of things I would like to know about your life and experiences on board, but by the time you get this most of the questions will have become out of date. I wondered yesterday for example as I was crossing the Harbour Bridge whether you had seen Coogee on your way South, or was it already too dark? And did you have nice views of the land around the Australian coast? Also I want to know lots more about your Melbourne days. Perhaps you will have had some time to report between Melbourne and Fremantle. I also wonder whether you still go to bed with the children or whether you have begun to take any part in evening activities. Whether you have met any nice people, and so forth. You will probably answer anyhow in your letters. How is No. 3 getting on? I hope you have not been sick any more, whether because of No. 3 or seasickness. How is Nicky's eczema? And Chris's asthma? Do you have any trouble in stopping them falling overboard? (I confess I find it quite easy to think about that in wild day-nightmares.) How is the washing getting on—and drying? Do you send anything to the laundry—in fact, is there one to send things to? Have you so far had time for reading? And all the sewing you were going to do?

When he received Ruth's letter from Perth, informing him of the various illnesses that she and the children had experienced between Sydney and

Fremantle, and dreading the fact that the worst of the voyage was yet to come, Heinz responded as follows

> Your long awaited letter from Perth came today—and I am rather depressed. You poor old Darky, what a terrible time you are having, and there is nothing I can do about it. I do hope things have got better since Fremantle. I wish you could quite frankly appeal for a little help to some of your fellow passengers, e.g. one or other of the girls you mention. Perhaps you got someone nice on board at Fremantle. I shall worry about you until I hear from you again from Colombo. And I am terribly sorry for the two boys if they are so unhappy.

It did not get any better as the *Esperance Bay* crossed the Indian Ocean and passed through the Suez Canal on its way to the Mediterranean and Europe. Ruth, exhausted and despondent, finally reached England on 14 April. In London, she had difficulty coping with the weather and was too tired to visit everyone she had planned to see. Happily, she was able to alter the conditions of her entry visa to Germany, arriving there on 1 May. She travelled across the North Sea on a small cargo boat carrying a dozen passengers and stayed with her family at Cuxhaven for just more than a month.

Of her trip to Germany, Ruth wrote to Heinz

> As far as my family went, I think I can say that the joy and happiness which all showed made up for the complicated preparations for the journey and the trials of the trip. But to come home after 14 years was in many ways a great strain, especially as it meant coming back to such a small place where not much had changed and where the war had not affected the people unduly. …I can only say that I was quite overcome with the general impression that things there are so much better than we had expected after looking at it all from so far away. But the same is true of things here in England. Everything here seems to have improved a lot since we left three years ago. It seems to show that one does get isolated in these far-off places, where news of the rest of the world is scarce and probably prejudiced.

Heinz, meanwhile, was keeping Ruth informed of his daily life in Sydney. Noel Butlin had won an ANU travelling scholarship to undertake a PhD at Harvard, and he and Joan were planning to visit Ruth in England on their way to Boston. After the Butlins' departure, Heinz's former student Alan Barnard had moved into the Arndts' half of the house with Heinz, while Alan's girlfriend, Pat, and a female friend of hers had moved into the Butlins' half. To his father, Heinz wrote: 'Our ménage continues to function very well and I am leading a remarkably untroubled and placid life.'

He told Ruth that he had inaugurated a series of monthly lectures sponsored by the Fabian Society, was undertaking a research project for the Commonwealth Treasury, had written up a lecture he had given the previous year in Melbourne for publication in a new Italian journal of international economics and had been elected president of the University Economic Society. Also, he had been appointed president of a local music club, replacing a Mr Perrin, who had been deposed for embezzling the club's funds. Heinz told Ruth that he hoped 'we shall leave Hurstville before long and provide a decent excuse for resigning that honourable office'. From time to time, he reported to Ruth that he had posted food parcels, including packets of jelly, chocolate and sweets, and soap.

For Ruth, things appeared to improve once she and the children arrived at Shap. She wrote to friends

> Since the sea journey has receded into the background it has lost many of the horrors it has meant to me. I had known before we left that I would not enjoy the trip much, as I have never liked long journeys, but to have to face storms and cold weather when we were all very seasick, as well as extreme heat, and poor little Nicky was so sick that I sometimes thought he would not survive, was more than I had bargained for. There was nothing wrong with the boat, except that it was so slow, and that we mothers did not get any help from the crew in looking after the children. But the worst was that there was what I considered to be the most disgusting collection of Australians on the boat, and it all became more of a nightmare as the time went on.

At Shap, Ruth and the boys enjoyed the open spaces and the country air. They got on well with Tom Baily and his housekeeper; they met the locals, who probably thought it strange that this fatherless family of two small boys and one pregnant mother, all of them Australian citizens but with German accents, were living with their vicar, himself a bachelor. While the villagers no doubt discussed among themselves this strange ménage, to Ruth and the boys they were friendly and exhibited no malice. Chris attended the local school and enjoyed it. It was natural, however, that Ruth should find the circumstances far from ideal: about to give birth to her third child within five years, a long way from home and without Heinz. Though she was always interested in Heinz's news and waited eagerly for his letters, she wrote on one occasion to friends: 'Heinz has used this period of grass-widowerhood to do a lot of work, catching up with his research, and also doing some of the outside things which I used to frown upon, as I always thought he had quite enough to do with his university duties. I would like to think that he will feel that family life has compensations, even if it means that he cannot sit down and write and read when he feels like it.'

Heinz waited eagerly for news from Ruth, her letters often containing short notes and drawings by Chris. As if to disabuse Ruth of any impression she might have had that his life lacked hardship and adversity, he wrote three letters in quick succession at the end of June. These informed her of the floods in the coal-producing region of the Hunter Valley and of the crippling coal strike, both events causing severe shortages of power and fuel in New South Wales more generally. From his letter of 26 June 1949

> The fuel restrictions are really fantastic. All that one is allowed to use is two electric lights, cooking facilities in the morning and evening, and the electric jug three times a day: no radiators, no washing, except in cold water—(and it's much too cold for that); trains at hourly intervals; no electricity at all for industry, nor for public buildings such as the Public Library or the University. Hence no evening lectures…The immediate cause of all this is the floods which wrecked the railways from the northern coalfields around Maitland and Cessnock. But there is also the threat of the general coal strike which is due to begin tomorrow unless last minute negotiations can stop it. It looks as if we shall be with these difficulties, if not in quite this severe form, for the rest of the winter.

He added in a letter the next day

> You can congratulate yourself that you are not having the baby here. The coal strike has really started today and things are getting a bit thick. The restrictions are all still on—no baths, no hot water supply of any sort; cooking for two meals a day, no radiators (and it is lousily cold—39 degrees [Fahrenheit; 3.8 degrees Celsius] yesterday and today), no coal to be had, transport severely restricted, and all industry shut down. There were no evening lectures tonight, but we had been given a lecture room or two in the engineering department where they generate their own electricity…Hospitals were shutting down except for emergency wards…I was living on a small stock of coal from last year; crouching around the fire. I'm sure you wouldn't like it much here right now. Neither would the children.

He informed Ruth on 30 June that

> Things here meanwhile are going from bad to worse. The coal strike goes on (though the Government is taking quite unprecedented measures—unprecedented for a [Labor] Government—e.g. freezing union funds) and every day restrictions become more severe. Cooking periods have been further reduced; electric and gas hot water systems are to be cut off altogether (because the ban has not been adhered to properly), transport will be further cut, also street lighting; unemployment is increasing—already about 500,000 in NSW are affected. Our coal supplies are finished, but we are cutting up the wood behind the garage; there is still lots…The ban on the hot water is the worst business—no baths (I sneaked a tiny shower—the last one—on Tuesday) and no washing; I am wearing my last shirt but one; unless I get some washing done (the laundries are, of course, not functioning) I shall have to lecture in still white shirts next week! And even if I do get the washing done, we are not allowed to iron. I did manage to wash an accumulation of socks this afternoon and shall darn some of them tomorrow. But it's all rather complicated. Supplies of food are also getting short; no potatoes, little meat, milk supply cut (that was because of floods); no candles, little kerosene, and no

canned meat to be had; electric lights in homes are banned after 9pm. I managed to give some evening lectures this week, because we got a room in electrical engineering where they make their own electricity.

On 1 August, Ruth gave birth to Bettina. Before the baby was born, Ruth and Heinz, in their correspondence, often talked about possible names for the baby. Since both believed they were going to have another boy, much of the discussion centred on boys' names, though they did not discount completely the possibly that they might have a girl. Both of them desperately wanted a girl, and they agreed that if their latest child did turn out to be a girl, they would call her Bettina, after Heinz's sister. As soon as the baby arrived, Tom Baily sent Heinz a cable telling him the good news that Ruth and the baby were well.

Heinz could scarcely believe his good fortune. He cabled Ruth immediately, assuring her that he was delighted that they now had a daughter to complement the two boys. The day after the birth, Ruth felt able to write to Heinz, giving him all the details

> It started on Sunday night, all day I had had enough of it. Mrs Houguez [Tom Baily's housekeeper] and I took the boys for a walk and she made me climb over a stone wall, and it did the trick. I just managed to bath the boys and put them to bed, but felt pretty sick all the time. I then went to bed, but there was still no pain. I went to sleep but woke up about 10.30 and we left about 11pm by car. Then a long business started. The baby did not come until 6 o'clock the next morning (1 August). Anyhow it is all finished and done with now...Baby has lots of dark hair, weight 8 lbs 7 ozs!!!

In a second letter she wrote the same day, Ruth provided Heinz with further information about the baby

> It was really not so bad looking back on it, though I longed for some ether as they had in King George V!...Of course, the first surprise was that it was a girl. I wonder what your reaction was. I thought of you getting a cable read out to you over the phone

> and felt so sorry for you being all alone, and I cried. But maybe you were very pleased with your family which will be very nice and just right as long as everyone does not spoil the little girl too much…She is very sweet, awfully comic at times, but quite pretty. Lots of black hair, much more than either of the boys and much darker, a round head and face, fat cheeks, beautiful skin and will probably have very dark eyes. I am very amused by her; she often looks as if she is laughing. Being fat, she is also lazy and snoozes away peacefully and really does not bother to eat, but as she is only one day old that does not matter. She knows what it is all about and can suck when she is bullied.

To Joan and Noel Butlin (who had arrived in London), Ruth wrote after Bettina's birth: 'Except for the fact that there are nappies in the Vicarage garden you would not know we have her. I am doing everything for the boys and her and it is surprising how little difference she makes to our life here. She…[has] dark skin and [looks] half Chinese and half Mexican, goodness knows what thriller I must have been reading at the time she decided to come along.'

The Butlins decided to travel up to Shap, to take a look at the new arrival for themselves. In one of his circular letters to family and friends, Noel wrote of their trip to Shap as follows

> We had a very enjoyable time, seeing the inside of a village, a country inn and a vicarage. The vicarage was a gem, with a perfect Cold Comfort Farm touch down to an illegitimate housekeeper with an illegitimate daughter, a duck, dog, fowls, cats and pigeons in the kitchen, the house a great store barn with attached graveyard and a little stone church. The Arndt family was flourishing and well it might in that climate with stocks of food. We were able to go walking a bit with Tom Baily the vicar and were introduced to the general layout of the old Shap manor. In addition to this we went for a bus ride with Ruth, Christopher and Nicky to Kendal, almost 16 miles from Shap, and got some better idea of the general scenery on the edge of the [L]akes district.

After the Butlins left Shap, Joan Butlin wrote to Heinz: 'Bettina Mary's wonderfully well behaved and although she has not yet had time to become beautiful she has distinct possibilities. She is very long, with long fingers. By the way, she can hold her head up surprisingly well for such a young baby.' Noel added, 'Ruth seems very well—much better than she was before she left. Certainly she picked the right spot in staying in Shap.'

Ruth was now preparing for the long return journey to Sydney. With the traumas of the voyage to Europe still indelibly imprinted on her mind, she was scarcely looking forward to the voyage back. She gathered some comfort, however, from the fact that Heinz was able to book her and the children on a new, and much faster, Orient liner, the *Otranto*, which was due to leave Tilbury on 20 October. There was also the possibility, at first, of Heinz joining the ship at Adelaide and accompanying Ruth and the children to Sydney. Inquiries were made about this, but it ultimately proved impossible.

There was something else for Ruth to look forward to. Heinz's colleague John La Nauze had been appointed Professor of Economic History at the University of Melbourne and would be leaving Sydney at the end of the year. Ruth did not want to continue living in Hurstville, with the Butlins away, and now with three children crammed into half a house that had been too small even with two children. She put pressure on Heinz to see whether the unexpired portion of the lease on La Nauze's house at Chatswood, in Sydney's north, could be transferred to them. He found that it could and, thus, the Arndts moved into the house early in the new year of 1950.

With a berth on the *Otranto*, and with good reason to believe that they would be moving to a better house and neighbourhood soon after she returned to Sydney, Ruth felt in better spirits. Noel Butlin, having returned to London from the journey to Shap, wrote to Heinz, hoping that Ruth 'gets through the trip [all right] and I should think she will be in much better shape to start this one. She looked much better than she did in Hurstville before she left.' Though Ruth now had three children to contend with, one of them not yet three months old, the return journey proved to be far less of a burden than the voyage to Europe had been. Even so, it was not without its difficulties, and Ruth eagerly awaited the *Otranto*'s arrival in Sydney. Of course Heinz, too, looked forward with great expectation to that moment.

9
NEW HORIZONS

While Ruth was in Europe, Heinz considered his career and where it might take him. In particular, he wondered whether he should remain in Sydney, seek positions at other Australian universities or return to England. Even before Ruth had left for Europe, he had written to Tom Wilson, who, after graduating from Queen's University, Belfast, had become a Fellow of University College, Oxford. He asked Wilson whether he should apply for one of the vacant positions at Belfast, where the Australian Keith Isles was head of the economics department. Wilson replied that he appreciated Heinz's 'difficulties in Australia—the more so because of the uncertainty I have experienced myself…no roots, family, etc'. He told Heinz that there were posts available, but he was unsure about Heinz's chances of securing one of them. He recommended that Heinz should ask Isles himself: 'Put it to him that Sydney looks very doubtful and ask him whether he could advise you to apply for Belfast.'

It appears that this advice went unheeded, for, at the end of 1948, Heinz was corresponding with officials at the United Nations Commission for Asia and the Far East (ECAFE) about the possibility of an appointment there. These inquiries did not proceed very far because ECAFE had recently moved from Shanghai to Singapore ahead of the communist takeover and was now in the process of arranging more permanent headquarters in Bangkok. Thus, it was not immediately seeking new appointments to its staff.

One of the problems at Sydney University, to which Wilson had alluded in his letter to Heinz, was Sid Butlin's reluctance to fill the vacant second chair in economics. Heinz was ambitious to get ahead, telling his father soon after Ruth had left that 'I have no intention to end my life as Senior Lecturer at Sydney. Unless, therefore, a chance of promotion should come along here fairly soon, I may well begin to look around for a new job elsewhere—quite probably in other Australian universities, but conceivably also in England.' Had Butlin offered him the vacant chair, Heinz would have been quite content to stay in Sydney. Butlin, however, was not disposed to make decisions precipitately, and Heinz was not prepared to wait while Butlin prevaricated.

Two positions—one in England, the other in Australia—tempted him to submit applications while Ruth was away. He learnt from friends that Manchester was soon to advertise two readerships, one in economic theory and the other in international trade. He wrote to Arthur Lewis,[7] who had recently been appointed to the chair that Jewkes had vacated and who had been at the LSE when Heinz was there. Lewis encouraged him to apply for the post in international trade, yet he did warn Heinz about the problems the latter had experienced before at Manchester, with Jewkes and Hicks. 'The difficulty that we are afraid of here,' Lewis wrote

> …is that we do not know what may have been said by Jewkes or Hicks when you were last here. At these selection committees there is always a majority of ancient professors from other faculties, some of whom have long memories. Jewkes was not popular at the end, and the fact that you and he did not get on may be counted by some in your favour. Anything you can let me know about the episode would be helpful, in case any of the committee wishes to make things up.

Lewis added that it would be useful if Heinz could get Hicks to write a letter supporting his application since, after all, Hicks had been one of his referees when Heinz had applied for the senior lectureship at Sydney.

At the same time that he was considering the Manchester job, Heinz heard from Brian Tew, Professor of Economics at the University of Adelaide, that Tew had accepted the chair at Nottingham and would be leaving Adelaide at the end of 1949. Tew, who had become a close friend, urged Heinz to apply for the Adelaide chair. Heinz wrote to Ruth saying that he was now confronted with three choices: to apply to Manchester; to apply to Adelaide; or to have it out with Butlin about the Sydney chair. He asked Ruth for advice, recognising that the thought of the long voyage back to Australia might well influence her views. For Heinz, such a voyage would be an important consideration when deciding whether to apply for the readership at Manchester. Ruth, however, wrote back saying that she would not be disappointed if Heinz were to reject an offer from Manchester. All the same, she did not dissuade him from submitting an application.

In the event, Heinz applied to Manchester and to Adelaide. He also decided to tackle Butlin about the Sydney chair and to ask him about the readership that was soon to be vacated by La Nauze. Butlin made it plain that Heinz's chances of securing either of the Sydney posts would be enhanced if he could show the selection committees that he had an offer from Manchester or Adelaide. Heinz, however, was not convinced that he should apply for these reasons. He made it clear to Ruth that he was 'not very fond of this sort of poker game', because it could lead to offers from the three institutions, leaving him with an embarrassing choice.

Of the Sydney chair, he told Ruth that Butlin would be happy if he were appointed to it, but that he was unsure whether the university was now in a position to fund it. Butlin reckoned that Heinz should not be optimistic about Sydney and should seriously consider applying for the posts at Adelaide and Manchester. For Heinz, it was the insecurity about Sydney that finally made him decide to apply for the positions at the other two universities.

In his application for the readership in international trade at Manchester, Heinz set out his case for appointment

> My interest in international economics developed naturally in the course of my work at Chatham House. The history of international economic problems during the interwar period formed the central theme of my book, and much of my other work at Chatham House involved international economic issues. International economics, and particularly international monetary theory, have since then become my chief interest. During my three years in Australia I have had the opportunity of becoming acquainted with the problems of a primary producer country and the many international economic problems which are of special importance to a country in Australia's position. I have made a point of developing international economic theory in the course for which I am responsible and have largely concentrated on this field in the special course for honours students.

When describing his current research, Heinz referred to the project on foreign investment in Australia between 1865 and 1914. He emphasised, for the benefit of the Manchester selection committee, that 'the primary motive for [this research] is a desire to throw further light on the causes of economic fluctuations in the British economy during the nineteenth century'. Although there had not been much progress on the project, because of all the work that he and Noel Butlin were undertaking on national income estimates for New South Wales, he said: 'if I should return to England, I should hope to have the opportunity of continuing work on some aspects of this problem.' He gave as his three referees J.R. Hicks, Tom Wilson and Sid Butlin.

Tew was far more encouraging about Heinz's chances of selection for the chair at Adelaide than either Lewis or Butlin had been about his chances at Manchester and Sydney. In a letter to Heinz, Tew commented, 'while selection committees are queer things…[my] inquiries have so far not revealed anyone available who in my opinion is in the same street as you, and I think Adelaide would be mad not to select you, but in these matters you cannot be sure, can you?'

Nor did Tew think that anyone in England, who could be regarded as appointable, would apply for the Adelaide chair. Of possible Australian candidates, he considered that Heinz's only serious rival might be Dick Downing, but he was confident that the selection committee would support Heinz ahead of Downing. Later Tew was to inform Heinz that he had contacted Downing, who had told him that he was not interested in the position at Adelaide anyway.

Tew had also raised with Heinz the possibility of the Ritchie Chair at Melbourne University, which Ben Higgins was holding at the time on a two-year appointment, but which was about to expire. He suggested that Heinz should consider applying for that as well as for Adelaide. Though Heinz told Ruth that he thought the Ritchie Chair was well beyond his reach, he confessed nevertheless that 'it's all very exciting—and strictly secret'.

There then followed several months of agonising letters from Heinz asking Ruth for advice as to what he should do if he were offered all or any of these positions. On 29 April 1949, he wrote to Ruth: 'I still don't know at all what I shall do if the Manchester job is offered to me, nor is there any prospect that any further information about the possibilities here will come to hand in time to help me solve the problem. It would be rather absurd if I had to toss coins on an issue like that.'

Nevertheless, his optimism about the Manchester post was soon shaken when Ruth wrote to him in the middle of June. She told Heinz of having heard that, according to what Arthur Lewis had assured one of their London friends, Hicks had written an unfavourable referee's report. Ruth naturally was upset when she was informed about this, telling Heinz that

> It would be too silly if you gave Hicks's name again for future applications…It seems to me that all you have to do is to write to Arthur Lewis and ask him what has happened…It all seems

rather silly, can you explain it? Didn't he give you such a favourable testimonial for the Sydney job? However, that can probably be explained. I shouldn't get worked up over this, and for goodness sake don't go and tell everyone about it, it might spoil your chances for future promotion, etc. Just say that you haven't heard anything, write that letter to Arthur and then wait for what he has to say…I shouldn't tell Sid [Butlin] for one. It is rather a nuisance as Hicks would also be the obvious choice for you if you for instance have to apply for the Adelaide chair, so where do you get other references from?

Heinz wrote back to Ruth saying that the news about Hicks 'puzzles me'

> The most likely explanation seems to me to be that Hicks, in his unimaginative way, wrote to the effect that I was rather young and inexperienced while he knew me at Manchester and that he does not really know anything about my work since I left. It is just possible that he was annoyed that I did not write to tell him that I had given his name to Arthur, but since it was a private letter to Arthur, I do not think he would have expected that. However, the whole business does not worry me; in fact, I confess I am rather relieved not to have to reject the offer.

What appears to have worried Heinz much more was the fact that he had given Hicks's name as a referee for the Adelaide job as well as for the Manchester one. But he was relieved when Tew, after Heinz had informed him about Ruth's information, replied thus: 'As to Hicks, I may say that I heard confidentially that he might rat on you, and therefore [I] didn't write to him.' Instead, Tew had asked Leslie Melville to support Heinz's application. Melville, who had been the inaugural Professor of Economics at Adelaide, had 'agreed very willingly', having been greatly impressed with the research that he had commissioned Heinz to undertake for the United Nations. Heinz's other referees for the Adelaide chair were Tom Wilson, Paul Rosenstein-Rodan and Sid Butlin.

Now out of the reckoning for the readership at Manchester, and with little optimism justified about the chair at Sydney, Heinz rested his hopes on Adelaide. Brian and Marjorie Tew kept him regularly informed about the progress of the selection process. Marjorie wrote to him on 25 August saying that 'I am to tell you that your most serious competitor so far is J.S.G. Wilson [an Australian, then at the University of London] and he is a doubtful starter'.

Noel Butlin, on his way to Harvard via England, wrote to Heinz informing him that 'I looked up Brian [Tew] in Adelaide. He tells me that the selection committee reacted very favourably to your application.' With his friends reporting that events were progressing strongly in his favour, Heinz again asked Ruth for her views—'i.e. your personal preferences, on the understanding that I shall not necessarily treat them as decisive, so that you can give them freely without worrying that I shall disregard other considerations'.

Before he had a reply from Ruth, however, he received a depressing letter from Tew. This contained a warning: 'things are not going too well as concerns the chair, and in my opinion you should not rule out other jobs solely because you would prefer Adelaide. Your claims *qua* economist are not disputed, but I am constantly told that our Council is solidly and homogeneously right wing and that prudence demands that we render under Caesar, etc.'

Tew had, in fact, learnt that the Vice-Chancellor was unhappy with all of the candidates and was hoping that others would turn up. 'So far,' Tew told Heinz, 'I've nothing definite to report, only my feeling about the atmosphere—and I may be quite wrong.'

A month later, Tew wrote to Heinz again, saying that the short-list was down to three

> Baster (the 'international banking chap'), [Donald] Cochrane [of Melbourne] and you…I am afraid, however, that at present you are the least favoured of the three probably because of the conservative majority in the selection committee, possibly because of a highly adverse report from an eminent economist whom I think to be an irresponsible, prejudiced ass, but who is listened to by other members of the committee, despite the uniformly favourable nature of the other testimonials. (The wicked one was not one of your own referees, so don't blame Sid. In fact, he doesn't live in Australia.)

It is not clear whether Tew was alluding here to Hicks or Melville (now Australia's executive director at the IMF and World Bank in Washington), but probably the committee had contacted Hicks in Oxford. At any rate, shortly after this letter, Tew wrote to Heinz again. 'The selection committee has not yet definitely pronounced but I judge (with regret) that you are now out of the running.' In the event, Peter Karmel, recently returned to Melbourne from Cambridge, where he had completed a PhD, was appointed to Adelaide.

While Sydney, Manchester and Adelaide were Heinz's preferred options, they were not the only possibilities that came his way at this time. In June 1949, and without any warning, he received a telephone call from John Burton of the Department of External Affairs in Canberra, who had previously helped with the permit enabling Ruth to visit Germany. Burton asked Heinz if he was interested in taking a job in Yogyakarta.[8] The Indonesian government had recently established the position of Economic Adviser and had asked the Australian government whether there was anyone in Australia with suitable qualifications who might be interested in taking on the job for a number of years, or at least for six months.

Heinz doubted that six months would be long enough for a person to become fully acquainted with Indonesia and its economic problems. Besides, he could not leave the University of Sydney in the lurch, and he doubted whether it would grant him the necessary leave. As to the longer term, Heinz told Burton: 'extraordinarily attractive as it is in some ways, I doubt whether I am the person for that sort of job and whether, from my own point of view, I could hardly make so far reaching a decision without consulting my wife who…will be in Europe for another three months.'

He mentioned that Gerald Firth or Dick Downing might be interested, though he doubted whether the job would hold for them the 'political appeal that it has for me'.

To Ruth, Heinz wrote that 'the idea has its attractions. But you will be glad to hear that I gratefully declined.' Ruth replied that she was 'glad I don't have to go and live with you in [Yogyakarta], however romantic it might have been. But I shall be glad to get back to Sydney and have already proclaimed that for the next six months after we get back home we shall just stay put and go nowhere!'. For good measure, she added

> The other night I had such a wild dream about you and a French girl that I woke up in the early hours of the morning and made frantic plans to come back straight away by plane and tried to work out whether the next three months we have to spend here would

be quite as expensive as the air trip home! However it is probably quite healthy for me to wonder after all this time what you are doing.

There was also the possibility of a job in the public service in Canberra; Trevor Swan had raised this notion in conversation with Heinz. Though it appeared to be an attractive offer (so much so that Heinz discussed it at some length with Swan and others), it was not a permanent position. Heinz considered that, were he to take it, and in the event it did not work out satisfactorily, it might be difficult for him to return to academic life. Even so, he didn't discount it completely, as he explained to Ruth

> Yet another excitement yesterday: a telephone call from Canberra as I was in the middle of my seminar, from Trevor Swan (the very good young economist who has recently come back from England and is due to head the new Economic Secretariat which is to be set up—on the lines of the Robbins-Meade[9] set-up): could I be persuaded, on any terms, to enter the Public Service? The point clearly is that Trevor as prospective head of that new department is looking for staff; the job he would offer me is presumably second-in-command to him; very interesting and probably as well paid as a chair; but it would mean giving up the academic career, and on the whole I don't think I want to do that. Anyhow, Trevor wanted no definite answer; nothing concrete is likely to emerge until after the federal election…I merely told him that the answer would probably be NO, but that I would be quite ready to listen to more detailed suggestions. Think about it and let me have your reactions some time.

In the meantime, a new possibility had emerged, and this too appeared to be very appealing. On 24 June 1949, Heinz wrote to Ruth saying:'Canberra University College are [sic] about to advertise a Chair in Economics; I think I shall apply.'

10
CANBERRA UNIVERSITY COLLEGE

Canberra University College (CUC) was established in 1929 and took its first students in 1930. This was not an auspicious time to establish a public institution of higher learning in Australia, especially in the new national capital. Cost cutting by governments, including the Commonwealth, was the order of the day. In fact, expenditure on and in Canberra came to a sudden halt with the onset of the depression. Originally a college of the University of Melbourne, CUC had been promoted by a group of senior Commonwealth public servants, led by Sir Robert Garran, the Solicitor-General, who was chairman of the college's council from its inception until the 1950s. Its purpose was to provide part-time degree studies for public servants, some of whom had been enrolled in state universities before their Commonwealth agencies were transferred to Canberra.

Not only were students studying on a part-time basis, almost all of the academic staff of the college were also part-timers, working during the day in the public service and taking classes in the evening. A major development occurred in 1948 when Associate Professor Herbert ('Joe') Burton, Head of the Department of Economic History in the University of Melbourne, was appointed inaugural principal of the college. This appointment, together with renewed growth in Canberra—and hence growth in the number of public servants transferring to Canberra from interstate and in the number of school-leavers wishing to study full-time at CUC—initiated a new era in the college's history. Another was to occur in 1960 when CUC amalgamated with the Australian National University (ANU).

One of Joe Burton's first decisions was to establish four chairs, one each in history, political science, English and economics. Burton himself had been offered the chair in economics at the time of his appointment, but had declined to accept it, on the grounds that he had no qualifications in economics. Instead, he was appointed to a chair in economic history. In 1950, Manning Clark, then a lecturer in Australian history at the University of Melbourne, was appointed to the chair of history; and Fin Crisp, Director-General of the Department of Postwar Reconstruction, was appointed Professor of Political Science. The next year, A.D. Hope, the eminent Australian poet, was appointed Professor of English, and Heinz was appointed to the chair of economics.

Heinz had first heard about CUC's intention to establish a chair of economics in June 1949. Eighteen months were to elapse before he took up the post on 1 January 1951. When he first learned of the new chair in Canberra, he was still resting his hopes on his applications to Manchester and Adelaide. Once it became clear to him that these would fail, he turned again to the possibility of the second chair at Sydney.

He wrote to Ruth on 21 October 1949 to say that he had

> …got involved in a rather nerve-wrecking [sic] one hour's talk with Sid [Butlin]…I touched in passing on the question of our second chair here, but he did not bite at all. On the other hand he is anxious to know whether I shall be here next year; for the time being I am content to let him ponder the possibility of my going to Canberra. Perhaps if he considers that seriously, he might still investigate the question of the Chair more earnestly. It is pretty clear that, while he quite approves of me, he is not keen on having any second professor by his side.

Having got nowhere with Butlin, Heinz set his sights on Canberra. It was while waiting for the college to advertise the position that Heinz and Ruth moved from Hurstville into John and Barbara La Nauze's former home at 53 Centennial Avenue, Chatswood. They were now in a house to themselves, and for the first time they felt settled in Australia. Ruth in particular was ecstatic, welcoming the space and stability after the turmoil of the previous year. Heinz, on the other hand, was ready to move on, or more precisely, to make an upward move in his career, a fact that he freely made known to friends and colleagues.

La Nauze, now Professor of Economic History at Melbourne University, wrote to Heinz in March 1950 to tell him that Wilfred Prest (Dean of the Faculty of Economics and Commerce) had suggested that he might be interested in a vacant senior lectureship at Melbourne. Prest had indeed urged La Nauze to write to Heinz. Knowing that Heinz would not be interested, La Nauze nevertheless went through the motions of contacting him, but in his letter to Heinz he doubted 'whether the slightly greater pay (£950 plus £132 cost of living) would compensate for the bother, with no increase in status'. He was correct in thinking that Heinz would not be interested in moving simply from a senior lectureship at Sydney to the same position in Melbourne.

Heinz had now decided to apply for the Canberra chair and wrote to La Nauze asking him if he would act as one of his referees. La Nauze replied that he could 'with good conscience write one of my best and most judicious letters of the kind which always seem to me to be quite conclusive'. He wondered whether Heinz intended to invite anyone in England to act as a referee. La Nauze thought that while such references might 'not be absolutely necessary…if there is someone whose name is likely to impress the selection committee it always helps. Your name is known, I think, pretty favourably in Australian economic circles and it might be advisable to have this view supported by one overseas referee.'

The whole business of overseas referees was, of course, a sensitive issue as far as Heinz was concerned. After all, it was Heinz's belief that Hicks had sabotaged his prospects for the readership at Manchester and possibly for the chair at Adelaide, too. He was not going to fall into that trap again—and he concurred with Ruth that Hicks should not be asked to act as one of his referees for the Canberra post. Instead, he chose three of his Sydney colleagues: Sid Butlin, P.H. Partridge (Professor of Government, and later Professor of Social Philosophy and Director of the Research School of Social Sciences at the ANU) and La Nauze.

In his letter of application to CUC, Heinz summarised his academic qualifications and his work at the LSE, the Royal Institute of International Affairs and Manchester University. He stressed that he had lectured principally on money, banking, the theory of business activity, public finance and international economics, with some limited teaching in value theory. Also, he mentioned that from October 1946 at the Sydney post, he was responsible for the third-year course in economics, which covered monetary theory, the theory of business activity, international economics and public finance. Of his research at Sydney, he noted in his application: 'Such research work as I have found time to do has been mainly in the field of Australian economic history and, more recently, in interest theory.'

All three of his referees wrote strong supporting letters that highlighted not only Heinz's exemplary record as a teacher at Sydney and his impressive research productivity, but his human qualities: his undeniably strong character and undoubted integrity. La Nauze wrote that he had known Heinz as a colleague and close friend ever since his arrival in Australia and believed that he would 'hold a professorial position with dignity and competence in the general duties of administration and University life'. Indeed, he would 'regard him as, in every way, an exceedingly strong candidate for such a position both on personal grounds and on academic ability. He is an excellent teacher, a good theoretical economist, a man of wide culture and interests, and of attractive and impressive personality.' Most academic economists would view Heinz as 'one of the most prominent economists in University life in Australia at the moment'.

About Heinz's course in macroeconomics at the University of Sydney, La Nauze had no hesitation in saying that it was the best of the economics courses presently taught at Sydney, and that he had reached this conclusion through conversations he had conducted with staff and students. La Nauze ascribed this superiority to two factors: Heinz not only prepared himself thoroughly for his lectures, he possessed an outstanding ability to articulate in lucid terms even the most difficult economic concepts. He highlighted also Heinz's contributions to public affairs outside the university and was confident that he would undertake similar work in Canberra, recognising that this was 'a valuable attribute in a Professor of Economics at Canberra'.

At the same time, he made it perfectly clear that Heinz's activities as a public commentator had in no way interfered with, or compromised, the quality of his teaching and research. On the contrary, he was adamant that '[u]nlike some people within universities whose public activities are prominent, Arndt's university work has always come first'. (Here La Nauze might have been alluding to one of his own colleagues in the Department of Economic History at Melbourne, Jim Cairns, future Treasurer and Deputy Prime Minister, who at this stage was already beginning to make his mark as a future politician.)

Of Heinz's personality, La Nauze said that he was 'completely anglicised', pointing out that since the age of 18 he had been 'a member of a society with which he is now completely identified. He came to us in Sydney as an Englishman, not a German who had lived for some years in England.' And, more to the point, La Nauze emphasised, 'since arriving in Australia, Heinz had made a complete adjustment to conditions and attitudes here, and is indeed extraordinarily well informed about Australian life and institutions'.

This, as La Nauze admitted to the selection committee, was a glowing reference, full of positives and devoid of criticism. Regardless of how the committee responded to it, La Nauze wanted to stress that, based as his report was on his knowledge of the field of Australian economists, he was sure there was 'no one who does not at present hold a Chair who would be better qualified to fill a new Professorial Chair than Arndt. Unless some applicant from overseas should appear to be superior I think you will find that most people concerned with economics in Australian universities would express a similar opinion.'

Professor Partridge, in his reference, highlighted the fact that while he had known Heinz longer than the other referees, his own academic field was political philosophy, so he was unable to comment with any authority about Heinz's capabilities as an economist. He recalled having met Heinz in 1939 when they were both postgraduate students at the LSE. There they had been members of the same seminar group. Since Heinz's arrival in Sydney, Partridge had engaged in long conversations with him and had 'no doubt about his competence as a student of contemporary politics. His earlier training has given him a good knowledge of the literature of the subject and of the main schools of thought; and, in discussing current questions, he invariably shows that he has a firm grasp of theoretical issues and that he is well informed about recent political developments.' Partridge gave Heinz top marks as a public speaker, and in private discussion, for the acuity, rigour and cogency of his thinking. Of Heinz's recent article in *Public Administration*—on the interpretation of the defence power in the Australian Constitution—Partridge judged that it 'shows the care and competence with which he can deal with a problem outside the field in which he now specialises'.

For all Partridge's reluctance to describe Heinz's technical proficiency as an economist, he happily mentioned in his report the claim he had repeatedly gathered from students—and not only the more able ones—namely, that they had gained more from Heinz's lectures than from those of any other member of the Department of Economics. Of Heinz's contributions to public debate, Partridge noted that he had been 'very active and energetic, he expresses himself easily and skilfully both in speech and writing'; he doubted 'whether anyone in Sydney University has been more prominent or influential during the last few years in stimulating a critical interest in contemporary political and economic trends and problems both within the university and in adult education and other circles outside. His competence, together with his obvious seriousness of purpose, has made him a respected public lecturer and writer on current problems.'

When he came to comment on Heinz's character and personality, Partridge's views were particularly perceptive

…everyone in Sydney has been deeply impressed by his outstanding qualities of honesty, sincerity and integrity of mind. And also by his conscientiousness: he has a very high sense of public duty, and in his university work he adopts a rigorous conception of his duty to his students and in the general work of the Faculty. He approaches every task of teaching and administration, however irksome, with the same sincerity and earnestness; he is most generous in sacrificing his time to the demands made on him by students and colleagues. It is known that he has strong political views and there are, of course, others on the staff who dissent strongly from his views; but I think it is true to say that there is no one who does not admire and respect his character as a university teacher and as a citizen. I myself regard him as being a man of very fine character; he is frank and direct; modest and unpretentious; entirely disinterested and without any trace of self-seeking; and, as I have said, he has a quite exceptional quality of sincerity.

…I have never felt that his attachment to his political views in any way impairs his quality as a teacher or student. He has enough detachment and intellectual candour to be able to examine and to expound opposing views fairly. He is tolerant and good-humoured; I have noticed that he is generous in admitting the ability of some of those who strongly disagree with the positions he himself holds. Although he is a vigorous controversialist, he is always fair in argument and is, indeed, always anxious to apply to himself, as he applies to others, the highest moral and logical standards of intellectual activity.

…I am sure that Arndt's departure would be a serious loss to this university; apart from the qualities I have mentioned, he is mature and has a pretty wide academic experience now so that his judgment always carries a great deal of weight in the affairs of the Faculty. I am sure that a man with his qualities, and his experience of university teaching, would be a valuable acquisition in Canberra; and that all teachers of the social sciences there in particular would get a great deal from association with him.

Because Heinz's colleague Kingsley Laffer had also applied for the Canberra chair, and had asked Sid Butlin to be one of his referees, Butlin's report on

Heinz was expressed largely in the form of a comparison between the two. Butlin wrote that Heinz and Laffer had been 'congenial and helpful' colleagues and were 'completely dependable and conscientious' about their work. 'On questions such as these,' Butlin said, 'I could not distinguish between them, and would regard either as personally suitable to direct a department of Economics.'

Butlin, however, was in no doubt that Heinz possessed a more impressive record of publication than Laffer, and was confident that this would continue to be the case. Both men had completely different approaches to their research, Laffer being 'intensely self-critical, not morbidly so, but in the sense of holding back from thrusting on the world imperfect ideas or work which is merely [a] new presentation of accepted material'. Laffer had given greater priority to his teaching than to research and that, too, according to Butlin, would explain his meagre research output. Heinz, on the other hand, revelled 'in public discussion and deliberately puts work into print to provoke discussion of ideas which he wants to try out'.

Butlin was aware that Heinz was 'much better with honours students than Laffer for this reason, but Laffer would be more patient and more successful with pass students—and less inclined to over-rate their capacity to handle difficult work'. He considered that Laffer might be more effective than would Heinz in handling the time-consuming and often tedious administrative demands of a head of department. Yet he conceded that Heinz would provide better leadership in stimulating members of the department to conduct and publish research.

Butlin touched briefly on the entirely apposite question of which candidate would work better with Trevor Swan, who recently had been appointed to the chair in economics at the ANU. He believed that it was appropriate to consider this point, because quite probably the ANU would soon incorporate the college, so as to make one university in Canberra. In these circumstances, he felt that the relationship between the work of the two professors of economics should matter to the selection committee. As he pointed out, 'Arndt's interests are exactly along the same lines as those of Professor Swan.' As enigmatic as ever, however, Butlin concluded that, depending on the way the council of the college wanted the Department of Economics to develop, this might be 'an argument for or against Arndt'. He could envisage Heinz and Swan collaborating on joint research projects and together furnishing advice on macroeconomic policy to the public service and government. On the other hand, Laffer's strength in microeconomics would serve to balance Swan's command of macroeconomics.

By July 1950, the selection committee—which comprised the council of the CUC—had met and short-listed the candidates. Burton was overseas in the middle months of 1950 and participated in the selection process by correspondence. One of the applicants was Dr Karel Maiwald (later Maywald), a Czech economist and statistician, who at the time of the communist takeover of Czechoslovakia was a Social Democrat member of that country's parliament. He had escaped from Prague in October 1949 and arrived in Britain early in 1950, having been sponsored by the University of Manchester. Burton thought Maiwald would probably stand at the top of the short list, since he had held distinguished academic and government positions in his native land and was soon to be associated with the Department of Applied Economics at Cambridge. Burton, however, did not expect him to last the distance, largely because his command of English appeared to be poor.

Burton had spoken to P.D. Henderson of Lincoln College, Oxford, whom Maiwald had listed as one of his referees, but he discovered that Henderson had never met him. He had wanted to talk with Hicks about Maiwald's candidature but found that Hicks had left for Nigeria; in Hicks's place, Burton had written to James Meade, Professor of Commerce at the LSE, asking him to comment on Maiwald's strengths and weaknesses. Meade reckoned that the selection committee should not take the risk of appointing him.

With Maiwald's application put to one side while further investigations were made, Burton's short list comprised, in alphabetical order, Heinz, Burgess Cameron,[10] Donald Cochrane,[11] Laffer and Eric Russell.[12] Of these, Burton recommended dropping Laffer first. Next he would eliminate either Cameron or Russell, and probably both of them. For him, the choice boiled down to Cochrane or Heinz. And of the two, he clearly preferred Heinz.

A few days after furnishing this advice, Burton lunched with Maiwald in London. While he gained a favourable impression of him and thought Maiwald's English was somewhat better than the summaries of his publications had indicated—Burton had earlier thought it was 'really dreadful'—he would not put him any higher than number four on the short list. He still regarded Heinz and Cochrane as clearly superior to Maiwald on all counts, and there remained the language problem and how well Maiwald would adapt to academic life in Australia.

There was, however, now another problem with Maiwald. Burton asked: 'how are we to assess him as a security risk?' He had discussed the matter with Maiwald himself, telling him frankly that the CUC's council 'would hesitate...even if they did think he was a very good economist'. No details of the 'security risk' were disclosed, but Cold War tensions in Canberra at the time were particularly acute; Maiwald's involvement in *émigré* politics would doubtless have raised concerns among Western security agencies and in the Australian Department of Immigration.

Ultimately, Maiwald failed to make the selection committee's short list, which turned out to be Burton's list minus Maiwald. Burton again informed the selection committee (through the college's registrar, Tom Owen) that Heinz was number one in his estimation. Should the selection committee not agree with him, Burton said that he wanted to be consulted. In any event, he thought that Wilfred Prest, as Dean of the Faculty of Economics at Melbourne, and John La Nauze, as a former colleague of Heinz and now a professor at Melbourne, should be asked to rank the short-listed candidates. Burton had now communicated with Hicks about Maiwald and had also spoken to Arthur Lewis about him; both knew him because of their association with the University of Manchester. Neither Hicks nor Lewis spoke of Maiwald in glowing terms. Burton had also communicated with Lewis about Heinz, who said that he doubted whether the college would get anyone superior; certainly there was no one better in Britain who might be interested in going to Australia. What Hicks told Burton about Heinz is not recorded, but whatever it was, it failed to dissuade Burton from thinking that Heinz should be regarded as the frontrunner.

Responding favourably to Burton's suggestions, the selection committee then asked La Nauze and Prest to make comparisons between Heinz, Cameron, Laffer, Cochrane and Russell. The first three had been at Sydney during the time that La Nauze was there. Since he knew very little of Cochrane or Russell, he declined to make any comparison between them and the Sydney trio. While La Nauze thought that Cameron possessed a somewhat higher analytical ability than Heinz, and 'for sheer originality he is, or will be, a better economist in the purely technical sense', he thought that Heinz was 'all-round a stronger candidate for a position which requires not only ability in the subject of economics, but personal qualities of tact, administration ability and a capacity to work well with other colleagues and with subordinates'. In short, regarding Heinz's candidature, La Nauze informed the selection committee that 'it is unlikely that there is a better candidate in Australia, taking into account not only competence as an economist but personal qualities and experience desirable in administering a department'.

Wilfred Prest, in his comparison of Heinz and Cochrane, concluded that 'on balance Arndt's greater seniority and experience probably outweighs Cochrane's merits in other respects'. He felt, however, that Cochrane was superior to Heinz as a technical economist, being familiar with modern statistical techniques and econometrics. Cochrane was also developing an expertise in national income analysis and in Keynesian economics, as a result of teaching third and fourth-year students at Melbourne. In fact, Prest thought that Cochrane was quite at home in all fields of economics and 'I doubt whether Arndt has the same grasp of economics as a whole. Arndt probably has more publications to his credit, but I think that Cochrane has an equal facility for writing and he has already published several able papers.' He agreed that the selection should boil down to experience. Here Cochrane's two and a half years of teaching, and no real opportunity to take any administrative responsibilities, meant that Heinz would have to be put ahead of him.

As to Russell, Prest thought that, from an intellectual point of view, he was probably the best candidate of all; as an undergraduate at Melbourne, his examination results were consistently better than Cochrane's, but Prest had doubts about Russell's ability to write up material for publication, and Russell seemed to be plagued by unfortunate personal problems.

The committee then went back to Partridge, asking him if he could comment on the respective merits of Heinz, Cameron and Laffer. Since he knew nothing of Cameron, Partridge confined his comparison to Heinz and Laffer. The latter had published little, perhaps because of his conscientiousness as a teacher. At any rate, Partridge doubted that Laffer would ever produce anything original. He found it difficult to make a confident comparison between the pair because he was unable to judge their work in economics, but in

> …the discussion of political and other topics of general interest, Arndt makes the stronger impression; he thinks more quickly, expresses himself more fluently and forcefully (certainly a lot more copiously), and is more assertive…On the matters where I am competent to judge, Arndt seems to have the more critical mind… Because he is more forceful and more articulate, Arndt exercises a stronger influence on the general intellectual life of the Faculty.

With Prest and La Nauze agreeing with Burton's assessment of the candidates, Burton then took the opportunity while he was in London to ask Robert Hall for his opinion of Heinz's suitability for the chair. Like Burton, Hall had been a Queensland Rhodes Scholar and was now the Head of the Economic Section in the British Cabinet Office, later the British government's Economic Service. He had been Heinz's economics tutor at Oxford. Hall had 'expressed great appreciation of Arndt's quality' at a dinner with the Burtons in London, and it was this opinion that led Burton to ask him if he would mind writing a note for the selection committee about Heinz's strengths and weaknesses.

Though he had had no contact or communication with Heinz for some years, Hall wrote that, in his years at Oxford and before he left for Australia, Heinz 'seemed to me a man of great ability, and with a particular facility for expressing himself clearly both on paper and in conversation. He was a good economist and even as an undergraduate he had managed to relate his economics to the wide field of social studies, which is I think the most difficult of the steps which a student has to take.'

After his degree, Heinz had worked in the field of political institutions. Here, Hall said, '[w]hat I saw of his writings at that time, and what I heard about him, supported my early views and these were confirmed on the occasions when we met'. When he wrote in support of Heinz's application to Sydney, Hall said that his only hesitation was that he did not know how Heinz would get on with Australian undergraduates. Otherwise, he would have no hesitation in concluding that Heinz 'would be a very strong candidate for your Chair'.

By August, Heinz was beginning to hear reports that he stood a good chance of being offered the chair. With past experience firmly planted in his mind, however, he was not going to take anything for granted. Mick Borrie, a former colleague at Sydney and now about to join the ANU, wrote to Heinz on 24 August, citing a conversation he had recently had with Burton in London. Borrie was 'given to understand that at that stage you stood very favourably [with Burton]…I take it this is his [Burton's] opinion, but I trust that it is also the opinion of the others who will have a hand in the matter.' Tew likewise confirmed in a letter to Heinz from London that Burton 'seemed to be impressed' with his qualifications for the Canberra chair.

At the end of September, the college finally advised Heinz that it proposed to offer him the chair. Burton, when announcing Heinz's appointment officially, highlighted the fact that the largest enrolments in the college were in subjects taught by the Department of Economics and that it was therefore gratifying that a scholar of Heinz's standing and ability, especially as a teacher, had been chosen as the inaugural professor of economics.

The students of the college, in their newspaper, *Woroni*, congratulated the college on its decision, deserving as it did 'the highest commendation. In making what may be considered a controversial appointment, the Council has shown that unlike the Adelaide authorities when faced with a similar appointment, it has not allowed political prejudice to override academic qualifications.' While it was true that 'Prof. Arndt may be called a left-wing Keynesian', and while 'Prof. Arndt is somewhat doctrinaire', nevertheless *Woroni* believed that 'his sound knowledge of modern economic theory and the significance of its application to such spheres as banking, public finance, business activity [and] international trade, will enable him to exert a considerable influence upon his students, and in the long run upon the public service' (*Woroni*, 2/11/50).

Once Heinz's appointment had been announced formally, a flood of congratulatory letters arrived at his office at the University of Sydney. Among them were congratulations from some of the other leading contenders for the chair, including Cochrane and Russell. The latter even apologised to Heinz for having had the temerity to submit an application knowing full well that Heinz would be an applicant. Russell revealed to Heinz that it was Prest who had talked him into applying for the chair. Heinz answered by making it clear that there was no need for Russell to apologise, particularly since Heinz himself had never been confident that his application would be successful and he still did not know why the selection committee had chosen him over Cochrane.

La Nauze, having been given advanced information about the appointment from Burton, wrote warmly to wish Heinz well, adding that it 'will be a rather staggering blow to the teaching of economics at Sydney, but that is inevitable'. He hoped that Heinz would like Canberra, not necessarily a foregone conclusion in La Nauze's mind. Indeed, he thought that Heinz 'may well get ill with indigestion, being so close to the source of the abominations of a Liberal Government'. He also feared that Heinz might have problems with the prevailing quality of the students, who might not be of a sufficiently high calibre to stretch Heinz's intellect, though it would be up to Heinz himself to attract talented students to the study of economics.

Tew wrote saying that he was especially delighted with the news 'because on several occasions I believe you have been the victim of blind prejudice and now at last a job has gone to the right man'. Bruce Miller, an associate of Heinz's from Sydney University's tutorial classes, and later a colleague at the ANU, was quick to point out that Heinz's departure from Sydney would remove a 'provocative force that has done a great deal to stir up ideas and activity during the few years you have been here. I hope you will perform the same function in Canberra; in fact, I am sure you will.' Dick Downing wrote from Geneva, perhaps with tongue in cheek, proposing that Heinz would 'now be able to write provocative letters to that most provocative of all newspapers—the *Canberra Times*'. His appointment, Downing thought, was 'indeed a victory of left over right'. Gerald Firth wrote more ominously, saying that '[o]nce you have got a house, I am sure you will find Canberra a very good place to live in'. Others, too, including Downing, had alluded to the chronic housing shortage in Canberra.

Heinz's colleague-to-be for nearly 40 years, Trevor Swan, wrote to express his 'delight at your appointment. I can't tell you how pleased I am, from a purely selfish viewpoint, that you will be here to keep my ideas in order and to sharpen my wits. But I hope you will believe also that I am pleased for your sake, even if running the College may turn out to be rather a bore (it couldn't be worse than Sydney).'

Noel Butlin sent a letter from Harvard, saying that Heinz's friends would now sit back and watch him wasting his time on providing policy advice to the public service (Butlin and others had heard Heinz criticise Swan similarly). He asked how Ruth had taken to the thought of living in Canberra. 'From my own experience,' Butlin said, 'she should like the place very much, except for minor disturbances such as monopoly prices for all household goods, long distances to carry purchases, and the fact generally, as one Englishman put it, Canberra is a pleasant little village.' For all that, Butlin thought the best reason he had for considering an appointment at the ANU was that Heinz and Ruth would once again be his neighbours. As for his brother, Sid, Butlin said: 'Sid has been done in the eye…He could have done something about his confounded second chair some time back, and presumably would have done if he hadn't been so frightened of competition and concerned about respectability. However, Sidney now has a nice collection of mugwumps to carry on the Faculty.'

The only sour note about Heinz's appointment came from one of his former students, William McMahon, now a member of the House of Representatives and soon to begin the ministerial path that eventually led to the Prime Minister's Lodge. In a question without notice to Prime Minister Menzies, McMahon asked in the Parliament the following questions

> Can the Prime Minister inform the House whether the gentleman named H.W. Arndt, who was recently appointed as a professor of economics at the University College, Canberra, took a very prominent part, both in University circles and in public, in opposing the Communist Party Dissolution Bill? Is this gentleman a prominent and dogmatic member of the Fabian Society and did he support the Chifley Socialist Government in its attempt to nationalise the trading banks? Did Sir Andrew McFadyean of the Royal Institute of International Affairs annex an appendix to a book by Mr Arndt, which was published under the auspices of that institute dissociating himself from Mr Arndt's views? Does the Prime Minister consider that people of known and biased views should be appointed to a faculty in which complete impartiality and freedom from political bias is absolutely essential? Will the Prime Minister ensure that the appointment is reviewed? (*Commonwealth Parliamentary Debate*, Vol. 209:591–2).

Menzies answered simply by saying that he knew 'nothing of this gentleman beyond what I read in the newspaper this morning' and asked that the question be placed on the notice paper. When the Prime Minister replied some time later, he said that it was nothing to him 'whether a man appointed to an academic position were [Labor], Liberal or Country Party' (*Commonwealth Parliamentary Debate*, Vol. 210:1,562–3). With such appointments, he was in favour of academic freedom, and he strongly upheld the view that it was the quality of a person's academic qualifications and not an individual's political views that should be the determining factor. Menzies reminded McMahon that Heinz's appointment had been made correctly, according to processes laid down by the University of Melbourne, of which CUC was a part; these procedures were of no concern to the Commonwealth Government, particularly since the University of Melbourne came under state jurisdiction. But '[e]ven if it had been the National University to which the appointment had been made I could not be called upon', Menzies said, 'to examine the political position regarding it'—though he added that 'if somebody raised the security aspect that would be a different matter'.

There were many who were shocked by McMahon's attempt to deny the freedom of a university to appoint its academic staff. Trevor Swan quickly told Heinz that he had registered a strong protest, but he urged Heinz to refrain from any attempt to defend himself in public until the Prime Minister had replied to McMahon's question.'I can't predict exactly what the reply will be,' Swan wrote,'but I do think you will make it harder to give the right reply…if you fan the flames…but I think I am at least as angry as you must be (if interpersonal comparisons are possible in this sphere).' Noel Butlin simply made the point to Heinz that '[i]t just shows how careful one should be in selecting one's students'.

As to Heinz himself, he heeded Swan's advice, writing later to McMahon to congratulate him on his appointment as a minister. Heinz said that, whereas McMahon had declared that the decision to appoint him to the chair of economics at CUC was entirely political, Heinz hoped that McMahon's ministerial appointment would not be purely academic. McMahon replied in good humour, revealing that Heinz's letter was the first of the congratulatory letters he had opened. He assured Heinz that 'your contribution to my intellectual development was not negligible'; he was 'glad I was your first Cabinet Minister. I hope,' he added, that 'they are not all as difficult as me—though time does temper one's judgement and makes you tolerant of other's views'.

Heinz was farewelled at a dinner attended by his University of Sydney friends and colleagues on 29 November 1950. Addressing a trade union conference on education soon after he learnt that he had been selected for the chair in Canberra, Heinz was reported by the *Sydney Morning Herald* as saying that he was 'proud to be the first socialist professor of economics in Australia' (*Sydney Morning Herald*, 31/7/51).

11
CANBERRA

Heinz was 35 years old when he took up his appointment at Canberra University College on 1 January 1951, the fiftieth anniversary of Australian Federation. In the national capital, it was a day of special significance and celebration. Canberra then had a population approaching 20,000. The war had initiated a new spurt of growth, after the stagnation experienced during the depression years. As Australia's political nerve centre during the conflict, Canberra had become the true capital of the nation. After the war, with a Prime Minister (Chifley) and Cabinet dedicated to centralisation, Canberra's expansion was expected to continue rapidly. Anxiety arose with the election in December 1949 of Menzies' Coalition, dedicated to a federal system rather than a centralised one, and committed to smaller government. As it turned out, the new Prime Minister was Canberra's greatest champion. The city grew at unprecedented rates during his tenure and that of his immediate successors.

In 1951, the only buildings in the Civic Centre of Canberra were the two colonnaded blocks (the Sydney and Melbourne Buildings), the Civic Hotel, the Soldiers and Citizens Club, and the old weatherboard Census Building and police station. CUC occupied part of the Melbourne Building above the Trans Australian Airlines office and the Bureau of Mineral Resources. Its accommodation consisted of a small number of passageways with offices on each side, a staff common room and two larger rooms, one containing the library and the other serving as a lecture theatre. There were about 10 full-time staff, of whom five were professors: Joe Burton, Manning Clark, Fin Crisp, Alec Hope and Heinz. The students numbered about 600, all of them part-timers. The first full-time students were not enrolled until 1954.

In the early hours of Easter Sunday 1953, a fire broke out in parts of the Melbourne Building occupied by the college, destroying most of the libraries owned by Hope and the Professor of Law, John Fleming. Fortunately for Heinz there was no significant damage to his office, though his secretary, Margaret Easton, suffered some loss of possessions, for which she received compensation from the insurers. As a result of the fire, the college had to move into what at the time were considered to be temporary quarters, the disused workers' hostel in Childers Street. In reality, the college stayed there until the Hayden-Allen Building was completed in 1960; the economics and law faculties remained at Childers Street until the Copland Building was finished in 1966. By then, Bruce Hall, the first residential accommodation built for undergraduate students, had been completed and various other buildings had been constructed for departments in the Faculty of Science.

When Heinz arrived in Canberra, the shortage of housing was acute, just as many of his friends had predicted it would be. Before securing a house, Heinz lived for several weeks at the Hotel Kurrajong, while Ruth and the children remained in Sydney. Staying at the Kurrajong was a bonus for Heinz, because Chifley, by this time Leader of the Opposition, lived there and Heinz got to know him well. The Kurrajong was one of a number of government hostels catering to single people and married couples without children. Most Canberra families lived in houses located in the half-dozen suburbs grouped around Civic Centre to the north of the Molonglo River, and around Parliament House and the government buildings south of the river.

In February, Heinz acquired the lease of one of the 'Tocumwal' houses in north Ainslie, then considered to be on the northern fringes of the city (it was sometimes referred to as 'South Yass'), though it is now an inner suburb of Canberra. These houses had been constructed during the war in the southern NSW town of Tocumwal, as quarters for RAAF aircrew undergoing operational training on B-24 Liberator heavy bombers. After the war, the houses were brought to Canberra in an effort to ease the housing shortage. Their foundations were made of brick, the walls of fibro and weatherboard and the roofs of corrugated iron.

The interior of the house that the Arndts acquired (at 6 Lang Street, Ainslie) was in a state of disrepair and required extensive repainting. Shortly after they moved in, they applied to have an electric stove installed, as well as water heaters in the kitchen and bathroom. Delays occurred, because of the excessive load on transformer capacity at the time in Canberra. At first, there were no electrical appliances at all: the Arndts needed to use firewood to heat the copper in the laundry, the stove in the kitchen, the fireplace in the lounge and the chip heater in the bathroom. The house was rather large, easily big enough for a family of three children, and was cool, with wide verandahs. In the large backyard, Ruth and Heinz quickly planted a vegetable garden. Since there were no footpaths, the surrounds of the house often became a quagmire after rainstorms.

Until Heinz purchased a car, the family depended on the home delivery of services. As well as milk, bread and ice deliveries, J.B. Young's, a local department store, later taken over by Myer, collected grocery orders and delivered them the next day. Greek, and later Italian, greengrocers delivered fruit and vegetables. The Arndts had the first telephone in Ainslie and owned the first car in their street. The telephone and the car were used frequently by neighbours requiring a doctor or an ambulance.

The children went to the North Ainslie preschool and primary school. Heinz and Ruth often attended concerts in the Albert Hall and plays performed by the Canberra Repertory Society. They also attended social functions at the CUC, but more frequently they entertained in their own home or attended parties at the homes of colleagues and neighbours. They were to live at Lang Street until 1956.

In their early years in Canberra, Heinz and Ruth wrote frequently to friends about the pluses and minuses of the city; however, neither of them regretted the move from Sydney. Within six months of their arrival in Canberra, Heinz wrote to a former colleague in Sydney

> On the domestic front everything is going well. We managed to get the house into sufficient shape a fortnight ago and to have an enormous housewarming party with 30 people treading on each other's toes in our combined sitting and dinning rooms. The children are flourishing. They have found two neighbours' children with whom they play happily and far more satisfactorily than with the respectable neighbours at Chatswood, and beyond a further deterioration in Christopher's accent, the evil influences of our 'poor locality' have not so far been in evidence.

At the same time, he wrote to his colleague Burge Cameron, then undertaking doctoral studies in Cambridge, to say that they were 'finding Canberra a very pleasant place to live in. An economist, in particular, would get as much intellectual stimulus and knowledge of at least one angle on Australia here as in Sydney or Melbourne.' In an earlier letter he had sent to Cameron, Heinz had said that he was 'well pleased with my new academic environment', though he added that he was 'pretty appalled at the quality of our students'. Of the 48 students he had taught, 'about 5 are fairly good, another ten might just pass and the rest should not be wasting their time at university'.

To Tommy Balogh in Oxford, Heinz wrote that 'after a term's experience, [it] seems to have been a very wise step'. After a year in Canberra, he informed Professor Frank Mauldon, at the University of Western Australia, that '[w]e have thoroughly enjoyed our first year in Canberra, and I, my first year in the College. A short holiday trip to Sydney, from which we have just returned, has not caused us to revise our judgment that the move from Sydney to Canberra was a sound one, even though we enjoyed the Sydney beaches and meeting our Sydney friends.'

In August 1951, Heinz expressed his preliminary views ('these are very superficial impressions which I am foolish to commit to paper') about Canberra in an article for the magazine *Highway*. His major theme was that Canberra was 'very new and, for all its expanse, a very small place'. It was, he wrote, a place where one could live scarcely four miles from the city centre in a house that bordered the bush; where the circulation of local gossip was exhausted after 48 hours; where the local newspaper had a few days earlier published correspondence from 'two not very old gentlemen disputing each other's claim to have been the first to suggest this site for the city'; and where an 'American magazine editor recently made the pardonable mistake of selecting a photograph of the centre of Canberra to illustrate Australia's wide open spaces'.

Other characteristic features of Canberra to which Heinz drew attention were its planned nature and the fact that it was run by the Commonwealth Government through the Department of the Interior. It might be thought by some that the dead hand of government would be the subject of common debate and ridicule among Canberra's citizens, but Heinz was inclined to take a contrary view, contending that '[b]y almost general consensus, the worst feature of this socialist city is its private enterprises, though there are a few notable exceptions to the general tendency towards inefficiency and exploitation'. What surprised him most was how remote the average Canberra citizen was from politics, parliament and government, even though the 'good-looking white elephant [Parliament House] is visible from almost every corner'.

What did not surprise him was the vigorous social and intellectual life of the city. While it had no more cinemas or halls for dances and concerts than other cities of 20,000 people, and no nightclubs and virtually no restaurants

> Canberra people do not seem to miss these facilities unduly, because, thrown on their own resources, they have managed to organise for themselves an almost incredible number of societies and clubs for the cultivation of almost every conceivable interest: not only sport of every kind, but music, repertory, dancing, languages, chess, philately, politics and good causes of every description. This almost embarrassing profusion of social and cultural activity is the product, and satisfies the needs, of an abnormally large proportion of well-educated people.

Indeed, he thought that Canberra had more university graduates among its population than almost any other city in the world, though not perhaps as many as Oxford or Cambridge.

Of his colleagues at the CUC, Heinz wrote to Kingsley Laffer in the middle of 1951, referring to them as 'hardworking, peace-loving, and respectable people who do not lay themselves open to scandal and I am as yet too much outside the hallowed circle to be told any of the no doubt ample and juicy scandals which are said to abound in the higher reaches of the Civil Service'.

Ruth was able to use her skills and experience as a social worker to teach English to European migrants, mostly to women, but occasionally to men as well. State governments funded the teaching of English to these migrants; in Canberra, the classes were organised by the Education Department of Sydney University. Ruth at first held classes in her home; after 1960, migrant teaching became more formalised and teaching at home was no longer permitted. In the early years, she walked around the neighbourhood encouraging so-called 'new Australians' to attend her classes. Soon she had between 20 and 30 people enrolled. She began with two evening classes a week, but this proved unsatisfactory. Men complained that they were too tired to attend classes after work, or had to leave early because they had to be up early the next morning. Since they found it difficult to attend evening classes, many of them would not allow their wives to go to classes on their own at night. Ruth then began an afternoon class for women.

These English classes led her to branch out into providing a wider range of assistance to migrant women. They came to her for personal advice. For many of them, she became a confidante: she found work for them; helped them to sort out problems their children were having at school; acted as a go-between with government departments; drove them to doctors' surgeries and to the hospital; and was a marriage guidance counsellor.

Later, students from Asia and the wives of diplomats would attend her classes and she provided counselling to them when she thought they needed it. Some of her pupils came from Government House and Dame Pattie Menzies asked her to hold a special class for foreign-born staff working at The Lodge, the Prime Minister's residence.

On the basis of all this work, Ruth was invited to join the Good Neighbour Council as an independent member. These councils had been established throughout Australia by the Commonwealth Government in the early 1950s, to welcome newcomers to the country and to assist them with their assimilation into the Australian way of life.

From a teacher of English and social worker, Ruth was later to teach economics at the boys' and girls' Church of England grammar schools. She would often invite to her Deakin home various students who were preparing for examinations. There she, and sometimes Heinz, would give tutorials in the sitting room. After this teaching, Ruth found herself employed by the Department of External Affairs (later the Department of Foreign Affairs and Trade) for 15 years in the Economic Relations Division. Ruth's job was to instruct Australian diplomats about to be posted overseas for the first time on how to prepare economic reports. From External Affairs, she became associated with various women's groups at the ANU, providing assistance and guidance to wives and students who had come to the university from overseas.

When the Arndt children were young, Ruth took an active part in the preschool at north Ainslie. She chaired a committee of residents who were appointed to raise funds for interior fittings and furniture. The committee quickly managed to collect £700 from cake stalls, raffles and dances. For several years, she chaired the preschool's committee of parents and citizens. When the building was not being used as a preschool, Ruth often held her English classes there.

On top of all this, she also for a while worked as a research assistant to Pat Pentony, who lectured in psychology at the CUC. He had secured a research grant to undertake a study of the relationship between parental attitudes and child behaviour at school, and he hired Ruth as an interviewer–assistant. Her task, as she put it, was to 'ask hundreds of indiscreet questions of some 200 parents of pre-school children'. She also accepted a temporary job in the Department of Demography at the ANU, which involved reading and reporting stories in German-language newspapers published in Australia; this was for a study of attitudes among migrants living in Australia.

Before his arrival in Canberra, Heinz had little need to purchase a motor car, as public transport in Britain and Sydney were adequate for his and the family's needs. He soon discovered, however, that living on the edge of Canberra was no place to be without a car. In September 1951, he borrowed just more than £400 from the Industrial Finance Department of the Commonwealth Bank to purchase a new Ford Anglia two-door sedan, the net price of which was £698. To save money for the down payment on the car, he decided that he would not go to the ANZAAS meeting in Brisbane that year.

Never the best of drivers, he was soon writing to friends about various motor accidents in which he was involved. Ruth had an accident while she was still learning to drive, Heinz informing friends that she had suffered the indignity 'of having a big Chevrolet knock a hole into the back of our car during one of her driving lessons'. In September 1954, he informed his former colleague Ron Barback that he was

> …extremely lucky to escape from the car almost entirely unhurt (just a cut over my eye and a pulled muscle in my chest, both of which have cleared up very well). The other poor devil was very badly hurt and will be in hospital for 3–4 months; although he was indubitably at fault (crashing into me from the left at 35–40mph) you can't but feel very sorry for him.

For Heinz, the worst aspect of this accident was that he would be without a car for several weeks, including the school holidays. The insurance company estimated the repair costs as £150 (a very large amount in the early 1950s) and for a while he contemplated trading in the car for another. In the end, he had more urgent calls on his savings. In January 1958, he wrote to friends to inform them that he had exchanged 'the old and decrepit little Ford Anglia', which had clocked up 50,000 miles, for 'a new (second-hand) and, by our standards, enormous car, a Ford Zephyr, which at the moment thrills Ruth and me with as much awe and trepidation as pleasure (the Americans among you are permitted to indulge in a condescending smile)'.

In 1954, the Arndts decided that it was time to purchase a home. Two German carpenters had secured a block in Deakin that had been passed in at auction. They planned to build a house on the block in the evenings after work, and on the weekends, over 18 months. Heinz and Ruth agreed to buy the house and hoped to move into it during the summer of 1955–56.

There were, however, initially delays connected with the bank loan they had negotiated and with the college's guarantee of part of the loan.

Heinz wrote in March 1956 to Barback, informing him that the delays were 'very annoying not only because we are paying rent here [in north Ainslie] while the new house stands empty, but because our home life has been thoroughly unorganised by premature preparations'. It took some months to resolve these problems and when they finally were a thing of the past, Heinz and Ruth were able to move into 14 Hopetoun Circuit at Easter 1956.

Soon after they moved in, Heinz wrote a circular letter to friends about the new house

> We are very happy with the house. It is no larger than our previous (rented) one [they were later to add an extra room], but much solider, handsomer and in a much nicer part of Canberra. We did not venture on a really modern design—butterfly houses of every variety abound in the neighbourhood—but we managed to get most of the features on which we were really keen: large windows, large sitting and dining rooms connected by glass doors which fold right back to the walls, lots of built-in cupboard space, very nice front and back terraces, a pleasant kitchen in the front of the house where Ruth gets the splendid view when she looks up from the stove or sink (with a breakfast corner for family meals) and a good-sized garage. We also shocked the builders and painter by choosing two different shades of green for different walls of the sitting room and bright flamingo for the three outside doors to liven up the otherwise too sedate white of the house and green–grey of the roof.

Deakin, in Canberra's affluent southern suburbs, close to The Lodge, the grammar schools and foreign embassies, was only 15 minutes by car to the university. The Arndts' new house was opposite a local shopping centre and petrol station and close to bus stops. Heinz and Ruth were happy there and never wanted to move; fortunately, they never had to.

Though Heinz's Oxford degrees were predominantly in politics, and while he wrote and spoke frequently on political issues after he came to Australia, his only experience as an elected official was his membership of the ACT

Advisory Council, one of the forerunners of the present ACT Legislative Assembly. He was unsuccessful in 1955 at his first attempt to win a place on the council, but was successful when he stood again in 1959. Except for a brief period in 1960–61, when he was on leave in Geneva, he remained a member until 1964.

The Advisory Council was not a local government body, such as a municipal council. Rather it was a statutory authority, established by the Commonwealth Parliament to advise it on matters concerning the Australian Capital Territory. It could advise the Minister for the Interior (who had portfolio responsibility for the Australian Capital Territory) on legislative proposals relating to the Australian Capital Territory, and it could recommend alterations to ACT ordinances. But it had no legislative or executive responsibilities. Nor was the minister obliged to accept the Advisory Council's advice.

In 1955, the Canberra branch of the ALP endorsed three candidates to contest seats in the Advisory Council; Heinz was one of them. Nominations closed on 31 August and the election was held on Saturday 16 September. Heinz was at first reluctant to stand, but friends and party members encouraged him to do so.

Before becoming a candidate he needed to seek permission from the CUC council, which considered his nomination 'inadvisable but not improper'. This was not an entirely positive response, but neither was it an entirely negative one. In the event, he chose to proceed with his candidature, though he was far from confident that it would be successful. When Julius Stone, Professor of Law at the University of Sydney, contacted him in May 1955 to ask whether he would consider writing an article on the economic aspects of decisions relating to Section 92 of the Australian Constitution, Heinz replied that he was too busy: 'I have been induced to put up as a candidate for the ACT Advisory Council. While it is unlikely that I shall get in, the elections will make some claims on my time between now and September.'

During the election campaign in 1955, Heinz concentrated on housing, education, employment, social services and 'general amenities for the citizens of Canberra'. The demand for housing in Canberra continued to exceed supply, and the Labor team advanced a four-year plan for the construction of 5,000 houses. Related to this target were policies aimed at providing adequate housing finance and essential infrastructure, such as roads, footpaths and street lighting. Labor also highlighted the need to attract new industries to Canberra, to provide greater and more diversified employment opportunities, especially for young people.

There was a policy to re-establish the ACT Industrial Board to deal with wages, hours and working conditions, the Labor candidates claiming that standards had declined since the board was abolished. The ALP team pressed for a more realistic basic wage for Canberra, in line with the Australian Capital Territory's cost of living—which was higher than in most other parts of Australia—and for the appointment of an Apprenticeship and Industrial Inspector to enforce award conditions. In rural affairs, Labor promised to promote land settlement and protect small farming. It advocated a more favourable attitude to war service land settlement in the Australian Capital Territory; and it called for a fair deal for Jervis Bay, which legally (despite its location) was part of the Australian Capital Territory, and which, according to Labor, had been too long considered a plaything of 'service politics'.

In his policy speech for the election, Heinz declared that he was standing for the Advisory Council because he was a member of the ALP and supported its principles. He believed that the democratic system worked best when it operated through organised parties, 'which unite those with common ideas and a common political outlook'. Why, he asked, was a university professor standing for election? The answer was that he, as he put it

> …believe[d] people who have received a special training in fields relevant to local government have a special duty to take on some share of the work. Canberra has, among its citizens, a lot of highly educated and knowledgeable people. It seems to me rather a pity, to use no stronger word, that so few of them play an active part in the public life of the city. I happen to be an economist, and I hope that as such I shall be able to make some contribution to the good government of our city…I am particularly anxious to see that the progress of the last year in the school building programme is maintained and, if at all possible, surpassed. Classes are already much too large and unless school accommodation and facilities are rapidly extended, there is real danger that Canberra's school system will be overwhelmed by the growth of the city's population in the next few years.

He wanted to see the construction of a modern technical college and the creation of a faculty of science and a residential hall at the CUC. Concerning social services in Canberra, he announced that: 'We shall see what can be done to give Canberra a minimum of professional social welfare services, including provision for psychiatric treatment, child guidance, and an advice bureau on family, legal and other problems which the New Australians among us, in particular, need badly.' There was a need to improve bus services, particularly feeder services to and from the outer suburbs; a speeding up in the supply of electric stoves—three hot plates instead of two—for all but the smallest houses; an additional recreation ground beside the Cotter Reserve; improvements to Manuka Oval and other sports grounds; and the provision of water supplies to the villages of Hall and Tharwa.

As an Advisory Council member, Heinz always favoured widening the range of local government in the Australian Capital Territory. In May 1962, he foreshadowed the introduction of a motion that 'the Minister be advised to establish a Legislative Council for the Australian Capital Territory'. He explained that a legislative council might retain at first the advisory functions of the current Advisory Council, but should then move gradually to acquire full municipal powers and responsibilities.

The next year, he proposed the building of a cultural centre in Canberra. Such a centre, he argued, should include a home for cultural clubs and societies—along the lines of what later became the Griffin Centre in Civic—and a theatre and ancillary accommodation for the Canberra Repertory Society and other local theatrical groups. This theatre would be in addition to the one being built in Civic Square, which Heinz considered to be primarily a commercial enterprise. What he proposed was a venue to house performances by amateur groups. He quoted Menzies, who, on many occasions, had said that Canberra should be regarded not only as the political centre of the nation, but should be its cultural heart. In Heinz's final year as a member of the Advisory Council, he chaired a committee that recommended the development of a Canberra Public Library Service in association with the National Library of Australia.

Heinz's career as a local politician came to an end in 1964, shortly after he took up his appointment to the chair of economics in the Research School of Pacific Studies. In his letter of resignation, he cited pressure of work and his intention in the years to come to spend extensive periods of time overseas, especially in Asia.

12
SOUTH CAROLINA

By 1954 Heinz had spent more than seven years teaching at Australian universities and was eligible for what was then known as sabbatical leave. He decided to take six months' leave, the bulk of it to be spent in the United States. For this, he would need external funding to meet travel and living expenses.

He began applying for grants as early as 1952, when he wrote to the British Dominions and Colonies Fund of the Carnegie Corporation in New York asking for a study and travel grant to the United Kingdom and the United States. While waiting for the outcome, he applied for and was offered a John Hay Whitney Fellowship, which he rejected because he was confident of securing the Carnegie grant and because he would be committed to teach at two American universities for a semester each. He was not prepared to spend a year away from Canberra; and, in any case, it was unlikely that the CUC would grant him a full year's leave.

His application for the Carnegie grant, however, was unsuccessful. He decided to apply again in 1953, his three referees being Paul Rosenstein-Rodan, Leslie Melville and Ben Higgins. To Melville, he wrote: 'After six years in Australia, I have begun to feel the need for a (temporary) change of air.' In his application, he declared that the reason he wanted to visit Britain and America was 'to renew contacts and exchange views with universities and other economists and to obtain a personal impression of economic conditions in these countries and of the operation of international economic institutions'. The second application met the same fate as the first.

Meanwhile, the Australian committee of the US Educational Foundation had recommended him for a joint Fulbright and Smith-Mundt grant. The Fulbright provided him with funding to meet his travel expenses, while the Smith-Mundt grant provided funding for study leave at universities situated in the smaller and more remote states. One of the universities on the list was the University of South Carolina, a small state university in the state's capital, Columbia. It was not a distinguished university (ranked according to Heinz about forty-seventh among the forty-eight state universities in the United States), and South Carolina itself had some notoriety for racial segregation and religious fundamentalism. Heinz's brother was, however, now chairman of the Department of Linguistics, Slavic and Oriental Languages at the University of North Carolina at Chapel Hill in the adjoining state. Heinz had not seen his brother since before the war, so when the University of South Carolina nominated him for a six-month term as Visiting Professor, Heinz decided to accept the offer.

He left Canberra immediately after the completion of examination marking in November 1953. His first destination was Turkey, where he spent a fortnight with his father and gave three lectures at the University of Istanbul on 'The role of monetary policy'. These lectures extended some of the themes that he had adumbrated in his inaugural lecture at the CUC (discussed in Chapter 14); they were later published in the *Revue de la Faculté des Sciences Economiques de l'Université d'Istanbul*.

On the flight to Istanbul via Beirut, Heinz had the good fortune to sit for part of the journey next to the distinguished Swedish economist, politician and later Nobel laureate, Gunnar Myrdal, who boarded the plane at Jakarta. They shared a hotel room in Singapore, during an overnight refuelling stop, and struck up a friendship that was renewed in 1957 when Myrdal toured Australia as the Dyason Lecturer. Myrdal proved instrumental in securing appointments for Heinz at the Indian Statistical Institute in Calcutta and New Delhi in 1957–58 and at the Economic Commission for Europe in Geneva in 1960–61. The meeting with Myrdal in 1953 was of particular significance, helping as it did to refocus Heinz's intellectual interests on his later specialisation in development economics.

Having left Turkey, he spent a week in Germany, where he lectured at the universities of Frankfurt and Kiel on monetary policy and the theory of foreign exchange rates. After this brief German visit, he went to Britain and spent Christmas with relatives and friends. As well as visiting Sheffield, Manchester, Cambridge and Oxford, he gave a lecture at Chatham House on postwar developments in Australia. He attended the annual conference of British University Teachers at Sheffield, and at Oxford he dined with Tommy Balogh and Paul Streeten at Balliol and with Howard Florey at Lincoln, not to mention catching up with Harold Cox at Lincoln, and with Donald MacDougall, David Bensusan-Butt, Tom Wilson and J.R. Hicks at Nuffield.

At Oxford's Institute of Economics and Statistics, he talked with David Worswick and Colin Clark. In Cambridge, he lunched with R.F. Kahn, Joan Robinson, Richard Goodwin and Robin Marris; met Brian

Reddaway and Laslo Rostas at the Department of Applied Economics; lunched with Kenneth Berrill at St Catherine's; and tried unsuccessfully to catch Maurice Dobb at Trinity. In London, he met Hla Myint, Nicky Kaldor, Alan Peacock, Robert Hall, Peggy Joseph, Stuart Wilson, Norman McKenzie, Keith Murray, Brian Hopkin and Tibor Scitovsky. He also ran into a number of Australians in London, including Trevor Swan, John La Nauze, Perce Partridge and Bruce Miller. He even managed to fit in a visit to Manchester, where he lunched with Dick Spann, Tom Baily, Eli Devons and Arthur Lewis.

From London, Heinz flew to New York, where he spent a few days at the UN Secretariat. There he presented a seminar on the lessons of economic development in Australia (subsequently published in *Welwirtschaftliches Archiv*) and renewed an acquaintance with the development economist Hans Singer, whom he had first met during the war when they were both at Manchester. At the United Nations, he was introduced to Michal Kalecki, Folke Hilgerdt and Marcus Fleming, and re-encountered Arthur Lewis and the Australian Reg Heywood. He also visited Columbia University, where he met Abram Bergson, J.M. Clark and Arthur Burns.

In Boston, Heinz stayed with Paul and Margaret Rosenstein-Rodan. He met Arthur Smithies, J.K. Galbraith, James Duesenberry, Arthur Schleshinger and Alexander Gershenkron at Harvard, and Paul Samuelson, Max Millikan, Charles Kindleberger, Everett Hagen, Ben Higgins, R.L. Bishop and Walt Rostow at the Massachusetts Institute of Technology (MIT). He gave a seminar at the latter on the Australian economy and was introduced to the work being undertaken on development economics at the new Centre for International Studies, 'a magnificent new outfit', according to Heinz.

At Harvard, he arranged to meet two of his former students and colleagues who were undertaking graduate studies there: Roy Cameron and Noel Drane. Alvin Hansen, America's pre-eminent Keynesian, who had reviewed *The Economic Lessons of the Nineteen-Thirties*, took Heinz to lunch at the Harvard Club. In a conversation with Samuelson and others over coffee at MIT, Heinz was urged to take advantage of his time in South Carolina to examine the nature and causes of the recent rapid economic development of the American South. He duly accepted this idea.

From Boston, Heinz travelled by train to Washington. There he visited the Bureau of the Budget, the Conference Board, the Federal Reserve Board (where he met his fellow LSE student Sam Katz), the IMF and the World Bank; he was able to talk with A.G.B. Fisher (now at the IMF), J.J. Polak,

Raymond Goldsmith, E.M. Bernstein and Leslie Bury (later the Treasurer of Australia, but then a Treasury official serving as Australia's Executive Director at the IMF and World Bank). He also spent a couple of days at the 'lovely campus' of the University of Virginia at Charlottesville, which had been founded by the third President of the United States, Thomas Jefferson. At Chapel Hill, he visited his brother, Walter, and his family, and gave a talk on Australia to students at Guildford College. He finally reached Columbia early in February 1954.

His four months at the University of South Carolina were occupied fully with teaching, research, public talks and lectures. He lived on the campus at the Faculty Club, which had recently been converted from a professorial residence. Since the Department of Economics at the university provided few postgraduate courses, he was asked to take two courses of lectures for junior and senior undergraduates in monetary theory and international economics. He set and marked examinations for both courses; during the last month of his stay he took, in addition, a class dealing with the history of economic thought.

A letter Heinz wrote to Ruth shortly after his arrival in Columbia conveyed his first impressions of South Carolina and of its state university

> The University, of course, is confined to white students. South Carolina has the most rigid segregation. There are separate schools, indeed, there is much excitement over an impending Supreme Court decision which will declare segregation in public schools unconstitutional; the State of South Carolina is already planning to turn all public schools into private ones, so that segregation can be maintained. You see quite a lot of coloured people in the streets, drivers, servants, school children, but they probably live in parts of the city I have not seen yet. Almost everyone [with] whom I have got into conversation has raised the subject of segregation; it clearly worries them all the time, they want to defend it to the foreign visitor (though one feels that half the time they are trying to defend it to their own consciences). The people I have talked to, however, are not representative. One gathers that it is among middle class and upper class people that you find doubts (and more) about the morality and wisdom of it, while the extreme insistence on segregation and prevalence of race hatred is to be found mainly among the poorer and more ignorant whites. The most common argument one hears is that segregation is necessary

until 'the Negroes are more educated'. One's reaction is rather to feel that progress requires a higher income and more education for the southern whites, for it's their poverty which makes them fear coloured competition and their ignorance which sustains all the prejudice.

He soon found teaching a frustrating experience, as the students were conspicuous for their lack of intellectual ability and enthusiasm for learning. Heinz's efforts to raise the intellectual standard of his classes—by setting items of reading beyond the standard textbook—quickly led to difficulties with the university authorities when the students complained. 'The University', Heinz explained to Ruth

> …has about 3,500 students. You see them roaming about the 'campus', many of them looking rather like farm yokels, not superficially very attractive. There is a fair sprinkling of girls, also pretty daft looking, but well dressed. A fair proportion of students ride about in their smart big American cars. In our department there is [sic] hardly any graduate students, and the lecturers certainly complain bitterly about the ability of the students—both native IQ and interest in their studies; but I suppose that is, in part, to be discounted as a widespread prejudice of University teachers.

When it came to the examinations, his worst fears, as he wrote to Ruth, were confirmed

> I returned the test papers to my classes, and when I went through the questions…I got more and more irritated by the failure of some of the students to understand even the simplest points. I lost my temper as I have never, I think, done before with students. I shall have to apologise to them on Monday. The trouble is that they just haven't enough background to cope with the lectures. Their vocabulary is so limited that they often do not understand the words I use. (One of the students asked me yesterday what the word 'spontaneous' meant.) I am supposed to teach them international monetary theory, or value theory, all of which I must really presuppose, if I am to get anywhere. Then they don't read, certainly nothing that isn't in their one textbook; only one in ten

will ever look outside [the] reading you recommend. My colleagues are amused at my complaints; they have long resigned themselves to the situation.

In his third-year class, Heinz was unable to pass more than 45 per cent of the students, even though the questions he set were decidedly easier than the ones he would have set at home. Trying to improve standards, he added an optional class for those students experiencing difficulties. According to Heinz, most students had jobs and were enrolled in five to six courses each semester; the essence of the problem, as he saw it, was that students were unable to devote sufficient time to individual courses.

It was not only the poor quality of his own students at the university that drew Heinz's criticism. To Ruth, he mentioned his visit to the state women's college at Rock Hill, about 75 miles from Columbia.

> It was rather strenuous—2½ hours' bus journey each way—and hardly worthwhile. I talked to the whole assembly of about 1,000 girls on 'A Visitor's First Impressions of America'. For the first five minutes I managed to keep them amused by talking (shameless lies) about my impressions of American girls; thereafter, when I got on to heavier fare they fell in a sort of stupor. The next day, one of my students here told me that he had happened to speak to a girl from the college on the phone and she told him that some Professor had talked to them that morning—she thought he came from 'Asia or somewhere'. My chief impression was of the incongruity between the magnificent and lavish material equipment of the place—enormous solid buildings, lovely grounds, four auditoria (one holding 3,600 people) with organs, stages, etc; scientific laboratories, and everything you can imagine—and the miserable intellectual standards of teaching and curriculum. By our standards the place is not a university at all—a mixture between a public school (in the English sense) and a girls' finishing school, and a business or technical college where they learn a bit of typing and cooking, dressed up as 'secretarial science' and 'domestic science'.

Towards the end of his stay at the University of South Carolina, Heinz was invited by his colleagues to draft a memorandum setting out the problems he had experienced and proposing measures for improvement. The memorandum—entitled 'Notes on university education'—so impressed the president of the university that he asked Heinz for permission to circulate it widely among academic staff.

While his teaching experience at the University of South Carolina was not a happy one, Heinz found his colleagues friendly and hospitable; for the most part, they were competent and enthusiastic teachers, though lacking somewhat in the amount and quality of the research they were undertaking. He saw and spoke frequently with the Dean of the School of Business Administration (which included the Department of Economics), S.K. Derrick, and liked the economists Jim Blackman, Bob Paterson, Al Smith, Alf Geisenheimer and Gus Williamson. His closest friendships at the university, however, were with two historians, Bob Ochs and Howard Quint. Ochs was related to the founder of the *New York Times*; Quint later became a very successful chairman of the Department of History at the University of Massachusetts, Amherst.

Towards the end of his second month in Columbia, Heinz summarised his experience in a letter to Tommy Balogh

> This place, like most, has its good and bad sides. The latter includes the students, whose academic standards are appalling...the lack of any social life; and the relative lack of stimulus on the professional level. But there are compensations; I have two or three young colleagues who are pleasant and quite good economists; it is an interesting angle from which to see the USA; and I have plenty of time for my own work—far more than I usually have at Canberra with all the distractions there.

As well as teaching at the University of South Carolina, Heinz introduced and conducted a fortnightly staff seminar, at which he presented a number of papers himself. Most of them were not new, as the titles indicate:'Australia—economic problems and policies';'Wage regulation by compulsory arbitration in Australia'; 'Recent developments in trade cycle theory';'The role of monetary policy'; 'Economic development—lessons of Australian experience'; 'The determinants of international capital movements'. At the seminar on'The role of monetary policy', the subject of his Istanbul lectures, he reported to Ruth:'we had quite a lively discussion, though not at a very high level, because some of the older people kept on butting in with the Quantity Theory, the Gold Standard, etc.'

The main purpose of his leave, of course, was not to teach undergraduates, or rehearse or polish papers that he had already drafted, but to initiate a number of new research projects. One of them was an investigation into the nature and causes of economic development of the American South since the 1930s, the topic that Paul Samuelson had suggested to him in Boston. The subject matter was compatible with Heinz's newly developed interest in economic development and underdevelopment. He later explained how his work on the American South's economy began

> I went abroad fresh from writing a course of lectures on problems of under-developed countries. Wherever I went, in Istanbul, Kiel, Cambridge, Manchester, the U.N., the Fund and Bank, at Harvard and M.I.T., I found economists riding on the same bandwagon, and I was going to spend four months in a typically under-developed region which, in the last twenty-five years, seemed to have undergone that critical experience, the 'take-off', which plays the same role in the theory of development as a mystic revelation in hagiology. I was further motivated by a discussion in January at the new Centre of International Studies at M.I.T. in which Samuelson, Bishop, Rostow, Higgins, Rodan and others speculated on the factors responsible for this sudden 'take-off' of economic development in the South: some suggested the improvement in the terms of trade for agriculture, others the public works of the New Deal, others the war...
>
> When I got to South Carolina, therefore, I began to read what literature on the subject I could find.

He collected an impressive amount of quantitative and other material and engaged the views of his colleagues at the University of South Carolina. Having spent so much time on the project, however, he was bitterly disappointed to discover, shortly before he returned to Australia, that two papers covering much the same subject had just been published. Undeterred, he drafted a paper incorporating his work and submitted it to the editor of the *Review of Economics and Statistics*, Seymour Harris, who rejected it, as did the editor of the *Southern Journal of Economics*. Harris thought Heinz's paper was 'interesting and valuable', but he said that he had a 'tremendous backlog' of material. Instead of holding up its publication elsewhere, he decided to return it rather than sending it out to referees. Heinz, once back in Canberra, presented the paper to a meeting of the local branch of the Economic Society. The *Indian Economic Review* eventually published a version of the paper; in 1993, Heinz republished it in his *50 Years of Development Studies* (1993).

As well as carrying out his work on the American South, Heinz started researching and writing an article on the concept of external economies and its application to the process of economic development. This issue was drawing the attention of a number of leading economists at that time. During the previous year, Heinz had given for the first time, at CUC, a course of lectures on economic development in the context of developing countries. This was a new area of economics and he quickly saw its possibilities for future specialisation. Not only was the subject matter—poverty, trade, investment, national income accounting—of particular interest to him, it involved significant policy issues and was less mathematical and theoretical in its approach than recent work in macroeconomics had been. His discussions in Britain, New York and Boston had made the field still more attractive to him and he was impressed with the amount of research on the economics of developing countries that was under way around the world.

In Boston, he had remarked to Paul Samuelson that the concept of external economies was very mixed up in the current literature. Samuelson encouraged him to straighten it out. Heinz drafted a paper on the subject when he was in Columbia and sent copies of it to several leading economists, including Kenneth Boulding, Moses Abramovitz and Ragnar Nurkse. Though he had not met Abramovitz, Heinz had read his recently published survey of economic growth[13] and thought highly of it. Abramovitz's Stanford colleague Lorrie Tarshis, whom Heinz had met in London in December, had suggested that he should contact Abramovitz when he was in the United States. Abramovitz responded favourably to Heinz's draft, praising it as a 'very good job, indeed, and [the paper] brings together the various ideas to which people have been referring under this head in a very illuminating way'. He hoped that Heinz would publish it immediately for he thought that 'many economists will find your analysis useful'. Nurkse, too, told Heinz that he thought the paper was 'an interesting and useful piece of work' and was convinced that it would 'find a prominent and useful place in one of the journals'.

When Heinz sent a first draft to Roy Harrod at Oxford, who was editor of the *Economic Journal*, he explained that it 'has taken me from my usual stamping grounds in monetary and income theory, and I am anxious to have it looked over by someone who can be relied upon to spot howlers'. Harrod, though he sent back a number of minor criticisms and suggestions, thought overall that it was 'extremely well done and brings together a variety of interesting points'. If, however, Heinz was thinking of having it published in the *Economic Journal*, Harrod made it clear that he was fully committed for the next year and was not prepared to accept it for publication. It appears that the paper was also submitted to *Oxford Economic Papers*, which also rejected it. After extensive redrafting, it was sent to the *Economic Record*, where it appeared in 1955. It quickly became a minor classic in the literature on economic development.

As well as his teaching and new research projects at the University of South Carolina, Heinz was frequently asked by various organisations to lecture on Australia and on issues of contemporary economic significance. He invariably accepted the invitations with alacrity. The number and variety of these speaking engagements, and the range of topics discussed, was quite astonishing.

For example, within the university, he spoke to the Kosmos Club on 'British and American conceptions of democracy'. At the International Relations Club, he spoke on Australia. To the university YMCA, he gave his views on 'British and American universities'. At the Teachers' Organisation, he dealt with 'The dollar problem'. The Kiwanis Club heard him discuss 'The function of taxation'. To the Quill Club, he lectured on Australian literature. Outside the university, he gave a talk on Australia to the Columbia Merchants' Association, to the Columbia YMCA and to an association of black Americans; to the League of Women Voters, he covered 'World trade problems'; and to the Camden Rotary Club, he talked again about 'British and American conceptions of democracy'. He also spoke at other universities in South Carolina, including Allen University, The Citadel (the famous military academy) at Charleston and at Winthrop College at Rock Hill. This last was where he gave the talk on 'A visitor's first impressions of America', which had not elicited the favourable response that Heinz had expected.

While in South Carolina, Heinz took a close interest in political and social developments in the United States, and particularly the movement to end segregation in public schools. The two-year struggle by the National Association for the Advancement of Coloured People in the Supreme Court challenging segregation in four states—South Carolina, Virginia, Kansas and Delaware—came to an end on 17 May 1954, shortly before

Heinz left Columbia. On that day the court issued its momentous and unanimous verdict (*Brown v. Board of Education*) that segregation in public schools was unconstitutional and that the practice violated the Fourteenth Amendment, passed in 1868. Heinz heard the decision from a news vendor as he walked past the Columbia Post Office.

It was on his own initiative that he talked to the students at Allen College, an Afro-American institution. He had expressed for some time a desire to visit one of the black colleges in Columbia and had tried to get the University of South Carolina to organise it, but without success. Therefore, he decided to contact the college himself and spoke to its president, who invited him to address the student assembly. He also conducted a discussion group at a recreation centre in Columbia for Afro-American soldiers. About 30 to 40 people attended; not many were soldiers. His audience consisted mostly of civilians from the city, but Heinz enjoyed it, telling Ruth: 'we had a splendid discussion…It was my first opportunity of meeting some of the more educated Negroes here, and I enjoyed it immensely.'

By the time he was due to leave South Carolina, he had clearly impressed his colleagues a good deal. They organised a well-attended farewell and presented him with an expensive gift. In his speech at the function, the senior university spokesman said that it had been 'a rare experience to have had you with us this semester. By your zest for living and learning, your scholarship you have been an intellectual stimulus to all of us. And more by your understanding, your tolerance and good humour you have endeared yourself to the whole university community.'

Three years after his visit to the University of South Carolina, in 1957, Dean Derrick wrote to inform Heinz that the school was establishing a graduate program and was seeking senior appointments; he wondered whether Heinz might be interested in accepting the position of senior economist. After giving the offer 24 hours' consideration, and while finding the suggestion greatly flattering, Heinz replied: 'I am happy in Canberra, in charge of a department in a rapidly growing university in the national capital of an admittedly small country. My wife and I have twice already gone through the process of adapting ourselves to a new country and are reluctant to embark on the process for a third time…I do not feel that I want to leave Australia for good.'

From Columbia, Heinz returned briefly to New York. In that city he attended—thanks again to Myrdal—an international conference of economists, held as part of the bicentennial celebrations at Columbia University. There he met a number of the world's leading economists, many of whom presented papers on the conference theme of 'National economic policies for welfare at home and abroad'. After the conference, he wrote to Tom Wilson, saying: 'I bet you have never seen Robbins, D.H. R[obertson], Ohlin, Myrdal, Knight, Hayek, Roepke, Arthur Lewis, J.M. Clark, Kuznets, A.F. Burns and J.H. Williams (and numerous others) in one room—though I grant that you may not particularly want to.' To Howard and Eleanor Quint, he wrote saying that it was 'quite a thrill, seeing and meeting almost all the world's leading economists, suffering the usual surprises…F.H. Knight a little man with a white goatee beard and a whisper; Fritz Machlup an Austrian dandy kissing hands over his bow tie; Roepke out-bellowing the "Road to Serfdom" with the rasping voice of a Prussian N.C.O., etc etc.'

He reported his pleasure at attending the 'gala junket at the Waldorf; Ike [President Eisenhower] bringing the house down with a mild denunciation of McC [Senator Joseph McCarthy]'.

After New York, Heinz took the plane to San Francisco, where he spent two weeks before returning to Australia across the Pacific. He visited Berkeley and at Stanford he gave a version of his paper on the theory of international capital movements that he had drafted before he left Australia; the paper was later published in the Italian journal *Economia Internazionale*. In 'A suggestion for simplifying the theory of international capital movements', Heinz explained why capital did not to any extent flow from countries where it was plentiful (and presumably cheap) to countries where it was scarce (and presumably dear), as conventional economic theory would suggest. The lack of flow was because of significant imperfections in the world capital market, such as the much higher degree of business risk within poor countries, their lack of factors of production complementary to capital and exchange rate uncertainty concerning the repatriation of investment funds.

On the flight to San Francisco, Heinz had the good fortune to sit next to Dennis Robertson; later he attended a seminar Robertson gave at Stanford on 'Utility and all that'. There he especially enjoyed an exchange of views between Robertson and Kenneth Arrow, M.W. Reder, Hendrik Houthakker, Bernard Haley and Tibor Scitovsky. He was well looked after in San Francisco by a cousin of Ruth's and her family; they took him around the city and the Bay district and drove him as far south as Carmel.

In San Francisco, he was also able to catch up with his father, who was spending some time in the United States as a Visiting Professor. Heinz arrived back in Canberra on 21 June and had 'an exciting family reunion, presents and all'.

There is no gainsaying the fact that Heinz's leave was highly productive. Not only had he written a number of research papers, subsequently published, he had been able to meet and talk with some of the leading economists in Britain and the United States about the latest work in economics—above all, in the economics of developing countries. And he came away from the United States with a more sympathetic understanding of the country and its people.

Before he returned to Australia, the Fulbright Grant Committee asked him to explain how his stay in the United States had confirmed or altered the views of American life that he had held before his visit. He responded by highlighting six issues that had impressed or surprised him.

Of the Cold War, he thought American public opinion tended to view the issues in more black and white terms than was the case in Britain or Australia. About the views and activities of Senator McCarthy, Heinz highlighted the 'unanimous hostility' towards the senator that he had observed among his acquaintances, though he readily admitted that this was 'a limited circle of educated and mostly academic people'. He stressed, too, the low academic standards of university education at the undergraduate level and 'the good and bad features of American business civilisation: the willingness to work hard, loyally and efficiently, on the one hand, and the dominance of valuations in terms of money-making and business success, on the other'. In America in general, and in South Carolina in particular, he had been surprised by the prominence of organised religion in private and public life and by the 'surprisingly liberal, at worst apologetic, attitude to the colour problem and segregation…among almost all educated white people'.

In some notes compiled for a talk after he returned to Australia, Heinz summed up his likes and dislikes of the United States. On his list of likes was his experience of Americans in general. He found them—especially those in the South—to be generally courteous people: 'They have a sort of unconscious naïve idealism; they are prepared to tell you what they believe in, without feeling either bashful like the English, or (genuinely or affected[ly]) cynical like the Australians.' He admired the American work ethic: 'they really work hard, at every level, to "get on"; but also I think quite genuinely, because that's what they get paid for. They are not frantic about it as Germans; neither, however, are they prepared to cut off their noses to spite their employer's face.'

Of the things that did not appeal to him, he said the 'worst…is the monolithic attitude to Russia and the Cold War…The almost universal resigned expectation of war…They see it, quite uncomplicatedly, as a question of self-defence against an unappeasable aggressor; ideological objections to communism hardly enter into it. Such hopes of peace as they entertain are based entirely on the chance of deterring Russia by superior strength.' But on the issue of McCarthyism, Heinz said that he had been 'pleasantly surprised. It is true that McCarthy is unspeakable and that he has an appalling amount of popular support…[but] the better newspapers are gunning for him all the time, and among the people I have met (mostly academic of course) I have hardly met any who do not fully share our point of view on this subject.'

Throughout his life, Heinz was a habitual compiler of lists. At the end of his visit to the United States, he drew up the following list of what most pleased and displeased him about America and Americans. He liked

>   The lovely University of Virginia at Charlottesville
>   The superb flowers in Columbia gardens
>   Spanish moss at Charleston
>   The excellent economists at MIT and Stanford
>   The view of Mid-Town Manhattan from the UN Secretariat
>   The attractive way American girls dress
>   American coffee
>   Good Southern Food
>   The courtesy of most southerners
>   The cultured, liberal and kindly people I met at Columbia
>   Walter Lippmann
>   The UN Building in New York
>   The New York Times
>   San Francisco
>   Central heating
>   The view of the Rocky Mountains from the plane

He disliked

> Public opinion on the Cold War and world affairs generally
> McCarthyism
> The indignation of segregation
> A Greyhound bus journey at Easter
> Tipping in New York
> The laziness, illiteracy and frivolity of undergraduates
> Talking to women teachers on the Dollar Problem
> The Bible belt

Yet however important Heinz's period of leave had been in stimulating his long-term interest in development economics, it is important not to overestimate the significance of his discussions with American economists. Nor should one exaggerate the impact of the research projects he initiated in the United States. He had begun giving a course of lectures on economic development in the semester before he went on leave, and he found the difficulty of getting his research published in leading international journals a frustrating exercise.

His immediate disillusionment—which was fairly soon corrected—can be gauged in a letter he wrote to Roy Cameron at Harvard shortly after returning to Canberra. 'Anybody who adds to the absurd flow of literature on economic development,' Heinz wrote, 'ought to be ashamed of himself. I cannot remember a fad of economists ever assuming such fantastic proportions. However, I haven't got the moral courage to burn the stuff I wrote at South Carolina. Some of it is likely to appear in various out of the way journals, in the next few months.'

To Ron Barback, who was now on leave at Oxford, Heinz complained of having trouble redrafting the external economies paper, because he faced 'the awful prospect of a very radical revision; I am now waiting to hear whether Tom Wilson might publish it in something like its present form [in *Oxford Economic Papers*], without forcing me to start chasing all the other hares'. For the time being, he proposed to shelve further work on economic development and 'to give serious thought to the long-run-away-from book on the Australian Capital Market. It is time I tackled something bigger; somehow people do not seem to consider a flow of little articles an adequate substitute to an occasional book.'

Looking back some decades later (in 1985), he regarded his leave in the United States in 1954 as a lost opportunity to develop the knowledge and skills of mathematical economics and econometrics

> In one sense…I never really succeeded in qualifying as a professional economist. I never studied statistics or mathematics. Later I picked up some rudimentary statistical methods as I needed them for empirical work. But my mathematics never went beyond high school level. I failed to take the opportunity of my first sabbatical in 1954 to plug the gap by a year's full time study of mathematics, and thus gradually acquired only just enough to understand, but not to use, elementary calculus and matrix algebra. In consequence, I found a growing proportion of the articles that appeared in the *American Economic Review* and other journals incomprehensible (Arndt 1985:101).

13
POLITICS

Heinz's career as a public intellectual, which had begun in Sydney on his arrival in Australia, continued when he moved to Canberra. There he joined the ALP, after meeting the requirements for Australian citizenship. Though he was to resign from the ALP in 1972—over its policies on the Vietnam War and, more immediately, its decision to recognise Communist China—his association with the party was always controversial. Declining affiliation with either the party's Left or Right, he preferred to be regarded as a moderate or non-aligned member. He opposed the powerful communist involvement in the trade unions; he also opposed the influence of elements of the Catholic Church on the Right of the ALP. Above all, he stood for the application of democratic principles in politics and was opposed to totalitarian methods, whichever quarter promoted them.

His support was, however, often requested by different groups in the party, who sought access to his sharp intellect and wanted to draw on his extraordinary energy. In December 1951, for instance, he was invited to attend a conference in Moscow sponsored by the Australian Peace Council. He declined, informing the organisers that he was unable to spare the time and in any case was too busy to prepare an address. While he made it clear that 'these are conclusive reasons for my inability to assist you', he added that 'I am very sceptical of the *bona fides* of the sponsors of this Conference. We are all for peace—including the Kremlin and the State Department. But I see no reason to believe that a Conference such as the proposed Moscow Conference would serve any other purpose but to strengthen one side, and I believe unbalance the worse side in the world struggle for power.'

In Canberra, Heinz soon established a branch of the Fabian Society, as he had done earlier in Sydney. Twenty-five people turned up to the inaugural meeting in October 1951, among them Allan Fraser and his fellow Labor politician Kim Beazley senior. John Burton, the Secretary of the Department of External Affairs under Evatt and later Labor candidate for the House of Representatives, was also present, as were Joe Burton and Fin Crisp from CUC. Geoffrey Sawer, the Professor of Law at the ANU, addressed the meeting on 'The Australian Constitution after fifty years'.

One of the major reasons for Heinz's disagreements with the ALP, even before he joined it, was its economic policy, which often conflicted with his own adherence to the economics of Keynes. Unlike many of his contemporaries, Heinz quickly saw the inconsistencies between the party's support for nationalisation and direct controls on the one hand, and the economics of Keynes's *General Theory* on the other. Here Heinz's views coincided closely with those of contemporary British social democrats, such as Anthony Crosland and Hugh Gaitskell, who were in the process of revising the British Labour Party's commitment to nationalisation and other outdated socialist dogma.

Heinz was particularly critical of Labor's failure to promote policies aimed at containing inflation. Rather than diminishing inflation, he thought the policies associated with Evatt (who succeeded Chifley as party leader when the latter died in 1951) would augment it. He never concealed his view that the Menzies government was likely to do better than Labor when it came to containing inflation, but Labor would do better than the government when it came to effecting a more even distribution of income and wealth. He never shed his support for greater economic and social equality, even after he formally broke with the Labor Party.

His position on these matters emerged from an article he wrote for a publication called *Voice*[14] in the run-up to the 1955 federal election. Under the title, 'Menzies and Evatt on economic policy' (1955), Heinz concluded

> A Labor victory would almost certainly mean rather more inflation and rather worse balance of payments trouble than a return of the Menzies Government. An anti-Labor victory would almost certainly mean still more inequality in coming years. But it would not be unreasonable to assume that, whereas a Labor Government would soon be compelled by events to tackle the economic problems of internal and external balance, a fairer social policy would probably have to await the removal of the anti-Labor Government at the next election.

'That is why,' he said, 'with many misgivings, I shall vote Labor.'

He was never afraid to condemn the trade unions when they acted irresponsibly to exploit the prevailing state of over-full employment. Equally, he reprehended the eagerness of Evatt to expand government expenditure when there was excess demand; at such times, there was clearly a need for wage and expenditure restraint. Heinz saw his role in the party primarily as an advocate of a more rational approach to economic policy. Whenever he criticised the party's leadership, which he often did when Evatt was its leader, it was usually because of its failure to adopt responsible economic policies. This was to be the essence of his critique of the leadership of the party presented in 1956 in his Chifley Memorial Lecture.

During the years immediately before this lecture, Heinz began to think seriously about the deficiencies of the party's economic policy and how he might set about educating its leaders. He informed Kingsley Laffer in April 1953 that he was 'quite out of sympathy on current economic policy with Evatt and Co'. He agreed to write on the shortcomings of Labor's policy in a chapter for the book *Policies for Progress* (1954), edited by Geoffrey Serle and Alan Davies for the Fabian Society of Victoria.

This chapter explained that there were limits to what could be achieved if the party won office again, because its agenda would be constrained by the availability of resources. In a full employment world, firm choices had to be made between competing political ends. As he put it, 'the first task of democratic socialists today is to get clear in their own minds what they can and cannot hope to achieve.' Excessive demands would clearly give rise to inflation, would impair the economy's productive efficiency and would create all sorts of arbitrary injustices to different social groups. Then, in an effort to regain stability, governments would introduce direct controls, which would further erode productivity and inhibit economic growth.

The purpose to which democratic socialists should work, Heinz maintained, was 'to keep the economy balanced between the twin evils of inflation and deflation'. Getting the balance right was 'an almost impossibly delicate task', but the ALP should not underestimate the evils of inflation. Nor should it put its faith in direct controls as the major weapon to combat inflation. Instead, the government's budget, aided when necessary by the credit policies of the central bank, should be the major instrument for keeping inflation down. As for the nationalisation of the means of production, distribution and exchange—and particularly the nationalisation of banking—he now believed that it was 'not essential to an effective policy for full employment'.

This appeared to be a major apostasy on his part, for scarcely six years before he had informed Mary Walsh, among others, that bank nationalisation was essential to keep full employment intact. But what had changed in the meantime was the realisation that belief in a postwar slump was false; by 1953, it seemed that full employment had become a permanent state of affairs.

As well as seeking to persuade the party to jettison its traditional dependence on direct intervention in the economy, Heinz set out to encourage the ALP to adopt measures that would improve industrial productivity. This was critical, since he was adamant that future advances in living standards among lower-income groups would depend much more on the efficient use of resources than on the redistribution of current income. Instead of replacing productive private enterprises with inefficient public ones, democratic socialists should strive to make private enterprise function more efficiently and responsibly. To achieve this, encouragement should be given to raising savings and increasing investment, improving management practices, restricting monopolies and monopolistic practices and enhancing the skills of the nation's workforce.

Though Heinz expressed these views with his usual confidence and clarity, he realised that many in the ALP would find them unacceptable. He did not find it easy to come out as boldly as he did against such cherished Labor principles as nationalisation and direct controls—particularly when he had himself supported them earlier. Nor did he relish censuring the economic orthodoxy of the party and the poverty of its current leadership. He was aware that friends would take him to task. When he wrote to Geoffrey Serle to say that he would write a chapter for *Policies for Progress*, he confessed that

> I am no more happy about the whole business than I was when I last wrote. The reason is simply that I do not know at the moment where I stand on some of the central issues. I feel extremely uncomfortable about, or have actually come to reject, some of the socialist ideas which I took for granted three or five years ago; but just how far I have progressed towards Babbitry I do not know. I have the gravest doubt whether this is a fit state of mind in which to write an inspiring socialist manifesto, or even a modest contribution towards clarification of socialist thinking. However, I am determined not to let you down and propose today to start the job.

Later, he admitted to Serle that he had intended to be deliberately provocative, because 'unless we are prepared to say this sort of thing, the book is not worthwhile. But you and others may well disagree.'

Of Heinz's friends, one who immediately detected a shift of political ideology was Gerald Firth, by this time Professor of Economics at the University of Tasmania, to whom Heinz had sent a draft of the chapter for critical comment. After reading it, Firth replied: 'I don't think you are any longer a "socialist", except in the very peculiar sense that "we are all socialists nowadays". I think it ought to be published, but I shall be very surprised if the Fabians will swallow it.'

Heinz snapped back: 'What I have said seems to me to follow logically and inescapably from one premise: rejection of revolution. Democratic socialism implies gradualism, respect for the interests of the non-working classes, and a compromise between freedom and efficiency; from all this, all else follows.' And, for good measure, he informed Firth 'that the Melbourne Fabians have swallowed the Chapter with mild enthusiasm'. But Firth remained unconvinced that Heinz could still call himself a Labor man. Such scepticism seemed to be confirmed a few years later when, after reviewing Heinz's book on *The Australian Trading Banks*, Firth wrote to him saying that '[p]age 199 leads me to fear your impending conversion to the Liberal Party',[15] to which Heinz replied: 'I am afraid my prejudices are too deeply rooted to fear any prospect of a conversion to the Liberal Party.'

There was talk of a sequel to *Policies for Progress* in late 1956 and early 1957, but it did not eventuate. Heinz was not enthusiastic about it, but the themes that he had adumbrated in the book were developed further, and with much greater publicity, in his Chifley Memorial Lecture. The ALP Club at the University of Melbourne was the sponsor of the lecture. Heinz was invited to speak on the subject of 'Socialist economic policy'.

Delivered in Melbourne on 27 July 1956, the lecture was the third in the series; Evatt had given the first. Copies were sent in advance to all the major Australian newspapers and to members of the federal parliamentary press gallery, with an embargo to be observed until the time of delivery. Hearing of the controversial nature of the lecture, the Federal Executive of the ALP asked Heinz for a copy a week before it was due to be delivered. He reluctantly agreed, but only on the understanding that the embargo would be preserved until the lecture was given.

Choosing as his title 'The Labor Party and economic policy' (the change of name from the one that the original invitation had proposed is significant), Heinz used the lecture to launch a blistering attack on the party's leadership. He drew a sharp contrast between the quality of Ben Chifley's tenure of the party leadership and Evatt's. This attack on Evatt was to attract strong criticism from many quarters and for a while Heinz's membership of the ALP was threatened.

The lecture began with the assertion that, in the 'ten years since I came to Australia, I have encountered no other public figure for whom I can feel the same unreserved admiration than I did for Mr Chifley', who

> …combined in a remarkable way the qualities we should want to see in a leader of the Australian Labor Party and the Australian nation. Personal integrity, firm leadership made palatable by personal modesty and homely courtesy, a sense of solidarity with working people so natural and inborn that he found no difficulty in adopting a wider national outlook, a broad humanitarian idealism tempered by commonsense but not by mere party-political expediency, a strong sense of responsibility about principles and affairs coupled with engaging willingness to take neither himself nor other personages too seriously.

Even if there was an element of exaggeration in Heinz's singling out of these characteristics of Chifley's character, a good deal of care went into his selection of them. They were meant to supply a sharp contrast with Evatt.

Heinz was to return to the central theme of failed leadership in the concluding paragraph of the lecture, in which he said that

> The Australian Labor Party cannot expect more than perhaps once in a generation to find a leader of the stature of Ben Chifley. It does not need a leader who, like Chifley, happens also to be a first-rate expert on technical matters of economics and finance. What it does need is a leadership which counts among its members, some at least who are technically competent to make judgments on matters of economic policy; a leadership which is prepared to make the intellectual effort to develop the Party's economic policy and re-assess it in the light of changing knowledge and circumstances; a leadership which, on Chifley's principle that 'an informed public opinion is vital to the welfare of a democracy'…makes it one of its major responsibilities to explain its policies and the need for them to the people; and a leadership which stands by its principles.

Labor, in short, had to define what it stood for. Some might consider the ALP's objectives to be fairly similar to those held by the current government, such differences as existed being simply of degree. To be sure, the ALP had a greater commitment to income equality and social welfare than the government parties, but whereas the government's economic policy was marked by clarity, Labor's economic policy was decidedly opaque. It needed urgently to clarify its goals and to understand that there were alternative means of achieving them.

Above all, it had to learn that the world had changed profoundly since the 1930s. Then, mass unemployment and falling living standards were the predominant economic problems. Now, inflation had replaced unemployment as the pre-eminent economic difficulty. This elementary fact of economic life had to be comprehended by the party—but there had been other changes as well. For example, only a few gaps now remained to be filled in the social security system; nationalisation in Britain and other countries was no longer considered to be the cure-all for the problems of capitalism; the Australian Constitution imposed strict limits on what could be nationalised; the instability of the American economy posed a much smaller threat to the international economy than it once did; and the incompatibility of socialism and democracy had clearly been revealed by the experience of the Soviet Union and its satellites.

The problem, for Heinz, was this

> ...these changes have as yet hardly caused a ripple on the surface of traditional Labor thinking in this country. Paradoxically, it is the Left that has become the stronghold of conservatism within the Labor Movement, content to repeat the old slogans, fearful of departures from the beliefs of its fathers.

In contrast with the conservatism of the Left, Heinz argued that '[s]uch fresh thinking as has been done in the last few years has come almost entirely from right-wing Labor men and has, for that reason alone, been condemned out of hand by the Left'. He had

> ...little sympathy with the Industrial Groups [which had been promoted and supported in the trade unions, especially by the Catholic Right of the party, to combat communist influence], and would strongly oppose many of the policies of Mr Santamaria [the founder of the Catholic Social Studies Movement], with

their glorification of the rural life, [which] seem to me to be more concerned with the fundamentals of his church and religion than with the fundamentals of the Labor Party.

Still, there were progressive forces present in the party, among them Lloyd Ross[16] and Laurie Short.[17] Heinz believed that their 'ideas on industrial and economic affairs should be considered on their merits, regardless of alignments in the internal Party dispute'.

Applying his critique specifically to Labor's economic policy, Heinz argued that while inflation had been the country's leading economic problem since World War II, Labor's response was blunted by its abiding fear of unemployment. As to economic policy instruments, the party

> …had done little more than advocate direct controls, which it knew to be impracticable without prior constitutional reform, and had made political capital out of the unpopularity of other measures to deal with the situation, such as tax increases and cuts in government expenditure. On banking and monetary policy, Labor's sole contribution since Chifley's death has been to demand cheap money and condemn credit restrictions. Its contribution to the problem of raising productivity has been confined to (often justified) resistance to proposals from the anti-Labor camp and half-hearted talk about nationalisation of industry.

Having dealt with domestic macroeconomic policy, Heinz then turned to economic development. Here, he enjoined the party to take up the cause of developing regions and countries. This was an issue that was already stirring in his imagination and was to dominate his attention from the 1960s. In the Chifley Lecture, he asserted that the development of Australia's territories was 'a field in which Labor could make a great contribution if it bent its energy and mind to it'. He pointed out that Eddie Ward, the current leader of Labor's Left in the Federal Parliament, had exhibited (when he was the Minister for Territories in the 1940s) a willingness to promote policies aimed at improving standards of living in Papua New Guinea and other Australian territories. Since 1949, however, Heinz observed

> I can scarcely recall an instance when Labor has betrayed the slightest interest in their problems. It has even left it to Tory back-

benchers like [W.C.] Wentworth to expose the Menzies–Fadden Government's neglect of the potentialities of the Northern Territory and New Guinea. To make use of the potentialities of the Northern Territory, and to build up the economy of New Guinea in a way which will advance the welfare of the native people, will cost money and energy. If Labor is the party of progress, here is an opportunity to show how progressive it is.

Heinz had hoped the lecture would stimulate debate in the party and lead to fundamental reform. He knew that his analysis would be controversial. Indeed, he intended it to be so. He assumed that his critics on the Left, including those who supported the present party leadership, would condemn the lecture root and branch. But he expected that after the dust had settled, a calmer and more dispassionate debate would follow and the party would eventually move in the direction that he was advocating. In the event, though there were some concessions in Labor's economic policy over the years, Labor was never to absorb the essential drift of Heinz's analysis.

The reaction to the Chifley Lecture was swift and furious. Dr Jim Cairns, newly elected to the federal seat of South Yarra, in suburban Melbourne, led criticism from the political Left. Few came to Heinz's aid; some who did, including External Affairs Minister R.G. Casey, were more of a hindrance than a help.

Future Cabinet Minister John Button, a former president of the ALP Club at the University of Melbourne, and in 1956 an industrial relations lawyer with an office in the city's Australian Council of Trade Unions building, wrote to Heinz soon after the lecture with an assessment of trade union reaction. 'I have been in a good position to assess their reactions,' Button told him, 'and generally speaking it has not been favourable. And their criticism runs along the lines voiced by Jim Cairns, whose attitude disappointed us a little. The [Victorian] State Secretary [of the ALP], Jack Tripovitch, informed me that there had been a number of complaints to him, based wholly of course on the press reports.'

The State Executive was shortly to discuss the lecture and Button hoped the ALP Club would not find itself in hot water. One party official had already warned him that 'the lecture should not be published or else. I suspect this is bluff, however, and whether this is so or not it will certainly have no effect on our decisions.' Ian Wilson, the president of the ALP

Club, told Heinz that the lecture 'has had quite a heated reaction down here…The State Executive of the Party is not very pleased about it and some efforts were made to discourage us from printing it. However, they seemed to have cooled down.' He mentioned that the State Executive had been 'egged on a bit by Jim Cairns', and that the references in the lecture to the reformist activities of Short and Ross were responsible for most of the negative response.

As might be expected, the newspapers generally supported the position that Heinz had taken in the lecture. *The Age* called it '[o]ne of the most thought-provoking and constructive examinations of present Labor party policy to be made in recent years…Professor Arndt…said a number of things which are, no doubt, unpalatable to large sections of the party's supporters. Nevertheless, he reflected a view which has been growing in the minds of many during the seven years the party has been on the opposition benches' (*Age*, 30/7/56).

The newspaper noted that after three successive losses, the party had exhibited little desire to review or revise its policies. What Heinz had done was to inject 'fresh, uninhibited thought and discussion'.

An editorial in the *Sydney Morning Herald* supported Heinz's call for a debate in the party, drawing attention to the stagnation of thought in ALP circles compared with the refreshing debate that was taking place in the British Labour Party. The ALP was, according to the *Herald*, 'always distrustful of "intellectuals", prefers to live in a strange aboriginal dreamtime of its own, where Communists are still good Labor men at heart, where all Americans are reactionary capitalists, where inflation can be cured by higher wages and shorter hours, and where the word "Socialism", undefined, unwanted and—fortunately—unconstitutional, is an inadequate substitute for a political and economic policy'.

Casey (*Age*, 6/8/56) and Cairns (*Age*, 7/8/56) wrote letters to *The Age*, the former supporting Heinz, the latter criticising him. Casey believed that Heinz had made an important contribution to Australian political life— 'and not in any narrow political sense' (*Sydney Morning Herald*, 28/7/56). He pointed out that Heinz had the 'advantage of familiarity with European politics', it being a 'deficiency in our political life that such matters as his find little objective public ventilation or discussion'. He offered to donate £5 towards the cost of publishing the lecture. One aspect of Casey's mischief making was a matter that elicited a quick response from Heinz. A deficiency of the lecture, Casey noted, was its failure to support the fight against communism. Heinz replied that he was tempted to give a simple answer: namely, that his lecture was confined to economic policy. But he admitted that he would be

> ...less than candid in doing so. Frankly, on this issue I continue to side with Evatt rather than with his opponents. I regard the virulent anti-Communists as almost as much a menace to our national life as the Communists. While I recognise that Russian and Chinese Communism, in so far as it is expansionist, may be a threat to our national security, I cannot persuade myself that there is any practicable alternative to the present regime for the Chinese people; and I do not consider Communism as a significant internal danger in Australia. Since I suspect the motives and detest the methods of the professional anti-Communists, inside and outside the ALP, I had no desire to join them in their agitation.

Cairns, in his letter to *The Age*, claimed that Heinz had not spoken 'as a Labor man but as an academic lecturer without responsibility for the solidarity of the Labor Movement'. To this, Heinz replied that Cairns knew full well that he had been an active Labor supporter since 1949. 'As an academic lecturer and a Labor man', Heinz said that he did 'not accept Mr Cairns's assumption that party solidarity is everything, that all public discussion of the party's policies must be stifled in the name of solidarity' (*Age*, 10/8/56). Another member of the Left, John Burton, attacked Heinz in the *Sydney Morning Herald* for condoning monopolies and opposing the nationalisation of industry (*Sydney Morning Herald*, 2/8/56). To the veteran Labor politician Les Haylen, Heinz replied that Haylen was 'quite wrong in thinking that I sympathise with the rabid anti-Communism of the Right Wing. On all points of principle, which were in dispute in the internal struggle [of the Right and Left in the ALP], my sympathies were, and remain, with the Left, but I am convinced that the Left must re-think its economic policy' (*Sydney Morning Herald*, 30/7/56).

It was reported that Heinz, shortly after presenting the Chifley Lecture, was physically assaulted at a meeting of his ALP branch in Canberra, though some of those present denied that this had occurred. On the contrary, they pointed out that standing orders had been suspended specifically to allow him to explain the nature and substance of the lecture and that his views had been received politely. Even so, it appeared for a while that Heinz might be expelled from the party. Many wanted that to happen, but the powerful state secretary of the Western Australian branch of the party, Joe Chamberlain, rescued him.

Why Chamberlain chose to do so has been the source of considerable speculation ever since. Perhaps he, like Heinz, wanted a change in the party's leadership. If he did, it is most unlikely that his motives were the same as Heinz's, since Chamberlain was a major figure of the Left and would no doubt have dismissed Heinz's revisionism as unacceptable. For Chamberlain, it was probably all a storm in a teacup. He is reported to have said simply: 'By and large, I have no serious quarrel with the overall objective approach made by the Professor to his subject.' Heinz was later to claim that it was Chamberlain's intervention that saved him from expulsion.

Of all the correspondence generated by the Chifley Lecture, four published letters—two from each man—between Heinz and B.A. Santamaria were by far the most significant. As testimony to their importance, they were published in the *Australian Journal of History and Politics* (AJHP) (May 1957). Heinz had first sent the correspondence to *Meanjin*, thinking that it might publish the letters, but it rejected them. He then sent them to *Quadrant*, where the editor, James McAuley, also rejected them. McAuley, saying that their length made them unsuitable for *Quadrant*'s purposes, suggested that Heinz might print them privately. Meanwhile, the editor of the AJHP, Professor Gordon Greenwood, expressed an interest, given the political importance of the letters. In a short introduction, Greenwood explained that, while it was somewhat unusual for AJHP to publish an exchange of letters, he decided to do so because the correspondence was 'a reasoned contribution to the discussion upon one of the most controversial issues in contemporary Australian politics'.

In the first letter, a response by Santamaria to the Chifley Lecture, Heinz was congratulated for a 'most reasoned and thought-provoking analysis of the present intellectual crisis of the Labor Movement'. Santamaria said that his purpose for writing was Heinz's admission that he 'would strongly oppose most of the policies of Mr Santamaria'. Whereas Heinz had declared his support for Dr Lloyd Ross and Laurie Short, both of whom were strongly opposed to communist influence in the trade unions, Santamaria was puzzled as to why Heinz had criticised him when his views were at one with the others. Where, Santamaria asked, was the distinction to be found between him and Ross and Short? As to the contribution by members of the Catholic Church to the difficulties now besetting the ALP, Santamaria expressed disappointment with Heinz's implication that

Catholics should not engage in the political and social issues of the day. On the contrary, Santamaria believed it was a healthy sign that younger generations of Catholics were bringing their ideas to the fore and involving themselves in matters of contemporary Australian life.

For his part, Heinz acknowledged Santamaria's 'careful and courteous letter'. He conceded that his reference to Santamaria was much too brief and possibly unfair because of its brevity. He admitted, too, that the distinction he had drawn between Santamaria and Ross and Short was perhaps too sharp, even inaccurate in some respects. Yet he remained implacably opposed to the position adopted by the Catholic Right on three issues: its social policy (particularly the promotion of agriculture at the expense of other sectors of the Australian economy); its 'hysterical attitude to Communism'; and its 'authoritarian policies'.

About the Catholic Right's attitude to communism, Heinz explained that he was himself opposed to communism, but his opposition was 'based not primarily on disagreement with its economic ideas, nor on its atheism, but on its totalitarian methods and objectives'. He dismissed the belief, held by many on the Right, that communism posed a serious internal and external threat to Australia. And he expressed his strong opposition to the totalitarian methods the Right was pursuing in the industrial groups that it had helped to foster for the purpose of curtailing left-wing influence in the trade unions. He regarded the

> …totalitarian, or authoritarian, tendencies of the Catholic Right-wing as a threat to liberal democracy in this country, differing only in degree from that of the Communists, though I would readily admit that the difference of degree is important. In numerous ways—in the methods of its anti-Communist campaign, in its support of compulsory trade unionism, in its attitude to censorship, in its day-to-day struggle for predominance within the A.L.P. —the Catholic Right-wing has seemed to me to reveal its illiberal authoritarian outlook, its willingness to subscribe to the basic evil fallacy of Communism, that 'the end justifies the means'. You may regard me as an old fashioned nineteenth-century radical, with all the prejudices of that breed. But I find it impossible to disassociate this authoritarianism from the authoritarian philosophy and government of the Catholic Church.
>
> Hardly a day passes when I do not get new evidence of the divisive activities of the Church and its more ardent supporters.

Catholic neighbours' children telling us that their teaching Sisters have forbidden them to play with public school children because they 'do not say their prayers at night'. Catholic priests using quite indefensible moral pressure to compel helpless migrants to send their children to overcrowded Catholic schools. Catholic priests organising their voting strength in packed meetings of Good Neighbour Councils and other voluntary bodies. Catholic extremists in our A.L.P. branch using precisely the same methods as the Communists to find procedural loopholes and other shady devices to make their viewpoint prevail. All these instances are taken from my personal experience. You may say they are unrepresentative; they do not represent official policy. But why shouldn't they? If these people believe that their religious faith (whose spread or survival presumably depends in large part on the political strength of their Church) is more important than anything else, including mere political institutions like those of political democracy; if they believe that it is wrong to set the individual conscience of fallible human beings above revealed truth authoritatively interpreted and laid down; and if they believe that the end justifies the means; what then is to stop them from doing all the things which I accuse them of doing and which I believe to be a menace to our national life?

Heinz, in fact, told Santamaria that he sided 'with Dr Evatt against the Catholic Right-wing'.

Of course, he could scarcely have expected Santamaria to accept this extraordinary outburst. Probably he was surprised that Santamaria even bothered to reply. He did take some time to do so. At first, he was inclined to think that Heinz's mind was closed to opposing points of view; certainly this was so of many of those in the ALP whom Heinz was criticising. But on reflection, and remembering that Heinz was a member of a university faculty, and therefore a person whose mind should be open to reason, he decided to reply to Heinz's critique of the Catholic Church's intervention in the labour movement.

According to Santamaria, Heinz had misunderstood the reasons for his anti-communism. It was not directly because of an alleged internal threat to Australian democracy, but rather because of 'the tremendous military development of China under Communism, allied with a parallel economic development over the next fifteen years, [which] will make China so overwhelmingly powerful in our near north that well within fifty years it must constitute a threat to our present national security'. Thus he concluded that a 'continuation of the present degree of Communist influence in the trade union movement…so increases our eventual political and military danger that it cannot be tolerated with equanimity'. No lesser person than Evatt himself, Santamaria recalled, had supported the moderate industrial groups in their opposition to communist influence in the unions.

Given its malign influence, and given Heinz's declared opposition to communism, Santamaria wondered how Heinz would set about diminishing communist influence. If Heinz had a better way of dealing with the problem, Santamaria promised that the so-called Catholic Right would willingly withdraw from its activities in the Labor Party and in the trade unions.

The particular grievances Heinz had voiced about the Catholic Church—for example, its support for the belief that the 'end justifies the means'—Santamaria dismissed outright. If the views and actions that Heinz had claimed were being said and done by members of the Church, Santamaria assured him that most Australian Catholics would condemn them. Similarly, if Heinz's allegations about practices adopted by teachers in Catholic schools towards children in public schools were true, such practices would not be supported by most Catholics. As to Heinz's use of the word 'divisive' in connection with Catholics, Santamaria believed it could be used about any minority group in a democratic society that wished to preserve its ethos within the rule of law and oppose laws that appeared to deny its right to exist. If this action was divisive, Santamaria concluded that there was 'only one remedy—to run the totalitarian steamroller over it and to compel conformity. The charge of being "divisive" was precisely the basis of Hitler's immoral and destructive attack on the Jewish community.'

Heinz swiftly replied to Santamaria. Again, he declared his support for Evatt's 'opposition to the Catholic Right-wing and, generally speaking, with his views on Communism, civil liberties and foreign policy'. Yet he was at one with Santamaria in his criticisms of the 'illiberal methods employed by his [Evatt's] supporters…as strongly as I criticise the illiberalism of the Catholic extremists'. Further, he said that he did not regard Evatt as 'a satisfactory leader of the party and could hardly have expressed this view more strongly than I did in my Chifley lecture'. He drew a contrast between Santamaria's 'sweet reasonableness' and 'the attitude more commonly exhibited, in word and deed, by the Catholic Church and its zealous adherents in politics'.

The touchstone of his criticism of the Catholic Right was 'the civil liberties issue', by which Heinz meant its support of the Menzies government's attempt to outlaw the Communist Party, 'with its drastic departures from traditional principles of civil rights'. He doubted that all Catholics would be so ready as Santamaria to condemn the doctrine that 'the end justifies the means', 'the doctrine of the commissar, the crusader and the inquisitor'. While he did not think that 'this is the state of mind of all Catholics or of the Church in its official policy', he maintained that 'this state of mind has strongly coloured the activities of the Catholic Right-wing in recent years and that it is a state of mind to which Catholic zealots, because they believe themselves to be fighting in the cause of God, are particularly prone'. For him, the tactics of 'Catholic extremists in various ALP branches and organisations in recent years was a reminder of the tactics used by communist trade unionists in England during the war'.

About his claims concerning the divisive influence of the Catholic Church in Australia, Heinz conceded that the Church could not compel migrants to send their children to Catholic schools. Nevertheless, he was convinced that the Church brought moral pressure to bear on migrant Catholic families; he could not 'regard this policy of the Church as anything but authoritarian and indeed immoral'. Further, he 'deplore[d] the insistence of the Church on separate education for Catholic children. I believe the separate education of Catholic children (like the separate education of English upper-class children in the old public schools) tends to create two nations.'

There seemed an important difference between

> ...the Catholic minority and other religious groups. Unlike all other religious groups, the Catholics insist on separate education (and indoctrination) of their children, they oppose inter-marriage or at least insist that the children of inter-marriages shall be brought up as Catholics. They refuse to cooperate with other Churches; they regard adherents of other faiths as 'heretics' or at least as morally inferior. It is the sum of all these policies, the attitude of mind from which they derive and their social effects, which, in my view, make the Catholic Church a 'divisive' influence in our society in a way in which this cannot be said of any other significant minority.

Clearly there was no meeting of minds here. Santamaria was convinced that communism posed a threat to Australian security. Heinz denied this, charging the Catholic Right with using totalitarian methods; this was dismissed by Santamaria. The fact that Heinz condemned Santamaria and his Catholic Social Studies Movement, while at the same time supporting Lloyd Ross and Laurie Short, seemed to Santamaria to be inconsistent since the three of them were seeking the same ends. Heinz rejected this accusation of incongruity on the grounds that, whereas the others were adhering to democratic principles and procedures, the Catholic Right was using totalitarian tactics to achieve its ends.

These were issues of great political importance in Australia at the time. Central to the correspondence between Heinz and Santamaria were the momentous split in the ALP and the creation of the Anti-Communist Labor Party (later the Democratic Labor Party); concern about communist influence in the trade unions and the activities of right-wing groups who were trying to contain the spread of communism; espionage activities in Australia associated with officials of the Soviet Embassy in Canberra; and, above all, the controversial figure of Evatt. That the debate between the two men remained focused on political issues and did not deteriorate into personal denigration says much about their standards of public discourse and behaviour.

In an unpublished letter to Heinz, Santamaria wrote

> I suspect that you enjoy a dialectical scrap as much as I do. At the root of our controversial problem is, I suspect, your feeling that my 'sweet reasonableness' is simply a carefully assumed disguise for the purpose of debate. Perhaps it is — no one can be sure of the objectivity of his own motives. In any case, whether it is or not, I would be very glad if on your next visit to Melbourne you would have lunch with me, so that we might tease some of these points out further under the mellowing influence of good food. I might not be able to convert you to my right-wing aberrations, but at least I can show you a first class Italian cuisine.

Heinz replied: 'I shall be happy to accept your kind invitation at the next opportunity.'

Though their views were miles apart in 1956, a warm friendship grew between the two men with the years and eventually they became close friends. In October 1991, Heinz was invited to attend the fiftieth anniversary celebration of Santamaria's National Civic Council, held at the National Gallery of Victoria. He was overseas at the time and could not attend, but he sent his personal best wishes and said that he hoped it would be 'a splendid occasion, above all, a tribute to you for all you have done in these fifty years. As you know, we do not always agree on everything, but what we agree on seems to me terribly important, and I value your friendship.' When Santamaria died seven years later, Heinz wrote to his widow, explaining that his 'friendship with Bob goes back forty years to his response, firm but courageous, to my Chifley Memorial Lecture. We have not always agreed, but I admired and indeed envied his sharp intellectual and moral courage.'

The Chifley Lecture, from which this correspondence arose, was not concerned for the most part with communism, but with economics. The correspondence itself, however, was concerned primarily with communism, its penetration of Australian trade unions and the ALP and the external threat—particularly communism in China—that it posed for Australia. These were matters of great concern to Santamaria, but for Heinz, as his remarks make clear, much of the alarmism exhibited by the Right, and above all by the Catholic Right, was hysterical nonsense. This was the view that he had come to soon after arriving in Australia, and he held to it steadfastly throughout the 1950s and into the 1960s. He expressed it in his correspondence with Santamaria and stated it even more forcefully in an angry letter he wrote in 1958 to the editor of the *Observer*, Donald Horne. His protagonists were two of the country's leading anti-communists, the poet James McAuley and the philosopher Frank Knopfelmacher. An article that McAuley had contributed to a previous issue of the *Observer* prompted the following complaint from Heinz

> What a sad commentary on the human spirit is provided by the anti-Communist zealots of our time!…Unlike the egregious Mr Knopfelmacher, Mr McAuley is not one of those who recently became Communists or professional anti-Communists (which of the two is largely a matter of accident) because they have never understood the principles or absorbed the spirit of liberal democracy. Mr McAuley is an Australian intellectual raised in the tradition of Western liberalism; he was, and perhaps still is, a distinguished poet. Yet, with what hubris he besmirches the traditions and values to which he once owed allegiance; how recklessly he flirts with the anti-Christ!

To this once fine intellectual the very word 'intellectual' has become a term of abuse. He never nowadays refers to 'Western Liberalism' or 'Liberals' save in tones of pitying contempt. The 'sacred right of self-determination' is mentioned only to be mocked. The British tradition that one of the purposes of political activity is to right wrongs is dismissed as old-fashioned nonsense, an expression of 'exaggerated' or 'pathological guilt-feelings'.

It seems hardly possible that a man of Mr McAuley's undoubted intelligence and integrity should not see how far his furious pursuit of anti-Communism is carrying him towards a psychological position as evil, in all essentials, as that of his Communist allies. Anyone who remembers the views of the great German and Italian exponents of anti-Communism of the inter-war years is bound to sit up when he reads Mr McAuley's proposition that 'political domination of weaker or more backward by stronger states' does not necessarily raise any moral issues but merely reflects 'the needs of their (i.e. the stronger powers') own development'; to them anyone who favours, or admits the possibility of, resolution of political disagreements by peaceful compromise is said to be suffering from the 'liberal mentality' which 'shrinks away from the sharp edges of real conflicts'.

Communists, it is well known, hate social democrats and other moderate reformers more than they hate capitalists. The anti-Communist zealots present a similar phenomenon: their attitude to Communists is that towards enemies whom they understand and, in a sense, respect: liberals (with a small 'l') are the vermin for which they reserve their most venomous fury. And just as Communists tend to forget their original ideals in the unprincipled pursuit of power for its own sake, so to the McAuleys and Knopfelmachers anti-Communism becomes an end in itself in the pursuit of which all other values and ideals fall by the wayside.

If liberalism was all a mistake, if the notion of morality in politics was a pathological aberration, what then is the ultimate point in all this anti-Communism? For all Mr McAuley tells us, it is 'security'—security from Communist aggression; but just what it is that it is worth 'securing' if liberty and decency are the prejudices of 'Western intellectuals' we can only guess' (*The Observer*, May–June 1958).

The effects of the ALP split in the mid 1950s were experienced not only at the national and state levels of the party, but at the branch level. Just as Heinz was drawn into the national debate, so he became embroiled in the divisions that were manifesting themselves in his own ALP branch in Canberra. In 1956, as a result of factional disputes, the Canberra branch—until then the sole branch of the party in the Australian Capital Territory—was divided into two new branches. The undivided branch had been predominantly anti-Evatt (that is, of right-wing persuasion). The new Canberra branch continued to be anti-Evatt, but the other branch, Canberra South, was evenly divided between pro and anti-Evatt forces. Heinz, though not typically right or left-wing (his career hitherto suggested that he was more comfortable with the Right on economic policy and with the Left on the question of communism), had been alarmed at the manoeuvrings in the former Canberra branch by the pro-Evatt side, led by John Burton. Eventually, the party was persuaded to create two branches in the Australian Capital Territory. Heinz was now living in Deakin and his branch was the new South Canberra branch, where the pro-Evatt forces were stronger than they had been in the undivided Canberra branch.

He opposed the creation of this new branch, writing to *The Canberra Times* in September 1956 to say that he favoured the retention of one central branch, since it was doubtful whether new suburban branches would attract additional members or stimulate greater interest among members in local and national affairs, as the advocates of new branches had argued (*Canberra Times*, 25/9/56). Burton proposed new branches as a way of freeing the ALP in Canberra from 'authoritarian control' by a group whose policies he opposed. This, Heinz believed, was 'an attempt by a faction to obtain, through a back door, that power in the Canberra ALP which they have failed to achieve by ordinary democratic methods'. There was 'no foundation whatever,' he argued

> …for the charge that the Branch Executive (of which I have never been a member), has used authoritarian methods to keep us in a minority or prevent our views from being heard. If Dr Burton and his friends took the trouble to attend Branch meetings and showed as much energy in recruiting new members as those whose views he opposes have done in recent years, his complaints would carry more conviction.

As it was, Heinz lost the battle, and the Canberra South branch was established.

By 1958, however, divisions in the Canberra South branch appeared to have healed. For the November election of that year, Heinz helped the branch to draft an economic policy platform, which was to feed into the national election planning process. He wrote that the economic policies set out in the platform

> ...do not constitute a socialist policy because the Branch believes that a Socialist program is not practical politics in Australia in 1958. Neither, however, are the proposals designed to catch votes by expensive promises which cannot be carried out; they constitute an honest program of reforms which can be defended on its merits, apart from considerations of political expediency.

This was nothing less than the approach to economic policy that Heinz had been trying to persuade the party to adopt for many years. Included in the detail was a proposal to establish a Royal Commission to investigate the Australian taxation system; restoration of the 1951–52 share of public investment in the gross national product (which had fallen from 10 per cent to 8 per cent between 1951–52 and 1956–57); the establishment of a Government Finance Corporation to invest in industrial enterprises; resistance to any further weakening of the Commonwealth Bank; the formation of a Commonwealth Development Bank; a request to the states to refer their powers over hire-purchase credit to the Commonwealth; and the creation of a monopolies commission.

Perhaps because the ALP adopted some of his proposals, Heinz wrote at the outset of the election campaign in October 1958 to congratulate Evatt 'on your excellent policy speech and to wish you and the Party the best for November 22'. He went on to acknowledge that 'I have not always seen eye to eye with you in economic policy matters in recent years', but he wished Evatt to know that he 'would go practically all the way with you on this program'. He mentioned that he would be in India in the weeks immediately preceding the election, and indeed on the day itself. 'However', he wanted Evatt to know that 'I shall be watching developments at home excitedly and look forward to great news on November 23'. Once again, however, Heinz was disappointed with Labor's defeat, writing to Wilf Salter[18] from India about the 'lousy stinking election result'. Though the result was disheartening, at least it meant the end of Evatt's leadership of the party (he had now led the ALP to three election defeats, two of them by wide margins) and, while his replacement, Arthur Calwell, was not a person for whom Heinz had much time, there was the chance of a fresh start.

By the time the next election came around in December 1961, the ALP's economic platform had moved even closer to Heinz's point of view. After the election, he wrote to David Rowan:[19] 'I confess that I am now much happier in supporting Labor on economic policy (than say, two years ago).' So pleased was he with the ALP's election platform and its vigorous campaign that he wrote to Calwell to congratulate him 'on your near-victory in the elections which has given us all new courage'.

Foreign policy appears to have attracted less of Heinz's attention in the years immediately after his move to Canberra than it had done in the years before. But there were two events about which he did make his views felt. He opposed strongly the actions of Britain and France during the Suez crisis of 1956. As he wrote to the American Bob Ratchford, an economist friend at Duke University in North Carolina

> …most of us academics do not see eye to eye with Mr Menzies in his avid support for Eden's maniacal adventure. Initially, it was difficult to find anyone in Australia who supported the British resort to force; gradually the tale that it anticipated Russian aggression in the Middle East was, as usual, successful in enlisting some support. As in Britain, so here, the conservatives who support Eden are working off steam in violent diatribes against the USA. I, for once, find myself in full support of US foreign policy on the immediate issue, though I agree with the critics that American failure earlier to take the Middle East problem seriously, the subordination of tactics in the Middle East to Cold War strategy, must bear much responsibility for the whole mess, particularly the dreadful position in which Israel found herself earlier this year.

Heinz was critical, too, of the position that Australia and other Western countries had taken against India's so-called 'police action' in Goa—an action aimed at dislodging the Portuguese, who had refused repeated requests by India to hand over the small colonial territory to the new nation. He was especially incensed by the position that Calwell had adopted. He admonished Calwell for attacking India's failure to act in concert with the United Nations. Heinz would have preferred India to have waited until it had secured the approval of the United Nations, but as a matter of principle, he believed that Portugal's rights to Goa were no better than Britain's rights had been to India or France's to Indo-China. He reminded Calwell that Goa had become an international problem because Portugal had refused to follow Britain and France in effecting a voluntary and peaceful withdrawal from India. Instead, it had maintained an authoritarian regime in the colony and, indeed, in all of its overseas territories.

Nehru, India's prime minister, had spent 14 years trying to settle the issue by peaceful means and on occasions had sought the assistance of the United Nations. Heinz thought that Calwell had been less than fair to India when he compared India's action in Goa with China's invasion of Tibet. 'I agree with you that the Labor Party must uphold the principles of the United Nations and condemn resort to force,' he said, '[but] I believe it is equally important that it should be fair in its pronouncements on disputes in which friendly neighbours of Australia are involved, and in particular that it should recognise the point of view of the countries that have recently gained national independence.'

When Heinz had moved to Canberra and had secured Australian citizenship he looked forward to joining the ALP. Once he became a member, he was never an uncritical adherent of party orthodoxy, yet he rarely questioned his continuing membership of the party. As the years passed, however, the party's position on foreign policy became an issue of increasing concern to him. On 16 July 1971, he submitted his resignation in a letter addressed to the president of the Canberra South branch. Heinz wrote

> In 1954, during the Petrov Royal Commission, the late Dr Evatt put a nail in the coffin of a distinguished political career by writing a letter to Molotov. It was an extraordinary lapse of political judgment, due perhaps to failing health, perhaps to the psychological consequences of excessive frustration of years as Leader of the Opposition. But, extraordinary as it was, the Molotov

letter was less serious, less damaging to Australia, than the behaviour of Mr Whitlam in Peking [Beijing] last month.

Dr Evatt merely wrote a letter. He did not go to Moscow to give Molotov an opportunity for a significant propaganda victory against the West. He did not display any gross servility, he did not openly take sides against the United States, he did not cast aspersions on Japan, ridicule the Philippines and Thailand, denounce the Government of Cambodia, and offer to sell Taiwan down the river. He did not give Molotov an opportunity to say how much he would welcome a Labor Government in Australia.

I have been a member of the A.L.P. for over twenty years. I still find myself in agreement with many of the domestic objectives of the Party and I have been heartened by the evidence of constructive and progressive policy making at the recent Federal Conference. I believe, with many others, that Australia urgently needs a credible alternative Government.

But I have been increasingly unhappy in the last few years about the drift to the left in the Party's foreign policy. Mr Whitlam's posturing in Peking, humiliating to any Australian, has finally convinced me that I cannot any longer remain a member of the Party.

With deep regret I must ask the Branch to accept my resignation.

While Whitlam's visit to China and his declaration in Beijing that a future Labor government under his leadership would recognise the communist government of China provided the occasion for Heinz's resignation, Heinz had for some years been a critic of the party's opposition to Australia's involvement in the Vietnam War. He supported the defence of South Vietnam by the United States and its allies on the grounds that it was 'both right in principle and in the interest of the West'. He wrote an article for *Woroni*, the ANU Students' Association newspaper, in which he endorsed the war. This led to questions being asked about the retention of his membership of the ALP.

At the time of his resignation he still supported the ALP's economic and social policies, but he became increasingly critical of these policies, too. When he was on leave at the OECD in Paris in 1972 he observed the failure of the 'Phillips curve' approach to macroeconomic policy as 'stagflation' began to take hold in industrial countries. The coincidence of inflation and unemployment led him to lose his faith in Keynesianism. He was to write in 1985: 'If the Phillips Curve trade-off between inflation and unemployment no longer worked, if expansionary monetary–fiscal policies were much more likely to accelerate inflation rather [than] increase output and employment, the centrepiece of the Keynesian prescription collapsed.'

The expansion of the public sector and the acceleration of inflation during the Whitlam years were also matters of great concern to him, leading him eventually to the writings of Milton Friedman, James Buchanan, Gordon Tullock, Friedrich Hayek and Colin Clark. As a consequence of reading the work of these and other economic liberals and libertarians, Heinz was 'gradually persuaded that the monetarist analysis was as essential to an understanding of the inflationary process of the 1970s as the Keynesian analysis had been for our understanding of under-employment in the 1930s'.

He was ready to become a public intellectual once again. He joined the advisory boards of organisations such as the Centre for Independent Studies (a conservative think-tank established by a former Sydney schoolteacher, Greg Lindsay) and the Australian Lecture Foundation (which sponsored lecture tours in Australia by well-known conservative thinkers). When Zelman Cowen was appointed Governor-General of Australia in 1977, Heinz succeeded him as president of the Australian Association for Cultural Freedom. This organisation sponsored the monthly politics and cultural magazine, *Quadrant*. Heinz had begun to write for the magazine in 1969, later becoming a regular contributor; in 1981, he was appointed its co-editor. He continued to write for the magazine until his death.

14
ECONOMICS AND POLICY

At Canberra University College, Heinz continued to teach macroeconomics. At first, he took responsibility for the Economics B course, which covered in the first term the theory of income determination and trade-cycle theory. The second term included money and banking, while the third term included international trade and international finance (some lectures on economic development were added later). But as the college gained greater autonomy from Melbourne for the courses it taught, Economics B became Economics 111; by this time, Heinz was also giving lectures in Economics 1 (the first-year economics course). He lectured as well on public finance, took some honours classes, did more than his fair share of supervising candidates for the Master of Commerce degree and taught the economics component of Manning Clark's course on Australian affairs for diplomatic cadets working in the Department of External Affairs. He was scarcely exaggerating when he told Ron Barback that he had 'rather a lot' of teaching to do during his early years at CUC.

This heavy teaching load did not, however, diminish his publication record. On the contrary, between 1951 and 1963, he wrote one book and edited another, contributed three book chapters, published 34 articles and gave three high-profile public lectures. In all, this amounted to some 42 publications, at an average of 3.5 publications a year. And that total excludes various *ad hoc* lectures and talks, regular contributions to weekly and monthly publications, commentaries for ABC radio and the unpublished work he undertook while on leave in India and Geneva.

It also omits the articles he prepared in the early 1950s for a popular Australian encyclopaedia. The publishers of the *Melbourne Herald* had purchased from the London *Daily Mail* the rights to a British encyclopaedia that had been published in the 1930s. It had to be updated and a considerable number of entries on Australia were to be added. Heinz was commissioned to write entries on economics and finance. While he subcontracted some of the work, he did the bulk of it himself and it absorbed much of the 1952–53 summer vacation. He estimated that he had revised some 40,000 words and had written from scratch 47,000 words on 120 different topics. For his pains, he duly received, as he put it, 'a fat cheque'. When he completed the work, however, he wondered whether it had been worthwhile. To Geoffrey Serle, he lamented that he felt 'like a row of exhausted volcanoes'.

When Heinz had arrived in Canberra he was disappointed that the Workers' Educational Association did not operate in the national capital. With others, he helped to arrange adult education classes at CUC; later the classes were to become part of the ANU's Centre for Continuing Education.

In 1953, as a result of his interest in adult education, he arranged a short series of lectures on 'The economic background to life in Australia today'. Several of his colleagues agreed to participate, with Heinz delivering lectures on banking, full employment, inflation and the balance of payments. Three years later, he organised a public seminar on 'Australia's external trade', for which he engaged several prominent speakers, among them James Meade (who was visiting the ANU from London) and Trevor Swan; Heinz summed up. In 1958, he organised a conference on Australia's import policy and the next year he arranged a public seminar on 'The developing Australian money market', to which he presented a paper with the title 'Some questions about an Australian money market'. Also in 1959, he was invited to give the prestigious ES&A Bank Lecture at the University of Queensland. His subject was 'The banks and the capital market', in which he examined the recent diversification of the Australian capital market, including the emergence of hire-purchase companies, finance companies and investment banks. Meanwhile, he continued to contribute to Allan Fraser's *Australian Observer* and, when that ceased publication, he wrote for *Voice*.

In addition to teaching, research and various outreach activities, Heinz proved a diligent administrator. Now, as the head of an academic department, he was responsible for its academic programs and staff recruitment. His colleagues in the Department of Economics included at various times throughout the 1950s Burge Cameron (who was eventually to succeed him as head of department and Dean of the Faculty of Economics), Roy Cameron, Ron Barback, Hugh Hudson, Ron Heiser, John Head, Max Neutze, Ian MacDougall, Keith Sloane, Colin Forster and John Pitchford. Slowly, the number of full-time students at CUC increased. In April 1957, Heinz told Barback, with some pride, that the college that year had been 'remarkably transformed' by a sudden jump in the number of full-time students to about 50. A buttery, serving meals to students, had been established, the library was 'full of students working during the day' and the place was generally 'a hive of activity'.

Often he was called on to serve on the CUC council. There he made his mark by opposing the council's attempt to suspend study leave for financial reasons. He urged the council to adopt the principle that each application for leave should be treated on its merits. He also resisted an attempt by the council to have general staff sign a time book when they arrived at work, and again when they departed for the day; he thought it should be left entirely to supervisors of individual staff to make rules about such matters.

Offers occasionally came his way to take up positions at other universities, but he never seriously considered leaving CUC. In September 1954, Dick Downing informed him that he was being considered for the Sidney Myer Chair at the University of Melbourne. Heinz thought about it, prompted by the parlous financial state of the college, the uncertainty about its association with the University of Melbourne and the possibility of CUC being absorbed by the ANU. In the end, he told Downing that he had little desire to move to Melbourne.

Before Heinz went to Canberra, he thought that one of the great benefits of working there would be the opportunity to attend seminars and participate in discussion groups at the ANU. This turned out to be the case. He quickly became a member of a group assembled by Trevor Swan, who had been appointed Professor of Economics at the ANU just a few months before Heinz's appointment at CUC. The group included all the academic economists in Canberra, together with five or six senior economists employed in the public service. In 1951, under Swan's direction, the group decided to focus its discussion on the two-volume *Surveys of Contemporary Economics* (1948) edited by Howard Ellis and Bernard Haley, a collection of essays by various authors aimed at summing up the state of the discipline at the midpoint of the twentieth century.

A member of the group was selected before each meeting to present opening comments based on a chapter from the book. When Heinz's time came to open discussion, he chose as the subject of his talk 'Interest as a functional share of income'. He thought his introductory remarks were 'a complete flop', claiming that 'Trevor [Swan] and Horrie Brown[20] [had] demolished some of my arguments'. Even so, he welcomed the opportunity to discuss with his ANU colleagues and others contemporary theoretical issues on a more elevated plane than had been possible in Sydney. To Noel Butlin, he wrote that the discussion 'is on a fairly high level, with Trevor cracking the whip, and I am learning a good deal'.

As well as getting to know Swan, Brown and other economists whom Swan was assembling at ANU's Research School of Social Sciences, Heinz was able frequently to meet and talk with D.B. Copland, the ANU's Vice-Chancellor. On one occasion, Copland asked Heinz to prepare for him a paper that Copland had been invited to deliver at a conference in Brussels sponsored by the Economic League for European Cooperation, an organisation that Heinz thought was 'rather absurd'. For Heinz, another benefit of CUC's close proximity to the ANU was the opportunity to meet and talk with distinguished international visitors to Swan's department, including Meade, Balogh, Frank Paish, Donald MacDougall, Arthur Smithies, Eric Lindhal and Eric Lundberg.

Each time a new professor took up his appointment at CUC, he was obliged to present an inaugural lecture, which members of the public could attend. Heinz accepted this responsibility without hesitation. He chose 'The unimportance of money' as the title of his lecture. It highlighted the waxing and waning of monetary policy and drew extensively on the historical literature on the subject. Conforming to the dominant paradigm of the time, Heinz sought to downgrade the effectiveness of monetary policy for the purpose of short-term economic management.

It was unfortunate, however, that the lecture coincided with renewed support for monetary intervention, for on the same day that Heinz delivered his lecture, a general election was held in Britain, which was won by the Conservative Party. The new Chancellor of the Exchequer, R.A. Butler, soon announced a significant rise in interest rates, effectively ending the postwar era of cheap money. That was one embarrassment arising from the inaugural lecture. Another came from the London satirical magazine *Punch*, which, in its Charivaria column, made merry with the lecture's title and with an advertising notice announcing that entrance to the lecture was free. 'As if it mattered,' *Punch* commented (Arndt 1958:23).

Despite *Punch's* mockery, the lecture attracted considerable attention within the economics profession. Some of it was favourable and some of it was highly critical. Heinz sent copies to a number of the world's leading economists, among them Joan Robinson and Dennis Robertson. Robinson thought it was an 'excellent inaugural lecture', informing Heinz that she agreed 'pretty much with all you say'. Her only criticism was that, while Heinz was right to support the dethroning of interest rates, he had not accorded sufficient importance to the supply of finance, especially 'in connection with problems of development'. Heinz agreed, replying to Robinson that 'the comments of others, too, have convinced me that I failed to redress the balance of my argument, after tipping it unduly one way—chiefly, for the sake of vulgar dramatic effect. That is one of the difficulties of public lectures. Even as it was, two-thirds of my audience gave up the ghost halfway through.'

Dennis Robertson, too, wrote to congratulate him on the choice of his subject, saying that he had 'read the lecture with deep interest, and—as perhaps you will expect—alternating sensations of agreement and disagreement'. He endorsed the emphasis that Heinz had directed to the see-saw importance and unimportance of money—the central theme of the lecture—but he thought Heinz had exaggerated the amplitude of the swings in each direction. A similar criticism came from Frank Mauldon, who was convinced that Heinz had overplayed the twists and turns in intellectual fashion, declaring that he hesitated 'to believe that the downfall of monetary theory and policy is as complete and permanent as you suggest'. Heinz again conceded that he had probably 'overstated the downfall of money—tempted, I fear, by a vulgar craving for dramatic effect'.

Throughout the 1940s, Heinz had strongly supported the retention of cheap money, preferring fiscal policy to monetary policy for managing aggregate demand. After the inaugural lecture, however, he began to express doubts about the efficacy of cheap money, especially as it became clear to him that the fears he had held about the probability of a postwar slump were misplaced. In 1955, he confessed to David Rowan: 'You are probably right in saying that a more active interest policy in 1949/51 would have been a good thing, though I am acutely conscious of having opposed any such policy at the time.'

Even earlier, in his correspondence with Dennis Robertson, he had admitted that while 'I still do not like Bank Rate at 4%...I am prepared to be shown that at bottom my reasons have little to do with economics and they may not, in the last resort, stand up to cool rational dissection.' When, some years later, Heinz sent Robertson a copy of his Istanbul lectures on monetary policy, Robertson correctly detected a change in Heinz's position since the inaugural lecture. 'I think we are in closer agreement than we should have been some years ago,' Robertson wrote, 'though not perhaps very close, even now.'

Though Heinz might have softened his views somewhat on monetary policy, he was still convinced that fiscal policy should be retained as the dominant policy instrument for the management of aggregate demand. Governments, he felt, should consciously adjust taxation and expenditure policies to maintain full employment and control inflation. This belief drew him into a fierce debate with Colin Clark about the latter's contention that 25 per cent should be regarded as the upper limit of taxation on incomes. Beyond that rate, Clark had contended, incentives to work would plummet and income would consequently diminish. Clark's advocacy of a 25 per cent limit had been a direct response to the Menzies government's 'horror budget' of 1951, which sent taxes climbing, the intention being to reduce inflation and imports. Heinz had supported the tax imposts, asserting that it was better to raise taxes than to cut government expenditure on essential services. He was especially critical of those commentators—and there were many—who called for reductions in public spending without specifying the particular activities that should be cut; to him, this was intellectually irresponsible.

In a letter published in the *Sydney Morning Herald* in August 1951, Heinz challenged Clark's views, arguing that

> [The] question of the effects of taxation on the incentive to produce is essentially a matter of judgement. No doubt, beyond a point, taxation of marginal income has such effects but we have no concrete knowledge of their magnitude. It was very doubtful whether taxation has hitherto been a significant contributing factor to low production and whether even substantial increases in personal income taxation would make an appreciable difference to people's willingness to work. In some cases, increases in taxation (particularly indirect taxation), by increasing the effort necessary to secure a customary living standard, may actually increase people's willingness to work (*Sydney Morning Herald*, 6/8/51).

For Heinz, the central issue for government was the impact of taxation on aggregate spending. It was 'unquestionable', he asserted, 'that the deflationary effects of increases in taxation would far outweigh any inflationary disincentive effects of tax increases'.

Heinz had thought that being a professor of economics in Canberra would create opportunities for him to advise government agencies and even perhaps the government itself. His interest in contemporary macroeconomic theory and policy, and the relevance of this interest to an academic appointment in economics in the national capital, had been raised during the selection process that led to his appointment. He soon discovered that the new Coalition government had no intention of calling on his expertise. When he expressed his disappointment in a letter to Gerald Firth, he identified three possible reasons for the situation. One was the fact that the Commonwealth Public Service itself now employed some of Australia's leading economists, among them Roland Wilson, J.G. Crawford and Ronald Walker. Another was that a high proportion of the generation of economists who had graduated from universities in the 1930s—and Heinz was one—were on the left of politics, and were therefore out of tune with the current government. A third possibility was the new expectations of academics: the 'unwritten code of academic ethics which frowns on participation in public affairs'. This code, as Heinz explained it to Gerald Firth

> ...is a real difficulty because I have gradually become convinced of the truth (sad as it is) of the view that keen involvement in day-to-day controversy is inimical to the spirit of scholarship and scientific enquiry.
> ...The fact remains that anybody who does...incurs the displeasure not only of the community which dislikes what he tells them but also of the academic profession which regards all such activities as *infra dig*.

Nevertheless, Heinz refused to obey strictly the new code. Instead, he continued to express his opinions on issues of public policy and contemporary politics, but he was never asked to advise an Australian government until Malcolm Fraser's accession to The Lodge in 1975.

In his writing and commentaries on economic policy throughout his years at CUC, Heinz continued for the most part to express conventional 'Keynesian' views. For him, excess demand was the outstanding economic problem of these years. An active fiscal policy, assisted in a minor way perhaps by monetary policy, was necessary to reduce inflation. Not only did Australia suffer during the 1950s and early 1960s from internal imbalance, it experienced external imbalance. Again, he thought the principal reason for balance of payments pressures was excess domestic demand, though he conceded that a part of the problem was the slow growth in demand for Australia's traditional export products. Rather than clinging to import controls as a mechanism for shoring up the external accounts, Heinz advocated the replacement of controls by devaluation and supported regular adjustments to the exchange rate. It was important, he stressed, that any devaluation should be accompanied by cuts in domestic demand, otherwise the beneficial effects of devaluation would be dissipated by further inflation, thereby prolonging external imbalance rather than resolving it.

A significant aspect of Australia's problem of external imbalance was the shortage of US dollars. Heinz had devoted a good deal of his time when he was at the University of Sydney to thinking about this problem. He continued to do so in his early years at CUC. It was clearer to him now than it had been in his Sydney days that the dollar shortage derived from excess demand in countries such as Britain and Australia. In an article he sent to *The Argus* in January 1952 (though it appears not to have been published), he explained

> [The] remedy to the dollar problem in Britain, Australia and other countries is identical with the well-known remedies to domestic inflation, because fundamentally both are aspects of the same problem: trying to do too much with the resources we have.
>
> We must try to expand production, for export as well as for our own requirements. Meanwhile we must somehow or other cut down money demand (spending). And that means cutting down *either* consumer spending (by taxation or hire purchase restrictions or a brake on wage and profit increases) or civilian (business and government) spending on capital equipment for industrial expansion and development or defence spending—*or* a combination of all three.

During the late 1940s and early 1950s, he urged the government to adjust the exchange rate on a number of occasions. Not only did he consider that if sterling was devalued in the late 1940s (as it was) the Australian currency should depreciate against the US dollar, he believed that the Australian pound should be revalued against sterling. Among the measures he recommended in 1951, when inflation reached heights never before experienced (nor repeated since), was the revaluation of the Australian pound. In August 1951, he wrote

> The reason why I suggest that an appreciation of the Australian pound should contribute to the control of inflation is that it would reduce the incomes of primary producers, on the one hand, and would reduce import prices on the other. The first effect would help in cutting down one source of external demand and the second by counteracting one source of cost inflation…[however] I would not favour appreciation unless it was accompanied by a comprehensive set of anti-inflationary measures, such as all round increases in taxation, and further credit restrictions.

Even so, while he supported an adjustable peg regime for exchange rates, and while he supported exchange-rate adjustments in certain circumstances, he refused to endorse a free market for foreign exchange. This was because governments, he thought, would not be prepared to eliminate excess demand. In these circumstances, a free exchange market would lead to a depreciation of the Australian pound, further inflation would result and soon another devaluation would be necessary.

This interest in the exchange rate led him to consider the question of convertibility of sterling currencies, including the convertibility of the Australian pound. In 1954, Leslie Melville published a controversial article in *Australian Quarterly*, in which he proposed that the Australian pound should be made immediately convertible into other currencies. Dr H.C. Coombs, the central bank governor, asked Heinz to provide him with an independent evaluation of Melville's analysis, perhaps because Melville's protégés continued to dominate the central bank's Economic Department. Heinz was impressed at first with Melville's argument, reporting to Coombs that his initial reaction 'was to wilt under the persuasive power of Melville's style'. On reflection, however, he began to see difficulties with it. Melville had argued that inconvertibility, together with trade and payments discrimination by the Sterling Area,[21] was inhibiting the growth of the Australian economy. For example, there were difficulties in purchasing machines and materials in the cheapest markets, especially from the United States. Instead, Australia was forced to rely on inefficient, high-cost suppliers in the Sterling Area, particularly in the United Kingdom.

On balance, Heinz agreed that 'we should aim at the earliest practical restoration of full convertibility and elimination of the obviously restrictive forms of discrimination'. Hence, he supported Melville's general conclusion, but he disagreed with Melville's timetable. An immediate return to convertibility at the present exchange rate, he argued, would require a 'savage deflation' to preserve external balance. He agreed that some deflation was certainly warranted, since a state of over-full employment existed; prices were accelerating and there was pressure on the overseas reserves. But the degree of deflation that would be needed to achieve immediate convertibility, he concluded, would induce unacceptable levels of unemployment.

Heinz explained to Coombs that there were three ways by which Australian costs and prices could be reduced in order to achieve convertibility: deflation, devaluation and increased productivity. Melville's timetable, he believed, would require a drastic deflation: Australian industries would be 'hammered' into efficiency by 'the forces of US, German and Japanese competition'. In short, the 'gamble was too risky'. What Heinz preferred was a period of constructive preparation for convertibility. This would involve greater discipline regarding domestic policy, whereby appropriate fiscal and monetary policy would serve to eliminate inflationary pressures. Heinz also favoured promulgating a drive to enhance productivity, with priority given to investment over consumption, and he hoped that special efforts would be made to attract international capital into Australia on reasonable terms. Above all, a suitable date should be chosen for a devaluation of the Australian currency and a program devised for the gradual relaxation of discrimination and inconvertibility.

In the event, there was no immediate convertibility of sterling, or of the Australian pound. Rather, the finance ministers of Sterling Area countries set in place a gradual program aimed at restoring convertibility. This was exactly what Heinz had recommended to Coombs, though the actual timetable for convertibility had nothing to do with Heinz's advice. Full convertibility of the leading Sterling Area currencies was finally achieved by the end of the 1950s.

While it is true that Heinz was never asked to furnish advice to the government or its agencies before the 1970s, he was one of the senior economists from Australian universities who met regularly throughout the 1950s and early 1960s to advise the Governor of the Commonwealth Bank (later the Reserve Bank). The group generally met twice a year, though later the meetings were reduced to once a year. Each meeting initially occupied a day and a half and its purpose was to provide Coombs with independent advice about the state of the Australian economy and an assessment of current policy. Such advice, Coombs believed, would be particularly useful in his battles with the Treasury and its formidable head, Roland Wilson.

On the first day of these meetings, discussion tended to range widely over trends and events, in Australia and overseas. After dinner, it usually fell to Heinz to retire early to his hotel room to write up the major conclusions of the discussion. This task he happily accepted, though it often meant that he had to work into the small hours of the morning. On some occasions he would invite one or more of his colleagues to assist him. His summary would then lead to further discussion during the morning of the second day. In later years, one of the group would usually be invited, before the meeting, to prepare a paper surveying the state of the Australian economy. It would be circulated prior to the meeting and would form the basis of discussion. The paper would then be amended in the light of comments. After further revision and polishing, each paper was published in the *Economic Record*, as part of its famous 'Survey of the Australian economy' series.

These meetings were abandoned in the mid 1960s, when the number of professors of economics in Australian universities began to rise and it thus became invidious to invite some but not others. There was another reason why the meetings were terminated. The Treasury—and in particular Wilson, who was a member of the bank's board—had become increasingly suspicious about the purpose and nature of the meetings. The problem reached its apogee in the early 1960s, when Coombs on several occasions had the temerity to invite senior members of the Department of Trade to participate in the discussions. Why, Wilson wanted to know, was the Department of Trade represented at these meetings, which were meant to involve university economists, when the Treasury was not?

At any rate, the meetings, while they lasted, allowed Heinz to express his views on economic policy to the nation's senior central bankers. They also gave him special access to information about economic conditions in Australia and overseas.

It is unclear whether the views he expressed at the meetings had any long-term impact on government thinking. There was, however, one occasion when, in concert with other university economists, Heinz appears to have had just such an impact. In 1956, he signed the so-called 'Economists' Manifesto', a document drafted largely by Peter Karmel at the University of Adelaide. Published in April 1956 and entitled 'The Outlook for the Australian economy', its aim was to put pressure on the government to introduce measures aimed at curtailing domestic demand at a time of rising prices and imports. The government had tried to do something about these problems during the previous year, though in a rather half-hearted manner. In September 1955, Heinz reported to Balogh in Oxford: 'Economic affairs have suddenly leapt into the headlines here. Menzies is due to report in Parliament tonight on his get-togethers and gentlemen's agreements of the past fortnight and announce his Government's policy which, inadequate as it is, will be attacked for diametrically wrong reasons by Evatt.'

But the government failed to act in a decisive way. As economic conditions deteriorated into 1956, Karmel decided to produce what became the Economists' Manifesto. This called on the government to introduce measures to combat inflation and restore balance-of-payments stability. Karmel secured the signatures of eight of Australia's leading economists: Arndt, Black, Cochran, Downing, Firth, Prest, Swan and himself.

Heinz, and several of the others, had been arguing for some months that the government needed to increase taxation (so as to constrain spending on consumption) and to tighten monetary policy for the purpose of dissuading private investment (which had increased by 25 per cent in the previous two years). Demand had begun to spill over onto imports; import controls had been tightened, but the economists contended that this was dealing with a symptom, rather than with the problem itself. As government investment spending had not been rising rapidly, and because there was a desperate need to implement various infrastructure projects, the document opposed cuts in government spending. It also dismissed direct controls as a solution for excess demand. 'While some of us might favour resort to direct controls as [being] more effective and discriminatory than over-all monetary measures', the manifesto concluded that 'the climate of political opinion and constitutional obstacles make it highly unlikely that direct controls would in fact be introduced. In these circumstances, advocacy of direct controls is, in effect, a do-nothing policy.'

The immediate reaction to the call to reduce aggregate demand, principally by raising taxes and interest rates, was largely negative. Perhaps the best summary of the hostility the manifesto aroused came from the Sydney evening tabloid the *Daily Mirror*, which dismissed the economists' analysis and policy proposals by thundering that the 'theorists are at it again', and recommended that 'no one should take the slightest notice of them' (*Daily Mirror*, 1/2/56). Heinz was disgusted with this response and informed Barback

> None of the papers printed it [the manifesto] in full (except the [*Australian*] *Financial Review*) but they did print a spate of virulently or condescendingly hostile editorial comment and columns of solicited attacks by lobbyists, taxpayers' bodies, etc. In the more respectable papers, there ensued quite a lot of correspondence (almost all of it critical of us, except our own contributions to it), a long and vicious article specially written for the Sydney *Daily Mirror* by Colin Clark (saying among other things that all public works in Australia, other than those for agriculture, power and transport, ought to be completely eliminated), cartoons (about the 'woolly-headed' theorists), much comment in *Hansard*, etc.

Despite the unsympathetic public reaction, there was a significant outcome to the manifesto. The Prime Minister appointed a committee to advise the government on what it should do; the committee comprised Wilson, Coombs, Melville and Swan, with four businessmen to balance the four economists. It reported to the economic committee of Cabinet, which in turn reported to the full Cabinet. The result was that all the proposals in the Economists' Manifesto were hurriedly introduced, except, as Heinz put it, 'the not unimportant one that personal income tax has not been raised, so that the taxes actually imposed are, by and large, very regressive, particularly the additional excise duties on beer and tobacco and also petrol'. Evatt's reaction to the government's measures, Heinz was quick to note, 'has been as irresponsible as usual'. In fact, it was Evatt's response, economically illiterate and politically opportunistic, that led Heinz to comment in his Chifley Lecture a few months after the government's supplementary budget: 'It is high time Labor took the problem of inflation as seriously as it has always taken the problems of deflation and unemployment.'

When the next surge in prices and imports began in 1960, Heinz sought once more to persuade the government that it should take appropriate fiscal and monetary measures to deflate aggregate demand. In February, he sent a letter to *The Canberra Times*, in which he asserted that the Commonwealth should seek constitutional powers to control prices. His point was that such controls should be used to restrain monopolies, not to suppress inflation. To control inflation, he argued that the 'all-embracing system of controls that would be needed would involve great administrative difficulties. While price control could be used to squeeze profits, it could not keep the price level stable if the level of wage costs were allowed to rise significantly faster than productivity' (*Canberra Times*, 22/2/60).

Instead of favouring price controls, Heinz remained adamant that the 'answer to price inflation is a budget and monetary policy which prevents the level of spending from outrunning available supplies of goods and services.' And rather than adjusting wages for cost-of-living increases— which would simply increase prices still further—he argued that the growth of wages should be confined to the growth of productivity. He tried to enlist Karmel in another economists' manifesto, but Karmel declined. He then consulted Coombs, Swan and Horrie Brown, telling Karmel that Coombs 'seemed sympathetic to the idea of another economists' manifesto'. Swan had reservations, though he was not opposed to it providing he did not have to do any work, while Brown 'was very abusive indeed'.

Heinz's most important single publication during the 1950s was his book *The Australian Trading Banks*, which appeared in 1957. He had thought about writing a substantial work on the Australian capital market ever since he began to lecture on money and banking at Sydney University in the mid 1940s. In the event, the book covered only a part of the capital market, but he managed to publish several articles on other aspects of the capital market before and after the book was published. One of these was an article with Philip Shrapnel, one of his postgraduate students, on consumer credit in Australia; another article covered the Australian bond market.

The earliest reference in Heinz's papers to what eventually became *The Australian Trading Banks* was a note of November 1952 headed 'Framework for a study of the capital market'. This was an outline of a proposed investigation of Australian capital markets, the stated objective being 'to present a national picture of all significant aggregates of lending and borrowing transactions which accompany the process of production, distribution and disposal of national income'.

More specifically, the idea was to start with consumer credit, and since there was very limited information about that, he decided to construct a questionnaire to elicit the information himself. The results, however, were disappointing. He mentioned to Roy Cameron in October 1952 that, as a result of a shortage of data, he would have to rely 'on rather roundabout and precarious procedures. What I will do next, I do not quite know yet.' He thought he might try to obtain a direct estimate of the sources of lendable funds, including personal and other saving. In December 1952, he wrote again to Roy Cameron

> I am now contemplating, as a further instalment of the projected long-term study of the Australian capital market, a sort of annual series of aggregate balance sheets for the economy as a whole, as a framework for an estimate of credit transactions. I am interested in working out the principle of the thing even though it will obviously be impossible to fill more than a small proportion of the squares of the matrix.

Heinz made little headway with the project before he left for the United States at the end of 1953, and by the time he returned to Australia in the middle of 1954 he still had not achieved much towards it. By the end of that year he decided that he would have to put his head down and make a strong effort to finish the project. In December, he wrote to Gordon Bruns, at the ANZ Bank: 'I am hoping to get on with the main work now, which is intended to be a fairly comprehensive work on the Australian financial system and capital market.' At much the same time, he was informing Roy Cameron that he had 'made some effort, since my return, to get down to work on the long projected book on the Australian financial system, but the distractions are numerous'. These distractions included a talk he gave to the Canberra branch of the Economic Society on the development of the American South; the preparation of a course of lectures on public finance (which he shared with Burge Cameron); the reply to Melville's article on convertibility; a note on balance-of-payments equilibrium for the *Economic Record*; a paper for the Australian Institute of Political Science Summer School in January 1955; and work on a paper on 'Immigration and the post-war economy', which he hoped to deliver at a conference of the International Economic Association in August. In February 1955, he announced to Barback: 'I have been going on with my work on the capital market and am now in the throes of bringing together some information on the trading banks. A visit each to Sydney and Melbourne has been very fruitful in that direction.'

In an effort to hasten the work, he successfully applied in 1955 for a Social Science Research Council (SSRC) research grant. Originally, he intended to have another try at working with a research assistant, but he failed to find one with the necessary experience and qualifications; consequently, he decided to return the grant. He had stated in the grant application that his aim was to undertake a 'comprehensive descriptive and analytical study of the present-day financial system of Australia, to serve as a textbook for students and for the interested public'. Despite the research assistant's absence, Alan Hall, Heinz's former pupil at Sydney and now a member of Trevor Swan's department, agreed to collaborate with him in preparing those sections of the book that would deal with the new issues market.

On a Melbourne visit in May 1955, Heinz met Dr Andrew Fabinyi, the head of the publishing firm F.W. Cheshire. During the meeting, Fabinyi asked him whether he had a book in progress that Cheshire might consider publishing. When Heinz returned to Canberra, he considered Fabinyi's question and wondered whether he would ever complete the planned work on the Australian capital market. He had just finished a major section covering the foreign exchange business of the trading banks. The material was so extensive that he came to the conclusion that he could produce a book devoted solely to the trading banks. He wrote to Fabinyi asking whether Cheshire might be interested in publishing such a book. Nothing comprehensive, he pointed out, had been written about the Australian banking system since the Royal Commission of 1936–37. He thought the book he had in mind could be completed in about 12 months and he was confident that it would attract a wide market, including bankers, students and the general public.

In the wake of this proposal, Heinz informed Fabinyi that he had a second book for Cheshire to consider: a book of essays on aspects of Australian economic policy. Some of them had already been published as articles in *Voice* and the *Australian Observer*, but a few were entirely new. Altogether, Heinz listed 13 essays and sent them to Fabinyi, admitting that this volume would probably not attract as large a readership as the book on the banks. Fabinyi was impressed with the essays, thinking that they constituted 'a more humanistic and more civilized approach to the subject than I have come across in such reading of economics as I have done'. He did not think that such a book would be commercially successful and predicted that if it ever made it into print, it would sell fewer than 1,500 copies. Heinz was disappointed with this response, though it came as 'hardly a surprise'. 'The problem of teaching economics without tears,' he admitted, 'has yet to be solved.'

It was an entirely different matter, however, with the book on the trading banks. Fabinyi was enthusiastic from the start. Once the decision had been made to publish the book, Heinz worked on it at a furious pace. He had the first draft completed by October 1956, telling Barback that he had 'put everything else aside'. The contract was signed on 7 March 1957, with Firth and Karmel writing endorsements and guaranteeing the publisher that they would recommend the book to students as a text for courses at the Universities of Tasmania and Adelaide. Heinz corrected galley proofs at the end of May and the book was published in September 1957. In subsequent editions, Heinz enlisted co-authors, including C.P. Harris, D.W. Stammer and W.J. Blackert.[22]

There were yet other books that Heinz worked on during his years at CUC. A year before the publication of *The Australian Trading Banks*, he had conceived a plan to write a book on Australian economic growth since 1920. The draft of an unaddressed letter, dated 1956, included an outline of the book, which he predicted would take about a year to complete and would be based on existing data, published or unpublished. He sent around Australia, in November 1956, another letter that referred to this book; recipients were asked for assistance with relevant data. There were a number of responses and their authors showed considerable interest, but there is no evidence that anything was actually written.

In 1960, Heinz put together yet another book of essays, entitled *Essays in the Economics of Labor*. He sent the manuscript to Cheshire, informing Fabinyi

> You may have noticed Mr Calwell's recent attack [Calwell took over, that year, from Evatt as Federal Opposition Leader] on intellectuals in the Labor Party, and on John Button and me in particular. I confess I am unrepentant. I still believe that there is a need for intellectuals in the Labor Party and more need than ever now for the few Labor intellectuals there are to speak up and try to educate the Party…I have attempted to do so from time to time.

The collection of essays—headed by the Chifley Lecture—was meant to enlighten members and supporters of the ALP, though Heinz aimed also to educate the general public. Fabinyi agreed with Heinz that there was a desperate need to reform the Labor Party, but he considered that what was required was an entirely new basis of attack, not the regurgitation of past criticism. He concluded that the publication of Heinz's essays would attract few sales and would incur a substantial loss to the publishers. 'I am not entirely satisfied that the publication of these essays,' Fabinyi told Heinz, 'while bringing together very valuable material into a handy volume, would really assist in those major problems in which you and most of us at present are concerned.'

A distraction that faced Heinz and his colleagues at CUC for much of the 1950s was the question of whether the college should become an autonomous University of Canberra, or amalgamate with the ANU. The act that had established the ANU provided for the possibility of some form of incorporation, by the ANU, of CUC. Copland, the ANU's Vice-Chancellor, had refused to contemplate any such thing until the ANU had reached the stage where it could be confident of its own future. The University of Melbourne, however, was pressing to terminate its association with CUC. It informed the Commonwealth government of its intention to do so, but agreed to maintain its links on a short-term basis until CUC became either an independent university or joined the ANU.

These were the two options that faced CUC in the mid 1950s. Opinion in the ANU and CUC was divided on which option to take. Those at the ANU who opposed incorporation seemed to have the upper hand, while those in CUC who wanted an independent University of Canberra appeared to be in the majority. In the event, the Prime Minister (under pressure from members of his government, who saw little sense in having two universities in a city of fewer than 100,000 residents) decided that the two institutions should merge. This meant, in effect, that the ANU should incorporate CUC.

Heinz at first declined to enter the debate, though (as has been noted earlier) he was a member of the CUC council for brief intervals throughout the controversy. He found himself being drawn into it, however, through his friendship with *Sydney Morning Herald* editor, John Douglas Pringle; the two men had been undergraduate students together at Lincoln College in the 1930s. In April 1953, Pringle mentioned to Heinz that the *Herald* intended to support amalgamation in a leading article. Pringle believed amalgamation would 'meet a very urgent need for more universities and might perhaps save the National University from complete futility'. He urged Heinz to write a draft editorial setting out a case for amalgamation, which Heinz agreed to do. When Pringle read it, however, he thought it was unsuitable to be published on the paper's leader page. He suggested instead that Heinz might write a joint letter signed by those of his CUC colleagues who supported amalgamation, with the *Sydney Morning Herald* endorsing the letter in a small article in the same issue of the paper.

Heinz demurred and informed Pringle:'It would look too obviously like an attempt by College staff to put pressure on the Government. Besides, it is always difficult to get a group of academics to agree completely on the draft of a joint letter.' He let Pringle know that if the *Sydney Morning Herald* wanted to publish a version of the original article that Heinz had sent him, Joe Burton, the Principal of CUC, would be happy to write it. Pringle opposed this idea and preferred that one of his own reporters do the revision. Burton, however, went ahead and rewrote Heinz's article, sending it instead to the *Age* under his name.

In 1954, while Heinz was in America, Burton wrote informing him of the impending battle over what would happen to CUC. Burton mentioned that a cabinet submission by the Minister for the Interior, whose department literally ran Canberra, had prompted discussion about CUC's future. Some of the details of the submission had been leaked, including a proposal to give CUC the status of an autonomous degree-conferring university. This led the ANU's academic board, the Board of Graduate Studies, to recommend as a matter of urgency that the ANU should consider the incorporation of the college in the near future. The recommendation then went to the ANU council, which decided that it should not make an immediate decision, but which agreed, instead, to accept the recommendation of the Vice-Chancellor (now Leslie Melville) that a working party of four people from each institution should examine the question and report back to a future meeting.

Burton told Heinz that he had 'little doubt that the ANU will be prepared to incorporate us before our present association with Melbourne runs out in 1956', adding: 'The question of the nature, however, is still a thorny one to be overcome.'

The Board of Graduate Studies then decided to vote against incorporation. This decision, together with negative comments about CUC, its staff and students by a number of leading ANU academics, including Sir Mark Oliphant and two economists, Trevor Swan and Noel Butlin, led Heinz to change his mind about incorporation. He wrote to Roy Cameron in December 1955: 'there is nothing but trouble on the "ANU Incorporation" front; at the ANU there is much opposition to any association with the College, numerous different factions each having its megalomaniac reasons, and there is some danger that we shall be pushed into another renewal of the association with Melbourne—till 1960!'

In March 1956, he wrote to Barback: 'No progress at all on the ANU amalgamation front. The ANU Council was to have considered the matter at its March meeting, but never put it on its agenda; it will now have to wait till the May meeting. Meanwhile our Council will probably have to ask Melbourne for a further extension. It is a frightful mess.'

As a CUC council member (having replaced Manning Clark, who was on leave in Oxford), Heinz wrote to Clark in April 1956: 'The whole business is so exasperating that one cannot sustain the same degree of anger month after month…I am finding my membership of the Council quite the most disagreeable job I have had to take on in my ten years in Australia.'

He decided to switch sides. Henceforth, he supported those in CUC who wanted to see it become an independent University of Canberra, catering to the needs of an expanding city and its surrounding region. Nonetheless, he never became a vociferous campaigner for this view.

The CUC council recommended to the government that the college be granted independent status as the University of Canberra, but the request was held over, pending the report by a committee chaired by Sir Keith Murray,[23] which the government had established to review the Australian universities. Heinz knew Murray well because Murray, like Pringle, had been at Lincoln College. Heinz was appointed to the team that drafted CUC's submission to the Murray Committee.

This submission set out the case for the college becoming an autonomous University of Canberra. Heinz appears to have been confident that Murray would support autonomy, since he wrote to E.F. Penrose,[24] mentioning

> …the endless committee meetings and other activities connected with the impending grant of autonomy to our College. The Murray Committee looked into the matter and there is to be another meeting next week, chaired by the Prime Minister, to decide whether the College is to be given independent university status or in some way associated with the National University. After all that has happened, we now all favour the former course.

The Murray Committee, however, saw merit in the argument that Canberra should have only one university, though it did not go as far as to recommend incorporation. In any case, the government decided that Canberra could not justify two independent universities.

When Menzies forced the issue—the so-called shotgun marriage between the two institutions[25]—and demanded that the ANU and CUC come up with a plan for an ANU–CUC 'association' over the summer of 1959–60, several CUC staff members publicly opposed the government's decision, but Heinz was not among them. When the association took place in September 1960, he was on leave in Geneva and took no part in the administrative procedures for the ANU's takeover. After he returned to Canberra 12 months later, he expressed disquiet about some aspects of the association with the ANU, though his general irritability probably owed more to the difficulties he faced in coming to grips with life in Australia after the excitement of working with the United Nations Economic Commission for Europe than to the new university that had been created while he was away.

The seemingly interminable rows over association were not the only problems that Heinz had to endure when he was at CUC. Another was the poor quality of its students. Though the number of full-time students direct from school was slowly increasing, most students continued to be part-timers, who worked in the public service during the day and attended classes after work. Many of Heinz's friends had predicted that he would not find the students at CUC to be of the same calibre as those whom he had taught in Sydney, yet there were exceptions. One was Chris Higgins, who was to become the head of the Commonwealth Treasury. There were also the diplomatic cadets. Most of them had taken first-class honours degrees at Australian universities and some had been Rhodes Scholars. Heinz found teaching them a bonus, compensating to some degree for the difficulties he experienced with most of the undergraduates.

One student, not his own, to whom Heinz provided considerable advice and assistance, and who later received the Nobel Prize in economics (with John Nash, whose life was featured in the Academy Award winning film *A Beautiful Mind*), was John C. Harsanyi. When Heinz first met him, Harsanyi, a refugee from Hungary, was embarking on a master's degree at the University of Sydney. Hermann Black had encouraged him to contact Heinz for advice about his research. Harsanyi explained to Heinz the rudiments of game theory and Heinz in turn suggested that Harsanyi might consider applying game theory to the Australian arbitration system as a case study. Harsanyi agreed, making it the topic of his master's degree, which was the first empirical application of game theory in Australia. Harsanyi later asked Heinz to support his application for a Rockefeller Fellowship, to undertake doctoral studies at Stanford under Kenneth Arrow's supervision. Heinz wrote that Harsanyi 'shows as much promise as any of the younger economists in this country of making original contributions to this field of economic theory', highlighting the fact that he was the only person in Australia taking serious interest in the theory of games and its application to economics. He was particularly happy that Harsanyi had chosen to undertake his doctorate at Stanford because, as Heinz wrote, 'I do not think that any other American University I saw [in 1954] appealed to me so much.'

Harsanyi first met Heinz when visiting Canberra in 1955, not long before leaving for Stanford. Once in the United States, Harsanyi sent Heinz copies of his papers that had been accepted for publication in the *Journal of Political Economy* and *Econometrica*, including his classic article on 'The bargaining problem'. Of these papers, Heinz commented

> I am like a new-born lamb in the Theory of Games…any inexpert comments of mine, therefore, are unlikely to be of much use to you… The points you make seem to me valid and useful, though I can never resist the feeling that, in this present state of development, the theory of games employs an enormous opportunity for the solution of the problem which common sense can handle without much difficulty.

The two men continued their correspondence after Harsanyi returned from America to join the Department of External Studies at the University of Queensland. Heinz wrote to him in 1957 to congratulate him on having successfully finished his doctorate

> I am having a messy year, doing all sorts of odd jobs I have let myself in for. My book on the Australian Trading Banks is coming out this week. But my next project, a similar book on the Finance of Public Investment in Australia, on which I worked during the past vacation, has had to be put aside ever since. A paper on overseas post-war investment in Australia is coming out in the next *Record*, one on 'The Dangers of Big Business'…[and] the Consumption Function which you have seen; it is my turn to write the next survey article for the *Record*; and so on. A good deal of time has also been taken up by preparations for and meetings with the Murray Committee on the Australian Universities.

When he completed his book on the trading banks, Heinz began to direct his attention to the Australian public sector. He commenced a major project on the financing of public investment, informing E.F. Penrose in January 1958 that he had started work 'on the next instalment of my studies of the Australian capital market. It is to cover all those aspects concerned with the public authority sector as a borrower, the finance of public investment, national debt management, etc.' In August 1957, he read a paper to the NSW branch of the Economic Society; this was the 'Dangers of big business' lecture, which he had cited in his letter to Harsanyi. 'If big business has come to stay,' he observed in this paper, 'I prefer it to be publicly controlled and in some though not all cases publicly owned. The experience of TAA and ANA shows that public enterprise need not be less efficient [than private sector enterprises].'

In 1959, he opposed the government's plan to create a separate central bank—the Reserve Bank—by separating the Commonwealth Bank's commercial activities from its central banking functions. He was 'convinced that the case for reform is not strong enough to warrant arousing political controversy, and diverting attention from more important aspects of monetary and economic policy'. The experience since the war of dealing with inflation had demonstrated to him how the Commonwealth Bank could apply its policy of curtailing inflation by leaning on its commercial activities, thereby limiting the process of credit creation. Although '[t]here is a case for [bank] separation', he said

> ...there is also a case for the present system. It is very doubtful whether the proposed reform would, on balance, be in the national interest, even if it could be effected quickly without legislation. The case against arousing new political controversy over banking, taking up parliamentary time, and diverting the time of ministers and their expert advisers from more important matters for so doubtful a gain seems to me overwhelming.

This was a reasonable point for Heinz to make. Australian economists, including the Governor of the Commonwealth Bank (H.C. Coombs), generally did not support the creation of a separate central bank. Rather, the support came for the most part from private bankers, who believed that as a competitor to the private banks, the Commonwealth Bank possessed an unfair advantage by being both a commercial bank and the central bank.

While Heinz opposed the separation of the central banking functions from the commercial trading and savings bank activities of the Commonwealth Bank, he did support the creation of a new Commonwealth Development Bank. He urged Arthur Calwell to include the idea in Labor's program for the 1961 election. Such a government-owned bank, Heinz thought, would be useful as a means of channelling private savings into strategic areas of the economy. He cautioned, however, that such a proposal should be expressed in a form that would not 'arouse the wrath of financiers and others'.

By the end of the 1950s, Heinz was starting to re-examine some of his long-held beliefs on economic theory. One was the question of free trade and protection. He had never been an advocate of free trade. In fact, he thought it eminently possible to justify protection on various grounds, particularly as a means of creating and preserving employment. He was sceptical of theoretical arguments for free trade, believing the assumptions on which such arguments were based were unrealistic.

Nevertheless, he began to rethink his position after reading a paper that Max Corden (his eventual successor as head of the Department of Economics in the Research School of Pacific Studies at ANU) had presented to the ANZAAS conference in 1958. He contacted Corden to congratulate him on his paper, judging it to be 'one of the best applications of theoretical reasoning to an important policy problem I have ever seen'. 'As you know,' Heinz wrote

> ...my prejudices make me less partial to reliance on the price mechanism than your paper suggests I should be. I have always felt uncomfortable about the smug assumption of free trade theorists that, if all the rest of the world is protectionist, it must be that all the rest of the world consists of fools and knaves. Yet I am not sure that I can really pick any substantial holes in your argument. I am almost entirely carried away by the persuasiveness of your concluding recommendations.

Heinz was about to embark on an extended visit to India, a country where the ideology of protection was rampant. Helped by Corden's theoretical analysis, and witnessing with his own eyes the ill effects of protection on the Indian economy, Heinz was now ready to bring into greater alignment his long-established antagonism to controls and his revisionism towards protection and trade policy.

28. With Sir Robert Menzies, circa 1958

29. On the ACT Advisory Council, 1961 (rear, fourth from left)

30. Heinz's office at Coombs

31. Such a happy man

32. In Delhi

33. Heinz with Premier Sun of Taiwan

34. Heinz with Yip Yat Hoong and Kiyoshi Kojima

35. Heinz with Jan Tinbergen

36. With SA Premier Don Dunstan and US economist Paul Samuelson, 1973

37. In Banda Aceh

38. With Raj Krishna, Bangkok

39. In Indonesia, with Dennis DeTrey (World Bank), Ir Tungky Ariwibowo (Industry Minister) and Marzuki Usman (later Tourism Minister)

40. L-R: with Ross Muir, Peter Drysdale, Toshi Kinoshita, Hal Hill and Kazuo Imai

41. L-R: Juwono Sudarsono (current Indonesian Defence Minister), Clara Juwono (CSIS, Jakarta) and Moh Arif (the latter a close friend from Malaysia)

42. Heinz and Professor R.M. Sundrum, staff member of Economics RSPAS, 1971–90

43. In Indonesia, one of many happy dinners

44. Heinz with students

45. A good mix of (mainly) former students. L-R: Back: Helen Reid, Hal Hill, Ross McLeod. Front: Chris Manning, HWA, Howard Dick, Andrew Elek, Anne Booth, Tony Reid and Peter McCawley

46. Heinz at the home of Bessie and Vic Camino, Heinz's closest friends from the Philippines

47. In 1995 Gadjah Mada University, Yogyakarta, one of Indonesia's leading universities, launched the Arndt Scholarship Scheme

48. With Professor Nopirin, Dean, Faculty of Economics, Gadjah Mada University and colleagues.

49. HWA, Stuart Harris & Ross Garnaut

50. The academic family, including Ruth as ANU council member, at Bettina's ANU graduation, 1971

51. At Bettina's wedding to Dennis Minogue, 1977

15
GENEVA

In 1959, Heinz began to make arrangements for his next sabbatical leave. He wrote in June to Bob Ratchford at the Commonwealth Studies Centre at Duke University to ask whether there might be any possibilities there for him to teach and engage in research during the northern academic year of 1960–61. As he told Ratchford, he had recently embarked on an examination of the financing of public expenditure in Australia and would be interested to pursue the project further during his leave. Ratchford had recently been in Australia, to collect material for a project on Australian government expenditure, and had met Heinz in Canberra. In his letter to Ratchford, Heinz remarked that there might be an opportunity for them to collaborate, since their research appeared to be traversing similar ground. Duke had another attraction for Heinz: its close proximity to Chapel Hill, where his brother was still at the University of North Carolina. They had not met since 1954, when Heinz had visited Walter and his family on his way to South Carolina.

Duke, however, was not the only possibility. An alternative was the University of California at Berkeley, which Heinz's friend Tibor Scitovsky had proposed as a place for spending his leave. Heinz wrote to Lorie Tarshis at Stanford, too, asking him whether there might be funding available for a visit of 12 months in 1960 or 1961. There was also an offer to spend some time at the United Nations Economic Commission for Asia and the Far East (ECAFE) in Bangkok, but Heinz turned that down because Ruth and the children would have to live in Europe while he commuted between Europe and Thailand. He then sounded out the possibility of a temporary appointment at the United Nations in New York, but this came to nothing.

While Heinz was making plans to take leave in the United States, Gunnar Myrdal suggested to him that he might consider occupying a visiting research professorship at the new Institute for International Economic Relations in Stockholm. There he would be able to participate in a project involving the study of economic relationships between the industrialised, the underdeveloped and the communist worlds. This, however, would take more than 12 months to complete. Heinz declined the offer because he doubted whether CUC would approve leave without pay for a period longer than 12 months.

Of all these possibilities, Duke appeared to be the most promising. From there came an invitation for Heinz to take a graduate course in international trade in the second semester of 1960–61, with some supplementary undergraduate teaching if he was interested. He drew up tentative plans to leave Canberra in November 1960, travelling by sea to London and spending a week or two in Hamburg with his father before assuming the appointment. Difficulties arose, however, over funding. Heinz wanted to take the family, but housing and schooling in the United States were expensive. He also wanted to buy or hire a car for the family's use while they were away—and that would add to the cost of going to America. In the event, he turned down the offer from Duke, informing Frank de Vyver, the Chairman of the Department of Economics, that he did so 'with great heartburning and difficulty'.

Towards the end of the negotiations with Duke, Heinz received a letter from Nita Watts, Deputy Director of the Research Division of the United Nations Economic Commission for Europe (ECE), inviting him to spend a year in Geneva. Myrdal was probably responsible for bringing about this invitation. He had been the ECE's Executive Director at the time it was founded and was largely responsible for the excellent reputation that it had acquired for the quality and scope of its research. Myrdal had recruited first-class economists: Nicholas Kaldor and Hal Lary,[26] for instance, were the first two directors of the Research Division. When Heinz received the offer of appointment, the head of the division was not as distinguished an economist as his predecessors had been, but was a bureaucrat with a background in American government administration. In practice, the effective head was Nita Watts, who had been a student at the LSE with Ruth, and whom Heinz knew well.

The offer from ECE was particularly appealing because the generous salary would allow Heinz to take Ruth and the family to Geneva. Besides, he and Ruth would be close to their families in Germany and they would be able to visit each other frequently. So, once the possibility of Duke fell through, Heinz had no hesitation in accepting the ECE invitation.

With the family, he left Canberra in the middle of 1960; he and Ruth rented out their house for the year to a young family from Tasmania. On their way to Geneva, they spent some days in London. Though the weather was wretched, they all enjoyed seeing the musical comedy *My Fair Lady*. Heinz was able to spend a day in Oxford, where he met Paul Streeten, Ian Little, David Worswick and Max Hartwell, though not Hicks, who was ill.

In Geneva, they leased a flat in the Rue du Leman and the children were enrolled at the international school. They were to find Geneva an entirely congenial city. The ECE was located in the Palais des Nations, built for the League of Nations during the interwar period, and now it housed many of the European-based agencies of the United Nations. Heinz found his work at the ECE rewarding and his colleagues stimulating. During the winter and spring, the children enjoyed skiing and other winter sports in the mountains above Geneva, while Heinz's main diversion was watercolour painting. He told John Head, one of his ANU colleagues, that 'I could take all five days off for it, there are so many attractive subjects'.

The Research Division had a staff of 30–40, including economists, statisticians and assistants. Heinz's post was designated officially as Economic Affairs Officer, a position that Myrdal had created in the early 1950s. He had conceived it as a kind of visiting professorship. Over the years, it had been occupied by well-known economists, such as R.F. Kahn of Cambridge and Frank Burchardt of Oxford. The division's main tasks were to produce an annual survey of the European economies (containing reviews of economic developments in Western and Eastern Europe during the previous year, plus one or two special studies) and an economic bulletin published three times a year.

In the early months of the visit, Heinz undertook some work for the 1960 survey on monetary policy and balance-of-payments issues. He was then assigned to a project on trade preferences for developing countries. This study had been commissioned in the expectation that the United Nations would create a Trade and Development Commission (UNTAD). It was to be a precursor of a paper on an Australian scheme of trade preferences for developing countries, which Heinz wrote when he returned to Australia. The Australian government later adopted a modified form of Heinz's proposal, though Heinz himself came to take a jaundiced view of the Australian scheme.

Throughout his year at the ECE, Heinz acted as one of the four section heads of the Research Division. He took part in discussions with visiting economists, attended divisional meetings, supervised various research projects, tendered advice to other divisions and paid visits to the OECD in Paris, the European Economic Commission in Brussels and the Dutch Planning Commission at The Hague. Such duties brought him in touch with a number of distinguished economists, including the co-winner of the first Nobel Prize in economics, Jan Tinbergen (at The Hague), James Tobin of Yale (another Nobel laureate, then a member of President Kennedy's Council of Economic Advisers), Robert Solow, a later Nobel laureate ('with whom I have had a very useful discussion on my growth study'), George Jaszy, Gregory Grossman and the chairman of the perspective planning department of Gosplan.

Heinz acted also as secretary to a meeting attended by Western and Eastern experts on the measurement and analysis of labour productivity and wrote a paper for the secretariat on the subject. In addition, he became secretary to a meeting of senior economic advisers of European governments on the sources of economic growth and wrote a preliminary report on the discussion.

His major work in Geneva was to direct a project on the sources of economic growth in European countries. Initially, this project was to be published as part two of the *Survey* for 1961. Unfortunately, it was not published until 1964, due to delays caused by the diverting of resources to other activities. Heinz took responsibility for the statistical work (which was required on a uniform basis for each of the European countries included in the study) and for the analysis of sectoral data on output, investment and employment for some 20 Western and eight Eastern countries.

This work turned out to be far more time-consuming than he had expected, largely because national statistical offices were continuously revising their national accounts. At first, he had only one assistant working for him, though towards the end of his stay virtually the entire division was assigned to the project. It was June 1961 before he was able to begin the drafting of the statistical chapters. By July and August, shortly before he returned to Australia, he had completed only the first drafts of three chapters on the Western European countries. When he left Geneva, he agreed to continue to assist with the drafting process—commenting, revising and polishing the various drafts.

The work that Heinz performed for this study was in a similar vein to, though entirely independent of, Edward Denison's *The Sources of Economic Growth in the United States and the Alternatives Before Us* (1962). Heinz aimed to examine the different growth experiences of European countries since the war. Because he was somewhat sceptical of the aggregate production function approach to identifying the sources of economic growth (whereby the marginal products of labour and capital are measured by the share of national income accruing to each of the two major factors of production), Heinz developed a different methodology. As he was to write in 1985

> We first calculated incremental capital-output ratios (ICOR) from investment ratios and growth rates, as a measure of the marginal productivity of capital, and then divided each country's ICOR by the growth rate of its labour force to obtain what we called ICOR(L)—the acronym LICOR having been ruled out as too frivolous—as a proxy measure of total factor productivity. It was an extraordinary [sic] crude procedure but seemed worth trying as a first shot (Arndt 1985:49).

Heinz drafted the overall and sectoral chapters himself using the ICOR-ICOR(L) framework. Other members of the team were responsible for writing the qualitative chapters on technical progress, education and other components of the residual, together with a number of country-specific chapters. In the end, only Western Europe was covered, although the intention had been to include Eastern Europe as well. Uncertainties about the comparability of data and interminable political disagreements were among the reasons why the study finally dropped all consideration of the centrally planned economies.

While taking a somewhat different route from the conventional one followed by pioneers in growth accounting, such as Odd Aukrust, Edward Denison and Angus Maddison, Heinz and his team obtained results similar to those that other studies had achieved. The principal conclusion of all the studies, including Heinz's, was that somewhat more of the increase in national output could be attributed to so-called residual factors than to increases in labour and capital inputs. These residual factors were considered to be largely productivity-inducing ones, such as the introduction of new technology, the reduction of trade barriers, increased competition and, above all, improvements in education and health.

Heinz made the most of his time in Geneva, as he had done on his previous leave in South Carolina. It was frustrating for him that he was unable to complete the growth project before he returned to Canberra. It was otherwise a fruitful year and a happy one, with Ruth and the children being with him. Indeed, so enjoyable was it that they had great difficulty accepting the fact that their year away had come to an end. As it was, Heinz could not meet his commitment to resume teaching at the beginning of 1961's third term. This was because the United Nations insisted that he see out his full year in Geneva; otherwise, he would have lost his 'repatriation rights', by which was meant return airfares for the family.

Burge Cameron (who had taken over from Heinz as head of the department and dean of the faculty) approved the extra leave and asked Trevor Swan to take Heinz's lectures in Economics 111. Ruth and the children left Geneva a week ahead of Heinz and returned to Australia via New York, Washington and Santa Fe, staying with former friends from Canberra at each place. Heinz returned via Cairo (two days' sightseeing), New Delhi (where he spent three days attending the first ECAFE conference of Asian economic planners) and Singapore (one day in transit), arriving in Canberra at the end of September.

In his obligatory report to the ANU council on his Geneva sabbatical, he wrote

> I can say that my year's work with ECE in Geneva was not only most enjoyable but an extraordinarily valuable experience. After some 15 years in Australia, I was able to renew and bring up-to-date my acquaintance with the economy of Europe. The growth study compelled me not only to familiarise myself more intimately with the current literature on the theory of economic growth but also to relate it to concrete facts of particular national economies. I learned a great deal about the problems of handling and evaluating macro-economic statistics. Finally, through the experts of the planned economies section, I obtained, for the first time, some insight into the operation of the planned economies of the communist countries, their remarkable successes and hardly less astonishing failures; and through the frequent meetings with delegates from these countries some insight into their mental processes.
>
> I am confident that the varied experience I gained during the year will be most useful to me in teaching and research in Canberra. This is not the place even to attempt to summarise any of the conclusions of the growth study, though some of them, I believe, are not irrelevant to Australia. But I may mention two other impressions which I have brought back. One is that Australia can ill afford the purist attitude of its official statisticians which, however noble in intention, has in recent years resulted in Australia being almost alone among significant countries in lacking many major series of official economic statistics constantly used in international comparisons. I am sure this factor reinforces distance and inconvenience of classification (Australia belonging

neither to the 'developed countries of Europe and North America', nor to the 'underdeveloped countries', nor to the 'communist bloc') as a cause of general neglect of Australia in comparative and world wide economic analysis. The other lesson is that Economics Departments of Australian Universities cannot much longer afford to ignore so completely the study of the communist planned economies. The concentration on the economics of market economies which has been and remains customary in the teaching of economics at Australian universities is already out of touch with what is happening in the most rapidly developing part of the world and will increasingly lose in relevance as more and more countries, even of the 'mixed economy' type, turn towards overall economic planning of their economies.

The reference to economic planning is significant. When Heinz returned to Australia, he brought with him an enthusiasm for indicative planning, of the type that had been adopted since the war by several Western European countries, especially France and the Netherlands. For many observers, planning was a major reason why the Western European economies had recovered quickly after the war and were now experiencing more rapid rates of growth than countries such as the United Kingdom and the United States. The British government, under Harold Macmillan, had recently begun to experiment with a form of industrial planning, through the newly established National Economic Development Council, in the hope of accelerating its annual rate of growth. Australia's growth performance appeared to be more like that of Britain and the United States than the rapidly growing countries of continental Europe.

Heinz's work in Geneva on comparative rates of economic growth led him to consider planning as a possible explanation for why some countries were growing faster than others. Back in Australia, he found the country experiencing its highest rate of unemployment since the war. He doubted that this was simply the result of the 'credit squeeze' that had followed the government's monetary and fiscal measures (taken in late 1960) to reduce inflation and restore external balance. In addition, he thought that he could detect the fading of a number of key elements of postwar growth, including investment opportunities, pent-up consumer demand and immigration.

He gave a paper to the annual summer school of the Australian Institute of Political Science (AIPS) shortly after his return. There he declared that Australia should think seriously about planning as a means of accelerating its rate of economic growth. 'Because,' he said, 'I am rather concerned about the danger of stagnation, I regard a serious examination of national economic planning as an urgent task.' He proposed a four-year national plan, similar to the one in France.

In the lecture, he explained that the success of French planning derived from the stimulus to industry that came from setting clear targets and from the confidence inspired by the coherence of the plan as a whole. He thought the adoption of a four-year or five-year investment and development plan might make a decisive difference to the business and economic climate of Australia. 'The task of drawing up a national plan would compel us systematically and coherently to measure what we want against the resources at our disposal.' As it was, macroeconomic planning in Australia was a confusion of 'bits and pieces'. Also important in France's case were the microeconomic elements of planning, for the French plan promoted technical progress through scientific research, training and the exchange of know-how.

After the summer school, Heinz tried to persuade the ALP to adopt planning as a key element of its economic policy for the next federal election. He targeted Gough Whitlam, then deputy leader of the federal parliamentary party, rather than Arthur Calwell. Writing to Whitlam in February 1962, Heinz said that the ideas that he had expressed at the summer school were deliberately put

> …in a form suitable for public consumption and therefore free of any party political leanings…[but] I need hardly say that I have little hope of the idea being taken up by the Menzies Government. My hope for it rests on a Labor victory in the next election. Indeed I believe that adoption of longer-term planning by the Labor Party as a major plank in its election platform might help greatly to attract the extra votes needed.

He told Whitlam that he had been 'surprised to get quite a flow of letters from businessmen asking for copies and expressing keen interest. I believe a carefully worked out version of the proposal, which combines an air of responsible realism with some fire and enthusiasm, could be an election winner.'

An Australian four-year plan, he estimated, might take at least a year to prepare, though in other countries it had taken closer to two or three years. He was convinced that 'the mere decision to adopt the principle of planning and the period of preparation of the plan would have a beneficial effect on the whole business and economic outlook'. 'It is of the essence of the notion of planning,' he wrote, 'that correct policy decisions (on longer-term resource allocation) cannot be reached without careful inquiry and analysis of a wide range of relevant facts and except within the framework of a coherent plan for the economy as a whole.'

The central planning authority should be located within a government department, under a responsible minister, not outside the traditional government structure in some semi-autonomous council having merely advisory functions. 'On balance,' he felt

> ...this department should be the Treasury, not a new and separate department (of 'Planning' or 'Economic Affairs'). The Treasury has traditionally performed the function of co-ordinating financial and economic policies, even though its exercise of this function has too often been conceived narrowly as one of 'prudent house-keeping', or financial control of spending. I do not think an attempt to separate these traditional functions of co-ordination of financial and short-term policies from the function of long-term planning could lead to anything but muddle and frustration.
>
> Of course, some drastic changes to the existing Treasury structure would be needed: for example, a new division devoted to longer-term planning would have to be created. Other government departments would also have to be brought into the planning process. State governments, too, including Treasury departments and private businesses, trade unions and consumer groups, should all be part of the planning process.

While he was communicating with the ALP through Whitlam, Heinz was informing the business community of the merits of indicative planning, using as his vehicle the Institute of Public Affairs (IPA), a conservative think-tank. Throughout the 1950s, there had been ephemeral correspondence between Heinz and the IPA's director, C.D. Kemp,[27] usually concerning requests for each other's publications. Heinz wrote to congratulate Kemp in January 1958 on two articles that the IPA had published on funding public expenditure. The two men were to meet briefly in Canberra later in the same year when Kemp made it evident that he would be 'delighted' to talk with Heinz whenever he was in Melbourne. By the end of 1961, the relationship had moved to the point where Kemp was inviting Heinz to write for the *IPA Review*. He wondered whether Heinz might contribute an article for the March 1962 issue, referring in particular to a paper that Heinz had recently read to the Economic Society on economic growth in Western Europe. Instead of addressing the subject of economic growth in Western Europe, Kemp asked Heinz whether he might write an article on economic growth in Australia.

Heinz, however, sent Kemp a version of his lecture to the AIPS Summer School. Alarmed at the prospect of publishing an article that was complimentary to economic planning in a journal devoted to private enterprise, Kemp proposed alterations. He admitted to being

> …genuinely concerned about the 'acceptance' of the article, certainly among a good proportion of our influential readers who comprise probably most of the prominent businessmen in Australia. I take it that you want people of this kind to give full and fair consideration to the principles of national target setting and planning. Certainly I would wish the article to serve this purpose. But I fear that, in its present form, many business people will be inclined to reject the proposals in the article without this consideration being given.

Kemp acknowledged Heinz's admission in the paper that there was no coercion attached to French planning, but as far as Kemp was concerned, Heinz had then contradicted himself by saying that planning without teeth would be 'virtually useless'. Kemp thought this should be left unsaid, since it would frighten businessmen. It was his view that it would be better to take the issue of planning rather gradually, for it would be expecting too much of Australian society, business, government — and even trade unions—to rush suddenly into comprehensive planning of the type followed in France. After all, planning had been functioning there for 15 years and the French had come to accept it.

The most satisfactory approach, Kemp recommended, would be to leave the reader thinking that Australia might be able to learn from French planning and that a positive step in this direction would be to establish very broad production targets for some of the key sectors of the economy. Such an approach, Kemp believed, would receive a sympathetic hearing from the business community, not an antagonistic one.'In other words, we should go step by step, and learn as we go and not court possible failure and the rejection of the whole idea by being over-ambitious at the start.' He reckoned, in short, that Heinz had overplayed the success of French planning and he suspected it would be preferable

> …to leave the impression on the reader's mind that while planning can be a valuable adjunct to national economic planning, it is not a magic talisman which charms away all our difficulties; that we shall all the time be looking for improvements in the methods which we use to conduct our economic arrangements but we shall not expect miracles and that difficulties and disturbances are certain to arise from time to time under the best-laid plans.

As well as being convinced that Heinz should soften his promotion of planning, Kemp worried about Heinz's extensive criticism of the government's wider economic approach. Heinz had talked of the 'inadequacy of an excessively short-term approach to national economic policy of dealing with each internal and external crisis by *ad hoc* measures and leaving the pace and direction of the longer-term development of the economy largely to look after itself'. Since many *IPA Review* readers were among the government's leading financial backers, Kemp urged Heinz to tone down the adverse comments that he had made about government policy.

In the event, Heinz did make significant changes to the article, to meet Kemp's concerns. Kemp, in turn, agreed to publish the amended draft, but with an editorial that would clarify the IPA's own attitude to planning. The IPA believed that some benefits were likely to result from the introduction of planning, but it should not be regarded as a panacea, and should be considered dispassionately, analytically and fairly.

After the article had been published, Heinz wrote to Kemp saying that he was very happy with it and with Kemp's editorial. Thereafter a close and warm association developed between the two men, which endured until Kemp's death in 1995. The friendship was mutually beneficial. From Heinz, Kemp's enlightened approach to public affairs was reinforced; from Kemp, Heinz became better informed about the views of businessmen and supporters of the Liberal Party. Meeting Kemp, in fact, was to be a significant milestone in Heinz's political education.

16
A NEW LEASE OF INTELLECTUAL LIFE

After his year away, Heinz found it difficult to settle back in Canberra. Part of the problem was the excitement he had experienced in Geneva. The city itself was inspiring, an international centre at the heart of a great continent. That was one thing. More important, perhaps, was the excitement associated with the work at the ECE, especially the project he had been asked to lead on the identification of the sources of economic growth in Europe. In contrast, Australian issues now seemed to him to be insignificant and decidedly dull. Just before he left Geneva, he wrote to Dick Downing saying that

> …all of Australia has become appallingly remote. I can only hope that this will right itself quickly once I am back…Ruth asked me (and the children) what we were looking forward to in Australia. The children listed each a few features of their life in Canberra. I was horrified to find I could not think of anything except you and one or two other friends. (Ruth was herself in much the same position.) But as I say, this will change soon enough when we get back.

Quite apart from the exhilaration of living and working in Geneva, Heinz was unhappy with changes that had been occurring at home while he was away. By the time he returned to Canberra, the ANU had effectively absorbed the CUC and the aggressive application of mathematics and econometrics in the research and teaching of economics was now in full swing in his department. What he found particularly irritating was the insistence of his younger colleagues—and some of the older ones—that the teaching of macroeconomics, in respect of theory and its applications, should draw more heavily on mathematics than he was willing to accept. There was also disparagement of his research, which, it was claimed, was failing to keep up with the latest work in the discipline.

A month or two after his return to what was now the School of General Studies (formerly CUC), Heinz wrote to David Rowan admitting that he felt

> ...ill at ease in the new ANU set-up. I can't say I am looking forward to teaching, and it takes time to regain the feeling that Australian problems are important. Most of our former Canberra friends have left in the past year or two, and if it were not for Dick [Downing] and Peter Karmel, both of whom I have managed to see quite a lot since my return, I should feel even more disgruntled.

At the same time, Ruth was informing friends that

> Heinz has been very busy trying to settle back into University and public affairs. Lots of trips to various capital cities has made this process easier, but he is still very nostalgic about Geneva and slow in recovering his enthusiasm for the University routine. He has been re-elected to the City Council [the ACT Advisory Council] which adds to our social obligations but is also quite interesting. The children just love being back and have never once uttered one word of regret at having left Europe behind. They are very happy to be among their friends, even their schools, and above all they enjoy much greater freedom to roam, to be out of doors, to plan their own activities and entertainment, very largely independently of us.
> ...Although I, too, enjoyed Geneva and would like to see it again (and Europe generally), I am also beginning to feel once more that there is something very thrilling about life in such a new country as this one. There is the tremendous enthusiasm everybody shows about what is being achieved; here in Canberra especially they never tire to point out the new developments, new public buildings, new residential areas, new bridges and parks, and after you have been here for a while it gets you too!

One matter that gave Heinz some joy was the December 1961 federal election: Labor came within a single seat of dislodging the Menzies government. Calwell, though Heinz still felt little liking for him, had made the best of the economic circumstances—record levels of postwar unemployment and a resentful business community—and had performed creditably throughout the election campaign. Heinz expected that the government's tiny majority would force Menzies to the polls again within a year, and that when it did the rejuvenated ALP would win. He hoped, too, that the young and vital deputy, Gough Whitlam, would soon succeed the ageing Calwell as leader.

In a letter to a former Geneva colleague, Heinz explained what he saw as the causes of the dramatic election result and the changes it had brought about in the Australian political landscape

> The main reason for the huge swing to Labor…was undoubtedly the recession…resulting from the emergency anti-inflationary measures of November 1960. (The measures, as usual, came too late when the boom was practically over, they were perhaps too indiscriminate and tough and they caused so much business resentment as to lead to something like a 'strike on capital'.) But this has merely been the catalyst of all sorts of accumulated discontent with a Government too long in office, lazy, without any imaginative policies mainly concerned to ward off short-term crises, and with the increasing arrogance of Menzies.
>
> At any rate, the whole business has given a tremendous shot in the arm to Labor, which is all set for another early election in which it hopes to get into office. Calwell is rather old and not really much good (horrible in his pronouncements on foreign policy—all the old Labor chauvinism, White Australia, and all). But his deputy, Gough Whitlam, a barrister, young and sensible, may well take over before long. All this has helped to allay my own discontents because it has made public activity here seem a little more worthwhile.
>
> PS. In my article on Fiscal Policy published three months before the November measures, I said that the main problem in an effective anti-inflationary fiscal policy is 'sufficient courage by politicians' (or words to that effect). It slightly embarrasses me to think that Menzies has been taught what happens to politicians who show courage!

As had occurred after his return from South Carolina, so now after his return from Geneva, one of Heinz's major problems was his inability to focus on a sustained piece of research. In Geneva, he had scrapped his plan to write a book on the financing of public expenditure (as a complement to his work on private finance, of which the book on the trading banks was the chief legacy). To his former Geneva research assistant, Eduardo Merigo, he wrote in May 1962 that he was

> ...frantically busy without doing any real work. My teaching load this term is relatively light, only 5 hours (on economic dynamics and international economics), though it will get heavier next term. But there is a never-ending flow of public lectures (3 weeks ago in Adelaide, last week in Brisbane, next week-end in Melbourne); radio talks; committee meetings; etc. Such time as I have had for research has been spent looking at trends in interest rates and interest policy in Australia (which, as a by-product) involved me in reading the Radcliffe Report[28] and all the enormous debate that arose out of it and writing an article on Radcliffe Monetary Theory which will probably be published in the *Economic Record*. I also have a fair bit to do with our Enquiry into the Australian income tax system. Our fleeting hopes last December that a Labor Government might be returned at last has come to nothing; however, I do get consulted by Labor leaders on various matters of economic policy from time to time. I have been advocating some form of 'perspective planning' for Australia—it is in the air, and there is quite a lot of interest in the idea.

Some weeks later, he wrote again to Merigo: 'What I ought to do, as a colleague said the other day is to scrap all this nonsense [articles and lectures on current issues] and write something worthwhile. How does one do it?' To Nita Watts, he confided his 'wish [that] I had the moral fortitude to tell all supplicants for such papers to jump in the lake so that I can get down to something more substantial in the way of research'.

He made an attempt to attend the annual conference of the International Economic Association (IEA), which in 1962 was held in Vienna. The theme of the conference was economic growth, a field Heinz now intended to make his own. His former ANU colleague Wilfred Salter was giving a paper and Heinz was encouraged to write and present a paper himself on population and economic growth. He hoped the ECE might send him to Vienna, because of his Geneva work on economic growth in Europe, but it declined to do so. Then he hoped that he might represent the Economic Society of Australia and New Zealand. That hope also was dashed when the IEA withdrew a tentative offer of a return airfare. Ultimately, it was just too difficult to find the money and time to make the journey to Vienna. Besides, his heart was not in the topic of the proposed paper.

Ruth, too, experienced some immediate difficulties settling back in Canberra, though they soon disappeared. She was taking two adult education classes in German at home and teaching economics at Canberra Grammar School, with—as Heinz informed some friends in Geneva—'increasing disgust at the appalling quality of this typical (Church of England) school'. Ruth gave up teaching at the end of 1962, but then had some difficulty securing another job, until she landed one in the Department of External Affairs' economics division.

Some of the gloom dissipated temporarily when Heinz received a letter from Donald MacDougall, recently appointed by the British government to direct its new National Economic Development Office (NEDO). On leave of absence from Nuffield College, Oxford, MacDougall was looking for senior staff and had been told by Nita Watts that Heinz might be interested in working at NEDO for a year or two. He wrote offering him a job, but Heinz declined:'The idea of working in your new show for some time has great attractions, but I must say NO for the present.' It was unlikely that he would be granted leave so soon after his 12 months in Geneva and, for various reasons, he was not prepared to resign his chair for a longer-term appointment. Some time in the future, a one-year appointment might be possible and he asked MacDougall to keep him in mind should that possibility arise.

One research project that held out some promise (and about which Heinz exhibited some initial enthusiasm) was a commission from the Australian Social Science Research Council (SSRC) to investigate the Australian taxation system and formulate proposals for its reform. Economists—Heinz among them—had been calling for a review of the tax system for some years, but the government was opposed to the idea. The SSRC took the initiative and invited a group of four Australian economists—Dick Downing, Alan Boxer,[29] Russell Mathews[30] and Heinz—to undertake the review. Downing took it on himself to coordinate the work, with each member having responsibility for writing particular chapters. Heinz volunteered to draft several of them, some in collaboration with other members of the group. He also provided extensive comments on chapters that other members of the group had drafted. Melbourne University Press eventually published the report in 1964, but it had little immediate impact on taxation policy in Australia (Downing et al. 1964).

Ever since Heinz had returned to Canberra, the notion of returning to Geneva for an extended period, and perhaps even permanently, had been running through his mind. Early in 1962, scarcely six months after arriving back in Australia, he began to sound out Watts about the chances of securing a semi-permanent position at the ECE. It was clear to him that he would not be able to take further leave before 1963, and possibly not before the middle of that year. In March 1962, he wrote to another of his former colleagues in Geneva, Gisele Podbielski

> I am resigned to spending at least this and next year here (not a word from Nita or anybody about the situation in Geneva—but I assume that nothing is at all likely to come along for 1963). Maybe by then I will have settled into the groove here and won't want to shift. At the moment, the thought of not seeing anything but Australia for the next two years still irks me.

Watts soon replied, to say that the Executive Director of the ECE, Vladimir Velebit, was not prepared (at least for the time being) to face a row with his superiors over the appointment of a non-European to a senior position in the Research Division. But she hoped that Heinz might be available at a later date, possibly in 12 months. Heinz admitted to her his regret that nothing was currently available

> As the months go by, I am settling back into life here. Personally, I am still in a state of mind in which I would welcome the opportunity of a longer period with ECE (though I am not sure how Ruth feels, and the children are certainly unenthusiastic about any suggestion of leaving Australia). How I shall feel about it in another year I do not know. But I should certainly like to be kept in mind if a suitable vacancy exists in a year's time.

In June 1962, Watts wrote to tell Heinz that she had recently been talking to Velebit about the future of the Research Division. In the course of the conversation, he had disclosed that he was now willing to put up a fight for Heinz's appointment. He proposed to ask for a five-year appointment. Watts thought there was an excellent chance of Heinz taking over as director of the division some time within that period. The idea was that Heinz's appointment would begin towards the end of 1963. But Velebit had made it clear that he would want a definite commitment from Heinz before he was prepared to make a firm offer.

Watts told Heinz that everyone in the division wanted him to come back to Geneva: 'The year you spent here was tremendously stimulating for the rest of us and I am quite sure that you are exactly the kind of person we need to get in the Division for a long stay.'

Heinz then contacted Velebit, to tell him that he was interested in accepting an appointment on suitable terms. The major problem was that he had no accumulated leave available at ANU, so he would be unable to accept an appointment of merely one to two years, and he was not prepared to resign his chair for that period. He might be prepared to resign, however, should he be offered a five-year appointment. This would not be possible, however, before the end of 1963, as he would have to give the university six months' notice. For him to take up the post by late 1963, he would have to receive an offer before mid 1963, and the appointment would have to be at the director level. Velebit replied, saying that he could now begin firm negotiations within the United Nations. He wanted Heinz to start before the end of 1963 and the appointment would have to be at the deputy director level in the first instance. If Watts were to leave the division, Heinz was assured that he would be appointed to her position, becoming in effect the head of the Research Division.

There followed a long wait for the United Nations to approve: first, the position; second, Heinz's appointment to it; and third, the offer letter to be written and sent. The letter arrived on Heinz's desk at the beginning of November 1962. The question then was whether he should accept it. He quickly decided that he would agree to a five-year appointment at the deputy director level. This would mean that he would have to resign from the ANU. The thought of having to surrender his chair was difficult for him to contemplate, but that was a burden he would have to accept. A complication was that Joe Burton, the Principal of the School of General Studies at the ANU, was on leave in England and Manning Clark was the Acting Principal. Another was that Burge Cameron was also on leave and the Dean of the Faculty of Economics was the relatively inexperienced Graham Tucker, the head of the Department of Economic History. Clearly, Heinz would not be able to take up the appointment before the end of 1963, when Cameron would be back from leave and when it would be convenient to leave Australia from the point of view of the children's schooling.

A week after receiving the ECE's offer, and having made up his mind to accept it, Heinz wrote to Dick Downing saying that

I don't really know what makes me want to go: mainly (a) the feeling that, having held this job for 12 years, I cannot quite bear the thought of seeing out another 18 years; (b) increasing dissatisfaction with my competence as a teacher and academic economist—a feeling aggravated, almost beyond endurance, by my two dear colleagues Cameron and Swan; (c) increasing doubts about the usefulness of my role in public affairs and in the Labor Party and therefore increasing lack of interest in a possible career in that field; (d) sheer itchy feet, wanderlust, desire to do something different, see more of the world.

What I most fear is that you will think me lacking in loyalty and public spirit—in this, too, you would probably be right. As you know, you are my only close personal friend, and thus the strongest single argument against going to Geneva. But I have weighed this, too, and rationalised my doubts by the hope that we might see you there some time, and, if not, that we will be back.

To Gisele Podbielski in Geneva, Heinz wrote

We are definitely accepting…The decision itself is made in principle, but still surrounded by a number of uncertainties. When I broke the news to some of my colleagues last week, I was subjected to considerable moral pressure to stay here; but out of this also emerged a probable offer by the University of 3 years' leave without pay—in the hope that this might induce me to come back to the ANU in 3 years' time. I shall be glad to accept this offer…

As you can imagine, Dick [Downing] is very displeased with me, and so are the few colleagues who have been told about it. Every day I ask myself half a dozen times why I am doing this—it is a great mixture of motives, many of them quite irrational. But I have not really moved in my feeling that going to Geneva for a few years is what I want to do and Ruth is quite keen, too, [at] least in no way opposed to the idea.

Soon afterwards, he wrote again to Podbielski with doubts about his decision to leave Australia.'Goodness knows, why I am prepared to make the break here where in many ways I am very happy.' He admitted the'fact that I so much enjoyed my year in Geneva is probably the least rational or sensible of a variety of reasons since it would be a miracle if the second bite of the cherry did not prove a disappointment'. To another of his old associates at ECE, Zerzy Berent, he wrote

> I have no idea whether I was sensible in saying yes almost without hesitation when I was asked whether I would be available. I have told no one here except Ruth, not even the children: I fear they will be very hostile if and when it comes to the point. So will most of my colleagues and friends here; now that we have been back here almost a year, we are not even in any way unhappy here; we still like Canberra and Australia, and on the whole I like my job and my wide range of other activities. If I have any rational motive—beyond a vague nostalgia for Geneva—it is that I have been in this job for 12 years and cannot quite contentedly look forward to another 18 till my retirement. There is also a feeling of increasing inadequacy in teaching—more and more economic theory is beyond my comprehension, at least in the mathematical form in which it is presented. Both Ruth and I would go to Geneva…with the intention of returning to Australia after 5 or so years—though whether we would want to, and to what job, is in the lap of the Gods.

He contacted Joe Burton in London and told him

> I am not entirely clear even about my own motives. The main one perhaps is that I have now been in my present job for 12 years and have another 18 years to go. I feel like doing something else for a change. I liked Geneva and the work there, though I am prepared to admit that it may turn out less satisfactory for a longer period. I have become increasingly dissatisfied with my capacity as a teacher and theoretical economist as, every year, I fall more behind the current trend towards mathematical analysis and formulation. And I am too lazy to spend a year studying maths and catching up. All my kind friends, Dick [Downing], Graham [Tucker] and others, have used every argument that ingenuity could devise, and every form of kindly flattery, to tell me that I am wrong in this.

Burton, in fact, had heard from Manning Clark that Heinz intended returning to Geneva. He respected Heinz's decision and, while he regretted it, he was not at all indignant about it. But he rejected the claim that Heinz had become less effective as a teacher. 'I grant the need for mathematics for some of the branches of economics,' Burton wrote, 'but I cannot feel that without mathematics one is no longer useful.' He was not surprised to hear that Heinz wanted to return to Geneva, because Heinz had made it well known around the university that he had enjoyed working and living there. To Heinz, he said that he was willing to work out an arrangement of leave without pay for a year or two. 'I would be very happy,' he said, 'provided that it can be done without any detriment to students or the department as a whole.'

When Heinz informed the university of his intention to resign his chair, the Vice-Chancellor, Sir Leonard Huxley, asked Sir John Crawford, the Director of the Research School of Pacific Studies (RSPS) and fiscal adviser to the university, to see whether Heinz might prefer to take leave without pay, rather than resigning his post. Crawford told Heinz that the university might be willing to grant him three years' leave without pay, but there could be no guarantee that his chair would be available when he returned. Crawford explained that the university could not hold vacant a chair for such a length of time. What it could guarantee him was a senior post—a readership, or even perhaps a personal chair in Crawford's own department—when he returned. Crawford might also have given Heinz some indication that, were a second chair to be established in his department, he would regard Heinz as a strong candidate for it.

Heinz found all this satisfactory. It would probably mean that he would have to give up his chair in the Faculty of Economics, though Crawford had made it clear to him that if the chair had not been filled by the time he returned to the ANU, the university would not stop him reclaiming it. Also it would mean that he would have a senior position in the university if he wanted to resume his academic career when he returned. The sticking point now was whether he would be able to retain his membership of the Commonwealth Superannuation Scheme, were he to take an extended period of leave without pay.

He discovered that if he resigned from the ANU he would lose the accumulated employer contributions to his superannuation fund (amounting to roughly £12,000) and that he would have to work for the United Nations for at least five years to qualify for a UN pension. Even then, the pension would be small. It was clear that a three-year leave of absence without pay would be the best way to proceed. Accordingly, he wrote to Burge Cameron on 30 November saying that he had accepted the post in Geneva, had given notice to the university of his intention to resign his chair and would apply to the council at its meeting in January for three years' leave without pay.

In the same letter, Heinz said that he had canvassed with Tucker possible appointments to the chair that he would vacate. He believed there would be two outstanding candidates: Wilfred Salter, who had been in Swan's department in the Research School of Social Sciences but was now a senior economist in the Prime Minister's Department, and Max Corden, who had recently joined Crawford's department in RSPS from the University of Melbourne. Heinz told Cameron that he thought that

> Salter had perhaps the more original mind (though it is hard to know how many of his original ideas have been inspired by Trevor [Swan]). The strongest argument in favour of Corden is that Salter's interests overlap to a much greater extent with yours [Cameron's]. There is also some doubt how well Salter gets on with people—he has a reputation of being a little autocratic. Corden is first rate as a theorist and a superbly lucid lecturer—here again Salter is a *tabula rasa*. However, there is time to think about this—and of course there may be quite a large field.

As to who he thought should replace him, Heinz let Burton know that 'my present preference is perhaps for Corden'.

The process of accepting the Geneva appointment and leaving the ANU had progressed so far without great difficulty. From late November 1962, however, a number of major problems began to emerge. One was superannuation. It now seemed that the university might not permit Heinz to retain his superannuation entitlements, were he granted three years' leave without pay. But switching to the UN pension scheme was clearly unsatisfactory. Not only would it mean that he would have to be away for at least five years, the UN pension would be considerably less than he would receive were he to remain a member of the Commonwealth scheme. He mentioned to Nita Watts that '[i]f I were on my own, I would not worry about the security aspect. But everyone tells me I cannot be so irresponsible with a family.' Further, it was now clear that Nick and Bettina were 'violently opposed' to going to Geneva for five years or more. Again, as he informed Watts: 'while the family would be willing to go to Geneva for a short period—2–3 years—for my sake, they are all very hostile about leaving Australia for longer than that.'

Nor was that all, for when Burton returned to the ANU from leave early in 1963 he wrote immediately to the Acting Vice-Chancellor, Professor A.D. Trendall, saying that he 'recommended quite definitely that the University should not grant leave of absence for so extended a period [that is, for three years]. It would create a precedent that would, I am sure, cause us untold difficulties in future.' Trendall agreed with Burton and wrote accordingly to Heinz. It was also clear now that the Finance Committee of the ANU council—chaired by Crawford—would not allow Heinz to suspend his membership of the Commonwealth Superannuation Fund and that he would have to resign from it.

Naturally, the university's attitude infuriated Heinz. He was inclined more than ever to go to Geneva, but if he were to resign his ANU post it would mean that he would have to stay in Geneva for five years to be eligible for a UN pension. Five years' absence from Australia was clearly unacceptable to two of the children and probably to Ruth as well. While he appreciated the university's concern about the precedent that might be set were he to take three years' leave, he put it squarely to Crawford that the 'question is perhaps whether Council would be prepared to make a concession for someone who has been a Professor of the University for 12 years and is anxious to return to it after a spell of work elsewhere'.

Crawford assured Heinz that he was personally sympathetic to Heinz's request to take an extended period of leave, yet he doubted whether the Finance Committee would agree to allow Heinz to retain his membership of the Commonwealth Superannuation Fund in these circumstances. As well as the 'awkward precedent' it would set, Crawford said that he 'doubt[ed] if the Council would take quite a sympathetic view about three years' service in Europe as they would with, say, some Asian university or ECAFE'.

Heinz was clearly disappointed. He had known Crawford for at least 15 years, having met him for the first time on one of his first trips to Canberra, when he was at the University of Sydney. They had seen each other on and off during the 1950s, mainly in Canberra, and they appeared to get on very well. When Crawford left the Department of Trade and joined the ANU in 1960, they saw even more of each other, though Heinz's year in Geneva curtailed their opportunities to meet and talk. In 1962, they had both served on a committee established to plan a university for Papua New Guinea. It was then that Crawford had the opportunity to witness and appreciate Heinz's commitment to research and to observe his growing interest in the economics of developing countries.

After Crawford's frank acknowledgment of the difficulties that lay with any hopes of winning over the Finance Committee, Heinz decided to sound out the United Nations. Perhaps he could secure a higher salary to compensate for the loss of his superannuation entitlements. Alternatively, perhaps a shorter appointment than three years might be tenable. The answer was no on both counts.

On 8 February 1963, Heinz informed Watts that he would not be taking up the Geneva post, because the university had rejected his request for three years' unpaid leave. He explained that the ANU was fearful of setting precedents and of morally committing itself to finding him a job after he returned from Geneva, when there might not be money available to fund the post. In addition, he mentioned the Finance Committee's intransigence regarding his superannuation. The only way he could take up the UN offer now, as he told Watts, was by resigning from the university. But 'I have come to the conclusion that I cannot take this step', because

> I do not want to break my ties with Australia for good. The family are opposed even to a stay abroad of no more than three years. Yet, the superannuation problem would virtually compel me to commit myself to at least five years, and even during these five years and for some time longer the family would be very inadequately protected in the event of my death.

'It is all terribly disappointing', though he confessed to Watts that he was

> ...personally half relieved after these months of worrying and uncertainty. It has been very difficult—so much more difficult than I had foreseen. I have been under continuous pressure from my colleagues and friends here who, in their kindness, have thrown at me every possible argument against the move. Ruth has very firmly said that she would accept any decision I made, but I realised that she was not happy about any prolonged absence from Australia. Of the children, only Christopher was not hostile, and in his case the difficulties of organising his university studies satisfactorily were greater than he realised.

To Velebit, he wrote

> This is not only a great disappointment to me but also causes me the most acute embarrassment because I am virtually going back on the assurance I gave you last June. I appreciate that I have caused you and several of your colleagues much fruitless trouble and I will leave the Research Division short of the person they need and with little time to fill the post. I can only offer you my sincere and humble apologies.

Watts, however, wrote with some urgency to tell Heinz that Sir Alexander McFarquhar, the United Nation's Chief of Personnel, had been informed about his difficulties. McFarquhar had asked whether he might approach Australia's permanent representative to the United Nations to inquire whether the Australian government could apply pressure to the ANU to allow him three years' leave. Heinz was totally opposed to this idea, insisting that any such pressure on the university by the government would constitute for him an unacceptable breach of university independence.

What he did not tell Watts was that Crawford had indicated his willingness to appoint Heinz to a personal chair in his department, provided he could secure the necessary funding from the university. Given the heavy responsibilities that Crawford was carrying as director of RSPS, fiscal adviser to the Vice-Chancellor and chairman of the council's Finance Committee, he was finding it increasingly difficult to run a department that was growing in size as a result of the recruitment drive that he had recently initiated. Disappointing, too, for Crawford was the fact that he had been forced to scale back his own research program because of his administrative responsibilities.

Heinz at first was pleased that Crawford was prepared to support the creation of a personal chair for him in RSPS. But as he considered it further, he began to feel uneasy about such an appointment, which would be regarded by colleagues as somewhat inferior to a chair that was open to competition. He understood, however, that if a second chair—rather than a personal chair—were established, it would have to be advertised; competition would be strong, and in the event he might miss out to a more highly regarded candidate. Therefore, he would be reluctant to apply for the chair, though he would consider an invitation to fill it if the selection committee was unable to make an offer to one of the applicants.

Crawford now saw little point proceeding with the idea of a personal chair, since Heinz had made it clear that even if offered it, he would not accept. Accordingly, Crawford proposed to the Vice-Chancellor that a second chair, externally advertised, should be established in the Department of Economics, RSPS. The grounds for establishing a second chair, Crawford told Huxley, were simple: 'I cannot continue to do what is apparently expected of me without some relief. Moreover, my colleagues and students in Economics are entitled to the same attention as given by the Head of a Department in other Departments. This they are not getting and cannot get in the foreseeable future.' In addition, he said that he had

> ...regretfully concluded that for some time to come there will be need for a Fiscal Adviser. Likewise, my work on the Economic Enquiry [the Vernon Committee][31] will be heavy and has already meant an indefinite postponement of an eagerly planned study leave in January next year. I have had to abandon my interest in 'food and population' studies and hardly dare hope to complete my documentary study of post-1943 trade policy in Australia.

He suggested to Huxley that the second chair in the department—Crawford made it clear that he wished to retain his own chair—might be called 'Economic Development', 'Political Economy' or 'Economic Policy', though the name was of secondary importance to him compared with the establishment of the chair itself. And he added

> As you know, I would be happy to have Professor Arndt. Although I realise the loss of a good teacher this would mean [sic] for the School of General Studies, I am conscious also that my own Department is proving a popular one for post-graduate students of quality. A good teacher in charge will be an asset. Arndt's scholarship and research abilities are certainly adequate and I know it would be virtually impossible to choose anyone else in Australia. (I exclude Swan and Karmel from this calculation but know no one else whose experience could so quickly and usefully be brought to bear on the studies of my Department.)

'Arndt may not be an applicant,' Crawford told Huxley, 'but I would wish his qualifications taken into account when candidates, if any, were being assessed.'

The ANU council approved the establishment of the second chair in May 1963. The post was then advertised widely outside the university. The selection committee was Crawford (chairman), the Vice-Chancellor or Deputy Vice-Chancellor, Professor Mark Oliphant or Professor Hugh Ennor, Professors Burton, Noel Butlin, Karmel and Partridge. There were six applicants, but Heinz was not one of them. After short deliberation, the selection committee concluded that none of the applicants warranted appointment.[32]

Crawford then put Heinz's name forward as someone the committee might invite to fill the chair. It was agreed that he should seek further information from Gunnar Myrdal and Hans Singer (the United Nation's senior development economist) about Heinz as a suitable appointee. It was further agreed that, if the advice from Myrdal and Singer was favourable, there would be no need for the committee to meet again. Myrdal informed Crawford that he had been pleased to hear that the ANU was considering the appointment of Heinz to the chair. He thought it would be

> …an excellent choice and…a very good thing that in the new chair he will have his time free for research and supervising training on a higher academic level. I do not need to tell you that he is an excellent man meeting all the specific criteria you mention. In addition I have learnt to know him also as a hard worker and serious scholar without prejudices and therefore prepared occasionally to find out what he was not seeking which to my opinion is the mark of a scholar. As holder of the chair he will certainly have the stature to gain ready access to Asian universities.

It is not known exactly what Singer had to say. Whatever it was, it appears to have impressed the selection committee.

With both advisers supporting Heinz's appointment, the Board of the Institute of Advanced Studies approved on 27 September the electoral committee's recommendation that Heinz be appointed, and the Standing Committee of Council endorsed the recommendation on 11 October. Heinz took up the chair on 1 December 1963 at a salary of £4,700.

In his press release on the announcement of the appointment, Sir Leonard Huxley noted

> In the past thirteen years Professor Arndt has most ably built up a strong teaching department in the University. His new

appointment will, however, give him an opportunity to concentrate on research and the training of postgraduate research students in a department whose primary role is the study of the economies of developing countries, especially in Southeast Asia and the Pacific region, and Australia's economic relations with this area.

As soon as he heard that he would be invited to take the chair, Heinz wrote formally to Burge Cameron to let him know that he was about to be offered the chair and would be accepting it, 'partly because I have come to feel it is time for a change of job, partly because the problems of underdeveloped countries represent one area where mathematical moronism does not show quite so much'. On 14 October, he wrote to Joe Burton, saying that he had that morning received an official letter from the Vice-Chancellor offering him the new chair in RSPS. He told Burton he intended to accept it.

This was a painful letter to write, because it had been Burton, as the principal of the CUC, who had been responsible for bringing Heinz to Canberra 13 years before. Now he was leaving the CUC's successor, the School of General Studies, to join one of the original research schools of the ANU.

'I think you know my reasons for having decided to make this move,' Heinz wrote

> I need hardly say that I am making it with mixed feelings, after my many happy years here. I look back with particular pleasure to my early years at the College amongst a small group of congenial colleagues…I am very conscious of the fact that I owe much of my academic career, and therefore also this new opportunity, to you. For it was your initial confidence in me that gave me the chance of my appointment at the College, and your encouragement and friendly advice on many occasions has been of great help to me throughout these years. For all this, and for your constant kindness, I am most grateful to you.

Burton replied to Heinz a few days later

> I too look back with pleasure on our association over the past thirteen years, and in particular to the happy relations I have had with our four pioneer professors — Clark, and Crisp, Hope and

yourself. I am sure there is no better quartet in any university in this country, and doubt whether there is even outside it. It is remarkable to think that it has remained together so long. I shall always be grateful for the support I have had from you, and the others.

After accepting the chair, and once he had submitted his resignation to Burton, Heinz wrote to Myrdal, informing him that he 'had not applied for the job but was in the end invited after Crawford, on his own initiative, had approached you and Hans Singer for reports'. He let Myrdal know that it was his 'hope that by throwing myself into a new and interesting field I will give myself a new lease of intellectual life'.

PART THREE

17
ECONOMIC DEVELOPMENT IN PRACTICE: IT ALL BEGAN IN JAKARTA

Heinz's practical introduction to the developing world came about in India, where, from December 1958 to February 1959, he was a Visiting Professor at the Indian Statistical Institute (ISI), first in Calcutta and then in New Delhi. The appointment had been proposed by Gunnar Myrdal, whom Heinz had first met in 1953 when, in Jakarta, Myrdal boarded the plane in which Heinz was flying to Beirut (*en route* to Istanbul and eventually to South Carolina, as recounted in Chapter 12). This first acquaintance, and protracted conversations, with Myrdal was not only the start of a long and lively friendship, it served as Heinz's intellectual introduction to development economics. It was fitting, therefore, that Myrdal should later have been instrumental in getting Heinz started on the practical side of the subject; hence Heinz's observation that 'it all began in Jakarta'.

The route to Calcutta was via Singapore, where Heinz disembarked to spend three enjoyable days before going on to Kuala Lumpur for four more. Although free of business, Heinz spent most of his time in Singapore with academics. He was guided by Englishman Tom Silcock, long-time Professor of Economics at Singapore's university (originally the University of Malaya) and a prisoner of war in the notorious Changi camp ('Changi university') during World War II. Years later, Silcock joined Heinz as a colleague in the Research School of Pacific Studies (RSPS) at the ANU. Silcock handed Heinz over to the labour economist Charles Gamba (from Western Australia), who in turn introduced him to Ungku Aziz, the agricultural economist grandson of the aged Sultan of Johore. Aziz later headed the Economics Department in the University of Malaya, Kuala Lumpur, before becoming Vice-Chancellor of that institution. These contacts were to prove valuable to Heinz when he took command of Economics, Pacific Studies, five years later.

The university in Singapore appealed to Heinz—'[h]andsome campus, colonial style buildings laid out in [a] spacious park'—and he enjoyed meeting academic and other staff. Among them was a young lecturer in philosophy

Eugene Kamenka, a graduate of Sydney and the ANU, who later returned to Australia and grew into a renowned and respected Professor of Philosophy and head of the History of Ideas program at the ANU. Kamenka's wife, Alice Tay—'pretty, vivacious young law lecturer and barrister'—also later attained intellectual and public distinction in Australia, most famously as President of the Federal Human Rights and Equal Opportunity Commission.

To his disappointment, Heinz was unable to meet Goh Keng Swee, finance expert of the infant People's Action Party (PAP) and in later years the main architect of economic policy and development in the PAP government of independent Singapore under Lee Kuan Yew. But this miss was later made up for and Heinz formed a strong friendship with Goh. Rather ironically, Heinz recorded in 1958 the view that '[t]he Chinese realise that Singapore can never become independent outside Federation (with the Malayan peninsula)'. Lee Kuan Yew, Goh Keng Swee and others were soon to prove that view mistaken!

In Kuala Lumpur, Heinz was an honoured state guest, at the invitation of the Malayan Prime Minister, Tunku Abdul Rahman, in recognition of Heinz's years of teaching a special course in economics to Malayan diplomatic cadets sent to Canberra for postgraduate and in-service training. As befitted this privileged status, Heinz was treated royally and loved every minute of it, especially the 'large black limousine driven by [a] splendid uniformed chauffeur', which—together with the services of Max Garling, an Australian adviser to the Prime Minister—was at his disposal during his visit. Garling was an experienced, pleasant and influential man among a number of other such Australians whom Heinz met, befriended and valued in later life. They included Tom Critchley (High Commissioner in Kuala Lumpur and later Ambassador to Jakarta), Fred Fisk (who would become a close and longstanding colleague at the ANU), Bill Wilcock and Don McKenna (respectively, governor and central banking adviser in the infant Bank Negara Malaysia). Most of these men were to reappear in Heinz's later life as Professor of Economics in RSPS.

The state part of the visit began with a formal audience with Tunku Abdul Rahman ('the father of Malaysia' as he was later known). The Tunku was an aristocrat, substantially but not entirely Anglicised in culture and manner; he had an English wife. Heinz found him friendly, jovial and more interested in sport than any other subject: 'Professor, why don't you come to the races with me this afternoon?'. Heinz was well out of his depth here; except for tennis, he never showed any interest in sport and horse-racing was a particular anathema to him. Perhaps a puritanical streak in his upbringing had something to do with this but he was also never at ease among sportsmen. As he wrote years later, 'my failure to take the slightest interest in horse racing and betting shows that I am as yet imperfectly assimilated.' This after he had lived more than half a century in Australia!

The meeting concluded, Heinz spent most of the rest of the day—including an excellent lunch at the elegant Lake Club—with the banking and financial advisers to the government. They were mostly Australian or English expatriates, but Heinz also met several prominent local Chinese and Indian lawyers and MPs. He was particularly taken with the charismatic P.P. Narayanan, the Tamil secretary of the Plantation Workers' Union (PWU). Narayanan took him to inspect the offices and building of the PWU, which also contained a printing press, conference rooms, library, economic research unit, guestrooms and even badminton courts—all supported from the monthly subscriptions of 130,000 union members, virtually all of Indian race. The splendid day ended with a state dinner for some 50 guests. The Tunku was a jolly host and Heinz enjoyed himself thoroughly; he had a childlike relish of privilege and pomp though he never sought to become part of 'high society'.

On his last day in Kuala Lumpur, he was given a comprehensive tour of the highly professional Rubber Research Station (later Institute). He was impressed by the technological advancements but asked himself some basic questions: why not nationalise plantations? Does Malaya need new British capital? At this stage of his life, Heinz's political inclinations were still essentially socialist. One notices, too, that his affinity in Malaya and Singapore on this and later visits was predominantly with the Chinese, to a lesser extent with the Indians and little if at all with the Malays. The British expatriate community he generally treated with wary formality.

On 14 November 1958, Heinz arrived in Calcutta, then a city of five million people, sprawling over the 'immense, utterly flat area of Bengal formed by the joint delta of the Ganges and Brahmaputra rivers'. He overlooked much of this plain from his office on the sixth floor of the Indian Statistical Institute, some miles north of the city centre in a once-prosperous residential suburb overrun by impoverished refugees from East Bengal. The institute maintained one wing of its large main building on Barrackpore Trunk Road as a guesthouse. Here Heinz was billeted, along with a motley crew of other academic visitors, most notably J.B.S. Haldane, the distinguished English biologist of communist convictions, 'who wanders about the building looking, despite his Indian national dress, just exactly the eccentric English elderly don he is'.

The Indian Statistical Institute, founded in 1931, was the fiefdom of Prasanta Chandra Mahalanobis FRS, one-time Professor of Physics and an eminent statistician, described by Heinz as 'founder, secretary, director and *paterfamilias*' of the institute. Mahalanobis was a dedicated planner by conviction and temperament and at the time was immensely influential. The 1950s were the apogee of economic planning in developing (then styled 'underdeveloped') countries and India represented the biggest challenge of all because of its endeavour to reconcile parliamentary democracy with economic autarky, as well as the sheer size of the nation. Resource allocation was not made in accordance with market signals but by official fiat based on the not always clear socioeconomic values of the government in office. India's disposition was then, and for many years subsequently, strongly towards central planning. The institute supported these plans by its pioneering work in developing Indian statistics, especially of national income and agriculture but also including social and demographic data. The institute ran a major course in statistical training for about 400 graduate students at any one time. Cooperation between the institute and the government's Planning Commission was close, so there was much sharing of ideas between the two agencies and among the succession of international experts who came to work for either.

For his first two weeks in India, Heinz was underemployed, while his hosts decided how best to utilise his skills. He filled the time chiefly by writing, 'with brash discourtesy', a paper critical of the autarkical development philosophy of Mahalanobis's planning model because of its total neglect of the concept of comparative advantage. Despite this lack of tact, the paper was subsequently published in the institute's journal, *Sankhya*. Of this initial work, Heinz wrote to Wilf Salter in Canberra

> Import replacement caught up with me within a couple of days of my arrival in Calcutta—especially in the form of a number of papers by my host P.C. Mahalanobis. I was tactless enough to use my first week to write a critical note on one of his papers…The whole question is laden with politics here: the notion that India must follow the USSR example and go all out for heavy industry has become the No. 1 political dogma of Nehru and the people around him. I am not saying they are wrong—but I suppose it is the job of the economist to examine the validity of economic arguments even if the conclusion is politically inescapable and perhaps right.

Otherwise in Calcutta Heinz socialised with fellow boarders in the guesthouse, attended a tennis exhibition given by international professional players, including the young Australians Lew Hoad and Ken Rosewall, and undertook some local travel. A highlight was a train journey to Santiniketan, 160 kilometres northwest of Calcutta. Here, the poet Rabidranath Tagore had founded a combined school, technical college, rural university and community centre, 'a romantic world of patriotic fervour, moral and aesthetic ideals and religious contemplation'. Classes were held mostly outdoors, in the shade of great trees. Heinz was much taken with the mission and atmosphere of Santiniketan: 'the conscious expression of one man's personality and ideas.' The romantic side of Heinz was easily touched; his inclinations to music, art and communal endeavour would all have been aroused by the Elysian setting, style and spirit of Santiniketan.

After a fortnight in Calcutta, Heinz decided he would much prefer to be in New Delhi, working on the Third Five-Year Plan, to be launched in 1961. He wrote to Joe Burton

> It has now been decided that my work will consist of some aspects of preparation for the Third Five-Year Plan and that, for this purpose, I shall move to Delhi. I am not sorry for, although I have been quite well looked after at the Guesthouse of the Institute, Calcutta is not very pleasant, and there are hardly any economists here (nothing but mathematical statisticians!).

The ISI had a cell in the Planning Commission in New Delhi, known as the Perspective Planning Division. The head of this division was Pitambar Pant, a brilliant young civil servant and protégé of the Prime Minister, Jawaharlal Nehru. Nehru had asked Pant and Mani Mukerjee, of the ISI in Calcutta, to prepare an outline of the Third Five-Year Plan. That done, Nehru required Pant to prepare a fuller version for the May 1959 meeting of the National Planning Council. To help in this work, Mukerjee took Heinz to Delhi, where he met up with other advisers assembled by Pant into a small team. The group included Heinz's ANU colleague Trevor Swan and Oxford's Ian Little (who were among a number of visiting economists attached to an Economic Development Institute set up in Delhi by the Massachusetts

Institute of Technology), the Dutch econometrician Jan Sandee and, for a while, Amartya Sen (later a Nobel Laureate in Economics, who was on a visit home from his doctoral studies in Cambridge). This was all very congenial to Heinz. As he reported to Burton on his return to Canberra

> My assignment proved to be a piece of great fortune. Not only is Delhi a much more agreeable city than Calcutta, but the work on the Third Plan was a fascinating and invaluable experience. Nothing else could have given me so much insight in so short a time into India's economic problems and planning techniques.

Agriculture was the largest component of the Indian economy, yet it was taxed lightly. During the colonial period, land tax had initially provided a significant proportion of public revenue, yet, by the time of independence in 1947, revenue from agricultural taxes had dwindled to almost nothing. Pant asked Heinz to look first at the possibilities of 'resource mobilisation' from the agricultural sector (that is, higher taxes or, bluntly, squeezing more out of the poor peasants). Heinz was professionally—and perhaps personally—uncomfortable with this task, so he offered instead to undertake a more general approach to India's potential for generating savings and the mechanisms for shifting savings into productive use; in other words, the then new methodology of 'flow-of-funds analysis'. This is essentially a matrix statement of sources and uses of funds for the whole economy, classified vertically sector by sector, and the various financial instruments classified horizontally.

Such an ambitious task proved very difficult, not only because of a great deficiency of detailed data, but because some of the more highly aggregated statistics obtained from the Reserve Bank of India in Bombay were not consistent with those from the government's Central Statistical Organisation (CSO) in Delhi. Heinz, however, later wrote: 'I had the satisfaction of attending in my last few days a meeting at which representatives of the CSO, the ISI and the Reserve Bank agreed to set up a new section in the CSO national income division to develop flow of funds accounts on a regular basis, using my modest effort as a starting point' (Arndt 1985:45).

Heinz here is too modest. His pioneering work, despite its inevitable deficiencies and crudeness, caused the Indians to take the subject seriously and led to India being the first Asian nation—and one of the first in the world—to produce an articulated flow-of-funds matrix, published in 1963.

Aside from this main task, Heinz attended various meetings in the Planning Commission in Delhi, the Reserve Bank in Bombay and the All-India Economic Conference in Lucknow. He also managed to see several other parts of India courtesy of Mahalanobis and the Myrdals (Gunnar's wife, Alva, was Swedish Ambassador to India at the time). In all these ways, Heinz's observant eye and curious mind quickly gave him a sense of India's history and its condition of underdevelopment.

Jaipur was the destination for a Christmas 1958 driving tour with the Myrdals: Heinz the passenger in a big Chevrolet driven by Gunnar, the rest of the party going with Alva in the chauffeured ambassadorial black Mercedes. Gunnar Myrdal was regarded by Heinz as a talker of world-championship class (praise indeed!), and Heinz was subjected to a mixture of monologue and interrogation for the whole journey. It took a long day to get from Delhi via Digh to Jaipur, where the party put up in style at the Rampagh Palace Hotel, the former residence of the maharajahs of Jaipur. The palace was about 100 years old, in good taste and with very fine formal gardens and pleasant courtyards. Heinz thought that staying there must have been a little like staying at Versailles. The next day, Christmas, was devoted to a motor tour of Jaipur city and nearby Amber, the old capital of the state, concluding in time for Heinz to catch an evening plane back to Delhi for a brief respite before going to Lucknow for the economic conference.

Heinz thought that the formal sessions of the conference were not of a high calibre: 'the papers had all been written by relatively junior Indian economists and were very poor, while too many of the contributions to the discussion were, as always, by people who like to hear themselves speak.' Nevertheless, he enjoyed the opportunity to meet people, especially a few brilliant members of the younger generation and the top senior economists. Many Indian economists of the day had been to the London School of Economics or Cambridge and remarked that they had there read Heinz's *The Economic Lessons of the Nineteen-Thirties*. Heinz was further pleased to find his name known for his contributions to the *Economic Record*, the Australian journal unnoticed in the United States but evidently well-known in India.

Also at Lucknow and in Delhi were several accomplished foreign economists 'passing through' India on jobs of various length. They included

Harold Lydall (who was undertaking a savings survey), George Rosen (working on industrial finance), Nicholas Kaldor (revisiting the scene of his proposal for an expenditure tax) and Ted Wheelwright of Sydney, who later wrote a substantial book on industrialisation in Malaysia. There were also notable non-economists passing through, including from Australia Edward St John (distinguished barrister and Member of Federal Parliament) and Zelman Cowen (then Professor of Law at Melbourne and later a Vice-Chancellor (twice), knight and Governor-General of Australia).

On New Year's Day 1959, arising from an idle conversation and on merely one hour's notice, Heinz was offered the opportunity to accompany Mahalanobis on a car journey to Agra. He packed quickly and went along, experiencing four and a quarter hours of continuous talk by the great man. This was worse than Myrdal, who at least asked questions; Mahalanobis gave no room for interruption in his unceasing tirade against America, Britain, the West and capitalism. 'He must be nearly seventy, immensely vigorous, alert and intelligent, but also domineering, vain and bigoted, a Bengali aristocrat who in moving towards a Stalinist-type authoritarianism has completely by-passed democratic liberal notions, never in any doubt who would plan and who would be planned for (or against?)' (Arndt 1987:27). Arriving at the Laurie Hotel in Agra in the dark, Heinz went to bed depressed.

The next day was a different story. Mahalanobis arrived, with the Governor's splendid car, in bright morning sunshine, to show Heinz the Taj Mahal. Heinz was overwhelmed by the beauty of the 'exquisitely proportioned' building and counted himself fortunate to be shown it by mathematician Mahalanobis, who expertly explained the subtle geometry of the ground plan. Later in the day, Heinz was taken by others (but still in the gubernatorial limousine) to see the Agra Red Fort and the Itimal-ud-Duala tomb with its fine marble screens. The late-afternoon return drive to Delhi was better than the outbound experience because Heinz managed to keep Mahalanobis to subjects such as education and social problems in India and monetary theory.

Two weeks later, Heinz greatly enjoyed a professional and social visit to Bombay. The Reserve Bank of India arranged this trip so that Heinz could delve for statistics for his flow-of-funds project. The bank, as is the wont of such institutions, was generously hospitable. Heinz was installed in the luxurious Taj Mahal Hotel, situated at the Apollo Bunder, with a sweeping view across the bay to the mainland. He was charmed by Bombay: 'so much cleaner than Calcutta, so much more elegant and metropolitan than Delhi.' It is worth quoting Heinz here at length

> Imagine a peninsula as large as Sydney Harbour, with a wide sunny bay on one side and the Arab Sea on the other; an inner city, a little more provincial than the City of London, a little more imaginative than the centre of Melbourne, with wide clean streets, green parks and playgrounds, substantial English public buildings, modern bank and office blocks, red London buses and Manchester trams, Indian and American cars, and a great many smartly dressed people—the men in white, the women in saris or western dresses (and a high proportion with short hair); stretching north from the city, in a wide curve along the waterfront, a magnificent drive lined with modern apartment houses, leading at the northern end to the homes of Bombay's multi-millionaires on Malabar Hill; and further north still, a seemingly endless succession of suburbs for every variety of income group, gradually giving way to the textile mills and other factories of the industrial area of Worli, and beyond it to the most recent residential areas on the mainland around the new international airport of Santa Cruz (Arndt 1987:30).

In Bombay, Heinz spent five days working at the bank and lunched twice with its Governor, H.V.R. Iengar, whom he had met previously at a conference in Sydney. The second lunch was a private one between the two men and it soon became clear to Heinz why this was so: Iengar wanted, as Heinz wrote

> ...to quiz me about thinking among the Delhi planners concerning the third Five-Year Plan and to ask me to do what I could to explain in Delhi how disastrous it would be if a recent Congress Party resolution was implemented which demanded, in the name of grass roots democracy, the abolition of the Reserve Bank's network of rural co-operative banks. It seemed to me extraordinary, and illuminating, that the governor of the central bank thought it worthwhile to enlist an obscure foreign academic for such a mission (Arndt 1985:46).

There was, of course, rivalry between the orthodox Finance Ministry and Reserve Bank on the one hand, and the more free-wheeling and unorthodox Planning Commission on the other. Of that situation, Heinz noted: 'Clearly, the "Left" hand in Delhi does not always let the "Right" hand in Bombay know about all it is doing—and the "left" and "right" here means largely what it says' (Arndt 1987:30).

In Delhi at the end of January was the All-India Science Congress, in the presence of Nehru, his daughter and later prime minister, Indira Gandhi, Dr Sarvepalli Radakrishnan (Vice-President of India and Chancellor of the University of Delhi), Mudaliar (President of the Science Congress and Vice-Chancellor of the University of Madras), V.K.R.V. Rao (noted economist and Vice-Chancellor of the University of Delhi) and such foreign notables as the Duke of Edinburgh and Professor H.W. Arndt of Australia. Heinz lapped it all up.

Heinz's work in Delhi and Bombay, and his observations throughout his travels, confirmed the view he had formed earlier in Calcutta, namely, that India was overcommitting itself to industrialisation and import replacement. In contrast, he rightly saw the importance of agriculture, arguing that agricultural output in India would have to grow at 5 per cent a year to meet a population growth of more than 2 per cent and income growth of more than 4 per cent. He believed that the 5 per cent rate of growth of farm output was possible, but it would require better organisation, especially of rural extension services, and more irrigation and fertiliser than was discernible during his travels. He shared, too, Iengar's concern for the continued provision of cheap rural credit.

More fundamentally, Heinz thought the problems facing Indian agriculture were not only economic in nature, but included 'the caste-bound conservatism and illiteracy of the peasantry, lethargy, nepotism and lack of trained personnel in administration, and the vested interests of the kulak-landlords in the villages and state legislatures'. Land reform, improved diet and community development were also important. He was particularly interested in the last and spent some time visiting community development projects in the countryside around Delhi. Here was the possibility of conveying new knowledge and technologies to the overwhelming majority of the Indian population.

After his three months in India, Heinz appears to have taken very little interest in the country's affairs. His development interests were soon to be redirected to Southeast Asia, particularly Indonesia, and to Northeast

Asia, particularly Japan. The fading of his interest in India derived in large measure from his dissatisfaction with the path to development that India was taking. The hallmarks of Indian economic policy—direct controls, the lack of market incentives and extensive government intervention—were to become anathema to him.

Unfamiliar, and perhaps incredible to modern economists steeped in the conventional wisdom that resource allocation is best left to an unfettered market, are the strength and depth of the debates in the 1950s about economic planning, especially in India, which was rivalled in the huge size of its planned economy only by China and was probably unmatched in the intellectual articulateness and passion of its leading economists. The essence of the local debate at the time of Heinz's visit was 'big push' (espoused by the Planning Commission) versus 'hasten slowly' (favoured by the Ministry of Finance). The proponents of the big push advocated driving development with state-owned, large-scale and modern technology industries, while taking care to reserve government funds for the provision of education, health services and the alleviation of rural poverty. Such a strategy would obviously impose immense strains on India's supply capacity, domestic prices and balance of international payments, and thus lead to a myriad controls on prices, finance, foreign exchange, labour and capital mobility—hence the reservations of the other side.

With hindsight, it is now easy to condemn the waste, misallocations, inefficiencies, costs and corruption associated with the administration of central planning on such a huge scale. It should not be forgotten, however, that the planners were driven, heart and mind, by the noble desire to secure rapid alleviation of the desperate poverty suffered by the mass of India's population. As Heinz wrote: 'It was impossible to spend some months in India without being profoundly affected by the emotional experience of learning about the abysmal poverty of hundreds of millions of human beings.' The impact of his observation of this poverty was deep and lasting. It drove him into the further study of economic development as the chief professional interest for the rest of his life. In his report on his leave to the CUC council, he acknowledged that he had 'come back from India with a much better understanding of Indian economic conditions, of the basic problems of under-developed countries, than I could possibly have acquired by reading in Australia. I am confident that my teaching and research will benefit substantially from my visit to India.'

Heinz's first practical lesson in development had been a success and would pay handsome dividends for years.

By the middle of February 1959, Heinz was beginning to tire of India and its problems and was thinking of home. On 24 February, he wrote to his Canberra colleague A.J. Rose: 'It is remarkable, and quite shocking, how my concentration on the problems of India has, over the last three months, replaced all interest in world or Australian affairs. I cannot remember any other period since I was 16 when I have taken so little interest in what has gone on in the world at large.'

And to Burge Cameron in his department, he wrote: 'Not only has all this work been getting me down a bit, but I have become increasingly depressed about India, fascinating as it has been to learn more about it… I must say I am beginning to look forward very keenly to getting back home.'

Nevertheless, rather than returning directly to Australia, Heinz decided to fly first to Germany to visit his father, who was ill and had asked to see him. He left Delhi at the end of February and spent nearly a week in Hamburg—'an exercise in kinship rites', as he put it—as well as three days in London, before arriving back in Canberra on 5 March in time for the start of first term.

Ruth had not had the easiest of times while Heinz was away, with three children to look after for three months, of which half the time was school holidays. They kept in regular and frequent contact by letter, Heinz giving Ruth news about his work, the people he met and the places he visited. Ruth kept Heinz informed about the children and her activities. This was now the third time in less than a decade that he had been parted from the family for a prolonged period. While he was able to pursue his career without the day-to-day interruptions of family life, Ruth, on the other hand, had to cope with all the worries attaching to the care of three young children, without having the help of an extended family.

Heinz vowed that he would never again leave her and the family for any extensive period of time and he redeemed his pledge to take Ruth on future extended visits abroad. The whole family accompanied him when he spent a year in Geneva in the early 1960s and Ruth went with him to Paris when he worked at the OECD in the early 1970s.

18
THE DEPARTMENT OF ECONOMICS, RSPS, 1963–80

A Department of Economics had long been planned for the Research School of Pacific Studies (RSPS). The department became a reality in 1962, after the ANU's successful enticement of Sir John Crawford from the public service (where he was head of the Department of Trade) to be the first director of RSPS and, with the standing of professor, head of the new Department of Economics. Crawford went about his new responsibilities 'with vigour, indeed one might say in the grand manner', as Heinz later wrote.

Crawford, however, was so busy being director of the school and fiscal adviser to the university (an extra role to which he had been conscripted) that he could not give enough time to the Department of Economics. Crawford's time became even scarcer in 1963. In this period, not only were the causes of economic growth of paramount interest to economic theorists, the achievement of high rates of economic growth became a pre-eminent policy objective in industrial as well as developing countries. Following on from the French experience, the idea was floating around the world that 'indicative' long-term planning might be conducive to faster economic growth.

Although the government and treasury in Australia had little sympathy for planning, the Menzies government nevertheless appointed a Committee of Inquiry to examine ways and means by which Australia's economy might grow faster. Sir James Vernon, a prominent businessman (general manager of Colonial Sugar Refining Limited), served as chairman of the committee, with Crawford as his deputy (interestingly, another future Vice-Chancellor of the ANU, Professor Peter Karmel, also served on the committee). The inquiry lasted two years and took much of Crawford's energies away from the ANU. Realising that he could not do justice to several positions in the university, let alone to his substantial outside interests, Crawford sounded out Heinz on the proposal that he relieve Crawford of the headship of the economics department, of which Crawford would remain at least a notional professor. The proposal suited Heinz perfectly, for he was very happy to remain in Canberra if he could relinquish undergraduate teaching and concentrate on research leadership. So, retaining his status as professor, he took up the headship of Economics RSPS in November 1963.

The transition was accomplished behind the scenes (as recounted in Chapter 16). It had been known in the department that Crawford wished to be freed from the headship, but, at least among the junior citizens, there was much speculation about (although no awareness of) who would gain the post. Heinz was a prominent and well-entrenched figure in the School of General Studies (SGS), and he had not hitherto shown his hand as an Asianist. It was therefore to some surprise that Crawford presented his chosen successor at a cocktail reception for members of the department in the late afternoon of a glorious, early summer Canberra day.

The specific mandate of the Department of Economics, RSPS, was the study of 'underdeveloped and primitive economies, with emphasis on the building up of a systematic empirical knowledge of the Pacific and South East Asia'. Trevor Swan, Professor of Economics in the rival Research School of Social Sciences (RSSS), was reputed to have joked that with Crawford as professor it would be primitive economics all right! This was said without malice, for Swan had a long friendship with Crawford and great respect for him. Swan had been Crawford's junior assistant a quarter of a century earlier in the Rural Bank of NSW, and he had been influential in securing Crawford's appointment as director of RSPS when the professors of the school were disinclined to accept him. As Professor Oskar Spate, himself a subsequent director, wrote

> Then, like a *deus ex machina*, Trevor Swan, Professor of Economics in Social Sciences and an old friend of Crawford's, stepped in with an invitation to meet him over drinks at Trevor's house. We went, warily suspicious, and found a man of short stature, anything but an imposing presence, very quietly spoken; and before the evening was out we knew we had the man to lead us (Arndt 2000:33).

Crawford was always keen on Papua New Guinea and that interest was reflected in his initial appointments of Scarlett Epstein (a distinguished anthropologist) and Ric Shand, each working on aspects of the rural economy in the territory. Other early academic staff in the department included E.K. (Fred) Fisk, W.M. (Max) Corden, D.M. (David) Bensusan-Butt and G.B (Geoff) Hainsworth. Fisk, lately released from a senior economist post in the Malayan civil service, was to coordinate one of the department's first research projects on the economy of newly independent Malaya. Corden, a rising star in theories of trade and protection, was to give leadership in the field of international trade and payments, in which

Crawford retained a keen practical interest. Hainsworth, steeped in the then fashionable field of development economics, was to guide graduate students through the large and rich literature of that subject. Bensusan-Butt, on growth theory and taxation, and Shand, on agricultural economics, had little to do with the graduate students in class but were unfailingly approachable for discussion or advice. This, then, was the composition and character of Economics RSPS when Heinz took it over, as a result of a happy intersection of his and Crawford's individual career needs.

The department was in good condition when Heinz arrived. Crawford was seldom seen at academic seminars—except for those given by extremely distinguished visitors, such as Japan's Kiyoshi Kojima—and he generally had only tenuous contact with the individual members of the department and their work. He did, however, use masterfully his great network of the rich and powerful to the advantage of the department in general and to many of its individual research projects. Heinz took over a happy ship, and he kept it so. Heinz was bequeathed a good-sized department with a complement of senior and junior research fellows and a strong group of research scholars (PhD students). Apart from those already mentioned, the research staff by then included Ken Thomas, Bruce McFarlane and Tom Silcock. There was also a steady procession of medium-term visitors, and notable brief visits from academic luminaries such as Nicholas Kaldor and Kenneth Boulding.

The research scholars had come from Sydney, Melbourne, Adelaide, New England, Fiji, Singapore, Vietnam and Thailand. At any one time, several of them would have been in Asia or the Pacific islands conducting field research, but there were about eight working in the department at the time of Heinz's arrival. Malaysia/Malaya/Singapore and PNG were then the main fields of geographic interest. Fisk was the resident 'old Malaya hand', who was then developing a major interest in PNG, along with Shand and under the oversight of Crawford. One doctoral student was in PNG on field-work and another was in Malaya.

During 1962, the department had conducted a major research and seminar program on Malaya, to which departmental staff, other ANU scholars and visiting experts contributed. In 1963, the collected papers of the seminar series were edited by Silcock and Fisk and published, about the time of Heinz's arrival, by the fledgling ANU Press as *The Political Economy of Independent Malaya* (a title arrived at after much tea-room discussion, and thought to have maximum reader enticement). This volume drew attention to the high quality of the department, thus giving Heinz a strong platform for its further development.

In contrast with Crawford's rather invisible presence, Heinz was everywhere at once in his new department. It was then housed on the ANU campus in the former nurses' quarters of the old Canberra Community Hospital. The buildings were wooden, rambling in style and very cold in winter, but at least staff and students were all together and could be gathered easily for seminars and social events, of which the daily morning tea was something of a ritual.

Heinz wrote

> The departmental seminar, every Tuesday afternoon in term time, played a central role in the life of a department in which research was done in the main by individual scholars rather than as organised teams. Originally there were two series, a 'work in progress' seminar at which staff and students were expected to report on their work, and a theory and discussion seminar. Later they were merged, but both kinds of activity continued to be fairly equally represented (Arndt 1985:67).

Heinz quickly got to know his academic community, attended all their seminars—in which he was always a prominent contributor—and read countless drafts of articles, chapters, books and theses. In these ways, he truly put his intellectual stamp on the research work of the department, and that work flourished under his leadership. It was, of course, sometimes daunting to be on the receiving end of Arndt as professor: many speak of the experience of delivering a carefully crafted draft of a paper to his office of an afternoon and finding it returned in one's mail box next morning covered with critical and constructive comments (not neglecting grammatical improvements) in tiny handwriting somewhat resembling the path of a drunken fly. Also, Heinz expected all his colleagues to match his own enthusiasm for work and he had little patience with any who were reluctant or who lagged in pursuing work and opportunity. The result of Heinz's assumption of the leadership was a confident and energetic department, to which most people were proud to belong.

It should be mentioned, too, that in each of his ANU departments, Heinz enjoyed faithful support from his most efficient and diplomatic assistant:

'some time in 1951 a young secretary was assigned to me, a Canberra girl, Margaret Easton. She was still my secretary 32 years later when I found it difficult to reconcile myself to the prospect of her imminent retirement' (Arndt 1985:23).

Heinz's first move was to broaden the department's geographical span of interest, notably by making Indonesia a major project. Although Ken Thomas, as a Research Fellow, and Ingrid Palmer, as a PhD student, were engaged wholly on Indonesian subjects, and other members of the department had made occasional excursions into Indonesian issues, it was clear to Heinz that research on Indonesia could not be left at that level. 'Either we made a major effort or we left it alone for the time being.'

Almost everyone he consulted advised against the effort. It was, after all, the time when Sukarno's 'Guided Democracy' was in full flower and the Indonesian economy was in tatters. Moreover, Indonesia was in its state of confrontation—*Konfrontasi*—with Malaysia. The prospect of the ANU obtaining high-level cooperation for research in Indonesia was faint; it was also unlikely that research workers would be admitted to the country. Indeed, Thomas had already left South Sumatra when it seemingly became unsafe for foreigners. In the face of near-universal pessimism and encouraged only by the Australian Ambassador in Jakarta, K.C.O. (Mick) Shann, Heinz made an exploratory visit to Indonesia in late 1964. The result of that visit was the initiation of the department's major project on the Indonesian economy, which is still going strong 40 years later. That, however, is a story for the next chapter.

Meanwhile, developments in the department in Canberra cleared the way for a focus on Indonesia. After the very successful Malaya program of 1962–63, work on Malaysia declined. Clive Edwards and I completed our doctoral theses on that country, Fisk's interests shifted to PNG and other Pacific islands and no new recruits took up Malaysia. The department was well endowed with funds for staff positions and scholarships, so Heinz was able to direct much of these resources towards Indonesia.

The original staff had been joined by Conrad Blyth, Helen Hughes and Ramon Myers, none of whom worked directly on Indonesia, and by Alex Hunter, David Penny and Shamsher Ali, who did. None of the new doctoral scholars—Don Stammer, Malcolm Treadgold, Brian Lockwood and Gregory Clark—took up Indonesia, but within a few years a succession of young Australasian PhD candidates joined the department, attracted by the opportunity to undertake original research, including field-work, on the Indonesian economy and enjoying good supervision while doing so. They included Peter McCawley, Stephen Grenville, Anne Booth, Howard Dick, Hal Hill, Phyllis Rosendale and Chris Manning, all of whom turned their opportunities to very good account. Of these, Booth, McCawley, Hill and Manning were subsequently appointed to the staff of the department and continued to work on Indonesian subjects. It would be fair to say that, from 1965 until Heinz's retirement from the university in 1980, Indonesia was the main focus of the department—but by no means to the neglect of other areas.

A physical shift of the department from the old hospital buildings to the spanking new Coombs Building occurred in June 1964. The new quarters facilitated interaction not merely with other departments in Pacific Studies, but with departments of the Research School of Social Sciences, which occupied the other half of the honeycomb-shaped building. A huge common room for both schools was a natural meeting place for morning and afternoon teas, although Economics Pacific Studies preferred to have its own morning gathering in the department, on the corridor junction and adjacent balcony. Heinz showed up whenever possible, although his many duties often took him elsewhere. In these informal scenes, it was natural and easy to be aware of each other's work as well as to discuss larger local and international issues of the day.

A dominant presence was that of Helen Hughes, who could be described as the monarch of the coffee club. Helen had opinions on everything and did not hesitate to express them, right or wrong with equal authority, as Heinz observed. Helen was an informal leader among the staff and an adviser to the graduate students. They were encouraged by her positive approach to research and were deeply appreciative of her caring interest in their progress. Hughes had an illustrious subsequent career, first in the World Bank and then as the founding head of the National Centre for Development Studies located at the ANU.

The shift to the Coombs Building also meant that the department became better integrated into the Research School of Pacific Studies and the Institute of Advanced Studies. Heinz was inevitably drawn into the administration, and the politics, of these higher levels of the ANU organisation. Heinz never admitted publicly that he enjoyed administration.

It was time-consuming, diverting him from the more important activities of teaching and research, which centred on his department. Yet he never shied away from administrative obligations; they were part of the workload that academics had to carry. He always took his responsibilities as a head of department seriously and conscientiously, as he did with the duties of the directorship of the RSPS when he was called on occasionally to act temporarily in that role.

In 1976, he took on one of the most senior administrative roles in the university, that of Deputy Chairman of the Board of the Institute of Advanced Studies (known by its humorous acronym BIAS). When the amalgamation between the original ANU and the CUC occurred in 1960, it was agreed that the new ANU should have two academic boards: the Board of the Institute of Advanced Studies and the Board of the School of General Studies. The latter was to cater for the faculties of the former CUC and in due course it was renamed the Board of the Faculties. The chairman of each academic board was designated Deputy Chairman, simply because the Vice-Chancellor was *ex officio* the chairman of all university committees.

For many years, Heinz had been a member of BIAS as one of the representatives of RSPS. In August 1976, the Deputy Chairman, Professor Frank Gibson, resigned and Heinz was appointed to replace him on an acting basis. Subsequently, the Vice-Chancellor, Professor Anthony Low, persuaded Heinz to take the job for two years. In 1978, Heinz agreed to be reappointed for a further two years, which would take him to his due date of retirement.

Under the *ANU Act*, BIAS was responsible for all academic matters concerning the institute and was to advise the governing council on 'any matter relating to education, learning or research or the academic work of the University'. In practice, it advised the Vice-Chancellor and the council on academic issues such as new courses of study and the establishment of new programs and departments. It devoted considerable time to receiving and discussing major reports, and it recommended admissions to degrees; it made appointments to subcommittees, received study leave and electoral committee reports and advised the Vice-Chancellor on appointments in the research schools. As Deputy Chairman, Heinz acted for the Vice-Chancellor in approving academic appointments at certain levels and accepted resignations.

In the oblique reference in *A Course Through Life* to his work as Deputy Chairman of BIAS, Heinz said that although he had been 'saddled' with the job and had found it time-consuming, it had nevertheless been an interesting experience. He noted that it involved chairing 16 standing committees and countless *ad hoc* committees. The Deputy Chairman also sat *ex officio* on the governing council of the ANU, a body on which at various times Ruth and Bettina Arndt had served. At one stage, Heinz and Bettina were on the council simultaneously. Bettina was once accompanied by her newborn son, Jesse, who slept peacefully during the morning meeting; Heinz was most proud of three generations of Arndts being in the council room.

During the 1960s, Heinz maintained his industrious work for the *Economic Record*. The engine room of the *Record* had always been in Melbourne, with Professor Sir Douglas Copland the founding editor in 1925. Heinz's connection with the University of Melbourne and its economists began through his job at CUC, which taught for Melbourne's Bachelor of Commerce degree. Heinz had to follow the Melbourne curriculum and interact with Melbourne staff in setting and marking examination papers. These duties sustained his contact with Dick Downing, whom he had first met in 1948, and the friendship deepened as the years passed.

By 1954, the *Record* was still the only learned journal of the social sciences in Australasia. In that year, Downing succeeded to the editorship and he invited Heinz to join the editorial board, in effect as assistant editor. The job lasted 20 years and, for at least the first 12 of those years, Downing and Heinz between them read every article submitted to the *Record*, subsequently rewrote many of them and commissioned or wrote further pieces to fill out a balanced journal. The two worked closely and enjoyably. 'I probably read, on average, four or five contributions a month, so that Dick and I exchanged one or two letters a week' (Arndt 1985:29–30).

Another major professional collaboration was in the 1964 report on *Taxation in Australia: agenda for reform*, instigated by the Social Science Research Council and produced by Downing, as chairman, Heinz, Alan Boxer, Peter Karmel and Russell Mathews. Heinz's long and frequent correspondence with Downing and their meetings were not confined to economics subjects. They talked and wrote also about friends and colleagues, family matters, career decisions, music, literature and the arts, right up to Downing's sudden death in 1975. Heinz regarded Downing as 'my closest friend for almost 30 years'.

The Department of Economics, RSPS, came into full bloom in the late 1960s and the 1970s. During those years, Colin Barlow, Peter Lloyd, R.M. Sundrum, Audrey Donnithorne, Elizabeth Whitcombe, Martin Rudner, Eric Waring, Dan Etherington, Paul Luey, Malcolm Treadgold, Hazel Richter, Brian Lockwood, Ross Garnaut and Peter Warr were all appointed for various terms. Their interests and expertise encompassed China, India, Burma (Myanmar), Malaysia, the Philippines, PNG, Fiji and other Pacific islands, as well as agricultural economics, international trade and economic development generally. Simultaneously, there was an increase in the number of research scholars: a dozen or so Asian graduates came to the department as PhD candidates, as did another half-dozen Australasians. Heinz undertook the supervision of several of these scholars but, curiously, he never supervised an Indonesian.

His sole and notable protégé from Indonesia was Boediono, whose position in the department was as a research assistant of the Indonesia project. Boediono came to the department in July 1970, having previously submitted a thesis for the Master's degree at Monash University. The thesis required revision, which Boediono was able to do while holding his post in the ANU. Boediono later progressed through the Indonesian civil service to become Minister of Finance, Minister for Planning and Coordinating Economics Minister. In an obituary tribute to Heinz, Boediono wrote

> I never took a course with him, nor did I do my thesis under his supervision. Nevertheless, I consider him my teacher both about my profession and life…Heinz's writings on Indonesia and development influenced me directly and indirectly. He influenced my thinking about the problems facing the country, about the role of economics in the solutions, and about how an economist should define his or her role in public life (McCawley et al. 2002:183).

The department became a very lively and, at times, crowded place. There was no shortage of bright, interesting and attractive women in the department. Some had been appointed by Crawford and their number was increased by Heinz. Hughes has recorded

> A major factor in Arndt's ability to find staff and students and to develop contacts in the region was his evident race and gender blindness. At a Departmental meeting in the mid 1960s a University edict noting the absence of women in academic

positions in the ANU's Institute of Advanced Studies was to be discussed. Arndt's Department then had three of the four senior women academics at the Institute ranged around the table. One of these remarked: 'This is something that this Department doesn't have to worry about.' Looking around, bewildered, Arndt said: 'I don't understand what you mean.' He saw around him his academic staff, not men and women. The morale boost of a head of Department so totally unaffected either by discrimination or affirmative action can now hardly be imagined (Hughes 2002:484).

Heinz clearly liked female company. There was no sign of any particular attachment but the younger men (and perhaps the older, who were more reticent) observed that their female colleagues, staff and research students received more of Heinz's time and attention than they did.

The department was basically brim-full of research fellows and graduate students, research assistants and administrative staff. It also managed to find room for callers and short-term visitors, too numerous to identify here. It is worth mentioning, however, the visits of two very distinguished economists, Charles Kindleberger and Fred Hirsch, which occurred in 1966 and 1974 respectively.

Heinz had been a 'pen pal' of Kindleberger since the mid 1950s. After a scraped acquaintance during Heinz's 1954 sabbatical in the United States, Heinz wrote to Kindleberger a detailed and constructive critique of the latter's book *The Dollar Shortage* (1950). Kindleberger replied, most courteously, in detail and with gratitude. The correspondence, which began as 'Dear Professor Kindleberger/Dear Professor Arndt', soon progressed to 'Dear Kindleberger/Dear Arndt', and then to 'Dear Charlie/Dear Heinz'; it was maintained, with increasing frequency in their retirement years, until Heinz's death (Kindleberger died soon afterwards in July 2003).

The visit of Professor and Mrs Kindleberger to Canberra in July 1966 was a big professional and social event for Heinz and Ruth and the department. Kindleberger had held a visiting appointment at the University of Canterbury, Christchurch, and was returning home via Australia. As well as going to Canberra, he went to Brisbane to give a public lecture and to Sydney to meet with the governor and staff of the Reserve Bank. Heinz arranged a full and rich program for the Kindlebergers in Canberra. Charlie met the staff of Economics RSPS and Economics SGS, lectured to the local branch of the Economic Society and gave a seminar in Heinz's department. The Kindlebergers were also subjected to a heavy social program, which involved not only Heinz and Ruth and many of the department, but ANU notables and the US ambassador. Charlie did not stint in expressing gratitude to Heinz: 'Not only did I enjoy seeing Canberra and meeting your colleagues, but it was particularly enjoyable to make your close acquaintance after all these years of correspondence. I regard this as an impressive capital investment of the trip and one on which I shall expect to draw revenue for years to come.'

The visit of Fred Hirsch, British academic, former leading international economic journalist and IMF senior staff member, occurred in October 1974. Hirsch had been invited to PNG to advise on the introduction of its new currency, the kina, and was looking for knowledgeable opinions. Heinz assembled Fred Fisk and Malcolm Treadgold of his department, Peter Drysdale of the ANU's Faculty of Economics, SGS, Dr M.L. Parker of the Industries Assistance Commission (and an old PNG hand) and myself (from the University of New England). It was a very interesting occasion. Hirsch, who later wrote the splendid and seminal *Social Limits to Growth*, was surprisingly quiet and diffident, but he asked good questions and listened attentively to all the answers and opinions. At least two of the group were stimulated to undertake later work on the PNG monetary system. Sadly, Hirsch was dead within four years; at the time of his death he was Professor of International Studies in the University of Warwick, a post to which he had acceded shortly after his visit to the ANU.

In general, the academic staff of the Department of Economics were happy with Heinz's leadership and gave him loyal support. Frictions, however, developed in some cases; and it should be mentioned that he fell out with all three of his first appointees to the Indonesia project, Ken Thomas, Jusuf Panglaykim and David Penny. To some degree, this was a matter of them not being comfortable in full-time academic research; further, at least in the case of Penny, who had been Heinz's closest colleague in the early years of the Indonesia project, anyone interested primarily in politics, sociology and the welfare of the Indonesian peasantry would find it hard to stomach the sympathetic attitude that Heinz and others displayed 'towards the growth-oriented policies of the Jakarta technocrats'. Some other members of the department grumbled about the attention and resources devoted to Indonesia, fearing that a negative consequence would be to distort the department's mission (and belittle their work on other subjects and places). The non-Indonesia cause never gathered much momentum or became a major issue until after Max Corden returned to the department from Nuffield College, Oxford, in 1976.

Corden was undoubtedly the most intellectually renowned member of the department before, during and since Heinz's time. Corden was already in the department—as a Professorial Fellow—when Heinz arrived. He left in 1967 to accept a readership at Nuffield College and returned as professor in 1976. Heinz was very enthusiastic about Corden's return. They had collaborated over the years on aspects of Australian economic policy (including the 1963 jointly edited bestseller, *The Australian Economy: a volume of readings*, and a paper for the Vernon Inquiry on 'The interdependence of problems of economic policy') and Heinz had great respect for Corden's powers of analysis, criticism and exposition.

Before leaving for England, Corden had worked on applied issues pertaining to Australia and Asia, as well as pursuing his theoretical interests. Heinz, therefore, had no reason to suspect that Corden would not now be comfortable with the department's commitment to Asian, and especially Indonesian, economic development; and he failed to grasp that Corden's former interest in that field had cooled by 1976.

Other older members of the department had reservations about Corden's return and it is fair to say that it was far from universally welcomed. In the next three years, as Heinz, Corden and the others had to live and work as colleagues, disenchantment set in on all sides. What galled Heinz was that, as far as he could see, Corden had not only given up his former applied interest in Asian trade and development, he seemed to belittle the work of those who tilled such fields. Heinz began to fear that the most creative part of his life's work—the Indonesia project—was under threat, and that thought took root ineradicably.

Things came to a head as Heinz's retirement loomed and as the elevation to Head of Department of Corden, then the sole remaining full professor, appeared automatic. The appointment of Corden as head was opposed strongly by some members of the department and Heinz encouraged them in their resistance. (It is proper and usual for a retiring academic leader to play no part in the selection of a successor, and to refrain from subsequent interference in the successor's leadership.) Within and beyond the department, Heinz fomented opposition to Corden, to the extent that the Vice-Chancellor gave thought to appointing one or other of the senior, non-professorial staff to be head. In the end, Corden was appointed to the post.

As head, Corden at last had the opportunity to rebalance the work of the department. He was reacting to what, on his return in 1976, he regarded as undue pressure from Heinz to change his own interests. In a recent interview for the *Economic Record*, he said

> Heinz had built up a Department consisting primarily of experts on various countries—people who knew Indonesia, Malaysia, Fiji or something like that…Heinz wanted me to move in the direction of the Department's current main interests, and that I should only take on PhD students who would work in these areas, especially Indonesia. But by that time I was 50 years old and not inclined to move in anyone's direction…I expressed my own views…Heinz began to feel that I was threatening his little baby, namely the 'Indonesia project'. He felt that I might destroy it. Actually I was not intending to, though I thought it could be improved…So we fell out.

Heinz, however, became embittered and never really forgave Corden. As late as 1996, in a letter to Kindleberger, he wrote

> Max Corden. This is a sad story, a bit like a broken-down marriage. As you know, we worked together for many years, I got him the Chair in my Department and had, and still have, a high regard for his skill as a trade theorist and expositor. But he nearly ruined my Department in his years as Head (because he was not interested in Asia or economic development) and has been singularly unhelpful ever since.

And to Kindleberger again, in late 1997, he wrote:'We used to be colleagues and friends, but nowadays, as he told me last time we met, his "time is too valuable" to comment on what I send him.'

This is indeed a sad story because neither man lacked respect for the other's abilities. Corden thought that

> Heinz was a very sophisticated, civilised person. He was a very good economist; he had a lot more intuition than most more technical economists; he could see through an issue in an argument, and this was very apparent to me years earlier. Also he had many virtues. He was a man of high principle, which also meant he had strong convictions. He was very conscientious — if

a student gave him a draft of a chapter he would read it, and comment on it promptly in detail and not in a few words, so he was greatly respected among students…Let me also add that earlier he had been a member of the editorial board of *The Economic Record*, and he gave incredibly thorough comments on submitted papers. I benefited from this way back in 1954 before I had actually met him, when I sent a paper from the LSE, which was my first paper published in the *Record* (Coleman 2006:391–2).

So, two good men, each respecting the other as economists, each recalling fondly their early connection, collaboration and companionship, but unable to heal fully the damaged friendship before Heinz died.

Periodically, Heinz received extended relief from departmental responsibilities through study leave and special assignments. A good example of the latter was his visit to Chile in September–October 1970. Heinz encapsulated this experience thus

> In 1970, Claudio Veliz, the Chilean historian, organised a '*Conferencía del Pacífico*' in Viña del Mar. *Dependencía* was in the air, and Veliz and others had the romantic idea that [the] dependence of Chile and other Andean Group countries on the USA might be reduced through closer ties with countries of the western Pacific. It was a splendid conference, opened by the neo- (or at least near) Marxist economist, Osvaldo Sunkel, whose imaginative diagrams illustrating the relations between the 'Centre' and the 'Periphery' evoked gently amused comments by the chairman of the opening session, President Eduardo Frei. But the real excitement of that visit to Chile arose from the fact that it took place in the interval between the popular elections which gave Allende his plurality and his election to the presidency by Congress. All through the week, Viña del Mar buzzed with rumours about Allende's negotiations with the Christian Democrats on constitutional guarantees (which in the event he proved unable to honour), about Cabinet appointments and about the bombs that every night blew out shop and office windows in Santiago. Young radicals, neo-Marxists of various hues, were congregating in Chile from all over Latin America and were

very vocal at the conference. The Singapore Foreign Minister, Mr Rajaratnam, who was one of the participants, commented that they reminded him of the turtle that lays a thousand eggs but only one hatches (Arndt 1985:70).

This précis, however, omits some interesting sidelights such as the constant dogmatic warfare between left and right-wing economists on the conference floor, Heinz's consequently challenging role as rapporteur and summariser, and the highly unsettled and uncertain situation in Chile, which threatened armed conflict and economic disaster. There had been a large-scale flight of capital, a run on the domestic banks and desperate queues at the airports. A conservative young man told Heinz that there were two classes of Chileans: 'the cowards who are leaving and the idiots who are staying.' According to many, the tragedy for the nation was that, under Chile's constitution, the widely respected President Frei could not stand for a further term.

Heinz enjoyed associating in Viña del Mar with Rajaratnam, Yip Yat Hoong (academic economist from Malaysia, and a chess player), Kiyoshi Kojima (so influential in the development of the ANU's interest in the economies of Japan and North Asia), New Zealander Les Castle and the notable Australian political and economic commentators Bruce Grant and Ted Wheelwright.

After the conference, Heinz went on to Santiago, where he saw the political developments played out further and got involved, at the last minute, in another conference, on the *Prebisch Report* about economic development in Latin America. This conference was organised by the Inter-American Development Bank and the Economic Commission for Latin America and was held at the latter's new building, which Heinz thought 'a superb piece of modern concrete architecture'. Heinz ran into a number of distinguished economists and friends: Rosenstein-Rodan, Saburo Okita, Kojima, Thomas Balogh ('provocative as usual—about Indonesia: "So you are studying the economics of Fascism, how to murder 200,000 people"'), Wheelwright, Oskar Spate (ANU geographer), Dudley Seers, Edward Mason and Albert Hirschman (prominent development economists). He returned to Canberra a few days later, refreshed and stimulated by his experiences but confirmed in his judgement to confine his future professional work, and that of his department, to Asia and the western Pacific.

In 1965, Heinz went once more to Geneva, for a sabbatical leave spent in the secretariat of the newly established UN Conference for Trade and Development (UNCTAD). He was part of a team to prepare a shipping document for the second UNCTAD meeting in Delhi in 1968, '[b]ut the answers to all the major questions were already decided: our task was merely to prepare the argumentation'. The UNCTAD strategic objective was to bring about a fracture of the shipping conference cartels and clear the way for the development of national merchant navies by developing countries. Heinz did a statistical and analytical piece on the balance-of-payments effects of import substitution in shipping; it did not survive into the final draft because it gave unpalatable results. A 'passing health scare' gave Heinz the excuse to withdraw from the project. Nevertheless, he had enjoyed being in Geneva again, though now recognising that it held no future for him.

Heinz's next sabbatical was spent at the Organisation for Economic Cooperation and Development (OECD) in Paris in the second half of 1972. In May of the preceding year, the Australian government had accepted an invitation to become the twenty-third member of the OECD. Accession to membership was formalised when the Deputy Prime Minister, J.D. Anthony, attended the annual ministerial meeting of the OECD in Paris in June 1971. Previously, fearing that its high tariff levels and controls over the international flow of capital would come under close and critical scrutiny, Australia had been reluctant to join the OECD. This had been the view of the former Minister for Trade and Industry, John McEwen. With the retirement of McEwen and the accession of William McMahon to the prime ministership, Australia's position changed quickly. McMahon declared that membership of the OECD represented a significant step in Australia's foreign economic policy.

Heinz's appointment to the OECD arose because of the organisation's first survey of the Australian economy. To write the survey, the OECD required a person with a thorough understanding of the Australian economy and its economic and political institutions. Heinz's former research assistant at the UN Economic Commission for Europe (ECE) in Geneva, Eduardo Merigo, was now a senior economist at the OECD. Merigo recommended to Christopher Dow, the head of the organisation's Economic Department, that Heinz should be engaged to write the survey. Heinz was appointed as Deputy Director of the Country Studies Division to work specifically on Australia and generally on current economic developments in high-income countries. He arranged with the ANU to take sabbatical leave for six months.

Ruth accompanied Heinz for the first few months. On the way to Paris, they spent a day in Hong Kong and four days in Iran, where Heinz lectured at the University of Teheran and where, unfortunately, he and Ruth contracted severe gastric troubles: 'a souvenir from two marvellous days at Isfahan.' In Paris, they took a small flat in the Rue Eugene Manuel, close to the Château de la Muette, the Rothschild mansion used by the OECD as its headquarters. When Ruth returned to Canberra, Heinz obtained slightly better accommodation.

> No larger [than the previous flat], it was sub-sub-let to me, illegally, by a lady who had almost certainly used it professionally, in the oldest profession; but it was light and clean and had the great advantage of being in the Rue de Passy which, still following contours of the main street of what had once been Passy village, is one of the most charming streets in suburban Paris (Arndt 1985:85).

As well as drafting the survey of the Australian economy, which included an excellent economic history of the country since 1950, Heinz prepared a series of annexes on Australia's system of government, its economic policy instruments, its financial system and the system of wage determination and arbitration. The Australian economy at the time was experiencing a boom, based on high prices for commodity exports. Speculative funds were flowing into the country on the expectation of an appreciation of the Australian dollar, but the government would not agree to a revaluation. In an effort to staunch the inflow of capital, the government had introduced controls on investment from abroad. Heinz recommended in his draft an across-the-board cut in tariffs and the abolition of the capital controls. He was surprised when a team sent from the Australian Treasury (which included his old friend John Stone) to the OECD to vet the draft report insisted on only one change to it, a modification of his recommendation to abolish the capital controls.

Meanwhile, the government had changed and the incoming Prime Minister, Gough Whitlam, was at first reluctant to endorse a report that had been approved by the outgoing McMahon government. But, as recorded by Heinz: 'when his attention was drawn to the paragraph advocating an across-the-board cut in tariffs, he changed his mind: "This is how I can dish Jim [Cairns, his protectionist party colleague]." I like to think that the survey contributed to Whitlam's courageous decision to cut tariffs by 25 per cent, as well as to appreciate the dollar, in his first weeks in office' (Arndt 1985:85).

Heinz's work in the OECD was not confined to preparing the survey of Australia. He contributed also to surveys of Canada, Italy, Greece, Denmark, Norway and the United Kingdom. He attended meetings of the Economic Policy Committee, the Short-Term Forecasting Group and a working party on public expenditure in member countries, and he drafted the introduction for the December issue of *Economic Outlook*. He found discussion among the organisation's economists highly stimulating, especially their interest in inflation and the policies to combat it.

When he returned home, he reported to the university about his leave: 'in this way, and through some involvement in the work of various committees in the last few weeks, I gradually familiarised myself with the major issues of economic policy, domestic and international, of current concern in the developed countries.'

Above all, he found particularly attractive the OECD's strong commitment to the market economy, freedom of trade and international capital movement, and tight monetary and fiscal policies.

Heinz warmed to Paris as a city, spending much of his spare time sketching and painting the city landscape and its buildings. He attended concerts, visited museums and galleries, enjoyed restaurants and travelled outside the city. In his final weeks in Paris, there was talk that he might succeed Sir Ronald Walker as Australian Ambassador to the OECD. Walker had played a large part in convincing Heinz to accept his first Australian job at the University of Sydney, and he was keen for Heinz to replace him in Paris. It had been decided within the Canberra bureaucracy, however, that Walker's replacement should be a Treasury official, so Roy Cameron, who had been a member of Heinz's department in CUC days, was chosen for the post.

Towards the end of his time in Paris, Heinz was asked if he would act, for a short term, as the director of the ECE's Research Department in Geneva, where he had spent his leave in 1960–61. The idea was that he would begin this short appointment early in 1973 and hold the post until a new and permanent director arrived in June. This would be a busy time because the ECE's major annual publication, the *Economic Survey for Europe*, would be produced. Heinz was considered a natural for the job. He expressed considerable interest in the idea, and he had enough accumulated leave for a six-month appointment. David Butt, who was acting head of Economics RSPS, was willing to continue for that long; in the end Heinz chose not to accept the invitation.

Instead, he left Paris in December and returned to Australia via Canada, the United States and Japan. He attended the annual meeting of the American Economic Association in Toronto; he then held discussions about the Indonesia project and his department's work generally in New York with the Ford Foundation, the Asia Society and the UN Secretariat, and in Washington with the World Bank. From the United States, he flew to Tokyo, where he took part in the Fifth Pacific Trade and Development Conference and attended a meeting of the Joint Research Project on Australia–Japan economic relations, which had been established by Crawford and Okita but was the brainchild of Kojima and Peter Drysdale and was managed by the latter. Heinz's direct involvement in this long-term project was marginal but he maintained a strong connection to it, often acting on Crawford's behalf, participating in its Canberra meetings and in the project's seminars at the ANU, serving on its Australian research committee and monitoring its research.

Not long after he had returned from the Paris sabbatical, Heinz was approached to join the Board of Directors of Australia's oldest commercial bank, the Bank of NSW (nowadays Westpac Banking Corporation). In 1973, Sir John Dunlop, a leading industrialist, had resigned from the board of the bank in order to join the board of the new Australian Industries Development Corporation, a government authority. The General Manager of the bank, Sir Robert Norman, knew Heinz and his work on Australian banking and invited him to join the board. After much indecision, and consultation with many friends, Heinz decided 'to seek the view of one more friend whose judgement I trusted completely and to abide by his advice whatever it was. It turned out to be to decline the invitation, which I did. Five years later it might have been a different matter' (Arndt 1985:88).

In 1973, however, Heinz was too tender about his recent resignation from the Labor Party to sup at the table of the plutocrats, one of whom ironically had been portrayed in the press as going in the opposite direction and embracing socialism by accepting the position on the Industries Development Corporation.

For the next seven years, Heinz soldiered on with his work in the Department of Economics, his incessant writing and his many business trips to Asia, which are the subject of succeeding chapters. He continued to contribute to debates on economic and political policy in Australia. Yet, with the exception of letters to the editors of *The Australian Financial Review* and *The Australian*, he dealt with subjects of international rather than domestic significance. Even his longer essays in popular journals, such as *Quadrant*, and academic outlets were largely to do with international economic development. He did, however, publish new editions of *The Australian Trading Banks* with co-authors Don Stammer, in 1973, and Wes Blackert, in 1977. And he began to lay the foundations for his retirement.

Among the indicators of Heinz's success as an academic leader must be counted the significant later careers of the PhD graduates and other alumni of the department, whether in his time or later. Heinz has written that 'I enormously enjoyed the continuous intellectual and personal contact with the students I was myself supervising and have followed their subsequent careers, in many cases notable and even distinguished, with pride and pleasure' (Arndt 1985:68).

To run some risk of unintended oversight, among Heinz's own doctoral students were, in chronological order: myself (founding Vice-Chancellor, Australian Catholic University, and previously Professor of Economics and Principal, University of New England, Armidale); Don Stammer (investment banker and leading financial commentator, formerly Deputy Head of Research, Reserve Bank of Australia); Malcolm Treadgold (Professor of Economics, University of New England); Chirayu Isarangkun (Dean, School of Development Economics, Bangkok, and later Director of Thailand's National Institute for Development Administration); Peter McCawley (Vice-President, Asian Development Bank and Dean of its Institute in Tokyo, previously Deputy Director, AusAID); Anne Booth (Professor of Economics, School of Oriental and African Studies, University of London); Stephen Grenville (Deputy Governor, Reserve Bank of Australia, and earlier with the IMF); Howard Dick (distinguished economic historian of Southeast Asia, now at the University of Melbourne); Alan Stretton (Deputy Secretary for Arts and Sports, Commonwealth of Australia, Department of Communications, Information Technology and the Arts); Phyllis Rosendale (senior Treasury official, Victoria); Mingsarn Santikarn (Deputy Director, Thailand Development Research Institute); and Hal Hill (H.W. Arndt Professor of Southeast Asian Economies, ANU). Grenville spoke for us all when, at Heinz's funeral, he said

> [Heinz] not only opened the doors for us, his students, to new and mind-enlarging experiences that we would not have been

brave enough to undertake without him but as well he made us a bit braver and a bit more ready to push those doors by ourselves. We didn't learn as much as we should have from his example, but we learnt enough to change our lives. I don't doubt that this was the achievement Heinz was most proud of—not the shelf load of books he's written (although he certainly loved those) but rather the people who he emboldened to try just a bit harder to make the world a better place.

The list above, of course, does not include other distinguished doctoral graduates of the department who were not supervised by Heinz himself, such as Peter Drysdale, Ingrid Palmer, Andrew Elek and Chris Manning, and the many Asian graduates who returned to make fine careers and valuable economic and social contributions in their home countries or as international civil servants. Just as importantly the list also excludes those whose careers prospered after stints as research staff of the department. These would include Max Corden and Helen Hughes, already given particular mention, as well as Conrad Blyth, Ramon Myers, Geoffrey Hainsworth, Martin Rudner, Bruce McFarlane, Peter Lloyd, Kym Anderson and Christopher Findlay, who all became professors at other universities. Worthy of particular mention is Ross Garnaut, Heinz's much admired and respected junior colleague and protégé whose extremely distinguished later career included the posts of Ambassador of Australia to China and professor and head of Economics RSPS (fittingly inhabiting Heinz's former office).

Hughes, in her obituary essay for Heinz, traced the success of the department in making its work relevant to economic policy in Asia and becoming the nucleus (together with its offshoots, the National Centre for Development Studies and the Australia–Japan Research Centre) of an international hub of Asian economic studies based at the ANU. She drew attention to the fact that, as well as hundreds of graduates returned to Asia and the Pacific islands, '[i]n Australia, universities, the public service and business had been staffed with economics graduates specialising in development and Asian studies'.

At the time of Heinz's retirement, he could justly claim to have upheld the department's mandate for the study of 'theoretical and applied problems of economic growth and trade' and, as evidenced by a substantial output of quality publications, to have promoted effectively its primary interest in 'the economic development of the countries of Southeast Asia and the Pacific region, especially New Guinea, Malaysia and Indonesia, and in Australia's economic relations with these countries'.

19
SUKARNO'S INDONESIA

Heinz made his reconnaissance of Indonesia in October–November 1964. The lengthy diary that he kept and later published (in edited forms) shows how eager and delighted an academic visitor he was. It reveals idealism, optimism and great enthusiasm, but not zealotry or gullibility. His eyes were fresh, he went without preconceptions, and he travelled without hindrance.

On what in those days was a rather long flight from Sydney to Jakarta, Heinz spent much time trying to learn the Indonesian language. He had begun this task in Canberra, with the help of conversation classes and Yale language tapes. During his time in Indonesia, he adopted the discipline of reading, with the help of a dictionary, a local newspaper for half an hour every morning. He also constantly badgered his various Indonesian hosts and helpers for words and conversation. But—as is the fate of all passing visitors—he never really learned to converse in Bahasa Indonesia. As he wryly wrote: 'One of my friends once complimented me unkindly: "You know Heinz, you employ your vocabulary of 200 words with remarkable fluency." But my failure to learn Indonesian properly diminished my usefulness in Indonesia in many respects' (Arndt 1985:53).

Culturally, however, Heinz found Indonesian people congenial—'so much easier to be with than Indians'. He felt that the lack of urgency in the culture, despite its exasperating side, 'made for a friendliness which readily extended to foreign visitors'. He found the weeks of travelling through various islands of Indonesia's archipelago tremendously exciting and enjoyable, notwithstanding the poverty and abject mismanagement of the Indonesian economy.

Sukarno's Indonesia had problems aplenty. Not only was average income abysmally low; the country's roads, shipping and infrastructure were run down, the manufacturing industry was working at less than 20 per cent of its capacity, foreign trade was throttled by a complex of regulations and multiple exchange rates, and foreign debt had risen to a level that promised certain default. On top of all this, inflation had risen to an annual rate of more than 600 per cent, and endemic corruption further eroded domestic and foreign confidence in the economy. One anecdote of Heinz's epitomised the intellectual bankruptcy of the country's leadership at that time.

> In 1964, the effective head of government under Sukarno, Dr Subandrio, banned the publication of the budget or any related statistics. A little later he called a meeting of university economists. When he addressed them for 40 minutes on the 'Newly Emerging Forces', one of the economists asked whether they might be allowed to draw his attention to some of the country's economic problems. Dr Subandrio rounded on him and said: 'The fact that you think economic problems important shows how your mind has been corrupted by Western liberalism' (Arndt 1985:52).

The parlous conditions and repressive attitudes under the Sukarno regime were daunting for economic research, especially when foreigners were attempting it. Heinz refused to give up. He soon realised that he would have to begin by working diplomatically and carefully around the edges of the system. Therefore, he sought to establish viable connections with Indonesian officials, Indonesian university economists and the handful of foreign economists still working in the country. His first efforts with local officials, promoted with the help of Mick Shann, the Australian Ambassador, ultimately came to nothing because the 1965–66 change of regime removed Sukarno's men from office.

With academic economists, especially the younger ones at the University of Indonesia in Jakarta, Heinz had better luck. Sukarno's apparatchiks tended to regard them with some suspicion, because many of them had recently returned from postgraduate studies in the United States. They included Professors Mohamed Sadli and Widjojo Nitisastro, as well as Ali Wardhana, Emil Salim, Rahmat Saleh and Soehadi. Most of them achieved importance as senior economic bureaucrats in the Suharto government. So did Dr Jusuf Panglaykim (alias Pang Lai Kim), of whom more afterwards.

Among the precious few foreign economists left in the country, the one most helpful to Heinz was Don Blake, an American who specialised in studying labour markets. An old Asia hand, Blake gave Heinz great assistance in breaking the ice locally, and he and Heinz got on well. Heinz mentions a handful of other foreign economists: a group from the University of Kentucky, led by Howard Beers, based at the Institut Pertanian Bogor (IPB, the agricultural university) and working under the auspices of USAID, the main American aid agency; Ingrid Palmer, a doctoral candidate from ANU, who researched the textile industry; David Penny (an Australian); and Shamsher Ali (an Indo-Fijian). Heinz later recruited Penny and Ali to the Canberra end of the ANU's Indonesia project. How different was all this from the last years of the Suharto regime when Jakarta was swarming with economists from the World Bank, the IMF, other international agencies, foreign governments and merchant banks.

Once Shann and David Evans at the Australian Embassy had welcomed Heinz to Jakarta (along with Palmer and Blake), he spent almost two weeks in and around the city, with a lot of time to himself after the initial introductions were out of the way. He stayed at what was then the prestigious Hotel Indonesia, something of a flagship for Sukarno, who also lavished on the capital a rash of monumental statues in parks and at major intersections. In his leisure time, Heinz explored the streets, markets and shops (especially bookshops), experimenting with local food and reading or writing in his room at the hotel. He observed the poor condition of the city streets, the muddle of traffic (cars, trucks, trishaws, bikes, buses and military vehicles of every sort), the modern hotel and office buildings, and the comfortable older houses with their well-kept gardens. On Jalan Thamrin, the main dual carriageway that bisected the city, he noted 'an astonishingly thick flow of motor traffic, plenty of smart American cars, also Mercedes and smaller ones. Every so often a screaming siren from a motorcade which precedes and follows a large beflagged car carrying some general or one of Sukarno's ministers' (Arndt 1987:60).

Also on Jalan Thamrin, Heinz saw slogans painted in huge letters on posters, billboards, fences and walls. Many read '*GANDJANG MALAYSIA*' (crush Malaysia), in reference to the Sukarno policy of *Konfrontasi* towards Malaysia, which the president regarded as Imperial Britain's lackey, and hence contemptible for any self-respecting independent Asian nation. *Konfrontasi* was in a sense the bellwether of Indonesia's relations with Australia at the time. Of course, Australia wished to remain a firm supporter of Malaysia, its newly independent ally and fellow Commonwealth member. At the same time, it feared an open rupture of relations with Indonesia. That it avoided such a rupture was due in many respects to the exceptional diplomacy of Shann and his team at the Australian Embassy. These staffers also did much to ensure that Heinz pursued his research not only unhindered, but sometimes with active Indonesian assistance.

While staying at the Hotel Indonesia, Heinz dined with Dr Panglaykim's family, as well as with Blake, Palmer and George Hicks. This last figure was an Australian volunteer graduate who was working with the planning agency Bappenas. An able, independent thinker, Hicks always maintained good relations with Heinz, and had a distinguished subsequent career as an economist and commentator in various parts of Asia.

Most evenings, Heinz, left to his own devices, chose to spend his time reading and writing before going to sleep rather early. On one evening, however, he wandered into a vast hall next to the hotel. There he found himself in the middle of a large function organised by a local student association. The hosts made him welcome and he found the event pleasurable. Speakers included Ali Sastroamidjojo, a former prime minister, and General H.A. Nasution, the Commander-in-Chief of Indonesian forces. Ali worked the room 'like a French politician' (according to Heinz); Nasution was earnest and sober. After the speeches, entertainment and fraternising with the student leaders, Heinz met Nasution and his handsome wife, as well as Sukarno's daughter, Megawati, herself destined to become President 37 years later.

Heinz's important objectives in Indonesia included collecting current economic data and establishing channels to transmit to Canberra future relevant economic information and statistics. The Indonesian contacts he made in this quest enabled him to obtain copious data for use in the *Bulletin of Indonesian Economic Studies* (BIES), which first appeared in an 80-page pilot issue in 1965. Heinz founded the BIES (of which more in the next chapter) and produced it in his Canberra department. It has continued, without interruption, since then. Today it is recognised as the premier academic journal about the economy of Indonesia.

During his travels—not only in Jakarta but through rural Java, Sumatra and Sulawesi, then widely called the Celebes—Heinz made contact with Indonesian academics and officials in various universities and provinces. He introduced himself to several faculties and government departments by giving lectures and conducting seminars. He concentrated from the beginning on the topical subject of inflation (then, as already mentioned, rampant in Indonesia), which he approached from the theoretical side. Trying to strip away the veil of money from considerations of real income and asset values, he aimed to get his listeners to think about the underlying real resources. For example, he noticed that some peasants managed to hoard real resources, despite the accelerating inflation.

Inevitably, the discussions on these occasions turned from theory to the particularities of Indonesian inflation, and thence to Indonesia's general economic condition, above all its balance-of-payments difficulties.

Despite the great shortage of foreign exchange, Heinz noticed everywhere a profusion of imported goods. Not only were the shops in Jakarta well stocked, including with the latest television sets, so were shops in the provinces. In the northwestern Sumatran city of Medan, Heinz saw a grocery store in the main street with 'shelves to the roof laden with every kind of luxury food, bottles of liqueur, whiskey, smoked ham etc.' (Arndt 1987:93). Everywhere the well-to-do lived very comfortably. Who pays, and how, he wondered, for all those sleek new Mercedes and Chevrolets?

Of course, Indonesia's archipelago was perfect for smuggling, which was conducted quite brazenly. The abundance of expensive motor cars proclaimed the extent of corruption in official and financial circles and the very phrase 'black market' was a misnomer, since the relevant transactions were carried out so openly. Heinz wrote that 'the government system of economic controls is so inefficient that a (black) market functions reasonably effectively', and he quoted Panglaykim's marvellous remark: 'Professor, we are the most *laissez-faire* socialist economy in the world' (Arndt 1987:63). For foreign currency, the black market exchange rate on the streets of Jakarta in October 1964 was up to six times the official rate. This posed a moral problem for Heinz: where, and at what rate, should he convert his ANU allowance into Indonesian rupiah? He spoke of the problem but never revealed his solution.

As well as inflation, Heinz gave talks on other subjects: 'Central banking in less developed countries' and 'Foreign aid and economic development'. He delivered the latter lecture, by specific request, at Hasanuddin University in Makassar, on the west coast of Sulawesi. The rector of the university, Arnold Mohonutu, was a wily old politician who had turned his coat from the Dutch to the nationalists, become a friend of Sukarno and served as Ambassador to Peking. He was said to have been appointed to Hasanuddin to influence students and other groups increasingly hostile to Sukarno. Apparently, he had set up Heinz for a fall.

Before Heinz began his lecture, the rector delivered introductory remarks, in Indonesian and English, lasting some 40 minutes

> …giving me the official version of Malaysia and Confrontation, claiming that the West (including Australia) was out to 'crush' Indonesia by bringing about her economic collapse, arguing that all Western foreign aid was motivated by imperialist designs, warning me and Australia that we must choose between 100 million

> Indonesians and 10 million stooges of the British, reminding me of Indonesia's strong armed forces, quoting China's atom bomb as a great triumph of Asians over Europeans comparable in importance to the victory of the Japanese over the Russians in 1904, threatening, cajoling, shaking his finger at me, addressing 'Professor Arndt' over and over again with heavy irony etc, etc. (Arndt 1987:82).

The next evening, Heinz went, with some foreboding, to dinner at the rector's house. The outcome was more tolerable than he expected. He and the rector proceeded to enjoy an animated conversation—virtually excluding the three other guests—on all sorts of subjects.

In Medan, after spending time at the Faculty of Agriculture of the state university, Heinz visited the city's private, fee-paying, Lutheran institution, Nommensen University. There he successfully gave a theoretical lecture on the Swan diagram, to illustrate policies for the pursuit of both internal and external balance. He also went to other colleges outside Jakarta: the Institut Pertanian Bogor (at Bogor, Java), Padjajaran University (Bandung, Java), Sriwidjaja University (Palembang, Sumatra) and Gadjah Mada University (Yogyakarta, Java). During the couple of days at Yogyakarta, Heinz enjoyed visits to the wonderful sights of nearby Borobudur and Prambanan. He owed the Prambanan tour to the friendly and obliging Jack Golden, another old Asia hand, who was then helping at the Jefferson Library (recently taken over by the Indonesian government).

While being driven through Java's lush countryside and pleasant villages, Heinz remarked frequently on how fertile the island was. There was tea, coffee, paddi and fruits of all descriptions: 'hardly a square yard without something growing, a delightful sight.' He added: 'Pre-war Poland or Greece or Turkey looked *much* poorer, which makes the mess in which this economy now finds itself only the more incongruous' (Arndt 1987:71). Not only was the land fertile, so too was the population. Every woman of 15 years or more seemed to be carrying a baby.

After a month in Indonesia, Heinz spent a few days enjoying the view—political as well as scenic—from the other side of the Straits of Malacca. He went first to Singapore, where Param Ajit Singh, a former master's degree student in the ANU department, met Heinz and acted as his chaperon. Heinz was instantly impressed by Singapore: 'how clean, civilised, busy, booming and handsome after Jakarta!' He also noted the relative inconspicuousness of the military; the fact that many large buildings were not government offices; the vast infrastructure construction everywhere—roads, overpasses, tunnels; the rash of industrial plants and the thousands of new flats for the fast-growing population. Professionally, he called on Finance Minister, Goh Keng Swee, as well as several government economists and his academic friends in their then pleasant surrounds on Nassim Road. As always, he also found time for shopping, in this case primarily to search for information and catalogues about electric guitars. This was presumably for his son Nick, who was then performing in Canberra as part of a group called The Bitter Lemons. Heinz joked: 'I used to be known in Canberra as a university professor, but nowadays it is as the father of a Beatle.'

He then went on to Kuala Lumpur, on a pleasant late-afternoon flight of one hour from Singapore. He was met in Kuala Lumpur by Gordon Menzies, Deputy Governor of the Bank Negara Malaysia and a former student of Heinz in Sydney, Pierre Tu and myself, both graduate students from his ANU department, who were conducting field research in Malaysia. Heinz was quickly whisked away to Menzies' 'sumptuous' official residence in Kenny Hill, where he had only a little time to prepare for dinner, accompanied by Menzies, at the 'palatial' residence of the Bank's Governor, Dato Ismail bin Md Ali. Other guests included the Minister for Transport, the manager of Malaysia Airways and a few expatriate commercial bankers. The political flavour of the gathering was highly conservative, to Heinz's irritation: 'How pleasant and how disagreeable!' he wrote, and he attempted to provoke the others by referring with approval to his former acquaintance P.P. Narayanan, the firebrand organiser of the Plantation Workers' Union.

The next day began with a meeting of senior Bank Negara officials in their suite of offices in 'the old, grotesquely Moorish government office buildings which adjoin the cricket ground outside the Selangor Club—shades of Somerset Maugham!' Thence to the general offices of Bank Negara Malaysia, in those days situated in the upper floors of the handsome new Mercantile Bank building on Market Square. Heinz addressed an interested and interesting group of economists about the economic situation in Indonesia. As well as the Bank Negara senior and middle executives, the group included the distinguished Professor Arthur Bloomfield (University of Pennsylvania) and Warren Hunsberger (Rochester University, New York State). Bloomfield was assisting the Bank Negara and Hunsberger the government, and both were being supported in Kuala Lumpur by the Ford Foundation.

After a lengthy group discussion, Heinz enjoyed a private talk with Bloomfield before being taken to lunch with the Australian High Commissioner, Tom Critchley, and a small number of Malaysian government economists. Again, the talk was largely about Indonesia, including the interesting subject of the divergence of the Malaysian and Indonesian languages from their common root in Bahasa Melayu. After a quiet afternoon at the Menzies' house, Heinz dressed up for a splendid dinner, hosted by Gordon and Jean Menzies, at the super-elegant Lake Club. The other guests were Hunsberger, James Puthecheary, Siew Nim Chee, myself and our wives, and also Edgar Jones, formerly of the British Treasury and in Kuala Lumpur with the IMF.

The Siews were a very astute couple, who made a fortune in the casino/hospitality industry after Nim Chee resigned from his senior economist job at Bank Negara. James Puthecheary and his wife were lawyers. He had been something of a revolutionary intellectual under British rule in Malaya, and was gaoled for his pains, but had then quarrelled with his erstwhile leader, Lee Kuan Yew, who finally expelled him from Singapore. Heinz greatly enjoyed this swell occasion and the lively and varied company. He summed the evening up: 'Excellent European dinner, talk, even a dance with Joan Drake.'

The next day, Sunday, Heinz put himself in the hands of his ANU students. Joan and I, Gavin and Margaret Jones and Pierre Tu took him by car via Klang to Kuala Selangor, where the party had lunch at a resthouse by the sea. Heinz observed the fine roads and well-kept rubber plantations, but he disliked the labour lines of the plantation workers 'with the characteristically depressing appearance of Indian poverty', and he thought the Malay smallholder villages distinctly poorer-looking than those in West Java. The party was back in Kuala Lumpur in time for dinner with the Menzies and Joan and myself, in the modest rented house we maintained at 7 Jalan Bunga Rampai, Setapak.

Heinz's final day in Kuala Lumpur began with pouring rain, which, happily, had ceased by the time I drove him to the University of Malaya in Petaling Jaya. There he renewed acquaintance with the handsome and charismatic Professor Ungku Aziz. He was given a quick tour of the Petaling Jaya industrial estate and was then driven to the airport for departure to Singapore and Sydney. He returned to Canberra, fired with certainty about his planned Indonesia project, and bursting with enthusiasm to get on with it.

20
SUHARTO'S INDONESIA

Indonesia suffered bloody political upheaval during 1965 and 1966. Sukarno's presidency appeared, at first, to have survived a 1965 coup attempt, which led to the deaths of at least 100,000 people within weeks; but power gradually slid away from him. By late 1966, General Suharto had installed a military regime, which he headed himself. The new regime promptly made two remarkable policy decisions: economic development must have priority over all else, and civilian experts (rather than the military) would be put in charge of this goal. Indonesian academic economists thus attained great influence with, and indeed within, the Suharto government.

These economists were young, came mostly from Jakarta's University of Indonesia and had received postgraduate training in the United States. This last characteristic led to the group being referred to as the 'Berkeley Mafia', a sobriquet that they wore with wry pride, although it was originally coined as a term of abuse in a left-wing American magazine. The group—led at first by Professor Widjojo Nitisastro—had a profound and far-reaching influence. Indonesia's remarkable economic growth under Suharto owed a great deal to the group's development priorities and its policies of liberalisation. Heinz was lavish in praising its members: 'Their record of day-to-day co-operation, practical wisdom, technical competence and personal integrity, over a period of fifteen years, without a power base other than the confidence of the President and in circumstances, particularly in the early years, of appalling difficulty, has few if any parallels' (Arndt 1985:55).

As he grew older, Heinz's economic philosophy moved from Fabian socialist beginnings, through Keynesianism, to the Friedmanite position of 'free to choose'. In the 1980s, Heinz declared, in expressing enthusiasm for Henri Lepage's *Tomorrow, Capitalism* (1982), 'I am now a liberal if not indeed a libertarian.' This philosophic shift coincided with the Suharto administration's gradual acceptance of comparable advice from American free marketeers. Heinz found this acceptance increasingly congenial, and he had little difficulty in commending the Suharto era's economic policies.

Those policies had Indonesians' own initiative as their mainspring, but in later years foreign professional support played an increasingly large role. Often this support went through channels such as the IMF and the World Bank, which had established resident missions in Jakarta. Later, the Harvard Development Advisory Service sent many more American-trained economists to advise the Bappenas authority. The flavour of overseas expertise was, broadly, 'free-market American', but the ANU Indonesia project, though a much smaller presence, was of significant influence. This was because of Heinz's good connections, cultivated with energy and enthusiasm, and the emergence of the *Bulletin of Indonesian Economic Studies* (BIES) as the only authoritative, independent and regular source of information and analysis published in English.

The new intellectual openness after 1966, and the regime's hunger for economic research and analysis to underpin its development drive, greatly improved the prospects of the ANU's Indonesia project. Such official openness to advice had its disadvantages for Heinz, as well as its advantages. In some ways, as Heinz explained,'[it] rendered our task more difficult. As the World Bank, the Ford and other foundations, the Harvard Development Advisory Service and other well-heeled institutions moved in and bid for the limited number of professional economists interested in Indonesia, we were quite unable to compete' (Arndt 1985:55).

Nevertheless, two related strategies ensured that the ANU retained a small but valuable niche in Indonesian economic development discussions. First was the ANU's policy of giving its graduate students an extended period of field-work in Indonesia. Thus, in fairly quick succession, Ingrid Palmer, Peter McCawley, Anne Booth, Howard Dick, Stephen Grenville, Phyllis Rosendale, Chris Manning and Hal Hill lived in Indonesia, researched and wrote PhD theses on Indonesia and published their findings, and thereby established their own and the project's reputations for serious work. Palmer we have already met. McCawley, PhD graduate, later research fellow and subsequently head of the project, became the BIES's joint editor after Heinz retired. Booth was another PhD graduate and later research fellow. Hill, yet another PhD graduate and later research fellow, ultimately attained a professorial chair in Heinz's department.

Secondly, there was the sustained influence of the BIES. The first 80-page BIES issue, as previously mentioned, appeared in 1965. It included the first 'Survey of recent developments', which was to become standard fare in each issue of the journal. The survey was invariably written—whether by an Indonesian or an outsider—in Jakarta. This fact greatly added to its immediacy and credibility. Given the small amount of intellectual capital available in those days within the ANU (and indeed within other Australian universities) for work on the Indonesian economy, Heinz felt compelled to be an active participant in, as well as manager of, the Indonesia project.

Much of his own research contribution went into the BIES. 'Every year,' he recalled, 'I would contribute one or two surveys and an article or two of my own or written jointly…far more time was taken up editing contributions by others.' Very few contributions did not require some editing. Most needed a great deal. Problems of substance, presentation and expression abounded, especially, but not only, with Indonesian authors. Although Heinz was eager to obtain as many articles as possible from Indonesian authors, he found it remarkably difficult to do so. Those who could produce independent, publishable work usually occupied a rank so exalted, and so bound by proprieties, as to constrain them from publishing; or else they were so busy that they had no time for academic research and writing.

With great editorial diligence, Heinz found more junior Indonesian contributors who were making their way in the academic world; but their efforts required heavy editing, which was received 'with mixed feelings of resentment and gratitude'. Otherwise, the contents of the BIES depended greatly on the work of Heinz's Canberra department. Fellows, visiting fellows and PhD scholars all contributed to the *Bulletin*, and for the juniors it was often their entrée into academic publishing.

Some idea of the energy that Heinz put into the *Bulletin*'s production, and his resolution in setting a good example, emerges from this description

> The early surveys usually took the better part of a month to produce. With practice, I got this down to three and, for the last few of my seventeen surveys, to two weeks. I would aim to arrive in Jakarta on a Friday and use the first evening to phone friends—phoning in Jakarta became easier as the years went by—to make appointments for Monday and Tuesday. On Saturday morning I would collect all the available recent statistics and use the weekend to identify the more important trends and compose tables to illustrate them. Having reached some tentative conclusions, I would try them out on my friends in the course of ten to fifteen interviews, Monday to Wednesday, revising my ideas in the course of often lively discussion, picking up new ones, sorting out arguments pro and con, getting additional data. On Thursday afternoon, after another morning round-up (in the VW Beetle which the project kept in Jakarta) to fill gaps, I was ready to write

> my 'Summary' which also served as outline. Two 12-hour sessions on Friday and Saturday to write the draft, another on Sunday to retype it with a couple of carbon copies, and I was over the worst. On Monday morning I would give one copy, in exchange for three Xerox copies, to each of three well-equipped friends, so that by the evening I had up to ten copies in various hands. On Tuesday and Wednesday of the second week I was free to deal with other project business, on Thursday I would collect comments on the draft, on Friday I would revise it, and on Saturday fly home to Canberra. It was a strenuous business, but also exhilarating, and not all work. I had many friends, I enjoyed Indonesian food—especially the chili-hot West Sumatran version obtainable in one of the many *rumah makan Padang*—and for entertainment there was always chess. I never had any difficulty finding a partner, often the *jagah malam* (night watchman) at the gate of one of the neighbouring houses or one of the transport drivers of the Australian Embassy, all of whom played with enthusiasm, with Musa, the tall, friendly driver to the Ambassador, as their champion (Arndt 1985:58).

Peter Timmer—now a distinguished academic in the United States, but in 1970 the newest member of the Harvard group at Bappenas—affectionately recalled Heinz's determination to snare data for the *Bulletin*

> One morning, Bill Hollinger, our Project Director, called all the staff together to announce that Heinz Arndt, the editor of the *Bulletin of Indonesian Economic Studies*, would be visiting the office to talk with any of us who were available. He would have two missions—ideas for future articles for BIES, and information on the current state of the economy for the 'Survey of Recent Developments', which he was writing for the next issue…Bill turned to me and said, 'Peter, you don't know Heinz. I encourage you to talk with him about your work and the possibility of publishing something. But be very careful to hide all documents and data while he is in your office. Heinz is very good at extracting them when you aren't looking.'

Over time, as the BIES became known and respected for its editorial standards, better-quality submissions were offered to it. By 1990, its twenty-fifth anniversary year, it could justly claim 'the reputation of being the best source of information about the Indonesian economy publicly available'.

Heinz's work for the BIES enlarged and strengthened his network in Indonesia. His web attracted cabinet ministers, civil servants, university professors, lecturers and young researchers, visiting economists, bankers and businesspeople. Two pivotal contacts, especially in the early years, were Jusuf Panglaykim and Mohamed Sadli.

'Pang', an Indonesian of Chinese descent, had business interests in banking, insurance and trade during the 1950s. These suffered under Sukarno, so he went to study economics at Berkeley, then completed a PhD at the University of Indonesia, and duly became head of that university's Business Management Institute. He had befriended Heinz on the latter's first visit to Jakarta in 1964 and, in 1966—'equipped', in Heinz's words, 'with fascinating statistics, into the provenance of which I was expected not to enquire'—he helped Heinz write the survey for the June 1966 issue of the BIES, which covered the first policies of Suharto's 'New Order'. Pang had friends and contacts everywhere and Heinz benefited from many introductions. Heinz, still building up the Canberra staff of the Indonesia Project, persuaded Pang to take a Senior Research Fellowship and bring his family to Canberra. There, his daughter, Mari Pangestu (later a distinguished economist and research leader in Indonesia, and now an Indonesian government minister), received much of her education. Pang, however, was somewhat uncomfortable with the research style of the Canberra department and increasingly nostalgic for Jakarta. He returned there in 1969, and successfully rebuilt his business and communications activities. He died in 1986.

Heinz had first met Mohamed Sadli in Canberra and renewed acquaintance with him in Jakarta in 1964, when Sadli was Professor of Economics in the University of Indonesia. Later, benefiting from the increased levels of esteem given to intellectuals, which marked Suharto's rule, Sadli became very influential and achieved a cabinet post. Heinz had great respect for Sadli's intellect and integrity. They took to one another and Heinz stayed often with the Sadli family in their pleasant Jakarta house. There and elsewhere, Sadli introduced Heinz to many of Indonesia's leading economists, including Widjojo, who lived next door.

Beyond Jakarta, Heinz made lasting connections at Gadjah Mada University in Yogyakarta with Mubyarto, Sukadji, Ace Partadiredja and with the economics faculties at Hasanuddin University (in Makassar/

Ujung Pandang, South Sulawesi) and Andalas University (in Padang, West Sumatra). The last two campuses 'were situated in attractive cities— Makassar with its beautiful harbour and astonishing Portuguese fort, Padang the gateway to Bukittinggi in Minangkebau country with its singular art and culture'. Further afield, Heinz went to Syah Kuala University in Banda Aceh and Udayana University in Bali. Always his objects were to promote the work of the Indonesia project, to tout the BIES and to identify local talent for future cooperative endeavours.

As well as specific trips to Indonesia for the project, Heinz took every opportunity to stop over for a day or two on trips to Europe or Bangkok, and to attend conferences and seminars in or about Indonesia. These included conferences of the Pacific–Indonesian Business Association (Jakarta, 1967); the International Planned Parenthood Federation (Bandung, 1969); seminars on regional planning (Bandung, 1975), wages and employment (Jakarta, 1974) and transmigration within Indonesia (Jakarta, 1977); and the annual meetings of the Australia–Indonesia Business Cooperation Committee, which alternated between the two countries.

Heinz continued to maintain contact in Jakarta with the Ford Foundation resident office, the resident IMF and World Bank missions and the Harvard Development Advisory Service, as well as with Bank Indonesia, the Central Bureau of Statistics, government offices and foreign embassies. His vast network and accumulated knowledge must have attracted offers of paid consultancies, yet he commented that, before formally retiring from the ANU

> I never, with one exception [in 1979, to do some work in Washington for the World Bank on central banking policy in Indonesia], acted as a consultant for the Australian or Indonesian or any other government or any international organisation. In the early years, it was our deliberate policy not to set ourselves up as advisers or consultants on policy, although the 'Surveys of Recent Developments', it must be admitted, were not reticent in offering suggestions, at least between the lines (Arndt 1985:63).

The work of Heinz and the project in Indonesia was aligned with that going on in Canberra. From that base, staff and research students pursued empirical studies of the Indonesian economy, which were of analytical interest and were relevant to policy formation. No other centre in the world was doing this kind of work, intended for publication, on

Indonesia. Now and then, the project's independence and public nature caused problems that Heinz regretted: 'Many times, friends in the World Bank resident mission would explain how important they thought our work was and how they wished to help, but when it came to the point, natural bureaucratic caution, reinforced by confidentiality commitments to the Indonesian authorities, would almost invariably stand in the way' (Arndt 1985:60).

The staff and students of the Canberra department constituted the best repository of intellectual capital on the Indonesian economy that any institution outside Indonesia could boast. Heinz announced in 1985 that the doctoral graduates of the department's project accounted for half of all the non-Indonesian academic economists in the world who specialised in Indonesia. Invidious though it would be to mention many names, the self-identified Indonesianists in the department included David Penny, as well as the doctoral graduates who stayed on and other figures cited earlier. Additional members of the department would occasionally work on Indonesia, as would various visiting scholars from Indonesia, the United States, Europe and even the former Soviet Union. One Russian, Seva Archipov, was a colourful character, 'worthy of a novel' in Heinz's opinion. In a class of his own was R.M. Sundrum, who joined the department in 1970 and held a senior position until he retired in 1991. Sundrum did a lot of work on Indonesia, in his own research and in editorial/administrative tasks. He was, however, much more than an Indonesia specialist. He had impressive skills in economic theory and econometrics, which he could deploy over a vast range of subjects that captured his interest.

Although Heinz did not lightly decline invitations to lecture or write on Indonesia for Australian audiences, neither did he seem to have a goal to educate Australians at large about the economies of Indonesia and other Asian countries, in the visionary—if somewhat inchoate—way that J.G. Crawford did. And, unlike several political science, history and geography professors of things Asian, he never took an active part in the Asian Studies Association of Australia or its country-focused subgroups. Rather, Heinz preferred to advance Indonesia's cause through the media—principally newspapers and magazines, though at times radio and television appearances as well. Often his contributions were responses to carping criticism, by most of the Australian media, of Indonesia during Suharto's long reign. Heinz found himself a prominent defender of the regime, but by no means an uncritical one; he always acknowledged that corruption and authoritarianism existed in Indonesia.

Heinz took an especially prominent media role in 1986, a year that saw sustained criticism of Suharto in the *Sydney Morning Herald*, a very cool public statement on Indonesia–Australia relations by Bob Hawke (then in his second term as prime minister) and Indonesia's temporary refusal to permit the Royal Australian Air Force (RAAF) to land on Indonesian soil, an action thought to have been provoked by the criticisms made by a Perth-based academic Dick Robison. The flavour of Heinz's stance is best captured in his Shann Memorial Lecture, delivered at the University of Western Australia in September 1986, in which he claimed that sectors of the Australian public and media had intermittently soured relations between Australia and Indonesia

> Particularly after the death of five Australian journalists during the Timor fighting, the Australian public received a highly slanted picture of events in Timor and of Indonesia generally…Australian journalists, with the ABC well to the fore, have been only too eager to pillory the inequities of the Soeharto regime…part of the problem has been the Timor legacy…part of it has been sensationalism…no small a part has been ideological antipathy to the Soeharto regime.

The Shann Lecture appeared in *Quadrant* in November 1986. When challenged on this choice of outlet, because of its limited circulation, Heinz responded by letter

> Shann Lecture: I could not send it to *Australian Outlook*, the next issue of which is entirely devoted to a symposium on Australia–Indonesia relations edited by Dick Robison!…I agree in *Quadrant* I preach to a handful of converted. That is why I was so disappointed to get no coverage in the dailies [This is incorrect: the *Sydney Morning Herald* reported the lecture reasonably well as soon as it was delivered]. But Foreign Affairs [now the Department of Foreign Affairs and Trade] are also putting it into their monthly *FA Record*. That is not widely read by the general public, but it goes in 10,000 copies to every conceivable official agency at home and abroad.

Public debate in 1986 also reflected a long-standing, and indeed continuing, intellectual rift in the Australian academic community on the subject of Indonesia. For example, Monash University political scientists, led by Herb

Feith and Rex Mortimer, held views on the country that completely opposed the views of Heinz's ANU circle. Mortimer, in his critique of Indonesia entitled 'Showcase state of accelerated development', denounced Heinz as symptomatic of the intellectual and moral decadence of the Australian bourgeoisie. Non-governmental organisations and church groups—with an innate distaste for economic analysis—mostly leaned to the side of the political and historical radicals. A publication 'by the Australian Council on Overseas Aid, during a phase of radical management, showed up the Indonesia project as a reactionary, if not CIA-inspired, plot, of which donations by the Ford Foundation and multinationals were clear and blatant evidence' (Arndt 1985:65). Heinz noted, however, that, when corporate funds ran out, the Australian government made a substantial grant to the project.

There also was division of intellectual opinion internationally, especially among economists, about the relative importance in the developing world of economic growth versus interpersonal equity. Indonesia was an unappealing example for those who gave priority to the redistribution of income and wealth in the name of equity or social justice. Heinz remarked: 'At a conference of the Indonesian Studies Association at Berkeley in 1979, I was one of only three economists among a hundred sociologists, political scientists, anthropologists and historians, most of whom had no time for economic growth' (Arndt 1985:65).

Even within the Indonesia project, various shades of opinion coexisted. After all, experience in the field had shown staff and students plenty of corruption and conspicuous consumption within the regime. At the same time, the project members recognised objectively the evidence of a high GNP growth rate noticeably benefiting the otherwise impoverished peasantry and the workers in the new factories. The debate about development and equality was not conducted only in the departmental tea-room. Commendably, the project produced and published three substantial books on that theme in the early 1980s.

Heinz entered into retirement at the end of 1980 and handed over the BIES editorship at the end of 1982. Thereafter, his opportunities to visit Indonesia diminished. In late 1986, he bemoaned the fact that he had spent only three days in each of the previous two years in Indonesia. He never gave up on the country; he continued to write about Indonesia for academic and popular publications and managed at least one brief visit to Indonesia in most years until the end of his life.

21
OTHER PARTS OF ASIA

Despite Heinz's passion for Indonesia, it would be wrong to categorise him as merely an 'Indonesianist'. His early Asian engagements, as we have seen, were in Malaya, Singapore and India. For the rest of his life, he retained strong academic connections and friendships in many parts of Asia. (He never went to China or to Africa; and he visited Latin America only fleetingly.)

Bangkok especially interested him, largely because of his membership of the Governing Council of the UN Asian Institute for Economic Development and Planning (ADI for short). This institute was financed by contributions from the member countries of the UN Economic Commission for Asia and the Far East (ECAFE), with an annual supplement from the UN Development Program (UNDP). Heinz, under the patronage of Mick Shann, was elected to the council for two terms, from 1969 to 1974. He greatly enjoyed the council's annual Bangkok meetings. They usually occupied a couple of days, so there was plenty of time to cultivate and nourish friendships, such as with the Indonesians Widjojo and Sumarlin, and Gerry Sicat, an economist from the University of the Philippines in Manila. A social highlight of each meeting was an informal dinner at the house of U Nyun, ECAFE's Executive Secretary. On these occasions, more serious discussions were punctuated by friendly banter, such as the light-hearted argument about which country produced the finest mangoes. Heinz observed, wryly, that he 'did not feel called upon to bat for Queensland'.

As is often the case with such bodies, the ADI was torn between teaching and research. Its original mission had been clear—to serve as a training institution—so in theory teaching remained paramount. The contracted academic staff, however, and a succession of consultants favoured turning it into a think-tank. Heinz, rightly, thought this notion unrealistic because of the institute's inability to attract first-rate staff, who would be deterred by the UN rule against long contracts. He also had his reservations about the teaching (or, more exactly, about the six-month length of the course in development planning) and about the calibre of the student officials whom the member countries nominated. Such reservations prompted him to formulate 'Arndt's Law': the quality of participants was inversely proportional to the length of the course. He would have preferred courses of up to three weeks each, in which senior officials could learn some contemporary economics of relevance to their work at home, and in which they could also exchange the fruits of experience with one another.

In the end, the institute fell victim to financial problems and discontent in the United Nations and among member countries. Thailand went cold; Singapore (in the person of Lee Kuan Yew) aborted a planned rescue; Heinz accompanied the director and his deputy to Manila on another rescue submission to the Asian Development Bank. All these efforts failed. Finally, the ADI was subsumed into the new Asian Pacific Economic Development Centre in Kuala Lumpur, of which I, doubtless on Heinz's recommendation, was a founding director.

The demise of the ADI did not sever Heinz's connection to Bangkok. Several ECAFE expert groups engaged Heinz's services, thanks to U Nyun, whom he had first met in 1964 through the good offices of Colin Simkin. (A New Zealander by birth, Simkin later became Economics Professor at the University of Sydney.) Heinz made various other visits to Bangkok over the years for conferences, such as that on Pacific Trade and Development (held at Pattaya, about 160km southeast of Bangkok) in 1976—at which Heinz had the job of summing up—and on the Pacific Community in 1982. Heinz took part in many conferences of the Pacific Trade and Development (PAFTAD) group (in Honolulu, Sydney, Mexico City, Wellington, Pattaya, Canberra and Singapore), which he felt were among the most interesting and pleasant of all his professional experiences. He cherished the conditions they provided for 'meeting intelligent people and learning about significant issues in usually handsome and more than comfortable surroundings' (Arndt 1985:73).

An opportunity to see a little more of Thailand took the form of a 24-hour rail journey from Bangkok to Penang in 1973. The train went west from Bangkok through uninspiring suburbs, over the river and then wound through dense forest, market gardens, padi fields, swamps and nondescript villages for a couple of hours before stopping at Khorn Pathorn, a modest town of some 20,000 people. Then came more rural scenery and a change of direction—south towards the border with Malaysia, though the train did not arrive at that border until late the next morning. From Sungei Patani (on the Malaysian side), the train finally arrived at Butterworth. Heinz found the journey full of interest but also of discomfort, as he found the food and the sleeping arrangements unpleasant.

In later years, Heinz returned several times to Singapore and Kuala Lumpur, as External Examiner in Economics at those cities' universities. The initial invitation, in 1967, to work for the two universities was enormously flattering because his very distinguished predecessors in that role had been Sir Arthur Lewis, Hla Myint and Harry Johnson. The first two may fairly be called the founding fathers of development economics, while Johnson was the pre-eminent economist of the 1960s and 1970s. In tropical climates, during the days before air-conditioning, an external examiner had an arduous task. He sat, in humid and often uncomfortable conditions, poring over many bundles of examination scripts. As Heinz described it

> The duties consisted in first vetting the question papers which were sent to me in Canberra beforehand and later, first in Singapore and then in Kuala Lumpur, reading the scripts of a sample of honours students, all those whom the internal examiners were proposing for first and upper second class honours. The border between lower and upper second was of particular importance because an upper second was a prerequisite for a civil service appointment. I was also expected to report to the two Deans on any aspects of the curriculum, the quality of teaching or the performance of students on which I felt I had something to say. Marking papers, as always, could be onerous—I remember sitting for days on the balcony of the small old Orchard Hotel in Singapore and again in the old Majestic Hotel in Kuala Lumpur where, if one was not careful, monkeys would hop through the windows and steal anything edible they could find (Arndt 1985:77).

Subsequently, Singapore invited Heinz to take up the task again (Kuala Lumpur by then had a separate examiner). By this means, he maintained his contact with the island state, which he much admired for its capable and honest government (Goh Keng Swee's friendship with Heinz has already been noted in these pages) and progressive development, which Heinz attributed to 'a combination of intelligent government and enterprising private business'. In his retirement years, Heinz sustained his interest in Singapore through close academic contacts in its Institute of Southeast Asian Studies, where he spent two months in 1981 as a visiting professor.

OTHER PARTS OF ASIA

Partly because Manila is the home of the Asian Development Bank, Heinz paid many visits to the Philippines, especially in the later period of his career; however, he made his first trip there as early as 1965, *en route* to Japan. At that time, his reputation was as a monetary economist, so his few professional engagements in Manila were with officers of the central bank and academic economists with the same interest. Otherwise, he enjoyed his time with the Australian Ambassador, W. Cutts, and a private dinner at the splendid ambassadorial residence.

Typically, Heinz sought to learn as much about the history, society and culture of the Philippines as his limited time there would permit. He noted the dominance in that nation of the English language; the strong presence of the Catholic Church (especially in politics and education); the power of the great landowning and business dynasties; the orientation towards the United States; and the fact that, with all its imperfections, the country was democratic: 'at least there *are* elections which are taken seriously, and peaceful changes of government.' Conscious of the need for intellectual breadth in his new ANU department, Heinz escaped from the central bankers—but in their chauffeured car—for an afternoon, in order to see the International Rice Research Institute at Los Banos and the nearby Faculty of Agriculture of the University of the Philippines. On the last of his three days, he visited the Economics Department of the University of the Philippines at Quezon City, where he was impressed by the young head, Dr Jose Encarnacion. Like General Macarthur, Heinz left the Philippines determined to return. And he did so at every opportunity.

One of Heinz's visits to Manila—four days in 1969 for a conference on the Indonesian economy—turned out to be a great disappointment. Heinz joined a group of Indonesian economists (Sadli, Suhadi, Ismael, Emil Salim, Sarbini) and the American Bill Hollinger at Jakarta's Kemayoran airport. From there, they flew as a party to Manila and were accommodated at the garish Sulo Hotel. The next day began in discomfort. Heinz, having overslept, awoke to find that the hotel's electricity had been cut off. He therefore had to perform his morning ablutions without hot water or electric light, and as a result felt miserable. The misery was compounded when, on an afternoon sightseeing tour of a volcanic island on Lake Tagatay, a sudden and severe rainstorm soaked the party. They were obliged to suffer the long drive back to Manila in wet clothes. By the next afternoon, Heinz felt decidedly seedy with a gastric cold. This illness prevented him from taking much part in the conference, 'having to leave a number of times', or its formal dinner. Still indisposed, he struggled through one more day and a flight back to Sydney.

Of the western and central parts of Asia, Heinz visited Pakistan and, on one long trip in 1976, Nepal, Afghanistan and what was then Soviet Central Asia (Tashkent, Bukhara, Samarkand). The week in Soviet Central Asia was the second part of a fortnight spent in the Soviet Union, which had come about at the invitation of the Soviet Academy of Sciences. Heinz had spent the first week in Leningrad (St Petersburg) and Moscow. Ruth accompanied Heinz on this assignment and on the subsequent visits to Afghanistan and Nepal. Heinz's professional obligations on this tour were not onerous—he was essentially in the role of academic ambassador—so there was plenty of opportunity to see something of ordinary life in those places. He was struck by the low standard of living and the many commercial inefficiencies of the state economic system; and he later noted in Afghanistan a negative local attitude towards Russia and the neighbouring Soviet states.

Kabul was a challenge initially, because of a local misunderstanding about the dates and length of the Arndt visit. Unknown to Heinz, he had been billed to lecture on three days. To his embarrassment, that plan had to be abandoned, because he already had firm commitments in, and flights to, other places. Hosts and guest contented themselves with a meeting to discuss matters of mutual interest and a day and a half of hectic tourism and social events. Much of their activity revolved around the family life of Dr Abdul Sami Noor, of the Economics Faculty of Kabul University. 'Sam', as he became, was delightfully attentive to the Arndts. Heinz and Ruth responded to the warmth of his family and friends.

Each house block in Kabul was surrounded by a high mud wall, for privacy and protection. At the Noor house, nothing could be seen from the street except the white wall and a door; but the door opened to a beautiful courtyard and garden with fruit trees. As well as Sam's extensive family—Heinz remarked on the beauty of Sam's sisters—the lunch guests included several elderly men who spoke German or English, having studied or held postings in Europe. Heinz always had a particular yen for fruit and fretted if it was not a regular part of his diet. No fruit shortage threatened at the Noor home. There he was treated to an abundance of plums, apricots, cherries and apples: 'starved of fruit as we had been for the past three weeks, we had a great feast.'

Dr Noor took Heinz and Ruth to the bazaar of Old Kabul: 'no very interesting buildings but a fascinating scene of traditional oriental city life, thousands of people, many men in turbans, most women still veiled.' Eventually, they all reached the shop of Dr Noor's elderly father, where they parted with US$500 for an Afghan carpet. At the end of the day, they were taken further into the countryside to see a farm property of vineyards, flour mill and fruit trees. Again, they mixed with overseas-educated Afghanis of the professional class and enjoyed a feast of mulberries. At dusk, they were returned to the hotel, glimpsing there a large wedding party, and retired after 'a tremendous day'.

Dr Noor gave the Arndts the next day too, together with an American couple he had acquired: a 'Los Angeles rich dentist and fat, friendly wife, both orthodox Jews'. They went on another visit to the bazaar—'incredibly old, ramshackle, mudbrick buildings, held together by wooden props and struts'—where the American couple made the inevitable purchase of a carpet from the Noor shop. During an afternoon drive to the village of Istalef, along a good Russian-made road, Dr Noor treated his four guests to a diatribe about Soviet exploitation of Afghanistan. Beyond Istalef, they had a magnificent view of the Hindu Kush mountains: 'mauve-ochre, with snow-tipped peaks, beyond a wide flat plain, and the town of Istalef on the other side, mud houses—some very substantial—climbing up the steep hillside.' While the others went off to a nearby hotel for drinks, Heinz sat on a stone wall and did a quick painting of the picturesque view. It was his second artistic production of the day, as he had done an early morning scene from the Kabul hotel. In the evening, the Arndts were given dinner by the Dean of Economics, Dr Kasem, and his wife, in their modern apartment: a very different style of entertaining from that of the Noors' traditional household. The next morning, the Arndts were at the airport early to fly to Delhi for a social weekend. The visit to Kabul had been delightful, thanks to Dr Noor, 'whose kindness and hospitality had really been overwhelming'.

Nepal was the last stop in Central Asia. Dr Pant, a former Central Bank Governor whom Heinz had met in Canberra, had arranged the Nepalese trip. The arrival in Katmandu was disappointing. No one in the university seemed to be aware of Heinz's advent. After a fruitless effort to book academic appointments, Heinz and Ruth undertook some self-directed sightseeing, somewhat impeded by monsoonal rainfall, which made the streets uncomfortable. Heinz did manage a sketch of the Jarnagath temple, and recounted an amusing experience in dealing with one of the locals.'On the walk back to the hotel a shoeshine boy triumphed over my repeated rejection of his services by pointing to my shoes and saying several times: "cowsit". When I grasped what he meant—uncertain whether a cow or he had put it there—I laughed so much that I had to give in—at the price of 15c' (Arndt 1987:241).

On the whole, Heinz found the Hindu culture unattractive in its visual manifestations—'grotesque, horrible deities'—but he thought the young people of both sexes to be very good-looking and the old city fascinating, 'probably the nearer to what a mediaeval European city must have looked like than anything that remains elsewhere'.

Things began to improve on the academic front after a man from the rector's office phoned to say that a Land Rover and a lecturer from the Economics Department would be at the Arndts' disposal for the rest of their stay. The next day, Mr Dahal and Mr Sharma arrived in a fine-looking vehicle and gave the morning over to a conducted tour: the Monkey Temple, the National Museum and an industrial estate. In the afternoon, Heinz finally got to the university campus—out of town, across a river, over incredibly muddy and unpaved roads until, laid out amid padi fields, came the modern, low, brick buildings of Tribhuvan University. There Heinz lectured, to about 50 staff, on 'Problems of aid recipient countries'. At the end came a few cool comments and then a blistering attack by Dr Singh, Chairman of the Economic Studies Committee

> 'Let the Professor ponder why socialist countries are popular in LDCs [less-developed countries] and capitalist countries are not; what are "sensible" policies in Australian eyes are not necessarily sensible in Russian, Chinese or Indian eyes; India devalued in 1966 under IMF and American pressures and it proved disastrous'; etc., etc. I thanked him saying I would long remember the occasion not only because of the longest introduction but also because of the sharpest criticism of my lecture by the chairman (Arndt 1987:243).

Heinz escaped from a somewhat oppressive 'tea', thanks to a message that Mr Shastra of the Planning Commission wished to see him.

The next day more rain fell and this spoiled Heinz's 'pilgrimage' to the statue of a Hindu god perched on a hill high above the city. After rather perfunctory calls on the Governor of the Central Bank and the Vice-Chancellor of the university, Heinz was taken by Mr Dahal to Bakthapur. They were favoured with late-afternoon sunshine, which showed to advantage a dozen superbly picturesque views. Bakthapur itself, once the capital of a separate kingdom, moved Heinz to an eloquent description

> An amazing sight, a mediaeval town, red brick paved narrow streets with red brick houses, many very dilapidated and barely standing up, poor looking people, hundreds of ragged children. We stopped in the central square, with two tall pagodas on two sides (and two incongruously blonde children on bicycles!). From there we walked a couple of blocks and came out, quite unexpectedly, on a really magnificent, spacious rectangular square completely enclosed by palaces, pagodas and other interesting old buildings, an acropolis. A large central pagoda was pointed out by Mr Dahal as containing the famous erotic wood carvings. The proved rather disappointing, each carving only about 6 inches high and 10 feet above one's head, crudely carved and painted white and other faded colours. Of all the improbable positions, the most surprising perhaps was that where a man servant lifts the lady in his arms to a suitable height. We did a hurried tour of the ancient royal palace, surprising mainly for the smallness of the rooms and the low height of doors, barely 4½ feet. The best piece in the Art Gallery a fine marble bust of the Buddha; also a very old stone slab with Tibetan inscriptions. The sun was still shining and I greatly regretted that there was not time to paint any one of a dozen highly paintable views—everywhere one looked was supremely picturesque—and that Ruth had not come along to see it, definitely the highlight of our visit to Nepal (Arndt 1987:245).

Heinz's Asian itineraries also included Pakistan. In 1964, he received an invitation to lecture at a training course for 24 central bank officials of 17 SEANZA member countries (SEANZA stands for Southeast Asia, New Zealand and Australia), to be held in Karachi. Heinz went there via Bangkok, so that he could develop contacts with economists in Thai official agencies and in the secretariat of ECAFE. For much of this brief stopover, Heinz was chaperoned by his friend and colleague Colin Simkin. The program comprised a succession of meetings, lunches and dinners with the economics fraternity, plus a little touring, and some socialising with the Simkins.

In Karachi, Heinz duly carried out his teaching obligations and otherwise made the most of sightseeing in that city. Also in Karachi at the time was Gerry Gutman, a Canberra economist and friend employed as a consultant to the Harvard Advisory Group. Heinz remarked rather enviously on Gutman's living arrangements: a large and sumptuous house, four bedrooms (each one with its own bath) and six servants. Gutman gave Heinz a 'crash course' on Pakistani politics.

The State Bank of Pakistan arranged a conducted tour for Heinz and for the New Zealand Reserve Bank's Deputy Governor, Alan Low. This tour consisted of two stages. First, during a break in the SEANZA course, Heinz and Low went on a trip to Hyderabad. Their host there was Mr Kazi, a local landowner, entrepreneur and former Minister for Education in the Sind provincial government. Heinz found him very knowledgeable, lively and amusing. He and Low were lodged in the splendid 'Directors' Bungalow' of the local cement factory. The bungalow was elegantly furnished, including 'lovely Persian rugs which I am sorely tempted to take with me'.

At a formal dinner, they met all of Hyderabad's notables—males only, of course. Necessarily, the next day began with an inspection of the huge factory, which was very impressive to a layman. After that, they went for a brief look at Hyderabad more generally, before proceeding to Potari. In that city, they inspected an irrigation scheme on the Indus River and visited the military cadet school run proudly by Colonel Coombs (United Kingdom, Singapore, Changi). Finally, they were entertained at Kazi's farm on the Indus River, which was a real showpiece of what could be done with imagination and energy.

The second part of the Arndt–Low tour occurred at the end of the SEANZA course. It began with a first-class flight to Lahore, where they were met by the local manager of the State Bank and installed in Faletti's Hotel—'like Raffles, a memorial to an earlier age'. Heinz found Lahore more appealing than Karachi: spacious, green, with Mogul remnants, a handsome mosque and British colonial legacies. The next day, they made an early flight to Rawalpindi, where they were again taken in hand by the manager of the State Bank and given a busy day of sightseeing, including a detour to emerging Islamabad.

The next day, they flew to Peshawar, with regrettable results. Heinz confided his disappointment to his diary

> It has become sadly apparent that we could not have come to Peshawar on a worse day. Yesterday was the last Friday of Ramadan, today is Eed [sic], greatest Moslem holiday of the year. We are obviously a terrible nuisance to the poor bank manager and staff... The worst of it, from our point of view, is that after postponing most souvenir shopping to Peshawar (everyone's advice) we now find every shop firmly shut! It really is most disappointing. The weather also fails to co-operate. Another grey winter day, though not quite so cold (Arndt 1987:56).

Things did improve. Kausar Ali, 'rosy and rotund', arrived to arrange for Heinz and Low a successful expedition to a couple of shops that were open: 'he won't rob you while I'm here.' He then took them to an interesting and entertaining Eid party. Finally, now in sunny weather, they were driven to see Warsak Dam. So it was with good opinions of Pakistan that Heinz left the country the next day for Geneva.

Heinz first visited Cambodia, briefly, in 1967. He went there purely in a private capacity, on a detour from an ECAFE meeting in Bangkok, because he wanted to satisfy his long-held desire to see Angkor Wat. This lived up to his hopes. Guided first by his young diplomat friend and former student Tony Neylan, and in the company of a French couple (friends of Tony), Heinz travelled by car from Phnom Penh, northwest via Siem Reap to Angkor. The long journey (280km) began in daylight and ended in dark, but was rewarded by the 'stunning sight of spot-lit temples in brilliant moonlight'. They spent the next day on a long tour of Angkor, inspecting in great detail the many monuments and climbing to the top of the five-towered Angkor Wat itself. It was late by the time Heinz got back to Tony's house in Phnom Penh and recounted, over a glass of whisky, his delight at having seen this marvel for himself. The next day, he met various economists and diplomats in the capital and rounded off the visit with a pleasant dinner at the house of Australia's ambassador. Heinz kept his eyes and ears open during the few days he was in the country and, after he had left it, he wrote in his diary a shrewd appreciation of Cambodia's economy and politics

A country without economic problems! Or is it?…The peasants have plenty of land—the country is underpopulated—they are protected from moneylenders by the government which prohibits high interest rates and thus avoids dispossession of 'yeoman' peasants…Since there is no population pressure on land, and enough food and jobs for all, there is no great pressure for economic development. There is considerable pressure for social development, in health and especially education, but the drive here comes from the Prince [Sihanouk] himself. Finance for these purposes presents no great problems since much of the work is done voluntarily, voluntary donations of funds and voluntary labour by villagers who, e.g. build their own schools and merely ask the Government for teachers…

Others suggest that this is not the whole picture. There is an acute balance of payments crisis which will almost certainly lead to devaluation. The financial situation is deteriorating, the administration corrupt and inefficient. For some years the budget has shown large annual deficits…and there is large-scale capital flight abroad…there is a wide black market in foreign exchange…

Other adverse features: with the development of tertiary education there is increasing graduate unemployment…'voluntary' labour of peasants is largely provided under pressure by Bonzes (Buddhist priests)…Much land, especially in Siem Reap province, is not very fertile, largely sandy soil…Corruption is colossal; every transaction requires bribes of numerous officials.

In domestic politics, Sihanouk is a demagogue, autocrat and shrewd politician. In foreign policy a realist and opportunist… S[ihanouk] acts completely autocratically…But he also looks after popular support by indefatigable travel throughout the country, laying foundation stones, opening schools and hospitals, etc.

His primary concern is to keep his country intact and free from Great Power domination…the dominant fear is of the Vietnamese presence: expansionism by the more active, aggressive, smarter Vietnamese…

Fundamentally, Cambodia cannot afford to alienate China, but how much this conditions Cambodian foreign policy depends on China's power and intentions. Two years ago, Sihanouk believed the Vietcong would win, so Sihanouk backed the Communist

horse. Now there is increasing doubt. Should the US win in
Vietnam, Cambodian policy might shift completely, including the
whole 'socialist' line at home…and close economic relations with
the Communist Bloc (Arndt 1987:151–3).

Heinz visited South Vietnam three years later. Again, he went there from Bangkok (this time after a meeting of the ADI council) and, again, it was an Australian diplomat friend, in this case Lloyd Thomson, who was Heinz's host in Saigon. The visit lasted five days, a leisurely proceeding by Heinz's standards. It occurred, of course, during the Vietnam War. Heinz's account contains fascinating snippets of a war not yet lost, and he heard talk that it could yet be won by the South Vietnamese and their American and Australian allies.

Even before this visit, Heinz had reached an intellectual position of support for the United States and Australian military intervention. He had no doubt that the Vietnam War was a revolutionary one, initiated by Hanoi with the object of extending the northern regime to the south and thus uniting the whole country as a communist state. Such an outcome was anathema to him. He supported Western intervention on the side of the South Vietnamese government in Saigon, in the hope of maintaining a viable non-communist society there and because of the fear that a communist victory in Vietnam would weaken the anti-communist ascendancy in the rest of Southeast Asia.

Heinz's comprehensive perception of the favourable economic and political developments then proceeding in the Philippines, Thailand, Malaysia, Singapore and Indonesia heightened his alarm at resurgent communism, and increased his belief in the 'domino theory'. At the same time, doubts remained as to how long—or whether—outside forces could continue to prop up the Saigon government. Heinz worried on that score: 'so difficult has it been to sustain domestic morale in the United States in a war so far away, that it may well have been a mistake for the United States to get involved in Vietnam in the first place' (Arndt 1969:36–7).

While in South Vietnam, Heinz and Thomson accompanied the Australian Ambassador, Ralph Harry, and other embassy officials (including the Air Attaché and a naval commander) on a flight reconnaissance. At Tam Ky, in Quang Tu Province, they were met by the provincial chief, Colonel Tho, and given a briefing on the progress of 'pacification'; officials classified 70 per cent of the province as 'very secure'. Then Colonel and

Madame Tho provided a most excellent lunch at their home. After lunch, two helicopters whisked the visiting party away, first to a reoccupied coastal village near the northern border of the province, and then to the regional headquarters of the Australian troop contingent. The helicopters returned the party to Tam Ky, whence a Dakota flew them south to Da Lat. From Da Lat, they travelled by car to the air base at Phang Rang, and from that base they boarded another flight to Saigon.

Two of the next three days followed a similar pattern: military inspections interspersed with meals among Australian diplomats and advisers. Heinz did, however, succeed in devoting most of one day to economics: he managed a long session with a section head and several staff in the Planning Office. As well as trading questions, information and analysis about South Vietnam's economy, the gathering discussed possible involvement with the work of Heinz's department at the ANU. Later, over a lunch for 25 guests (given by the US coordinator of aid), Heinz gathered more economic facts and opinions. On his final morning in Saigon, Heinz talked again with two USAID officials, but to little effect. He found street shopping more productive than such discussions and came away with a 'quite pleasant oil painting, purchased from the painter himself'.

Heinz first visited Japan for a month in early 1965. Two local organisations, working jointly, had invited him: the Japan Foreign Office and the Committee for Economic Development of Japan. Those bodies, along with the Australia–Japan Business Cooperation Committee, arranged and financed the trip. The informal antecedents of the visit could, however, be traced to the activities of three men: Sir John Crawford, Professor Kiyoshi Kojima of Hitotsubashi University, Tokyo, and Peter Drysdale, a doctoral student in Heinz's department (who, at the time, was at Hitotsubashi conducting field-work under Kojima's guidance for his study of Australia–Japan trade relations).

On his first full day in Tokyo, Heinz met for the first time the formidable Dr Saburo Okita, the founder and Director of the Japan Economic Research Centre. Heinz's first impression of the Tokyo street scene was how greatly it resembled New York's, except for the absence of skyscrapers. The next day began at breakfast with Ramon Myers, later a very distinguished economic historian, who then was a research fellow in Heinz's ANU department and was in Tokyo for his own field-work. That same day, Heinz also met for the first time the vivacious and energetic Ryokichi Hirono, then only 33 years old, but with a great career ahead of him, including many more interactions with Heinz. From Hirono, Heinz gained several insights into the historically inextricable interweaving of Japanese social values, labour practices, mobility, wages and working conditions (such as life-long employment, wage structures based on seniority and education), which, by the 1960s, were under siege from market forces.

Among Japan's officials and economists generally, Heinz noted the excessive focus of interest on bilateral trade balances—another concept under pressure from increasing international market freedoms. Similarly, the Japanese were attached to government planning and incredulous of Australia's rejection of it as inefficient and impracticable.

Conversation with Reg Little, one of Ruth's young colleagues in the Canberra Department of External Affairs, who was in Japan to study the language and culture, added to Heinz's disquiet about his first impressions of the Japanese. He mused: 'How superficial is my picture of "like us" Japanese? How much is there in his [Little's] (and others'—indeed conventional) view of Japanese as having totally different outlook, mores, etc.?' (Arndt 1987:119).

The old hands saw entrenched Japanese attitudes: feudal, cohesive and disciplined, stressing loyalties to family, nation and company. Heinz worried that such attitudes would put a brake on economic change and growth. On the other hand, a visit to the Sony Corporation and its distinguished founder, Masaru Ibuka, left Heinz extremely impressed. Ibuka's firm was a model of rapid innovation and of keeping right up to the pace of technological change. It bothered Heinz that Australian industry seemed unable to do likewise. In similar vein, Heinz was taken with the quality of academic development in Japan. Hitotsubashi alone boasted a galaxy of economic talent and it was but one of many fine universities that he saw.

As well as visiting government departments, banks, universities and major industrial corporations (Toyota impressed him almost as much as Sony had), Heinz made a couple of forays into the rural sector, where he generally felt less comfortable than in city offices. He could not fail, though, to be struck by the Hokkaido Prefecture. In that region, the principal industry had once been horse breeding, mainly for the Japanese armies in times past. Horse breeding continued, but now took the form of a thoroughbred racehorse stud. The main contemporary rural industry was dairy farming and Hokkaido was home to the biggest dairy company in Japan, with factories in other parts of the country as well. Although the Hokkaido region produced a lot of rice, the Japanese believed that dairying represented the only real agricultural alternative to rice growing. Consequently, the dairy industry enjoyed substantial protection, enough to make an Australian economist wince. Although demand for dairy products was growing, given the country's increased population and its rising living standards, the Japanese still did not feel it was safe to open the gate to imports of agricultural products.

Heinz found the social demands in Japan heavy. Almost every business engagement came with lunch or dinner attached. Not only that: often, after dinner, there would be a visit to a bar or nightclub, which seemed to be more for the pleasure of the Japanese hosts than for hapless foreign guests. Heinz observed: 'how hard one has to work entertaining these geishas!' A related economic point was the remarkably large amount that Japanese men spent on entertainment. At times, this constituted fully 20 per cent of their personal income. Heinz learned that the men generally lived much better than the women, and that such large entertaining bills were to be expected. Moreover, the entertainment industry used a great deal of (cheap) labour, and company expense accounts were the norm (providing about 85 per cent of entertaining costs, according to a man from the Mitsui Corporation).

Later on, Heinz made brief visits to Japan in connection with Kojima's series of PAFTAD conferences, the Australia–Japan Project (established by Kojima and Drysdale, and successfully developed by the latter from an ANU base) and a 1982 colloquium organised by a Japanese newspaper on 'Japan in the world economy'.

Japan was not the only country Heinz visited on his 1965 trip. The Department of External Affairs asked him if he would supplement his Japanese trip with a week in Seoul, so as to investigate South Korean academic opportunities. In those days, very little academic contact of any sort existed between Australia and South Korea.

Among the first people he met in Seoul was David Cole, then serving as an assistant to Dr J. Bernstein, head of the US aid mission. Cole, a monetary economist, and Heinz later had a lot to do with each other concerning Indonesia's economy. Heinz came to South Korea at a particularly tense time. Students had just rioted over the country's 'normalisation' treaty with Japan, and a large US military contingent continued to occupy South Korean territory near Panmunjon, just outside the Demilitarised Zone (DMZ), which had resulted from the Korean War's armistice 12 years earlier. America had a large and powerful presence, civilian as well as military, in the nation as a whole and its influence dominated everywhere.

Heinz was taken to the DMZ by Major Finlay, the Australian Army representative on the Military Armistice Commission. The drive to Panmunjon took 90 minutes, 'through some pleasant country, mostly rice fields, some villages with spring blossom on fruit trees around thick rounded thatched roofs'. When they approached the DMZ, the land became barren and at the actual line of demarcation between the contending forces was a 'Security Zone', which both sides shared. 'This consists,' Heinz wrote in his diary, 'of a compound, about 100m by 200m, with a dozen or so huts, blue = "UN" (i.e. US & ROK [Republic of Korea]), green = "Communists" (North Korea).' Heinz was fascinated by the formalities with which the two sides communicated at set, regular intervals (Arndt 1987:140–1).

Like many other nations at that time, South Korea had put its faith in planning, so Heinz did the rounds of the Economic Planning Board, the Planning Coordination Office, the Central Statistical Bureau and others. Not surprisingly, agricultural product prices were controlled, for the benefit of consumers, and producers were subsidised. Efforts to raise agricultural productivity through research were in train, but not yet effective. The financial markets were, however, enjoying increasing freedom. The South Korean currency (the won) had lately been allowed to float and the market for it had behaved in textbook fashion: the won first depreciated from 250 to 270 against the US dollar, then rose back to 255, where it seemed fairly stable. At the time, Cole was sensibly arguing for a parallel deregulation of interest rates.

Student unrest had closed down many South Korean universities, however, a few remained open, including the private, Christian, Chung Ang University. There Heinz addressed the economics staff, as well as some 15 other economists from several of the closed institutions, and responded to questions. The discussion neatly reflected the issues of the day and the mood of the South Koreans: trade with Japan; US aid; the floating exchange rate; interest rate controls; price stabilisation; industrial strategy; P.L.480 aid from the United States; and trade with Australia. Though Heinz left South Korea much more knowledgeable about the place than he had been when he arrived, he never returned to the country.

On this particular tour, he returned to Tokyo, and, at the end of the week, went to Hong Kong.

The Hong Kong visit was brief—less than three days. Heinz stayed at the Park Hotel on Kowloon and was looked after with great diligence by Bob Beveridge, a former ANU student who lived nearby and who worked at Hong Kong University Press. In the short time available to him, Heinz managed to visit the two universities (the University of Hong Kong and the Chinese University of Hong Kong), where he saw a vice-president (registrar), an acting vice-chancellor and the acting head of an economics department.

He derived much more professional benefit from a meeting with the Financial Secretary of the Hong Kong Government, Sir John Cowperthwaite, who spoke authoritatively about the new banking ordinance, the effective working of the informal currency board and Hong Kong's trade difficulties arising from industrial countries' protectionism—all subjects of particular interest to Heinz. Something in Cowperthwaite's manner, and that of Mr Watt at the Government Information Service, must have got under Heinz's skin (which was always thin where the English ruling classes were concerned) because he concluded: 'Very interesting, but curious how, in contrast to the Japanese, both the Englishmen managed to convey, with all their impeccable manner, that you are a nuisance and wasting their valuable time' (Arndt 1987:146).

It remains to say a little about Heinz's connection to Australia's nearest northern neighbour Papua New Guinea (PNG): not strictly Asia, but certainly a large part of the Pacific islands. Curiously, despite the fact that Heinz's Department of Economics belonged in a Research School of Pacific Studies, it did only a limited amount of work on islands other than PNG. Perhaps that was because the Pacific never really captured Heinz's interest (as it had Crawford's). Even the PNG research, though at times substantial, was something of a minority interest in the department; it had been left largely to Fred Fisk, Ric Shand and Malcolm Treadgold in the 1960s and 1970s. Also, the establishment of the New Guinea Research Unit as a Port Moresby-based outpost of the ANU tended to diminish PNG-related activity in Canberra. Ross Garnaut, who later became such a productive and influential member of the department and professor after Heinz's retirement, had made an energetic and most effective contribution to PNG development when working in its Treasury during the 1970s. When he returned to academic life, however, the focus of his interests moved to Asia.

When Heinz went to PNG in 1969, the country was on the threshold of independence. Many argued, then and later, that this was granted prematurely; but the politics of the time, and in particular the prevailing rage against 'colonialism', would have made it very difficult for Australia to continue administering the country. The advent of independence threatened to impose excessive demands on Papua New Guinea's scarce professional resources, so the country was thick with Australian advisers doing their best to develop robust physical, governmental and commercial infrastructures before the handover of sovereignty. Heinz's specific mission was to advise the PNG Development Bank on interest-rate policy, particularly regarding its indigenous customers. His 'director' on this journey was the Manager of the Development Bank, Keith Crellin, 'a likeable, thoughtful person, clearly anxious to find ways to assist indigenous economic development but insistent on remaining practical'.

Other expatriates who influenced Heinz's approach to the job included Ron Crocombe, of the ANU New Guinea Research Unit, and Bill McCasker, economic adviser to the government and former executive officer to the Vernon Committee. The two did not always see eye to eye. According to Heinz, McCasker was 'very hostile about "ratbag" academics, who, determined to see the issues in terms of colonialist exploitation and race conflict, will not grant the Administration even their good intentions and dismiss all efforts to advance the interests of the indigenes as hypocrisy and tokenism'.

The expatriate industry advisers favoured low interest rates, because indigenes needed 'all the help they can get', and were hostile to the Development Bank, with its high rates. Heinz held a further fear that cooperative lending institutions would not be viable once the expatriate managers were withdrawn. Nevertheless, the strategy for indigenous financial development clearly centred on the cooperative movement as a vehicle for savings and investment finance.

At every point in his travels from Port Moresby through Rabaul, Lae, Mt Hagen and Goroka, Heinz saw the cooperative movement in various forms. The Reserve Bank was actively promoting this movement, despite some scepticism among certain bank staff. Heinz noted

> They [the cooperatives] start as savings clubs; once deposits
> pass the $2,000 mark, they become societies and make loans to

> members for trucks (not favoured by the Reserve Bank), land development, cattle, etc. Repayment is the main problem. The people have only rudimentary understanding of contractual obligations; what matters to them is the complex pattern of mutual clan obligations in which time plays little part' (Arndt 1987:164).

The traditional customary relationships of indigenous society caused great pessimism among expatriate business advisers who tended to think that, at best, it would take at least one generation to develop indigenous managerial and commercial skills. Yet the Reserve Bank persisted with efforts to draw indigenous agricultural producers into the cash and market economies. It thus achieved just enough success to sustain the policy.

Heinz greatly enjoyed the grandeur and variety of the scenery in PNG. He also found stimulus among the rich assortment of indigenous and expatriate people he met. The European missionaries he considered particularly inspiring, not only because of the social cohesion and strength of the communities in which they served, but because of the viability of their business enterprises. The Seventh-Day Adventist market gardens at Goroka formed a 'most impressive' example. Further, most of the Catholic and Lutheran missionaries were German; this faint connection to his native land pleased Heinz, enabling him to appreciate and savour the food, language and culture from which he had largely parted company for more than 35 years.

In 1970, Heinz returned briefly to PNG to inaugurate, rather incongruously, in Port Moresby a branch of the Economic Society of Australia and New Zealand. He gave the branch's first local public lecture on 'The future of New Guinea's monetary system'. In retrospect, he thought this paper too cautious, because in it he recommended 'nothing more adventurous than a currency board system'. The longer view has, however, shown this advice to be good, and the paper's analysis has stood the test of time.

52. Ruth with Nick's son Gregory, 1986

53. Heinz with Chris' girls Sara and Emma

54. Heinz at Cottesloe Beach with Sara and Virginia, circa 1980

55. Heinz with Bettina's older son Jesse playing tiddlywinks, circa 1986

56. Arndt family gathered for 50th wedding anniversary celebrations, 2000

57. Last portrait with Ruth

58. Heinz meets his great-granddaughter Charlotte, 2002

59. Recent Arndt gathering. L-R Bettina's daughter, Taylor, Nick's sons, Benjamin and Gregory, Nick's wife, Catherine, Bettina and sons Jesse and Cameron and brother Nick

60. Chris' daughters Sara and Virginia, Bettina with her sons Jesse and Cameron at the launch of the H.W. Arndt Building at The Australian National University

61. The H.W. Arndt Building, opened in 2005

22
RETIREMENT

As was usual in Australia in 1980, Heinz's job at the ANU was subject to mandatory retirement at the age of 65. Most reluctantly, Heinz accepted this rule and retired in the formal sense on 31 December 1980 (the last day of the year in which his sixty-fifth birthday occurred). For him, retirement could never mean idleness. He had to have something worthwhile to do and he needed to find it outside the structure of formal, continuing employment.

The answer—which he perhaps had a hand in preparing—came in the form of the Joint Research Project on ASEAN–Australia Economic Relations (AAJRP). This project was an initiative of then Prime Minister, Malcolm Fraser, who had put the idea forward at an Association of Southeast Asian Nations (ASEAN) summit meeting in Kuala Lumpur in 1977. Heinz was able to position himself for a leading role in the project, because the idea was being discussed when he travelled in Fraser's party on an around-the-world trip for the Commonwealth Heads of Government regional meeting in Delhi in August 1980, just four months before his retirement from the ANU. As Australia promised to meet all the financial costs of the project, the assembled heads of government in 1977 had agreed in principle to the proposal. Nevertheless, partly because the project required cooperation among six nations, and partly because the initiative lay squarely with the respective governments, the project took a long while to begin. In fact, it did not start operating until 1981. Before saying more about the AAJRP, one must digress at some length on related subjects, bound together with it by the interests of Prime Minister Fraser.

More or less in parallel with the AAJRP's conception was another international initiative of Fraser, in which Heinz played a central part. At the Commonwealth Heads of Government Meeting (CHOGM) in Lusaka, Zambia, in 1978, Fraser proposed the formation of an expert group to consider what might be done to revive economic growth in the OECD countries, and thus develop a 'Marshall Plan for the Third World'. The proposal was accepted; but, under the influence of CHOGM's developing-country members, its focus changed from 'growth' to 'development', with an emphasis on the related trade and investment issues of the so-called (and then fashionable) notion of a New International Economic Order.

Commonwealth Secretary-General, S.S. Ramphal, duly appointed an Expert Group in August 1979. It consisted of 10 eminent Commonwealth economists, including such luminaries as Amartya Sen and Alec Cairncross; six were from developing countries, four from industrial countries. As the initiative had come from Australia, Heinz was made chairman. The group met in London for the first time in February 1980 and twice more before delivering its report, *The World Economic Crisis: a Commonwealth perspective*, in June 1980.

In reasoned, sober style, the report worked its way through contemporary developments in the world economy; the relationship between the current slow-down of world economic growth and the problems of poverty, and often starvation, in developing countries; the difficulties of financing balance-of-payments deficits in those countries; the adverse consequences of protectionism for future world economic development; the problem of inflation; energy, resources and conservation. The report judged that many of the current problems were intimately related to the need for structural changes, which would accelerate economic growth in industrial and developing countries. It recommended collective action, because the world economy had become so interdependent that 'common economic problems can only be solved by concerted and mutually consistent action by all countries'.

Worthy though the analysis and conclusions of the report were, it sank without trace, perhaps because it was overshadowed by the almost simultaneous release of the Brandt Commission's report, to the UN General Assembly, on a 'New International Development Strategy' for the 1980s.

Of course, it was necessary for the Commonwealth report on the world economic crisis to be presented at a meeting of the Commonwealth Heads of Government. This was done at the regional meeting in New Delhi in September 1980. For this purpose, Heinz, as Expert Group chairman, was invited to accompany Fraser and his entourage. A customised RAAF Boeing 707 took off from Melbourne on 30 August, filled with the prime minister's staff, many other officials and selected journalists. All except Heinz seemed to have work to do in flight, and news cables were frequently passed around. Heinz sat on the plane with Owen Harries, who later became editor of America's *National Interest* magazine, and whose company he enjoyed, not least because they played chess. Prime Minister Fraser was last aboard, a towering figure walking down the aisle chatting to each in turn and later inviting all to his lounge for a 'nightcap'.

The party made stopovers in Honolulu and San Francisco. In the elegant Hotel St Francis, Heinz enjoyed being one of three at dinner with the prime minister. He took the opportunity to report to Fraser on a recent meeting with ASEAN officials. Otherwise, the conversation was about food, wine, sport and the honours system, of which it was said that Mrs Fraser and Mrs Arndt disapproved.

The next stop was Boston, so that the prime minister could attend the America's Cup yacht race at nearby Newport. In Boston, Heinz, not being interested in sailing, sought contact with family and friends in the New England area; he managed to speak by telephone to his brother, Walter, and to economist Gus Papanek, and to see his nephew David and his old friend and patron Rosenstein-Rodan. Rosi, then aged 78, reminisced about seeing Joseph Schumpeter in Vienna in 1913, and attending Vilfredo Pareto's lectures in Lausanne in 1919.

The next day, Fraser's party enjoyed a fine lunch in the Copley Plaza Hotel, before leaving for Washington. Heinz was able to rub shoulders not only with the prime minister but with Senator Robert Cotton and mandarins of the Australian Public Service Nick Parkinson, Geoff Yeend and Peter Henderson. The Washington stopover was brief, but Heinz fitted in dinner with Helen Hughes and Graeme Dorrance, her economist husband. On this occasion, there was much talk about developments in economics at the ANU.

During the next flight, to Delhi via Rome, Heinz did his first real work of the trip: with public servant Dick Rye, he prepared notes on international economic issues for the prime minister. Their first draft, taken forward by Rye, went through several revisions and additions on the run in the next two days and the intervening night, until Heinz and Rye met Fraser once they arrived in Delhi. Fraser asked questions, made comments and asked Heinz to prepare a further revision. He also proposed that Heinz join himself and Foreign Minister, Andrew Peacock, as a three-member Australian team at a Heads of Government session on international economic issues.

After the formal opening of CHOGM later in the morning, the heads mingled with their many attendants over coffee. Heinz ran into Ramphal, who introduced him to Indira Gandhi—recently reinstalled in the prime minister's office—and then left them to it. In his unpublished diary (from which the quotations in these passages are taken), Heinz wrote

> She made a pleasant comment on the Expert Group Report. I told her about my time here with Pitambar Pant ('he was a great loss') and meeting her father at the Science Congress. She said all our political and economic systems have to be changed—'they no longer work' and cited as an example the fanatical efforts to overthrow her Government as soon as it was elected. I asked her what should be done—she said 'I don't know'. I said I sometimes wondered whether, especially in huge countries like India, there might be a case for decentralisation of power from the Centre to the Provinces; she said that would make things worse; 'they are even more vulnerable to pressures by vested interests'.

After the coffee break, Heinz went into the meeting of heads of government on international economic issues. Around Gandhi in the chair—'like a small, alert bird with her fringe of white hair and black eyes'—sat Secretary-General Ramphal and the assembled heads of government. These were J.R. Jayawardene (Sri Lanka), Zia-ur Rahman (Bangladesh), Sir Robert Muldoon (New Zealand), Tun Hussein Onn (Malaysia), Lee Kuan Yew (Singapore), Sir Julius Chan (PNG), Father Walter Hadye Lini (Vanuatu), other Pacific island leaders and, of course, Fraser. This assembly was surrounded by attendant officials and advisers.

Heinz sat 'in the third row of chairs, behind Fraser and Peacock, taking notes and occasionally passing notes to Fraser via Peacock, as first Mrs Gandhi, then Muldoon, Lee Kuan Yew, Ramphal, Zia and Fraser made lengthy statements. Fraser followed our outline, adding supplementary points of his own. Most fascinating experience.'

At the end of the session, Heinz compiled a short report with which to brief the larger Australian contingent. After lunch, he travelled back to the next session with Fraser in his car, using the time to explain to him the 'recycling' problem, and then sat through a long and dull session. In the early evening, Heinz was summoned at short notice to the Australian contingent's debriefing session

> I was impressed by the extent to which issues were discussed in terms of tactics, manoeuvring for advantage from Australia's national interest point of view, with subtlety and a degree of cynicism which showed itself partly in a general air of hilarity, all this obviously at a high level of intelligence and professional competence. Interesting contrast of style: Owen Harries analytical

and forceful, Rob Merrilees sharp and in a way ruthless, Roger Holdich thoughtful and moderate, Peter Henderson relaxed, deliberately low-key, Geoff Yeend authoritative in an informal, friendly way, obviously in command.

The next day, Heinz was back in the role of onlooker. As there seemed to be nothing for him to do, he went shopping until the late-morning meeting of the communiqué drafting committee, where there was 'much wrangling over words'. The drafting committee worked on and off over the next two days, but Heinz found himself superfluous and unoccupied. He was reduced at one point to reading the *Holy Bhagavad Gita* (of which there was a copy in each room, along with the Bible).

The next day, it was announced, just before noon, that the communiqué had been approved. All delegations promptly began to depart and, by late afternoon, Heinz was airborne with the prime minister, the Australian contingent, Lee Kuan Yew and Singapore's Foreign Minister, Suppiah Dhanabalan, who were 'given a lift home'. In flight, Heinz managed a few words with Fraser and asked if he would publish in *Quadrant* the speech he had given in Washington. Fraser said he would be 'honoured'. When the bureaucrats got their hands on the proposal, however, they raised difficulties, mainly about the production of, payment for and distribution of off-prints.

After arriving late at night, the Australians enjoyed a one-day stopover in Singapore. The enjoyment was somewhat soured when they read in the local press an account of Lee Kuan Yew's Delhi interview with Australian journalists: 'he certainly did not mince words; Australia "more conservative, backward-looking and protectionist than the meanest Europeans"! No wonder Fraser was unhappy.' For Heinz, however, the final lap of the trip was unalloyed pleasure. He shopped in Orchard Road for himself, family and friends, lunched with Professor Lim Chong Yah and other Singaporean academic friends, and later discussed the AAJRP plans with K.S. Sandhu (Director of the Institute of South-East Asian Studies).

The day culminated in a formal dinner at the Istana (the palace) given by Lee Kuan Yew and Mrs Lee. Other guests included Fraser, of course, Professor Ray Vernon (Lee's American economics guru), Singaporean cabinet ministers Goh Keng Swee and Tan Hong Koh, and Captain B.G. Lee, Lee Kuan Lew's son and himself to become Prime Minister of Singapore some 20 years later. Over dinner, at which he sat next to B.G. Lee, Heinz took part in 'fascinating discussion' among Lee, Vernon and

Fraser about the OPEC oil-price crisis, its financial consequences, East–West relations and much else. He found himself supporting sometimes Fraser, sometimes Vernon. The next day, it was home to Canberra after an 'unusual dozen days. What an experience!'

Shortly after the prime minister's trip, the Joint Research Project on ASEAN–Australia Economic Relations at last set sail. The AAJRP was to be managed by two steering committees, one for Australia and one for ASEAN, with a joint steering committee to meet from time to time, in order to give overall direction. In Australia, there would be a research director with a research unit, and in ASEAN five such offices, one in each country; the six research directors were to provide operational coordination. Not until September 1980 did the Australian steering committee hold its first meeting. Meanwhile, in July 1980, Andrew Peacock made appointments: Heinz as chairman of the steering committee; myself, Peter Drysdale, Bruce McKern (Macquarie University) and Richard Snape (Monash University) as members; and Ross Garnaut as research director. Gerry Ward (Director, RSPS, ANU) was later added to this committee, and in 1983 Hal Hill succeeded Garnaut as research director. On the ASEAN side, the initial steering committee chairman was Tan Sri Ishak Pateh (later succeeded by Y.B. Dato Seri Radin Soernano Al-Haj), who served also as co-chairman (with Heinz) of the joint steering committee.

Despite his general distaste for committee work and administration, Heinz was good in the chair, eliciting contributions from everyone and, when necessary, coaxing them into a progressive consensus. He also much enjoyed the meetings of the joint steering committee in Malaysia; these were held at such delightful locations as Penang, Kuala Lumpur, Kuching and Kuala Trengganu. The Australian and ASEAN representatives mingled easily and happily outside the formal meetings. Incidentally, among the various excursions arranged by the Malaysian hosts on these occasions, as brief respite from the work at hand, was a visit to a longhouse in the Borneo jungle. There the aboriginal inhabitants, once headhunters, were discovered enjoying the delights of colour television.

The AAJRP was allocated $3.5 million and given an initial life of three years. Extensions occurred and, by the time the project closed down, almost 10 years had elapsed. It had by then produced and published some 15 books and more than 50 research papers on a wide range of subjects, including trade in services, food and manufactures; protection, regulation and structural adjustment; shipping; aviation; minerals; migration and labour markets. For Heinz, the project provided not only intellectual stimulus and achievement but pleasant offices in University House, overlooking the beautiful Fellows' Garden, secretarial and research assistance and, above all, a further opportunity to lead a program of applied economic analysis of Australian–ASEAN themes and relations.

When the AAJRP was nearing its end, Heinz was asked by Helen Hughes, then director of the ANU's National Centre for Development Studies, to establish and edit a new journal, *Asian–Pacific Economic Literature* (APEL). The idea of APEL had sprung from Peter McCawley, who, at the time, was working in the Australian International Development Assistance Bureau (now AusAID). The bureau provided a grant to get the project going. Hughes made the journal a major enterprise of the Development Studies Centre; it would be devoted to chronicling economics writings about the Asia Pacific region.

In a later unpublished typescript, Heinz wrote

> We defined the purpose of the journal as keeping busy people up with what was being written about economic developments in the Asian–Pacific region. There would be two or three commissioned literature survey articles in each of the two issues a year and…book reviews, annotated lists of new books, abstracts of journal articles, lists of working papers, etc. My role as editor [was] chiefly to commission and edit the literature surveys, choose books for review and reviewers, write 60–80 abstracts of journal articles for each issue and keep an eye on the whole operation.

Lest it be thought that Heinz did all this single handed, it should be noted that he always had the help of an associate editor and/or an assistant editor (of whom, over the years, there were several) and the support of an editorial advisory committee or board.

It fell to the associates and assistants to do the tedious work of abstracting hundreds of journal articles (300–400 per issue by the time of Heinz's death), preparing an annotated list of unreviewed books (80–100 per issue) and drawing up lists of countless working and discussion papers emanating from various universities, institutes and international organisations such as the World Bank.

The initial advisory committee was very much 'in house': Anne Booth, Drysdale, Hill, McCawley and Hughes, all sometime members of Heinz's old department. There were also corresponding editors in each of several

Southeast Asian countries. By 2001, the advisory board personnel had largely changed from the earlier committee but still contained a preponderance of members from RSPS. The corresponding editors were paralleled by a large international advisory board, composed of people so distinguished that they would have had scant time for editorial duties for APEL. None of these groupings ever exercised any real control over the structure and content of the journal. While the editorial board did meet, briefly, twice a year, it served primarily as a 'brains trust' to help Heinz identify authors for the magisterial survey articles. It was always very much as Heinz wanted it to be: specifically, empirical and policy oriented, devoid of mathematical economics and economic modelling.

Heinz took eagerly and effectively to the responsibility for APEL, which he regarded as a part-time job. He enjoyed the work greatly for the content itself, for the complex network of communication with so many authors, publishers, referees and reviewers, and for the companionship and support he received from clever, capable and friendly associate and assistant editors.

Like the BIES, APEL has earned a well-recognised place in the panorama of economics periodical literature. Heinz was justly proud of having established two such journals—a rare feat indeed.

The other part of his time was devoted to consultancies, conferences and writing on economics, history, politics and biography, for academic and public consumption. He maintained a voluminous and vigorous correspondence with friends all over the world, many of them his distinguished economics contemporaries. In addition, he managed to travel frequently to Asia and occasionally to Europe, and he took a keen interest in the flowering of the careers of his children and his academic protégés. To these activities we now turn.

An early retirement job was a one-month stint in the Department of Economics at the University of New England in Armidale, where his erstwhile graduate students, Malcolm Treadgold and myself, held the two chairs of economics. His task there was to teach international development economics to a class of 16 students—from Asia, Europe and Australia—who were pursuing the degree of Master of Economics by course work and dissertation. Heinz was worried that he would not be up to the job, because he had been out of the classroom for many years. As always, he was over-sensitive about his alleged inadequacies in the mathematical expression of graduate-level theory. He need not have worried; the course had a sound theoretical basis but it was not overly mathematical in style, and there was ample opportunity to analyse contemporary issues of international policy, which he enjoyed doing. Also, he found the students to be capable, interesting and lively. In turn, they responded keenly and with application to his formal and informal tuition.

He got on well with his academic colleagues and with the administrative staff in the department. Staying in one of the university's residential colleges, he made friends there too. For leisure, when not being entertained by the university community, he made a series of water-colour sketches of aspects of the beautiful campus and its buildings. He had half a dozen of these framed and he presented them to the university, in appreciation of his final formal appearance as a university teacher.

The consultancies were for international governmental organisations rather than businesses. Heinz had never taken to the money-making world and the idea of becoming 'a gun for hire' was anathema to him. The UN Industrial Development Organisation (UNIDO) was the largest and longest employer of Heinz as a consultant. UNIDO had its headquarters in Vienna, a fact that Heinz found particularly attractive. The mission of UNIDO was the provision of assistance to developing countries on their industrial policies and programs.

Heinz's first UNIDO job was as part of a team to advise the Indonesian government on the potential for developing a local capital-goods industry. The advice ran to four volumes, flavoured with caution, and warning against damaging nascent industries by requiring them to buy costly capital goods produced locally. Yet the document also laid positive emphasis on educating Indonesia's industrial workforce and on improving the country's engineering workshops. 'In the following years,' Heinz recalled in a 1992 typescript dealing with his retirement activities

> I gladly accepted UNIDO invitations to contribute to a new series of Industrial Development Reviews, to write a monograph on *Industrial Policy in East Asia* (which, sadly, was published in the not widely read UNIDO journal *Industry and Development*) and to join the Director-General's Special Advisory Group—not least because of the opportunities they provided for almost annual visits

to Europe and for the enjoyment of Vienna's concerts, museums and restaurants. Unfortunately, this role ceased abruptly in 1989 when the Australian Government was persuaded to end Australia's membership of UNIDO, ostensibly to save the $1 million subscription. The Director-General informed me that, with great personal regret, he had to dispense with my valuable services on his Advisory Group.

The Asian Development Bank was the other international organisation that called often on Heinz's services. His earliest connection with the bank was when it sponsored an important book called *The Economy of Southeast Asia in the 1970s*, for which Heinz provided background assistance. A decade later, the bank invited him to design and conduct a project on 'Financial development in Asia'. Heinz saw this as a major enterprise, which would engage a range of leading monetary economists. In the event, it was on a small scale and was carried out largely by staff of the bank, although it did include a paper by Heinz, which appeared in the first issue of the bank's annual *Asian Development Outlook*.

Heinz had a glorious year in 1984. It began with 10 days in Vienna, to help UNIDO complete a report of earlier work concerning industrial-sector development in Asia. After Vienna, he went to Paris, where he attended the investiture of a distant cousin as an Officer in the Order of the *Légion d'Honneur*, and where he also visited the OECD. Finally, he toured the Rhineland: his son Nick lived at this time in Mainz, while various relatives and friends lived in other cities not far away.

Almost immediately after he returned to Canberra in early March, he had a meeting of the steering committee of the Australia–Japan Centre, and needed to deal with planning for the July meeting of the AAJRP, to be held in Kuching, Malaysia. In May, it was off to Jakarta to join his UNIDO colleagues in discussions with Indonesian officials about the six-volume report on industrial development. He found this a disappointing experience, because of the low level of the Indonesian representatives. In June, Heinz was in Singapore, playing a prominent role in the very successful Pacific Trade and Development Conference. He returned to Kuching in July for the AAJRP meeting. He revisited Manila for 18 days during October, in order to write two chapters for an Asian Development Bank publication, and then went back to London, *en route* to Vienna once more. This London visit was to see David Bensusan-Butt (who had retired to Stamford Brook, in the house once owned by his uncle-in-law, the painter Lucien Pissarro, son of Camille Pissarro) and myself and my wife (we were on sabbatical leave). We lived on Parliament Hill in Hampstead, and Heinz's visit to our house was acutely nostalgic, because it was just around the corner from 1 Keats Grove, where Heinz and Ruth had their wedding reception in 1941. Heinz and David walked around to see that the house was still as Heinz had remembered it.

Indonesia always remained an absorbing interest for Heinz. He published articles on various aspects of the Indonesian economy in the BIES, in other academic outlets and in the popular press. A selection of these was translated by Heinz's Indonesian friend Mubyarto into Bahasa Indonesia and published in 1991 as a volume entitled *Pembangunan Economi Indonesia: Pandangan Seorang Tetangga* (*Indonesian Economic Development as Seen by a Neighbour*). Heinz also spent much time—indeed, more than 10 years—overseeing a Bahasa Indonesia edition of the large textbook of economics originally written in English by the Filipino economist G.P. Sicat. This involved not only guiding the translation but, with the help of colleagues, 'Indonesianising' some 150 pages of statistical and institutional material. The formal launch of the book in May 1992 gave Heinz another opportunity to visit Jakarta.

Heinz's 1986 public writings in defence of Indonesia have already been mentioned. He returned to the fray in 1991, trying to counter some of the more extreme anti-Indonesian propaganda in the Australian media over the issue of East Timor. His most cogent piece on that subject occupied two columns of *The Australian* on 6 December 1991. After recounting the history of Portuguese occupation of East Timor, and giving the lie to exaggerated statistics of East Timorese lives lost during Indonesian rule, Heinz argued that an independent East Timor would be a mendicant state, indefinitely dependent on foreign aid. His policy prescription was for East Timor to remain within the Indonesian republic, with some form of special status, including a measure of local autonomy, together with its own earmarked development budget. History, however, judged otherwise.

In his retirement years, Heinz wrote a good deal on economics. As had been the case throughout his academic career, he was eager to publish anything and everything he wrote. More than occasionally, he sought to do so as soon as the ink was dry. These habits resulted, first, in the publication of inferior pieces that might have had greater impact had they been subjected to rigorous revision; and, second, in reproofs from peers, colleagues and correspondents. One such reproof came from Charles Kindleberger (Emeritus of MIT and distinguished in international economics and economic history). Kindleberger wrote to Heinz, in 1992, with warm regards

> …your tariff history of the US [is] based on [Frank William] Taussig, who is out of date…I hope you will not be offended if I say that the material on England, France and Germany is pretty amateurish…the depression in Germany of the 1880s: you mean from 1873 and the famous Bismarck tariff on iron and rye was in 1879. Sorry to be blunt.

Heinz was honest and unabashed and did not hesitate to share this criticism with his friends. Ross Garnaut and I wrote in our 1995 citation of Heinz as Distinguished Fellow of the Economic Society of Australia: 'If Heinz had written less, had worked more on the presentation and logical clarity of his most important ideas, more of his seminal ideas would be around in contemporary footnotes.'

The crowning literary feat of Heinz's retirement was *Economic Development: the history of an idea*, published in 1987 by the University of Chicago Press. In this monograph, Heinz traced the history of thought about economic development as a policy objective. He started with the Western origins of the idea of material progress, from Adam Smith to the colonial theorists. He then focused on the 1950s and 1960s, when economic development and economic growth were treated synonymously and commanded popular respect—and when the engines of growth were seen as, successively, physical capital formation, human development and freedom of trade. From the late 1960s, growth and development were distinguished from each other, with the latter increasingly denoting social objectives such as employment, equity and basic needs. Heinz dealt with all this and considered left-wing and right-wing dissent on the subject of development. The book was read widely and well received.

As by-products or consequences of this work, Heinz wrote papers on structuralism, market failure in developing countries, globalism and sustainable development. He also returned to the fields of monetary and international economics, dealing with such topics as credit rationing, trade in financial services, exchange rates and what he called 'a controversial defence of the "old view" that external balance remains a necessary objective of macroeconomic policy'.

Such controversy was most notable in his 1989–91 dispute with John Pitchford of the ANU about whether a nation's current account deficit was of any importance to its economic policy. The 'Pitchford view', which undoubtedly enjoyed the support of most academic economists, was that in a world of—for the most part—floating exchange rates and freedom for the international movement of capital, foreign exchange markets would determine the market-clearing exchange rate for any individual currency. As those markets take account of current and capital transactions, it does not matter if the current account at any time is in deficit (and balanced by a surplus on capital account). Nor does a sustained current account deficit and consequent growing foreign debt need to cause concern, because the debt is essentially the result of private capital inflow, which can be presumed to yield a return sufficient to cover the costs of debt service, and in any case is an obligation of private-sector entities and not of the nation.

Heinz thought this view simplistic, particularly regarding the composition and motivation of capital inflows. He also considered that it ignored several negative externalities attaching to current account deficits (such as a possible loss of confidence among foreign lenders, which would lead to a diminished supply and/or a higher price of loans). Heinz fought for his opinion with great vigour and tenacity, but he did not prevail. In the end, the debate evaporated, since in later years Australia's official overseas debt was eliminated and private debt appeared to be within acceptable limits of commercial risk.

The issue of external balance was closely bound up with the idea of globalism or, to use the current jargon, globalisation. Heinz thought globalism was a truly awful word and devoted many hours and pages to showing its emptiness. 'But "globalism" is a fad notion. The sooner it disappears from economists' vocabulary the better.' So much for globalism. Unfortunately, globalisation is alive and well (if not universally admired), despite Heinz's efforts to dispatch that term too. He hammered away at globalisation and, in 1998, published an article in *Pacific Economic Papers* that sought to straighten out a lot of muddled thinking about the concept and the usage of the word.

Just as politics and political economy had been consuming interests for Heinz in his earlier life, so they remained in his retirement, if the word 'retirement' is really appropriate for his busy last years. He dealt with political economy in academic journals, as far as it was possible to do so, and beyond those outlets he repeatedly contributed to newspapers, especially on contentious or polemical issues. This leaning led to Heinz's involvement with *Quadrant* magazine. His first contribution to *Quadrant*, at the age of 54, was the remarkably open memoir 'Three times 18: an essay in political autobiography'. This piece attracted much attention and a frigid reception from Ruth.

Thereafter, Heinz wrote often for *Quadrant*, on issues of economic policy, such as anti-protectionism and tax reform, on Asia's development and Australia's engagement there, and a series of charming memoirs of his German family and his English associates of the 1930s and 1940s. This generous association with the magazine resulted, in 1981, in an invitation to be co-editor with Peter Coleman. Heinz brought distinguished contributors to the magazine and he organised conferences and seminars, including a celebration of *Quadrant's* twenty-fifth anniversary (also in 1981). In conjunction with his editorial role, Heinz managed the George Watson Prize for 12 years. This award was created and financed by George Watson, of St John's College, Cambridge, and administered by *Quadrant*; it offered an annual cash prize for the best political essay published in any Australian journal. Heinz selected and chaired a jury of editors and writers, and that panel chose a number of notable winners, including John Hirst, Michael James, Geoffrey Partington, Peter Ryan, Pierre Ryckmans, Clement Semmler, Sev Sternhell and Claudio Veliz. As Coleman wrote: 'It was the first essay competition of its kind in Australia and contributed something to the revival of the essay genre.'

In 1990, *Quadrant* underwent great changes: Coleman stepped down, Heinz relinquished editorial duties, the magazine was restructured and Robert Manne (who had briefly been co-editor with Coleman) became sole editor. Heinz had, meanwhile, joined the periodical's board of directors. In that role, he became increasingly uncomfortable with the illiberal drift of the magazine, in particular its lurch to economic protectionism. Continuing to be distressed by what was happening to *Quadrant* under Manne's editorship, Heinz wrote in April 1992 to 'The Editor' (Manne): 'In the past twelve months, *Quadrant* has published fourteen articles advocating or defending protectionism and eleven articles by present or former La Trobe academics. Should *Quadrant* be renamed the *La Trobe Protectionist Review*?'

The issue of the editorship came to a head in mid 1993, when Heinz resigned from the board of *Quadrant* as he felt no longer able, professionally or intellectually, to keep company with Manne and crew.

He had foreshadowed this resignation in a letter to Dame Leonie Kramer, chair of the board, in December 1992. In that letter, he identified two problems: Manne's relentless campaign, in *Quadrant* and elsewhere, against economic rationalism; and the image of *Quadrant* that this created in the public mind.

Heinz complained to Dame Leonie: 'It seemed to me that *Quadrant* retained a *raison d'être* in defending liberal economic values, as well as political. Instead it has become a propaganda instrument against economic liberalism. I could not have been more unhappy if the new editor…had turned out to be an extreme Greenie or anti-Semite.'

Another person from whom Heinz parted somewhat (philosophically but not personally) over protectionism was Bob Santamaria. As already described, Heinz, then a Laborite, and Bob, of the National Civic Council, had jousted in print in the 1950s and 1960s. Twenty years on, however, they warmed to one another and a strong friendship developed; each respected the other's integrity. On Bob's death in 1998, Heinz recorded, 'I liked him a lot, for his unfailing courtesy and intellectual curiosity.'

Heinz's later writings also included many pieces of biography. On the professional front, he wrote 'Keynes and Churchill', whose parallel lives intersected but little, despite the momentous times and English eminence which they shared. Regrettably, this paper was never published in widely accessible form, despite Heinz's many attempts to get it into either an international magazine or journal or within a volume alongside other biographical essays. It did appear 'by courtesy', together with some of the other late writings mentioned above, in his final volume, *The Importance of Money: essays in domestic macroeconomics, 1949–1999* (Ashgate, 2001). He wrote obituaries of economists Colin Clark, Robert Hall, James Meade, Gerald Firth, John Crawford, Richard Downing and David Bensusan-Butt. The last two essays were crafted with meticulous care, for he bore the subjects particular and deep affection. All but one of these obituaries, and half a dozen other short lives of economists, were collected into a dedicated supplement to the *History of Economics Review* (No. 32, 2000) entitled 'Essays in biography: Australian economists'.

Of more general interest were the memoirs of his family and early friends, published in *Quadrant* between 1981 and 1984. These are delightful little gems, each of two or so pages, which capture the times and styles of the subjects. These pieces—especially the moving 'Uncle Leo'—prove Heinz was a superb essayist. In addition, he wrote a longer piece about Fritz Georg Arndt, entitled 'My father: a personal memoir', which does not seem to have been published at all. Heinz writes not only of his father's academic career (and its setbacks occasioned by European politics and strife), but memorably of the Arndt family's life in Istanbul and Breslau. He does not shrink from mentioning the disintegration of his parents' marriage, or from alluding to the hurt he felt when his mother left in order to marry a member of an old Prussian family. 'The divorce shocked us children and probably contributed to my later puritanical attitude to sex,' he wrote. Fritz Georg engaged a divorcée, Hertha Brell, as housekeeper and three years later he married her. The children were not at first enthusiastic, but Hertha proved a staunch and devoted wife for 39 years. 'As we grew older we became more tolerant and in the last thirty years became quite fond of her.'

Fritz Georg lived in Istanbul with Hertha until, at the age of 70, he retired. In 1957, he spent five weeks in his elder son's adopted homeland, lecturing in Sydney, Canberra and Melbourne, on the invitation of the Royal Chemical Society of Australia. During the final years of his life, he was showered with honours by European academia. He had opted to retire to his hometown of Hamburg, where there were still many relatives and friends. Heinz dutifully managed to find some professional excuse for visiting Europe almost every year, and thus for spending a few days with his father. Fritz Georg died in December 1969, aged 84.

Heinz lived in some awe of his father's high academic reputation and, later, of the similar academic esteem enjoyed by his brother, Walter, who became a distinguished professor of Russian language and literature at Dartmouth College in the United States. There was no justification for this sense of inferiority, because Heinz stood as tall among economists as did Fritz among chemists or Walter among linguists. Heinz, however, could never shrug it off.

As Heinz often remarked in the 1990s, one of the consequences of living to a good age was to read and write obituaries and attend many funerals. Several colleagues to whom he paid literary tribute have already been mentioned. Heinz also saw off close Canberra colleagues and friends, including Trevor Swan, Noel Butlin, Gerry Gutman, Fred Gruen, Benjamin Higgins and Manning Clark. The spectacular obsequies of the last-named occurred at St Christopher's Pro-Cathedral in Manuka, and were conducted by the ANU historian Father John Eddy, SJ. More than 500 people attended, including Governor-General Bill Hayden, Prime Minister Bob Hawke, Treasurer Paul Keating and the rest of the Federal Labor Cabinet, various archbishops and bishops, and countless academics.

Heinz and Ruth had been friends with Manning and Dymphna Clark from the early 1950s, when the two men were the first professors of their subjects in the Canberra University College. Heinz and Clark shared high, but not always identical, principles. Clark said to Heinz in 1989, 'we are both men of moral passion.' Both loved to play with language: in 1980, Heinz received a telegram, 'HIC PARS TUI NUNQUAM MORIETUR. TUUS AMICUS. MANNINGUS CLERICUS.' (Incidentally, it is not well known that, between 1983 and 1998, Heinz sustained a correspondence with the editorial staff of the *Macquarie Dictionary*. Much of it consisted of queries or arguments about words, but he also made some contributions.) Both the Arndts were much affected by Clark's death. They had dined with the Clarks, at the home of a mutual friend, a week before Manning died and Ruth had spoken to him on the phone only the night before. Heinz wrote afterwards to a friend

> I liked him personally, however much I disliked his views and his influence on Australia—his anglophobia, his nationalism, his religiosity, his contempt (from a millionaire's comfortable perspective) for material progress, his peddling of trendy notions. He wrote marvellous English—built on the eighteenth century and the Authorised Version—and he carried off the role of 'secular prophet' with style. The adulation of a whole generation of Australians, amply demonstrated in media and newspaper tributes in the last two days, shows that people prefer a Tolstoy to a Hume.

The last death that affected Heinz deeply was that of Sir Leslie Melville. The two had known each other since 1948, when Heinz was in the University of Sydney and Melville in the Commonwealth Bank. Thirty years later, Heinz had the honour and pleasure of presenting Melville to the Chancellor of the ANU for the conferment of the degree of Doctor of Laws, *honoris causa*. (The citation is published in Heinz's 'Essays in biography: Australian economists'.) Among many other distinguished posts, Melville had been the second vice-chancellor of the ANU, from 1953 to 1960, and on retirement from full-time public service in 1966 he became an Honorary Fellow in Heinz's department. In old age, the two were very close. It was on his way to deliver a eulogy at Melville's funeral that Heinz met his own accidental death (see this book's Postlude).

The last period of Heinz's life was by no means all gloomy. Apart from the pleasures of travel and conferences, Heinz attained honours and respect. In September 1994, at a Surfers Paradise gala dinner of the Economic Society of Australia, Heinz was acclaimed as the Society's Distinguished Fellow of the year. (The citation for this award appeared in the *Economic Record's* March 1995 issue.) His acceptance speech included these observations

> I confess I find it hard to convince myself that I am in this league. Colin Clark and Trevor Swan were great economists of international stature; Roland Wilson and Leslie Melville were outstanding economist public servants. I suspect my main qualification is longevity, and even in this respect Wilson and Melville, well into their 90s, are way ahead of me. But I am glad that now, after fifty years, I am allowed to call myself an Australian economist.

Heinz turned 80 on 26 February 1995, and Ruth attained the same age about the same time. They celebrated with a joint 160th birthday party at home on 12 March. Heinz's academic friends, principally from the ANU, had earlier given him a very jolly lunch to mark his birthday. Later in 1995, the Government of Indonesia awarded Heinz a Presidential Medal (the *Bintang Jasa Pratama*), in recognition of his great contributions to promoting Indonesian economic studies. The award was conferred at the Indonesian Embassy in Canberra on 10 December 1995. Meanwhile, the Economics Faculty of Gadjah Mada University in Yogyakarta established an endowment to provide five H.W. Arndt Scholarships each year to talented, needy students in the faculty. Heinz received this news at the faculty's fortieth anniversary conference, which he attended in Yogyakarta in September.

Why did Heinz not receive any official Australian award? The answer is that he had been sounded out for such awards on more than one occasion, the last time in 2001, and each time he had declined, out of deference to Ruth's dislike of the honours system.

Perhaps this is the place to mention an honour that Heinz handed back. For more than 40 years, he had been a Fellow of the Academy of the Social Sciences in Australia, until he resigned in 1996 on a point of principle. The executive of the academy had excluded from the ballot for election of fellows the name of a man whom Heinz had nominated and whom several other eminent economists, male and female, from

Australia and abroad, had strongly supported. Heinz was livid. Despite being cajoled by the president of the academy, he refused to withdraw his resignation, because he saw the executive's action as an attempt to change the complexion of the academy. As he later observed: 'It has occurred to me that by resigning I make a modest contribution towards the objective of reducing the proportion of Fellows who offend by being over 60, male and economists.' Noble Heinz.

Heinz thought constantly about how he should be spending his time in retirement. It was obvious that he could not bear inactivity. At the end of a very busy 1987, he wrote to a friend

> For 1988 my program is as yet completely empty…I feel energetic enough to tackle another book but I have no ideas. Writing technical economics in the now approved fashion is beyond me. Economic history? Political economy? I am considering offering my services to the World Bank, OECD, [ADB] or other international agencies where I have personal contacts, but they usually want consultants for longer periods than I am willing to spend abroad… Of course, I could get myself involved in some charitable work or other NGO activities—or paint or play the piano. But I am reluctant, as yet, to give up the academic work I really enjoy.

In December 1991, he wrote: 'I find myself distinctly underemployed. Since no one wants my services for teaching or administration or advice of any sort, I do far too much writing.'

In January 1995, restlessness broke out again: 'I have no bright ideas for research…and I no longer have any other professional occupation (committees, consultancies etc.). I have been wondering whether to offer volunteer labour to some charity.'

On the whole, though, Heinz did enjoy his retirement, despite the occasional pinings for more activity and greater recognition. It was not in his nature to be without a project and even at the end of his days he was wondering where to publish a recent paper. He had, in 1992, conceded that 'I can strongly recommend retirement' and '[i]t has certainly been enjoyable'.

POSTLUDE
CHEZ ARNDT

In July 1970, a young Indonesian scholar arrived at a freezing Canberra airport with his wife and baby daughter. Heinz Arndt was there to greet him. The family was driven to the Arndt home and fed a hot breakfast before being taken by Heinz to their university flat. There Heinz lit a fire, left and then returned with a bag of groceries Ruth had organised for the family. 'He did all this when he was a famous professor and I a lowly research assistant,' wrote Boediono, who went on to become the Indonesian Minister of Finance, and afterwards attained the even higher rank of Coordinating Minister for the Economy.

Heinz's shift to Asian studies also brought changes to the Arndt household, with young Asian researchers now joining the steady flow of visitors enjoying Arndt hospitality. As she had done with her migrants, Ruth was notorious for mothering the young wives, finding cots for their babies and helping them find their feet in this strange new country. 'Ruth provided a haven for newly arrived immigrants and a window to Australia,' commented Professor George Zubrzycki at her funeral.

Ruth had spent a number of years teaching economics at the Boys' and Girls' Grammar schools, which also led to a steady stream of high school students visiting Heinz in the evenings for some remedial tutorials. A few years later, the Arndt living room played host to collections of foreign affairs cadets, befriended by Ruth in her new job working as a research officer at the Department of Foreign Affairs. Neither of these professional activities was particularly fulfilling for Ruth—her professional career was always a disappointment to her.

She got far more of a kick from some of her subsidiary activities, such as her membership of the governing body of the ANU. In the early 1960s, the ANU council consisted entirely of men, a cause of some embarrassment in a world increasingly sensitive to gender issues. To rectify this situation, it was decided that what was needed was a prominent Canberra woman whose name started with 'A', to put her at the top of the ballot. Ruth Arndt fitted the bill, was easily elected and went on to serve six years on the governing body, as well as becoming involved in some of the women's groups at the university.

Through all these varied activities, Ruth and Heinz acquired an enormous network of friends. They were both prolific correspondents, each day writing letters to friends all over the world. Aided by an extraordinary memory, which enabled her to retain the minutest details of the interests and personal lives of everyone she met, Ruth was renowned for her clipping service. Every day she would diligently troll the newspapers for items of interest and cut them out, to include in her correspondence.

Author Blanche d'Alpuget, who befriended Ruth when she was living in Canberra, was one of the recipients

> From the time I first met Ruth Arndt in the late 1970s, she began, unasked, to supply me with cuttings about literary subjects in which she knew I would be interested—many of them also being snippets about myself that I would otherwise never have seen—and continued to do this until the last years of her life. She was the most friendly and considerate of women, truly living up to her Biblical namesake, who stands in history as the personification of friendship. Ruth never asked, and never seemed to expect, anything in return for her kindness, which made it all the sweeter.

At Christmas, the ceiling of the Arndt living room would groan under the weight of many hundreds of Christmas cards, including those from some very well-known names. Ruth was an avid reader and for 30 years was a member of a thriving book club. 'She'd write to someone like Michael Ondaatje and these people answered and kept writing back. They responded to Ruth's genuine caring interest,' commented Dr Jan Appel, a member of the same book club.

Even as Ruth's health deteriorated—she suffered a badly broken leg after a fall in 1984—she kept up the informal counselling role she had long played for many in the Canberra community. At 82, she wrote in her regular circular about her unpaid work, 'which developed along the lines of my original training as a social worker—acquiring lame ducks who need informal help and advice, someone sympathetic to talk to'. She mentioned taking them to her regular spot in the local coffee shop and listening to stories 'which would…now fill a handful of books—separations, divorces, death of loved ones, cancers, drugs…the list is endless'. Sometimes she would refer them to a welfare agency, 'sometimes one can think of a remedy, sometimes just listening helps'.

When the census form that year listed her occupation as 'none', she wrote a letter to the local paper to complain.

She had quite a reputation for getting people to tell all, and the confidences naturally included a fair share of spicy sexual tales. Ruth was far from a shrinking violet about such matters. In fact, back in the 1950s when Australian censorship authorities were busy banning novels they deemed pornographic, Ruth would organise to have someone smuggle them into the country where they would be kept on the family's bookshelves. *Lady Chatterley's Lover, Peyton Place, The Group*—there they all were, discreetly covered in brown paper—a great help to the growing Arndt children seeking interesting reading material.

It was hardly surprising that Ruth reacted remarkably well when her daughter suddenly burst into the public eye as one of Australia's first sex therapists. Having originally trained as a clinical psychologist, I ended up specialising in sexual problems, and then joined the adult sex education magazine, *Forum*, as consultant editor. The Arndts suddenly found themselves having to deal with the shocked reaction of some of their friends at the explicit nature of the material. Mostly they took it in their stride.

Economist Graeme Dorrance remembered trailing around Perth with Heinz, as he went from newsagent to newsagent, trying to find a copy of *Forum* to show off to him. After I had spent my early life being asked if I was Heinz Arndt's daughter, Heinz was now bemused to find he was being asked if he was Bettina Arndt's father. He coped well, although he did like to grumble about the fact that speaking publicly about sex was so much more profitable than talking about economics.

Heinz's sister, Bettina, who became an eminent art restorer, once visited Canberra to give a lecture at the National Gallery. She was less than amused when she was introduced before her lecture as 'Bettina Arndt's Aunt Bettina'.

There were, however, a few sticky moments. 'My mother never told me anything about sex!' was the unfortunate headline of an interview I once gave to a newspaper. I had been asked by the journalist whether I received my sex education from my parents and I truthfully replied that I didn't remember any birds-and-bees talks. I received a plaintive note from Ruth: 'I told you everything but you forgot.'

That might be true, but I now know it isn't uncommon for children not to turn to their own parents, however liberal, for this type of discussion.

Despite the fact that my mother was confidante to half of Canberra regarding their love lives, I kept mine carefully hidden while I was still living at home. As a university student, I travelled halfway across Canberra to visit a GP I had found in the Yellow Pages, in order to obtain the contraceptive pill. I walked into the waiting room and there was our next-door neighbour. Sure enough, she promptly reported the visit to my mother. Not that I should have worried. Years later, Ruth told me she had known I was using contraception. Her reaction: 'I was pleased you were so sensible.'

So *Bettina Arndt's Guide to Lovemaking* ended up proudly displayed on the Arndt bookshelves, which by this time also included highly technical papers on geology. Both my brothers became geologists—Chris working most of his career for BHP, before managing the development of an enormous copper and gold mine in Pakistan, while Nick became an academic. He is now a professor at Grenoble University, having married a French geologist. Heinz always enjoyed trying to get his head around his sons' subject areas, displaying a curiosity that stemmed back to his teenage years. He often told the story of the Sunday lunches that were held at his father's home during the years he lived in Istanbul. When the food was finished, Professor Arndt Senior would give a lecture—invariably on recent developments in chemistry. 'I really looked forward to those lectures,' Heinz commented. 'They were always so interesting. My father explained everything so well.'

Heinz and Ruth took great delight in the progress of their nine grandchildren, with Heinz spending long hours on the floor with the younger ones playing tiddlywinks and later chess, while Ruth carefully quizzed the teenagers to try to find out whether they were behaving themselves.

Ruth died on 20 March 2001, on the morning of her eighty-sixth birthday, from medical complications after a fall. Immediately after her accident, we were swamped with flowers and cards from all her friends. Yet she insisted on no visitors. I tried to talk to her about it, asking if there was someone she would like to see. 'It is not a zoo,' she said firmly.

Her funeral presented difficulties. She had left us a note with instructions for her funeral: 'No religion, no speeches.' The latter we ignored. At the memorial service, Heinz quoted the American writer H.L. Mencken writing about his marriage: 'I can recall no single moment during our years together when I ever had the slightest doubt of our marriage, or wished that it had never been.'

After recovering from the shock, Heinz regained much of his usual good cheer. 'Heinz's happy spirit was unquenchable,' comments Maree Tait, who was involved in publishing journals with Heinz for more than 30 years. In his later years, his morning routine always started with a visit to Maree and the APEL staff who worked on his journal. Concerned about his health, Ruth had tried to keep him from dashing off to the office first thing in the morning. Once he was living alone, he revelled in his new freedom and set off at the crack of dawn to his office and then to check in with Maree and her staff, often carrying roses or sweet peas from his garden.

Increasingly frail but mentally alert, the 87 year old greatly enjoyed one last visit to Indonesia, where he was fêted by old friends and colleagues and was excited by the prospect of a trip to the Philippines, to visit his close friends, the former Philippine Ambassador Delia Domingo Albert and her husband, Hans. On a visit just before Heinz's death, Ross Garnaut noticed a French-language book on the side table: 'I need to brush up on my French,' Heinz told him.

The death of his close friend Leslie Melville came as a great blow. Three days later, on the morning of 6 May 2002, Heinz made his usual round of ANU visits and then set off in his car to deliver Leslie's eulogy. Driving past the University Chancelry, he appeared to suffer a blackout and slumped down. His car accelerated and ran into a tree. He died on the corner near his beloved Coombs Building, where he had worked for much of his career.

The shocking accident made news around Australia and led to a flood of tributes: from Prime Minister John Howard and many of his parliamentary colleagues, academics, ambassadors and business leaders from around the country. And from overseas came glowing eulogies from former students, now high-ranking officials and political leaders across Asia, and eminent academics and other heavy-hitters from across the world. Heinz would have been tickled pink.

NOTES

1. Nicholas (later Lord) Kaldor had been an undergraduate and postgraduate student, and later a Lecturer and Reader, in economics at the London School of Economics (LSE) in the 1930s and early 1940s; later he was a Professor of Economics at Cambridge. P.B. Whale was a Reader in Economics at the LSE in the 1930s and early 1940s, and later Professor of Economics at the University of Liverpool. Dennis Robertson was a Lecturer and then Reader in Economics at Cambridge in the 1920s and 1930s. In 1939 he was appointed Professor of Economics at the LSE. He returned to Cambridge in 1944 as Professor of Political Economy in succession to A.C. Pigou.
2. Gottfried Haberler, a native of Austria, was Professor of Economics at Harvard University from 1936 to 1971. The book to which Butlin refers is *Prosperity and Depression*; the first edition was published by the League of Nations in 1937.
3. Wilfred Prest was Professor of Economics at the University of Melbourne.
4. Roland Wilson was the Commonwealth Statistician and later Secretary to the Commonwealth Treasury. In 1931 he published *Capital Imports and the Terms of Trade* (Melbourne University Press, Melbourne). The book included work that Wilson had undertaken for two doctorates, one at Oxford and the other at Chicago (where his supervisor was Jacob Viner). Viner, a Canadian by birth, had undertaken a doctorate at Harvard under the supervision of Frank W. Taussig; the doctorate was later published as *Canada's Balance of International Indebtedness, 1900–1913: An Inductive Study in the Theory of International Trade* (Harvard University Press, Cambridge, Mass, 1924).
5. In *A Course Through Life* (p.15), Heinz wrote of this experience as follows: 'I even got a research grant to employ a research assistant, but this experiment, through no fault of hers, was a failure. Partly because of other distractions, partly because I was never quite sure what work to give her until I had had done some of it myself, she kept running ahead of me. After two years of waste of public money and her time, I shamefacedly dispensed with her services and have never had a research assistant since'.
6. Trevor Swan was Chief Economist at the Department of Post-war Reconstruction. In 1950 he became the inaugural Professor of Economics at the ANU. J.G. (later Sir John) Crawford was Director of the Bureau of Agricultural Economics. In the 1950s he was Secretary of the Department of Trade. He later became Professor of Economics, Vice-Chancellor and

Chancellor of the ANU. Gerald Firth was a senior economist in the Department of Post-war Reconstruction and later Professor of Economics in the University of Tasmania.

7   Arthur (later Sir Arthur) Lewis, the distinguished West Indian economist, who won the Nobel Prize for Economics in 1979.

8   At this time, Yogyakarta was the temporary capital of the newly independent Indonesia.

9   Lionel (later Lord) Robbins, Professor of Economics at the LSE, had during the war been the Director of the Economic Section of the British Cabinet Office; he was succeeded as Director by James Meade, who won the Nobel Prize for Economics in 1977. Chifley had planned to establish a similar group of economists in the Prime Minister's Department after the 1949 election, with Trevor Swan as Head.

10 Burgess ('Burge') Cameron, a graduate in economics of the University of Sydney, and later a PhD of the University of Cambridge, was lecturer in economics at Canberra University College (CUC). He was to succeed Heinz as Head of the Department of Economics and Dean of the Faculty of Economics at CUC/ANU.

11 Donald Cochrane was a graduate in economics of the University of Melbourne and of the University of Cambridge. He later became Foundation Professor Economics and Dean of the Faculty of Economics at Monash University

12 Eric Russell was a graduate in economics of the University of Melbourne and of the University of Cambridge. He lectured in economics at the universities of Melbourne, Sydney and the University College of New England (later the University of New England); he became Professor of Economics at the University of Adelaide.

13 This was a chapter in Haley (ed.), *Survey of Contemporary Economics.*

14 *Voice* was a short-lived monthly magazine edited by Harold Levien.

15 Firth appears to be alluding to the following comment by Heinz in *The Australian Trading Banks* (p. 199):'There is very little doubt that a firm central bank policy, which does not shy away from forceful use of existing powers of control while fostering and welcoming all mutual co-operation that the trading banks are prepared to offer, would serve the needs of monetary policy in Australia quite as well as central bank control of a nationalized banking system could do. Equally, there is good ground for thinking that, freed from fears of nationalization, the trading banks will increasingly accept their new role in the monetary system'.

16 Dr Lloyd Ross was NSW Secretary of the Australian Railway Union before he joined the Department of Post-war Reconstruction in 1943 as Director of Public Relations. A graduate of the University of Melbourne, he was awarded a Doctor of Letters degree from the University of New Zealand in 1935.

17   Laurie Short was a pioneer of Trotskyism in Australia. Later he was the head of one of Australia's most right-wing unions, the Federated Ironworkers Association; he gained control of the union by imposing a court-controlled ballot on the union leadership.
18   W.E.G. Salter, a graduate in economics of the universities of Western Australia and Cambridge, was a Research Fellow in Trevor Swan's department at ANU; he later joined the Prime Minister's Department.
19   D.C. Rowan was Professor of Economics at the University of New South Wales and later Professor of Economics at the University of Southampton.
20   H.P. (Horrie) Brown was Reader in Trevor Swan's department at the ANU. Before his translation to the ANU he was a senior economist in the Bureau of Census and Statistics.
21   The Sterling Area comprised colonies and self-governing states of the British Commonwealth (with the notable exception of Canada), together with the Scandinavian countries, Ireland and some other countries. It developed in a distinctive way after the devaluation of sterling in 1931, and was officially wound-up in 1979. Sterling Area countries pegged their currencies to sterling and kept their external financial reserves in the form of sterling balances in the London capital and money markets.
22   At the time of their co-authorship of *The Australian Trading Banks*, C.P. Harris was a senior lecturer in economics at the University of Queensland; D.W. Stammer was a senior lecturer in the School of General Studies at ANU (in Heinz's old department); and W.J. Blackert was a senior lecturer in economics at the University of New England.
23   Sir Keith Murray was Chairman of the University Grants Committee in Britain. He was a Fellow of Lincoln College, Oxford, from 1937 to 1953, and was the Rector of the College from 1944 to 1953.
24   Ernest Penrose, an American scholar, worked on Japanese economic and population issues before the Second World War; during the war he served as Economic Adviser to John G. Winant, US Ambassador to Britain. His wife, the distinguished economist, Edith Penrose, spent some time at the ANU in the 1950s. It was at this time that Heinz met Ernest Penrose.
25   In a paper delivered at the University of Melbourne in 1968, the Vice-Chancellor of the ANU, Sir John Crawford, wrote: 'These two strands [the ANU and CUC] came together in 1960 on the occasion of what is still rudely referred to as a "shot-gun marriage". The gun was held by the gentleman [Sir Robert Menzies] who, of all his titles, now undoubtedly enjoys most that of this University [of Melbourne]'. Here Crawford was alluding to the fact that Menzies was the Chancellor of the University of Melbourne.
26   Hal B. Lary, an American, had served in the Office of the Special Adviser on Foreign Trade to the President, and was employed by the U.S. Commerce Department in the 1930s and 1940s. From 1947 to 1957 he was a member

of the Secretariat of ECE; from 1949 he was the Director of ECE's Research and Planning Division.
27 Charles Kemp was a graduate in economics from the University of Melbourne. He became Director of the Institute of Public Affairs in 1948, having served for some years before as Economic Adviser to the organisation. Both his sons were to serve as ministers in governments led by John Howard.
28 The Committee on the Working of the Monetary System, chaired by Lord Radcliffe, reported to the British Chancellor of the Exchequer in 1959. It is generally considered to be one of the strongest statements of 'Keynesian' monetary theory and policy. The Report criticised policy approaches that concentrated on targeting the money supply, largely on the grounds that the velocity of circulation of money was unstable. It attached much greater significance to the 'wider structure of liquidity', or to the 'whole liquidity position'.
29 Alan Boxer at this time was a Reader in Economics at the University of Melbourne; later be became a senior member of the Treasury in Canberra.
30 Russell Mathews was Professor of Commerce at the University of Adelaide; later he was Professor of Accounting and Public Finance, and Director of the Centre for Research on Federal Financial Relations in Australia, at the ANU, and Member of the Commonwealth Grants Commission.
31 Following its near-defeat at the 1961 election, the government appointed a Committee of Economic Enquiry to report on how Australia might achieve faster rates of economic growth. The Committee was chaired by Sir James Vernon, an industrialist. It included two economists, Sir John Crawford and Peter Karmel.
32 The applicants were Alex Hunter, Professor of Economics at the University of New South Wales; T.H. Silcock, Professor of Economics at the University of Singapore; J.S.G. Wilson, an Australian economist then at the LSE (and later Professor of Economics at the University of Hull); E.S. Kirby, an economist at the University of Hong Kong; an applicant by the name of Johnstone (perhaps Bruce F. Johnstone of Stanford University); and an applicant by the name of Janus, about whom no details are known. Detailed records relating to the selection process, including applications, appear to have been destroyed.

REFERENCES

Arndt, H.W., 1939. 'Bentham on administrative jurisdiction' *Journal of Comparative Legislation and International Law*, 21(4):198–204.

——, 1940. 'The social outlook of British philosophers', *Science and Society: A Marxian Quarterly*, New York.

——, 1944a. *Economic Lessons of the Nineteen-Thirties*, Oxford University Press, New York.

——, 1944b. 'Productivity in manufacturing and real income per head in Great Britain and the United States', *Oxford Economic Papers*, November.

——, 1946. 'The monetary theory of deficit spending: comment', *Review of Economic Studies*, May.

——, 1946. 'Letter to the Editor', *Sydney Morning Herald*, 20 December.

——, 1951. 'Letter to the editor', *Sydney Morning Herald*, 6 August.

——, 1950. 'Impact of immigration on the Australian economy', commissioned by the Commonwealth Bank of Australia, *Statistical Bulletin*, October.

——, 1954a. 'Economic policy—stability and productivity', in A. Davies and G. Serle (eds), *Policies for Progress: essays in Australian politics*, F.W. Cheshire, Melbourne.

——, 1954b. 'A suggestion for simplifying the theory of international capital movements, *Economia Internazionale*, 3(3), August.

——, 1955. 'Menzies and Evatt on economic policy', *Voice*.

——, 1956a. 'Letter to the Editor', *The Age*, 10 August.

——, 1956b. 'Letter to the Editor', *The Canberra Times*, 25 September.

——, 1957. *Australian Trading Banks*, F.W. Cheshire, Melbourne.

——, and Santamaria, B.A., 1957. 'The Catholic Social Movement', *Australian Journal of Politics and History*, 2, May.

——, 1958. 'Letter to the editor', *The Australian Observer*, May–June.

——, 1960. 'Letter to the editor', *Canberra Times*, 22 February.

——, 1969. 'Three times 18: an essay in political autobiography', *Quadrant*, May–June.

——, 1987a. *Asian Diaries*, Chopmen Publishers, Singapore.

——, 1987b. *Economic Development: the history of an idea*, University of Chicago Press, Chicago.

——, 1985. A *Course Through Life: memoirs of an Australian economist*, National Centre for Development Studies, The Australian National University, Canberra.

——, 1993. *50 Years of Development Studies*, National Centre for Development Studies, The Australian National University, Canberra.

——, 1996. *Essays in International Economics 1944–1994*, Avebury, Aldershot and Brookfield.

——, 2000. 'Essays in Biography: Australian economists', supplement to *History of Economic Review*, 32, Summer.

——, 2001. *The Importance of of Money: essays in domestic macroeconomics, 1949–1999*, Ashgate, Aldershot

Ayer, A.J., 1936. *Language Truth and Logic*, Gollancz, London.

Balogh, T., 1947. *Studies in Financial Organisation*, Cambridge University Press, Cambridge.

Beveridge, W., 1944. *Full Employment in a Free Society*, Allen and Unwin, London.

Borkenau, F., 1940. *The Totalitarian Enemy*, Faber and Faber, London.

Burton, J., 1956. 'Letter to the Editor', *Sydney Morning Herald*, 2 August.

Cairns, J.F., 1956. 'Letter to the Editor', *The Age*, 7 August.

Casey, R.G., 1956. 'Letter to the Editor', *The Age*, 6 August.

Collingwood, R.G., 1939. *An Autobiography*, Oxford University Press, New York.

Commonwealth Parliamentary Debate, 11 October 1950, Vol. 209:591–2.

Commonwealth Parliamentary Debate, 31 October 1950, Vol. 210:1,562–3.

Coleman, W., 2006. 'A conversation with Max Corden', *Economic Record*, 82(259):379–95.

Corden, M. and Arndt, H.W., 1965. *The Australian Economy: a volume of readings*, F.W. Cheshire, Melbourne.

Davies, A. and Serle, G., (eds) 1954. *Policies for Progress: essays in Australian politics*, F.W. Cheshire, Melbourne.

Denison, E.F., 1962. *The sources of economic growth in the United States and the alternatives before us*, Committee for Economic Development, New York.

Dillard, D., 1948. *The Economics of John Maynard Keynes: the theory of a monetary economy*, Prentice-Hall Inc., Englewood Cliffs.

Downing, R.I. Arndt, H.W., Boxer, A.H. and Mathews, R.L. (eds), 1964. *Taxation in Australia. Agenda for Reform*, Melbourne University Press, Melbourne.

Drake, P. and Garnaut, R., 1995. 'H.W. Arndt—Distinguished Fellow', *The Economic Record*, 71(212):1–7.

Ellis, H. (ed.), 1948. *Surveys of Contemporary Economics*, Vol.1, Blakiston Company, Philadelphia.

Expert Group, 1980. 'The World Economic Crisis: a Commonwealth perspective', commissioned by the Commonwealth Conference, Pall Mall Press, London.

Fisher, A.G.B., 1935. *The Clash between Progress and Society*, MacMillan and Co. Ltd, London.

Frankel, H., 1940. *The German People versus Hitler*, Allen and Unwin, London.

Gottfried, H., 1937. *Prosperity and Depression: a theoretical analysis of cyclical movements*, League of Nations, Geneva.

Haffner, S., 1941. *Germany: Jekyll and Hyde*, E.P. Dutton and Co., New York.

——, 2002. *Defying Hitler: a memoir*, Farrar, Straus and Giroux, New York.

Haley, B.F. (ed.), 1952. *A Survey of Contemporary Economics*, Vol 2, Richard D. Irwin, Homewood.

Hansen, A.H., 1953. *A Guide to Keynes*, McGraw Hill, New York.

Harris, S. (ed.), 1947. *The New Economics: Keynes's influence on theory and public policy*, Alfred A Knopf, New York.

Harrod, R., 1933. *International Economics*, James Nisbit and Cambridge University Press, London.

Harsanyi, J.C., 1956. 'Approaches to the bargaining problem before and after the theory of games: a critical discussion of Zeultan's, Hick's and Nash's theories', *Econometrica*, 24(2):144–57.

Hayek, F.A., 1944. *The Road to Serfdom*, Routledge Press, London.

Hicks, J.R., 1937. 'Mr Keynes and the Classics: a suggested simplification', *Econometrica*, 5(2):147–59.

——, 1942. *The Social Framework: an introduction to economics*, Clarendon Press, Oxford.

Hirsch, F., 1976. *Social Limits to Growth*, Harvard University Press, Massachusetts.

Hughes, H., 2002. 'Heinz W. Arndt: economist and public intellectual', *Economic Record*, 78(243), December.

Jewkes, J., 1948. *Ordeal by Planning*, MacMillan and Co. Ltd, London.

Karmel, P. et al. 1956. 'The Outlook for the Australian Economy', *Adelaide News*, 17 April.

Keynes, J.M., 1936. *The General Theory of Employment Interest and Money*, MacMillan Cambridge University Press for the Royal Economic Society, London.

Kindelberger, C., 1950. *The Dollar Shortage*, Technology Press of Massachusetts and Wiley, New York.

Klein, L.R., 1948. *The Keynesian Revolution*, MacMillan and Co. Ltd., New York.

Koestler, A., 1937. *Spanish Testament*, Left Book Club, London.

——, 1940. *Darkness at Noon*, J. Cape, London.

Lafitte, F., 1940. *The Internment of Aliens*, Penguin Books, New York.

Lepage, H., 1982. *Tomorrow, Capitalism: the economics of economic freedom*, Open Court Publishing Co., La Salle and Illinois.

Mannheim, K., 1936. *Ideology and Utopia*, Routledge, London.

McCawley, P. and colleagues., 2002. 'Heinz Arndt: an appreciation', *Bulletin of Indonesian Economic Studies*, 38(2):163–78.

McFadyean, A., 1964. *Recollected in Tranquillity*, Pall Mall Press, London.

Myrdal G., 1968. *Asian Drama, An Enquiry into the Poverty of Nations* (3 Volumes), Pantheon Books, New York.

Nichols, B., 1993. *Cry Havoc!*, Jonathon Cape, London.

Orwell, G., 1938. *Homage to Catalonia*, Secker and Warburg, London.

Pigou, A.C., 1920. *The Economics of Welfare*, MacMillan and Co., London.

Plumptre, A.F.W., 1940. *Central Banking in the British Dominions*, University of Toronto Press, Toronto.

Robinson J., 1933. *The Economics of Imperfect Competition*, MacMillan and Co., London.

——, 1937a. *Introduction to the Theory of Employment*, MacMillan and Co., London.

——, 1937b. *Essays in the Theory of Employment*, MacMillan and Co., London.

——, 1942. *An Essay in Marxian Economics*, MacMillan and Co., London.

Sayers, R.S. 1938. *Modern Banking*, Oxford University Press, Humphrey Milford, London.

Strachey, J. 1940. *A Programme for Progress*, Left Book Club, London.

Viner, J., 1924. *Canada's Balance of International Indebtedness 1900–1913*, Harvard University Press, Cambridge, Mass.

Webb, S. and Webb, B., 1935. *Soviet Communism: a new civilisation?*, Longmans, Green and Co. Ltd, London and New York.

Wilson, R., 1931. *Capital Imports and Terms of Trade*, Melbourne University Press, Melbourne.

Wilson, T., 1942. *Fluctuations in income and employment, with special reference to recent American experience and post war prospects*, Pitman and Sons, London.

Wooton, B., 1979, c1945. *Freedom Under Planning*, Greenwood Press, Westport.

INDEX

ABC radio, 75, 80, 171, 272
Abramovitz, Moses, 138
Academic Assistance Council, 9, 10
Academy of Social Sciences, 310
ACT Advisory Council, 126, 127, 128
ACT Industrial Board, 128
Afghanistan, 278, 279
Alexander, Samuel, 9
Ali, Dato Ismail bin Mohamed, 263
Ali, Shamser, 240, 258
Allen University, 139
Allende, Salvador, 249
All-India Economic Conference, 230
All-India Science Congress, 233
ALP Club, University of Melbourne, 150, 154
American Economic Review, 53, 57, 145
Anderson, Kym, 256
Anthony, J.D., 251
Anti-Communist Bill, 80
Anti-Communist Labor Party, 162
anti-Semitism, 6, 7
ANU Act, 242
ANU New Guinea Research Unit, 291
ANU Press, 23
Appel, Dr Jan, 313
Arandora Star, 35
Archipov, Seva, 271
Arndt, Bettina, (H.W.'s sister), 11, 13, 314
Arndt, Bettina Mary, (H.W.'s daughter) 14, 88, 93, 216, 243
Arndt, Christopher, 54, 62, 91, 218, 315
Arndt, Fritz George, 2, 4–5, 10, 11, 196, 235, 307, 308
Arndt, Heinz Wolfgang
 Australian citizenship, 168
 British citizenship, 61
 correspondence with B.A. Santamaria, 157–163
 early years, 1–12
 at Canberra University College, 119–129
 at Chatham House, 42–55
 at the LSE, 27–31
 at Oxford, 13–26
 at RSPS, 236–256
 at University of Sydney, 68–86
 in Chile, 249–250
 in Geneva, 195–205
 in India, 224–235
 in internment, 32–41
 in Paris, 251–254
 in South Carolina, 130–145
 marriage of, 44
 naturalisation, 55
 resignation from ALP, 169, 254
Arndt, Leopold ('Uncle Leo'), 29, 307
Arndt, Marie, 3, 4, 8
Arndt, Nicholas, 65, 216, 263, 302, 315
Arndt, Paul, 3, 4, 8
Arndt (née Strohsahl), Ruth, 27, 123, 124, 243, 313, 315
 trip to Europe, 87-95
Arndt, Walter, 2, 11, 133, 195, 295, 308
Arndt–Eistert Reaction, 5, 9
'Arndt's Law', 274
Arrow, Kenneth, 141, 192
Aryan Laws, 10
ASEAN–Australia Economic Relations (AAJRP) project, 293, 297, 298, 299, 302
Ashton-Gwatkin, F., 44
Asian Development Bank, 275, 277, 302, 311
Asian Development Outlook, 302

Asian–Pacific Economic Development Centre, 275
Asian–Pacific Economic Literature (APEL), 299, 300, 316
Asian Studies Association of Australia, 271
Association of Southeast Asian Nations (ASEAN), 293, 295
Atatürk, Kemal, 10
Attlee, Clement, 21
Aukrust, Odd, 199
Australia–Indonesia Business Cooperation Committee, 270
Australia–Japan Business Cooperation Committee, 286
Australia–Japan Research Centre, 256, 288, 302
Australian Association for Cultural Freedom, 170
Australian and New Zealand Association for the Advancement of Science (ANZAAS), 72, 75, 125, 194
Australian Council on Overseas Aid, 272
Australian Council of Trade Unions, 154
Australian Department of Immigration, 112
Australian Financial Review, 255
Australian Industries Development Corporation, 254
Australian Institute for International Affairs, 75
Australian Institute of Political Science (AIPS), 185, 201, 204
Australian International Development Assistance Bureau, 299
Australian Journal of History and Politics (AJHP), 157
Australian Labor Party (ALP), 76, 77, 80, 86, 127, 146, 148, 155, 203
 the Catholic Right within, 157, 158, 160, 161, 163
 split within, 162, 165
Australian Lecture Foundation, 170
Australian National University (ANU), 76, 104, 173, 188
Australian National University Women's Group, 62
Australian Observer, 75, 85, 172, 186
Australian Outlook, 272
Australian Peace Council, 146
Australian Quarterly, 179
Ayer, A.J., 17
Aziz, Ungku, 224, 264

Baily, Mary, 23
Baily, Tom, 13, 24, 87, 90, 132
Baldwin, Stanley, 16
Ball, MacMahon, 25
Balogh, Thomas, 70, 122, 131, 136, 174, 182, 250
Bank of NSW, 254
Bappenas, 259, 266, 268
Barback, Ron, 125, 126, 144, 170, 172, 186, 187, 190
Barker, Ernest, 20, 26
Barlow, Colin, 244
Barnard, Alan, 71, 90
Barton, Gordon, 69
Baster, James, 44, 101
Battle of Britain, the, 40
Beazley, Kim senior, 146
Beeley, Harold, 20, 26
Beers, Howard, 258
Beloff, Lord Max, 66
Benham, Frederic, 27
Benson, George, 61
Bensusan-Butt, D.M. (David), 77, 131, 237, 238, 302, 307
Berent, Zerzy, 214
Bergson, Abram, 132
'Berkeley Mafia', 265
Bernstein, E.M., 133
Bernstein, Dr J., 288
Berrill, Kenneth, 132
Bettina Arndt's Guide to Lovemaking, 315

Bevan, Aneurin (Nye), 21
Beveridge, Bob, 290
Beveridge, Lord, 9, 50
Bintang Jasa Pratama, 310
Bishop, R.L., 132
Bitter Lemons, The, 263
Black, Sir Hermann, 68, 182, 191
Blackert, W.J. (Wes), 187, 255
Blackman, Jim, 136
Blake, Don, 258, 259
Bland, F.A., 61
Bloomfield, Arthur, 263, 264
Blume, Helmut, 40
Blyth, Conrad, 240, 256
Board of Graduate Studies, 189
Bodleian, The, 19
Boediono, 244
Bohr, Nils, 5
Booth, Anne, 241, 255, 266, 299
Borkenau, Franz, 36
Borrie, Mick, 114
Boulding, Kenneth, 138, 238
Boxer, Alan, 210, 243
Brandt Commission, 294
Brell, Hertha, 308
Breslau, 1, 2, 308
  University of, 2, 9,
Breslauer Neuste Nachrichten, 3
Bretton Woods Conference, 77, 78
British Dominions and Colonies Fund, 130
British Labour Party, 43, 53, 147, 155
British Museum, 19
Brogan, Denis, 20
Brooke, Henry, 44
Brown, Horrie, 174, 184
Brown v. Board of Education, 140
Bruce Hall, CUC, 120
Bruns, Gordon, 185
Buchanan, James, 170
Bulletin of Indonesian Economic Studies (BIES), 260, 267, 268, 268, 273, 300, 303

Burchardt, Frank, 197
Burlington House, 9, 10
Burns, Arthur, 132, 141
Burton, Herbert (Joe), 53, 64, 104, 119, 146, 189, 212, 214, 221, 222, 223, 228
Burton, John, 87, 102, 146, 156, 165
Bury, Leslie, 133
Butler, R.A., 174
Butlin, Joan, 94
Butlin, Noel, 65, 68, 72, 81, 90, 94, 95, 98, 101, 116, 118, 174, 190, 221, 308
Butlin, Sid, 58, 59, 60, 62, 68, 69, 96, 99, 100, 106, 109
Butt, David, 253
Button, John, 154, 187

Cairncross, Alec, 294
Cairns, Dr Jim, 107, 154, 155
Calwell, Arthur, 166, 168, 187, 194, 202, 207
Cambodia, 283–285
Cameron, Burgess (Burge), 111, 121, 172, 185, 200, 212, 213, 215, 222, 235
Cameron, Roy, 132, 144, 172, 185, 190, 253
Canada, 34
Canberra Bulletin of Public Administration, 85
Canberra Grammar School, 210
Canberra Public Library Service, 129
Canberra University College (CUC), 64, 76, 103, 104–129, 171, 188, 309
Carnegie Corporation, 130
Carver, Sir Stanley, 72
Casey, R.G., 154, 155
Castle, Les, 250
Catholic Social Studies Movement, 152, 162
Central Statistical Organisation (CSO), 229
Centre for Continuing Education, ANU, 172
Centre for Independent Studies, 170

Chamberlain, Joe, 157
Chamberlain, Neville, 16, 23, 24, 29, 32
Chan, Sir Julius, 296
Chatham House (Royal Institute of International Affairs), 42, 53, 54, 131
Cheshire, F.W., 186
Chifley, Ben, 81, 119, 120, 150
Chifley's government, 79, 85
Chifley Memorial Lecture, 148, 150, 153, 154, 156, 157, 163, 183
Childers Street, Canberra, 119
Chile, 249, 250
Chinese communism, 160, 164
Churchill, Winston, 32, 50
Citadel, the, 139
Clark, Colin, 131, 170, 176, 183, 307
Clark, Dymphna, 309
Clark, Gregory, 241
Clark, J.M., 132, 142
Clark, Manning, 25, 104, 171, 190, 212, 214, 308, 309
Cochrane, Donald, 101, 111, 112, 113, 115, 182
Coghlan, T.A., 72
Cold War, the, 85, 112, 142
Cole, David, 288
Cole, G.D.H., 20, 25, 26
Coleman, Peter, 306
'Collar the lot!', 31, 32
Collingwood, R.G., 30
Committee for Economic Development of Japan, 286
Committee on Post-War Reconstruction, 43
Commonwealth Bank, 73, 74, 76, 81, 181, 193
Commonwealth Heads of Government Meeting (CHOGM), 293, 295
Commonwealth Research Grant Scheme, 73
Commonwealth Treasury, 73, 74
Communist Party, 21, 29, 42, 43, 161

Communist Party of Australia, 76
Communist Party Dissolution Bill, 117
Congress Party, 232
Constantinople, 2
  Islamic University of, 2, 10
Coombes, Colonel, 282
Coombs, H.C., 77, 79, 81, 179, 180, 181, 183, 184
Coombs Building, ANU, 241, 316
Copland, (D.B.) Sir Douglas, 77, 80, 174, 188, 243
Copland Building, CUC, 120
Corden, W.M. (Max), 194, 216, 237, 247, 248, 256
Coronation, the 21
Cotton, Senator Robert, 295
Cowen, Zelman, 231
Cowperthwaite, Sir John, 290
Cox, Harold, 14, 15, 17, 131
Crawford, J.G. (Sir John), 77, 177, 215, 217, 218, 220, 223, 236, 238, 254, 271, 286, 307
Crellin, Keith, 291
Crisp, Fin, 104, 119, 146
Critchley, Tom, 225, 264
Crocombe, Ron, 291
Crosland, Anthony, 147
Current Affairs Bulletin, 75
Cutts, W., 277
Cuxhaven, 27, 87, 89

Dachau, 24
Dahal, Mr, 280, 281
Daily Mirror, 183
Daladier, Edouard, 29
d'Alpuget, Blanche, 312
Davies, Alan, 148
Dearle, N.B., 52
Denison, Edward, 198, 199
de Vyver, Frank, 196
Democratic Rights Council, 76
Derrick, S.K., 136, 140
Deutschland, 20
Devons, Eli, 56, 132

Dhanabalan, Suppiah, 297
Dick, Howard, 241, 255, 266
Dillard, Dudley, 70
Dobb, Maurice, 132
Domingo Albert, Delia, 316
Donnithorne, Audrey, 244
Donovan, Jack, 71
Dorrance, Graeme, 295, 314
Douglas, Isle of Man, 34
Dow, Christopher, 251
Downing, R.I. (Dick), 77, 99, 102, 116, 173, 182, 207, 210, 212, 213, 243, 307
Drake, Joan, 264
Drane, Noel, 71, 132
Dreyfus case, 1, 6
Drysdale, Peter, 246, 254, 256, 286, 298, 299
Duesenberry, James S., 70, 132
Duke University, 195, 196
Dunlop, Sir John, 254
Dutch Planning Commission, 197

East Timor, 303
Easton, Margaret, 119, 240
Econometrica, 192
Economia Internazionale, 141
Economica, 51
Economic Commission for Latin America, 250
Economic Journal, 72, 138
Economic League for European Cooperation, 174
Economic Outlook, 253
Economic Record, 64, 72, 139, 181, 185, 209, 230, 243, 248, 249
Economic Society of Australia and New Zealand, 75, 76, 185, 193, 204, 209, 292, 310
Economic Survey for Europe, 253
Economics RSPS, 238, 241, 244, 245, 254, 256
Economics SGS, 245
Economist Bookshop, 53

'Economists' Manifesto' the, 182, 183
Eddy, Father John, SJ, 308
Edwards, Clive, 240
Edwards, Harry, 71
Einstein, Albert, 5
Elek, Andrew, 256
Ellis, Howard, 173
Encarnacion, Dr Jose, 277
Ennor, Hugh, 221
Epstein, Leslie, 22
Epstein, Scarlett, 237
Erhard, Ludwig, 10
Esperance Bay, 87, 89
Etherington, Dan, 244
Ettrick, 34, 37
European Economic Commission, 197
Evans, David, 259
Evatt, Dr, 147, 150, 156, 165, 166, 168, 183

Fabian socialism, 76, 86, 265
Fabian Society, Canberra, 146
Fabian Society of New South Wales, 81, 90
Fabian Society of Victoria, 148
Fabinyi, Dr Andrew, 186, 187, 188
Fairfax, Warwick, 71
Feith, Herb, 273
Fernandez, Roy, 71
Feuchtwanger, Lion, 11
Findlay, Christopher, 256
Finer, Herman, 27
Firth, Gerald, 77, 102, 149, 177, 182, 187, 307
Fisher, A.G.B., 44, 51, 55, 58, 132
Fisher, H.A.L., 9
Fisher, Joyce, 64
Fisk, W.M. (Fred), 225, 237, 238, 246, 290
Fleming, J.M., 44
Fleming, John, 119
Fleming, Marcus, 132
Florey, Howard, 131

Ford Foundation, 263, 270, 273
Ford, John 15
Foreman, Ken, 71
Forster, Colin, 172
Forum, 13, 314
Frank, Leonhard, 6
Frank Cass and Company Ltd, 53
Frankel, Heinrich, 37
Fraser, Allan, 75, 80, 87, 172
Fraser, Malcolm, 177, 293, 294, 296
Frederick the Great, 8
French planning, 202, 204
Friedman, Milton, 54, 170
Front Populaire, 51
Fronterlebnis, 7
Fuchs, Klaus, 38
Fulbright and Smith-Mundt grant, 130
Fulbright Grant Committee, 142
Furtwängler, Wilhelm, 5

Gaitskell, Hugh, 147
Galbraith, J.K., 132
Gamba, Charles, 224
game theory, 191, 192
Gandhi, Indira, 233, 295, 296
Garling, Max, 225
Garnaut, Ross, 244, 256, 290, 298, 304, 316
Geisenheimer, Alf, 136
Gershenkron, Alexander, 132
Giblin, L.F., 76, 79
Gibson, Frank, 242
Goa, 167, 168
Goebbels, Dr, 11, 15
Goh Keng Swee, 225, 263, 276, 297
Golden, Jack, 262
Goldsmith, Raymond, 133
Good Neighbourhood Council, 124
Goodwin, Richard, 131
Grant, Bruce, 250
Great Depression, the, 47, 54
Greenwood, Gordon, 157

Gregg Revivals, 53
Grenville, Stephen, 241, 255, 266
Griffin Centre, 129
Grossman, Gregory, 198
Gruen, Fred, 308
'Guided Democracy', 240
Gutman, Gerry, 282, 308

Haffner, Sebastian, 8, 36
Hagan, Everett, 132
Haight, F.A., 52
Hainsworth, G.B. (Geoff), 237, 238, 256
Haldane, J.B.S., 226
Haley, Bernard, 141, 173
Hall, Alan, 71, 186
Hall, Robert (Lord Roberthall), 69, 114, 132, 307
Hampstead Police Station, 32
Hampstead Registry Office, 44
Hancock, W.K., 77
Hansen, Alvin H., 53, 70, 132
Harries, Owen, 294, 296
Harris, C.P., 187
Harris, Seymour, 70, 76, 137
Harrod, R.F. (Roy), 44, 71, 138
Harry, Ralph, 285
Harsanyi, John C., 191, 192
Hartwell, Max, 69, 86, 196
Harvard Advisory Group, 282
Harvard Development Advisory Service, 266, 270
Hasanuddin University of Makassar, 261, 269
Hawke, Bob, 272, 309
Hayden, Bill, 309
Hayden-Allen Building, CUC, 120
Hayek, Friedrich, 27, 52, 142, 170
Hayward, Dick, 64
Head, John, 172
Heidegger, Martin, 11
Heimann, Julia, 2
Heiser, Ron, 172

Henderson, Hubert, 44
Henderson, P.D., 111
Henderson, Peter, 295, 297
Henry Lawson College, 76
Heywood, Reg, 132
Hicks, George, 259
Hicks, J.R., 54, 56, 70, 97, 99, 101, 106, 112, 131
Higgins, Benjamin, 77, 99, 130, 132, 308
Higgins, Chris, 191
Highway, 122
Hilgerdt, Folke, 132
Hill, Hal, 241, 255, 266, 298, 299
Hindenburg, the, 15
Hirono, Ryokichi, 287
Hirsch, Fred, 245, 246
Hirschman, Albert, 250
Hirst, John, 306
Hitler, Adolf, 1, 6, 7
  appeasement of, 22, 30
  pact with Stalin, 29, 38
  invasion of Russia, 42
Hitler Youth, 7, 8
Hoad, Lew, 228
Holdich, Roger, 297
Hollinger, Bill, 268, 277
Hong Kong, 290
Hong Kong University Press, 290
Hope, A.D. (Alec), 104, 119
Hopkin, Brian, 132
Horne, Donald, 163
Horst Wessel Song, 8, 29
Houguez, Mrs, 93
Housman, A.E., 9
Houthakker, Hendrick, 141
Howard, John, 316
Hudson, Hugh, 172
Hughes, Helen, 240, 241, 256, 295, 299
Hunger Marchers, 17
Hunsberger, Warren, 263, 264
Hunter, Alex, 240

Hunter Valley coal strike, 91, 92
Huxley, Sir Leonard, 215, 220, 221
Huyton, 33
H.W. Arndt Scholarships, 310

Ibuka, Masaru, 287
ICOR-ICOR(L) framework, 199
Iengar, H.V.R., 232
Ilnicka, Countess ('Aunt Lala') 29
India, 223–235
  Third Five-Year Plan, 228, 232
Indian Economic Review, 138
Indian Statistical Institute (ISI), 131, 224, 226, 228, 229
Indonesia, 240
  Suharto's, 265–273
  Sukarno's, 257–264
Indonesia Project, the, 254, 258, 266, 267
Indonesian Studies Association, 273
Institut Pertanian Bogor (IPB), 258, 262
Institute of Advanced Studies, 221, 241, 242
  Board of (BIAS), 242
Institute for International Economic Relations, 195
Institute of Public Affairs (IPA), 203
Institute of Southeast Asian Studies, 276
Inter-American Development Bank, 250
International Economic Association (IEA), 186, 209
International Monetary Fund (IMF), 72, 78, 101, 259, 266, 270
International Planned Parenthood Federation, 270
IPA Review, 204, 205
IPEC, 69
Isarangkun, Chirayu, 255
Ismael, 277

James, Michael, 306
Japan, 286–288
Japan Economic Research Centre, 286
Jaszy, George, 198
Jayawardene, J.R., 296
Jefferson Library, 262
Jennings, Ivor, 25, 27
'Jewish republic', 7
Jewkes, John, 55, 56, 97
John Hay Whitney Fellowship, 130
Johnson, Harry, 276
Jones, Edgar, 264
Jones, Gavin, 264
Jones, Margaret, 264
Joseph, Peggy, 44, 57, 132
Journal of Comparative Legislation, 27
Journal of Political Economy, 192

Kahle, Hans, 38, 42
Kahn, Teddy, 56
Kahn, R.F., 131, 197
Kaiser Wilhelm Gymnasium, 5
Kaiser Wilhelm Square, 3, 7
Kaldor, Nicholas, 27, 132, 196, 231, 238
Kalecki, Michal, 70, 132
Kamenka, Eugene, 225
Kapp Putsch, 3
Karmel, Peter, 102, 182, 184, 187, 207, 221, 236, 243
Kasem, Dr, 279
Katz, Sam, 132
Keating, Paul, 309
Kemp, C.D., 203, 205
Kessler, Gerhard, 11
Keynes, John Maynard, 9, 17, 70, 147
Keynes-Hansen stagnation thesis, 53
Kindleberger, Charles, 132, 245, 248, 304
Klein, L.R., 70
Knight, F.H., 141
Knopfelmacher, Frank, 163
Koestler, Arthur, 21, 43

Kojima, Kiyoshi, 238, 250, 254, 286
Konfrontasi, 240, 259
Korean War, the, 80, 289
Kramer, Dame Leonie, 307
Kristallnacht, 24

Laffer, Kingsley, 68, 81, 109, 111, 123, 148
Lafitte, Françoise, 37
Lamberton, Don, 71
La Nauze, Barbara, 105
La Nauze, John, 68, 69, 95, 97, 105, 106, 112, 115, 132
Lary, Hal, 196
Laski, Harold, 25
Laqueur, Walter, 2, 7
Lee, Captain B.G., 297
Lee Kwan Yu, 225, 275, 296, 297
Left Book Club, the, 45
Lepage, Henri, 265
Leser, Conrad, 54
Leverhulme Research Studentship, 25, 43
Lewis, Arthur Sir, 97, 99, 112, 132, 142, 276
Liberal Party, 205
Lim, Chong Yah, 297
Lincoln College, Oxford, 13, 111, 188, 190
Lindhal, Eric, 174
Lindsay, Greg, 170
Lingen, Count, 37
Lini, Father Walter Hadye, 296
Little, Ian, 196, 228
Little, Reg, 287
Lloyd, Peter, 244, 256
Lockwood, Brian, 240, 244
London *Daily Mail*, 171
London School of Economics (LSE), 9, 25, 57, 108, 196
Loughborough Grammar School, 43
Low, Alan, 282
Low, Anthony, 242

Luey, Paul, 240
Lundberg, Eric, 174
Lutheranism, 1, 6
Luxemburg, Rosa, 6
Lydall, Harold, 231

MacDonald, Ramsay, 16, 45
MacDougall, Donald, 131, 174, 210
MacDougall, Ian, 172
Machlup, Fritz, 71, 141
Macmillan, Harold, 201
Maddison, Angus, 199
Mahalanobis, Prasanta Chandra, 227, 230, 231
Maiwald, Dr Karel, 111, 112
Manchester Guardian, 53
Manchester University, 54, 55, 56, 58
Manhattan Project, the, 38
Mann, Heinrich, 11
Mannheim, Karl, 19, 20, 22, 25, 27
Manning, Chris, 241, 256, 266
Marris, Robin, 131
Marshall Plan, the, 85
Mason, Edward, 250
Massachusetts Institute of Technology (MIT), 132, 229
Mathews, Russell, 210, 243
Maude, John, 17
Mauldon, Frank, 122, 175
Maxton, Jimmy, 21
McAuley, James, 157, 163, 163
McCarthy, Senator Joseph, 141, 142, 143
McCarthyism, 144
McCasker, Bill, 291
McCawley, Peter, 241, 255, 266, 299
McClure-Smith, H.A., 84, 85
McEwen, John, 251
McFadyean, Sir Andrew, 44, 50, 51, 117
McFarlane, Bruce, 238, 256
McFarquhar, Sir Alexander, 219
McGill University, 40, 57
McKenna, Don, 225

McKenzie, Norman, 132
McKern, Bruce, 298
McMahon, William, 69, 116, 118, 251, 252
Meade, James, 44, 111, 172, 174, 307
Mein Kampf, 1
Melbourne Building, CUC, 119
Melbourne Herald, 171
Melbourne University, 25, 77, 104, 150, 173, 188
Melbourne University Press, 210
Melville, Sir Leslie, 73, 79, 100, 101, 130, 179, 183, 185, 189, 309, 316
Menzies, Gordon, 71, 263, 264
Menzies, Jean, 264
Menzies, Dame Pattie, 124
Menzies, Robert, 117
Menzies government, the, 80, 119, 147, 176, 202, 207, 236
Merigo, Eduardo, 209, 251
Merrilees, Rob, 297
Michaelis, Anthony, 37
Miller, Bruce, 116, 132
Millikan, Max, 132
Mishan, E.J., 54
Modigliani, Franco, 70
Mohonutu, Arnold, 261
Molotov letter, the, 168
Monash University, 244
Mortimer, Rex, 273
Mubyarto, 269, 303
Mudaliar, 233
Mukerjee, Mani, 228
Muldoon, Sir Robert, 296
Munich crisis, 22, 23, 24, 44
Murray Committee, the, 190, 191
Murray, Gilbert, 9
Murray, Sir Keith, 132, 190
Myers, Ramon, 240, 256, 286
Myrdal, Alva, 230
Myrdal, Gunnar, 131, 140, 141, 196, 221, 223, 224, 230
Myint, Hla, 54, 132, 276

333

Narayanan, P.P., 226, 263
Nash, John, 191
Nasution, General H.A., 260
National Association for the Advancement of Coloured People, 139
National Centre for Development Studies, 241, 256
National Civic Council, 162, 307
National Economic Development Council, 201
National Economic Development Office (NEDO), 210
National Institute of Economic and Social Research, 57
National Interest, 294
National Library of Australia, 129
National Socialism, 18
National Socialists, 1, 7
National Socialist German Workers Party, 8
Nazi economic policy, 47
Nazi Labour Front, 8
Nazi revolution, 7
Nazism, 23
Nehru, Jawaharlal, 16, 168, 228, 233
Nepal, 279, 280
Neutze, Max, 172
New York Times, 136
Neylan, Tony, 283
Nichols, Beverley, 17, 32
Nissen, Rudolf, 11
Nitisastro, Widjojo, 258, 265, 269, 274
Nommensen University, 262
Noor, Dr Abdul Sami, 278, 279
Norman, Sir Robert, 254

Ochs, Bob, 136
OECD, 169, 197, 235, 251, 293, 311
O'Flaherty, Liam, 15
OGPU, 38
Okita, Dr Saburo, 250, 254, 286
Oliphant, Sir Mark, 190, 221

Onn, Tun Hussein, 296
Orwell, George, 20, 21, 42
Otranto, 95
Owen, Tom, 112
Oxford, 11, 12, 13–27
Oxford Economic Papers, 72, 139, 144
Oxford Labour Club, 21
Oxford University Press, 20, 50, 53

Pacific Economic Papers, 305
Pacific–Indonesian Business Association, 270
Pacific Trade and Development (PAFTAD) group, 275, 288, 302
Paish, F.W., 51, 174
Pakistan, 281–283
Palmer, Ingrid, 240, 256, 259, 266
Pangestu, Mari, 269
Panglaykim (Pang Lai Kim), Dr Jusuf, 246, 258, 259, 261, 269
Pant, Dr Pitambar, 228, 279
Papanek, Gus, 295
Papua New Guinea (PNG), 153, 217, 237, 238, 240, 246, 290–292
Pareto, Vilfredo, 295
Parker, Dr M.L., 246
Parkinson, Nick, 295
Partadiredja, Ace, 269
Partington, Geoffrey, 306
Partridge, P.H. (Perce), 106, 108, 113, 132, 221
Pateh, Tan Sri Ishak, 298
Paterson, Alexander, 40
Paterson, Bob, 136
Pauline, 17, 18, 20, 21, 23
Peacock, Alan, 132
Peacock, Andrew, 295, 296, 298
Penny, David, 240, 246, 258, 271
Penrose, E.F., 190, 193
Pentony, Pat, 124
People's Action Party (PAP), 225
Perutz, Max, 37
Petrov Royal Commission, the, 168

Philippines, 277
Phillips Curve, the, 169, 170
Pigou, A.G., 83
Pitchford, John, 172, 305
'Pitchford view', 305
Plantation Workers' Union (PWU), 226, 263
Plumptre, A.F.W., 70
PNG Development Bank, 291
Podbielski, Gisele, 211, 213
Polak, J.J., 132
Political and Economic Planning Institute, 43
Pollitt, Harry, 21
Power, Eileen, 27
Prebisch Report, 250
Prest, Marjorie, 64
Prest, Wilfred, 64, 105, 112, 113, 115, 182
Pringle, John Douglas, 13, 188, 189, 190
Punch, 174
Puthecheary, James, 264

Quadrant, 157, 170, 255, 272, 297, 306, 307
Québec, 38, 42
Queen's University, Belfast, 96
Quint, Eleanor, 141
Quint, Howard, 136, 141

Radakrishnan, Dr Sarvepalli, 233
Radcliffe Monetary Theory, 209
Rajaratnam, Mr, 250
Rahman, Tunku Abdul, 225
Ramphal, S.S., 294, 295, 296
Rao, V.K.R.V., 233
Ratchford, Bob, 167, 195
Rathenau, Walter, 6
Rech-Malleczewen, Friedrich, 8
Rechtsstaat, 25
Reddaway, Brian, 132
Reder, M.W., 141
Reichenbach, Hans, 11

Renwick, Cyril, 69
Research School of Pacific Studies (RSPS), ANU, 129, 194, 215, 216, 219, 220, 222, 224, 225, 236–256, 290, 300
Research School of Social Sciences (RSSS), ANU, 174, 237
Reserve Bank of India, 229, 230, 231
Review of Economic Studies, 72
Review of Economics and Statistics, 136
Richter, Hazel, 244
Robbins, Lionel, 9, 27, 141
Robertson, D.H. (Dennis), 141, 175
Robinson, Joan, 16, 44, 70, 71, 131, 175
Robison, Dick, 272
Robson, W.A., 27
Rockefeller Fellowship, 192
Roepke, Wilhelm, 10
Romanticism, 18
Roosevelt, Franklin, 16
Rose, A.J., 235
Rosen, George, 231
Rosendale, Phyllis, 241, 255, 266
Rosenstein-Rodan, Margaret, 132
Rosenstein-Rodan, Paul N. ('Rosi'), 43, 44, 46, 47, 52, 55, 73, 100, 130, 132, 250, 295
Rosewall, Ken, 228
Ross, Lloyd, 153, 155, 157, 162
Rostas, Laslo, 132
Rostow, Walt, 132
Rowan, David, 167, 175, 206
Royal Chemical Society of Australia, 308
Royal Institute of International Affairs (see also Chatham House), 50, 52
Royal Society, the 9
Rudner, Martin, 244, 256
Runciman Mission, 44
Russell, Eric, 77, 111, 112, 113, 115
Rutherford, Lord, 9
Rutherford, Stuart, 69
Ryan, Peter, 306
Ryckmans, Pierre, 306
Rye, Dick, 295

335

Sadli, Mohamed, 258, 269, 277
Saleh, Rahmat, 258
Salim, Emil, 258, 277
Salter, Wilfred, 166, 216, 227
Samuelson, Paul, 132, 137, 138
Sandee, Jan, 229
Sanders, Don, 71
Sandhu, K.S., 297
Sankhya, 227
Santamaria, B.A., 152–164, 307
Santikarn, Mingsarn, 255
Sarbini, 277
Sarpedon, 55, 60– 63
Sastroamidjojo, Ali, 260
Sawer, Geoffrey, 146
Schleshinger, Arthur, 132
Schlesische Zeitung, 3
School of General Studies, ANU, 206, 212, 222, 237
  Board of, 242
Schumpeter, Joseph, 68, 295
Scitovsky, Tibor, 132, 141, 195
Schwitters, Kurt, 37
Science and Society: A Marxian Quarterly, 31, 33
Seers, Dudley, 250
Semmler, Clement, 306
Sen, Amartya, 229, 294
Serle, Geoffrey, 148, 149, 150, 172
Shand, Ric, 237, 238, 290
Shann, K.C.O. (Mick), 240, 258, 259
Shann Memorial Lecture, 272
Sharma, Mr, 280
Shastra, Mr, 280
Short, Laurie, 153, 155, 157, 162
Shrapnel, Philip, 184
Sicat, G.P. (Gerry), 274, 303
Siew, Nim Chee, 264
Sihanouk, Prince, 284
Silcock, Tom, 224, 238
Simkin, Colin, 275, 281
Simpson-Lee, G.A.J., 69
Singer, Hans, 54, 132, 221, 223

Singer, Kurt, 69
Singh, Dr, 280
Singh, Param Ajit, 262
Sloane, Keith, 172
Smith, Al, 136
Smithies, Arthur, 132, 174
Snape, Richard, 298
Social Democratic Party, 11
Social Science Research Council (SSRC), 186, 210, 243
Soehadi, 258
Soernano Al-Haj, Y.B. Dato Seri Radin, 298
Solow, Robert, 198
Sony Corporation, 287
South Korea, 288–290
Southeast Asia, New Zealand and Australia (SEANZA) group, 281, 282
Southern Journal of Economics, 137
Soviet Academy of Sciences, 278
Soviet Union, 21, 30, 152, 278
Spanish Civil War, the, 20, 22
Spann, Dick, 67, 69, 132
Spate, Oskar, 237, 250
Spender, Stephen, 20
Stalin, 22, 86
  pact with Hitler, 29
Stammer, D.W. (Don), 187, 240, 255
Statistical Bulletin, 74
Sternhell, Sev, 306
Stone, John, 252
Stone, Julius, 127
Strachey, John, 45, 47, 52
Streeten, Paul, 131, 196
Stresemann, Gustav, 4
Stretton, Alan, 255
Strohsahl, Ruth, (see also Arndt, Ruth), 28, 30, 32, 42
St John, Edward, 231
Subandrio, Dr, 258
Sudetenland, the, 24
Suez crisis, 167
Suhadi, 277

Suharto, General, 265
Suharto's 'New order', 269
Sukadji, 269
Sukarno, President, 240, 265, 269
Sukarnoputri, Megawati, 260
Sumarlin, 274
Sundrum, R.M., 244, 271
Sunkel, Osvaldo, 249
Swan, Trevor, 77, 103, 110, 116, 118, 132, 172, 174, 182, 183, 184, 190, 200, 213, 228, 237, 308
Sydney Morning Herald, 13, 71, 75, 78, 84, 118, 155, 156, 176, 188, 189, 272

Tait, Maree, 316
Tagore, Rabidranath, 228
Tan, Hong Koh, 297
Tarshis, Lorrie, 138
Taussig, Frank William, 304
Tawney, R.H., 27
Tay, Alice, 225
Tew, Brian, 97, 100, 101, 114, 116
Tew, Marjorie, 100
The Age, 156
The Argus, 178
The Australian, 255, 303
The Australian Trading Banks, 184, 187
The Canberra Times, 116, 165, 184
The Economic Lessons of the Nineteen-Thirties, 45, 51, 53, 54, 64, 132, 230
The Informer, 15
The Listener, 52, 53
The Observer, 163, 164
The Spectator, 52
The Times, 9, 14, 58
Thysville, 41
Thomas, Ken, 238, 240, 246
Thomson, Lloyd, 285
Times Literary Supplement, 52, 53
Timmer, Peter, 268
Tinbergen, Jan, 197
Tobin, James, 197
Toller, Ernst, 11, 16

Toyota, 287
Treadgold, Malcolm, 240, 244, 246, 255, 290, 300
Trendall, A.D., 217
Trevelyan, G.M., 17
Tribune, 42
Tripovitch, Jack, 154
Truman Doctrine, the, 85
Tu, Pierre, 263, 264
Tucholsky, Kurt, 11
Tucker, Graham, 212
Tulloch, Gordon, 170

U Nyun, 274, 275
United Nations Asian Institute for Economic Development and Planning (ADI), 274
United Nations Commission for Asia and the Far East (ECAFE), 96, 195, 200, 217, 274, 282, 283
United Nations Conference for Trade and Development (UNCTAD), 251
United Nations Development Program (UNDP), 274
United Nations Economic Commission for Europe (ECE), 131, 191, 196, 200, 211, 251
United Nations Industrial Development Organisation (UNIDO), 301, 302
United Nations Trade and Development Commission (UNTAD), 197
University College, Armidale, 77
University College, London
University of Adelaide, 97
University of Istanbul, 131
University of Kentucky, 258
University of Manchester, 112
University of Marburg, 11
University of New England, Armidale, 300
University of Queensland, 192

University of South Carolina, 130–145
University of Sydney, 55, 58, 68–74, 107, 217
University of Tasmania, 149
USAID, 258, 286
US Educational Foundation, 131

Velebit, Vladimir, 211, 212, 219
Veliz, Claudio, 249, 306
Vernon, Sir James, 236
Vernon, Ray, 297
Vernon Committee, the, 220, 236, 247, 291
Verwaltungsrechtslehre, 25
Vietcong, 284
Vietnam War, 20, 169
Viner, Jacob, 73
Voice, 147, 172, 186
von Cramon, Freddie, 5
von Mises, Ludwig, 9,
von Mises, Richard, 11
von Papen, Franz
von Ribbentrop, Joachim, 29
von Stroheim, Erich, 7

Walker, E.R. (Ronald), 55, 58, 59, 69, 177, 253
Walsh, Mary, 82, 83, 148
Ward, E.J. (Eddie), 78, 153
Ward, Gerry, 298
Wardhana, Ali, 258
Waring, Eric, 244
Warr, Peter, 244
Watson, George, 306
Watts, Nita, 196, 209, 210, 211, 212, 216, 219
Weimar Judenrepublik, 24
Weimar Republic, 3, 7
Weinhold Academy, 4
Wells, H.G., 22
Wheeler, Fred, 74
Wheelwright, Ted, 231, 250
Whitcombe, Elizabeth, 244

Whitlam, Gough, 169, 202, 203, 208, 252
Wilcock, Bill, 225
Williams, J.H., 141
Williamson, Gus, 136
Wilson, Ian, 154
Wilson, J.S.G., 101
Wilson, J.V., 44
Wilson, Roland, 73, 76, 177, 181, 183, 310
Wilson, Stuart, 132
Wilson, Tom, 58, 70, 86, 96, 99, 100, 131, 141
Winthrop College, 139
Wood, Gordon, 72
Wootton, Barbara, 44
Workers' Educational Association (WEA), 50, 76, 172
World Bank, 77, 101, 241, 259, 266, 270, 311
Woroni, 115, 169
Worswick, David, 131, 196
Wright, Jack, 71

Yeend, Geoff, 295, 297
Yip Yat Hoong, 250

Zia-ur Rahman, 296
Zubrzycki, George, 312

www.ingramcontent.com/pod-product-compliance
Lightning Source LLC
Chambersburg PA
CBHW061123010526
44114CB00029B/2992